Minorities in West Asia and North Africa

Series Editors

This series seeks to provide a unique and dedicated outlet for the publication of theoretically informed, historically grounded and empirically governed research on minorities and 'minoritization' processes in the regions of West Asia and North Africa (WANA). In WANA, from Morocco to Afghanistan and from Turkey to the Sudan almost every country has substantial religious, ethnic or linguistic minorities. Their changing character and dynamic evolution notwithstanding, minorities have played key roles in social, economic, political and cultural life of WANA societies from the antiquity and been at the center of the modern history of the region. WANA's experience of modernity, processes of state formation and economic development, the problems of domestic and interstate conflict and security, and instances of state failure, civil war, and secession are all closely intertwined with the history and politics of minorities, and with how different socio-political categories related to the idea of minority have informed or underpinned historical processes unfolding in the region. WANA minorities have also played a decisive role in the rapid and crisis-ridden transformation of the geopolitics of WANA in the aftermath of the Cold War and the commencement of globalization. Past and contemporary histories, and the future shape and trajectory of WANA countries are therefore intrinsically tied to the dynamics of minorities. Intellectual, political, and practical significance of minorities in WANA therefore cannot be overstated.

The overarching rationale for this series is the absence of specialized series devoted to minorities in WANA. Books on this topic are often included in area, country or theme-specific series that are not amenable to theoretically more rigorous and empirically wider and multi-dimensional approaches and therefore impose certain intellectual constraints on the books especially in terms of geographical scope, theoretical depth, and disciplinary orientation. This series addresses this problem by providing a dedicated space for books on minorities in WANA. It encourages inter- and multi-disciplinary approaches to minorities in WANA with a view to promote the combination of analytical rigor with empirical richness. As such the series is intended to bridge a significant gap on the subject in the academic books market, increase the visibility of research on minorities in WANA, and meets the demand of academics, students, and policy makers working on, or interested in, the region alike. The editorial team of the series will adopt a proactive and supportive approach through soliciting original and innovative works, closer engagement with the authors, providing feedback on draft monographs prior to publication, and ensuring the high quality of the output.

More information about this series at
http://www.palgrave.com/gp/series/15127

Barzoo Eliassi

Narratives of Statelessness and Political Otherness

Kurdish and Palestinian Experiences

palgrave
macmillan

Barzoo Eliassi
Department of Social Work
Linnaeus University
Kalmar, Sweden

Minorities in West Asia and North Africa
ISBN 978-3-030-76697-9 ISBN 978-3-030-76698-6 (eBook)
https://doi.org/10.1007/978-3-030-76698-6

This Palgrave Macmillan imprint is published by the registered company Springer Nature Switzerland AG
The registered company address is: Gewerbestrasse 11, 6330 Cham, Switzerland

To Hawin and Hiwa

Acknowledgments

A book is rarely an individual accomplishment. First, I would like to express my deep gratitude to all the research participants for providing valuable knowledge about their lived experiences regarding statelessness and diaspora. Their testimonies are important to be considered in order to envision a new political order that is genuinely inclusive of ethnic, cultural and religious differences. Part of this research was funded by Leverhulme Trust while I was working as a researcher at International Migration Institute at Oxford University in 2014. The editors of Minorities in West Asia and North Africa (MIWANA), Dr. Kamran Matin and Dr. Paolo Maggiolini provided many insightful comments and suggestions to improve the outline and the content of the book. Dr. Kamran Matin has been my crucial interlocutor in relation to exchanging ideas and deliberation about Kurdish studies, statelessness, and nationalism. His ideas about undoing ethnic inequalities within the context of the nation-state have been highly inspirational during writing this book. I am especially grateful to the anonymous reviewer who provided a wealth of comments and important suggestions about how to expand my understanding of statelessness. Many thanks to Linnaeus University Center for Concurrences in Colonial and Postcolonial Studies for its support by providing me with research time that enabled me writing this book. Writing a book requires time, energy, focus and commitment and all these would not have been possible without a supportive family and kids who have encouraged me to finalize it. I dedicate this book to Hawin and Hiwa for their love and presence in my life.

Kalmar, Sardinia, Lund, Oxford
March 2021

Praise page *Narratives of Statelessness and Political Otherness*

"A powerful example of how attention to the institutionalisation of marginality illuminates socio-political processes that affect us all. Statelessness is far more than a legal status and Eliassi uses it to analyse the citizenship regime, the relation between nation and state, and how these produce subjectivities and rights. He combines engagement with theory and complex sensitive empirical work with Kurdish and Palestinian people to build a passionate argument for global equality and justice."

—Bridget Anderson, *Director of Migration Mobilities Bristol (MMB), University of Bristol, UK*

"Barzoo Eliassi's impressive, accountable and moving *Narratives of Statelessness and Political Otherness* leaves no reader untouched. Eliassi rewrites the geopolitical history of the present, connecting 'small stories' from the everyday lives of Kurds and Palestinians in Western Europe, with violent master narratives of place-based identities in a world of nation states. 'Where do you *originally* come from?' echoes the narrative power of governance in the everyday lives of marginalized non-white subjects across generations—subjects that resist through multiple complex stories about home, belonging and social justice. This is a book with long shelf life. It appeals to all readers interested in narrative power, suffering and resistance as an effect of nation and state building."

—Mona B. Livholts, *Professor of Social Work, Helsinki University, Finland*

"Despite the celebration of globalization as presumable borderlessness, the post-Westphalian and post-Potsdam world order remains a highly striated space divided into the increasingly impervious cells of nation-states. In this world statelessness means a political and ontological non-being, whereas having a formal citizenship cannot guarantee a real belonging to a nation/humanity. And even if the state cannot be democratized or decolonized and its very political form is downright outdated, the survival and well-being of people are still determined by their relative belonging to a nation-state which even in the most multicultural countries still continues to be defined by blood and by birth. Barzoo Eliassi's theoretically grounded and empirically rich study lets us feel what it means to be stateless in a contemporary world, what dreams, memories, fears, aspirations and hopes haunt people exiled from or made unwelcome guests in their own 'home'. Crucially, Eliassi achieves this effect not via abstract speculations but through an intense dialogue with many actual voices and opinions of Kurds and Palestinians living in the West. The outcome of this chorus of tragic human experiences and amazing resilience that the book forcefully presents, is a strongest argument against dehumanization of stateless people and their systematic defuturing."

—Madina Tlostanova, *Professor of Postcolonial Feminisms at Linköping University, Sweden*

"Written with rare verve that is as historical as it is theoretical, Barzoo Eliassi's book performs, embodies and thinks through the agony and the abjection of stateless-ness and stateless bodies from a perspective that is resolutely and non fungibly local and yet enables deep trans-local insights and conversations about the enforced condition of political alterity. Without ever losing focus on the specific plight of the Kurds and the Palestinians, Eliassi mounts a broad based migrant, diasporic, and 'post-humanist' critique of settler and racist regimes whose violence has been laundered and valorized as the hegemony of the western nation state. I applaud Barzoo Eliassi for his unwavering scholarship of rigorous resistance and search for alternatives."

—R. Radhakrishnan, *Distinguished Professor of English and Comparative Literature, University of California, USA*

Contents

CHAPTER 1

Theorizing Statelessness and Stateless Diasporas

This book engages with the experiences of statelessness and political belonging in a world of unequal nation-states and citizenship regimes. The study will investigate competing and conflicting conceptions of statelessness and statehood among Palestinian diaspora in Sweden and Kurdish diasporas in Sweden and the UK, and how to escape political subjugation and ethnic discrimination in the Middle East and in the context of migration. This problem area requires a combination of theoretical investigation of statelessness, minority and majority relations, citizenship and politics of belonging/home with empirical field research on the subjective experiences of the phenomena among the Kurds and the Palestinians, probably the two most debated stateless nations in the contemporary world. The comparative dimension of the investigation grounded in extensive sociological analyses of the experiences of statelessness, citizenship regimes across different nation-states and belonging among Kurdish and Palestinian diasporas gives an original character to the study as the first study of its kind.

Statelessness has been largely viewed as a lack of citizenship, with the acquisition of citizenship/nationality as the solution (Blitz & Lynch, 2009; Manly & van Waas, 2014; van Waas 2008). The main argument of this study is that citizenship rights and membership of an internationally recognized state are central to human rights of political subjects, but

B. Eliassi, *Narratives of Statelessness and Political Otherness*, Minorities in West Asia and North Africa,
https://doi.org/10.1007/978-3-030-76698-6_1

the structural conditions and subjective experiences of statelessness do not fade away with acquisition of formal citizenship, as the persistent political, legal and military struggles of the Kurds and Palestinian indicate (see Vali 1998; Butler 2012). There are different ways of experiencing statelessness, but a particular distinction needs to be made between statelessness as individual attribute—a legal category which invokes international protection—and statelessness of nations like the Kurds and Palestinians who are seeking political autonomy and sovereignty in the international comity of sovereign nations (see Gabiam, 2015). This study engages with the latter form of statelessness.

In this context, Kurdish and Palestinian diasporas constitute central actors in these struggles to establish political homes in order to maintain their collective identity through articulating their interests and needs in the face of state power. Unlike Palestinians who are conceived as a nation but denied effective sovereignty and return of its diasporic members, Kurds are often referred to as a minority within the framework of the current nation-states of Iran, Iraq, Syria and Turkey. The so-called Kurdish 'question' is framed and restricted to an internal affair of the existing states in which Kurds are coercively embedded, and hence denying the transnationality and cross-border vulnerability and subordination of the Kurdish population in the Middle East. However, without reducing their internal and external differences, historical constitutions and sensitivity to the dynamics of political challenges and changes that these two stateless nations encounter in the country of origin, I will define both Kurdish and Palestinian migrants as stateless diasporas with political goals to create political homes permeated by desire for sovereign agency in order to escape relations of subordination and identity-based political, cultural and economic subordination (see Markell, 2003).

The study highlights hitherto understudied subjective experiences of statelessness. Therefore, through narrative inquiry and in-depth interviews, I will draw upon the narratives of 50 Kurdish migrants living in Sweden and the UK and 20 Palestinians migrants living in Sweden to analyze how national consciousness emerges in the absence of a nation-state but also how the role of the nation-state shapes discourses about statelessness outside of the 'original' homelands (see Khalidi 1997). It is important to clarify at the outset that the focus of the study is primarily directed, but not only, on the experiences of Kurdish diasporas within the national settings of Sweden and the UK. When it comes to the experiences of Palestinian diaspora, the empirical data is limited to the Swedish context. Despite the imbalance in the empirical data, the Palestinian experiences and perspectives are both important and complementary to understand the complexity, commonality and differences of how statelessness is conceived and experienced within the political geography of the Middle East. This comparative approach, however imbalanced empirically, enables a better recognition of how different claims to statehood as a result of collective of sufferings and displacement within the context of nation-states are either punished and admonished or embraced and legitimized by the international community.

The study seeks to make an original and critical contribution to the politically contentious debates on Palestinian and Kurdish statehood aspirations in the Middle East and Western states. It also aims to contribute theoretically and empirically to the broader debates on minorities, nationalism, sovereignty, displacement and citizenship studies. Although Palestine was recognized as a non-member observer state in 2012 by the United Nations General Assembly, its territorial boundaries and political power remain insecure and indefinite due to Israeli occupation and continuous dispossession. The Kurdistan Region of Iraq is endorsed as an autonomous region by the Iraqi constitution since 2005 and the Kurds of Syria have built an unrecognized entity in northern Syria, called *Rojava* (Western Kurdistan) currently weakened due to Turkish military occupation of parts of Rojava following American abandonment of the Kurds. The future of Rojava remains unsecure given that Russia has gained the upper hand in shaping the reality of Syria and aiming to assert the Syrian regime's jurisdiction and power. Turkey views the destruction of Rojava as a tool to bury Kurdish dreams of political freedom and autonomy, and for achieving this, Turkey might make many painful concessions to appease Russia and the patronized Syrian regime.

Whereas the Kurdistan Region of Iraq flagged aspiration of statehood as a solution to political and sovereign freedom and carried out a referendum on independence in September 2017, which provoked retaliatory responses and sanctions by the neighboring states and the central Iraqi government, the political power of Rojava influenced and guided by the political thoughts of the imprisoned leader of Kurdistan Workers' Party (PKK) Abdullah Öcalan views statehood as an inadequate solution to the political subjugation of the Kurds. Kurdish Statehood based on ethnic dominance is assumed to reproduce a new master identity that leads to oppression of 'new' minorities and creation of ethnic strangers. The concept of democratic autonomy has been developed by Öcalan as a form of non-sovereign self-government within the context of existing states (Matin 2019, 2020; Öcalan, 2017), where different constituencies can live their identities relationally but not hierarchically.

In light of above discussion, it is important to investigate how political projects that guide political belonging and collective action of stateless peoples are constructed among nations without states. Political belonging creates collective goals to sustain, challenge or transform political order and precarious social conditions that characterize statelessness. Hence, this study accords attention to the complexity of statelessness in historical and geographical terms in the Middle East and diasporic contexts in West European contexts, through focusing on difficulties, hardship, possibilities, perils, antagonism, solidarity and agency that stateless individuals and peoples encounter and experience (see Gibney 2017).

More concretely, this study investigates what statelessness means to Kurdish and Palestinian diasporas and how members of these two diasporas frame their understandings and narratives about absence of 'land' and 'state'. Since gender is central to nationalist thought, this study will also examine how gender, political ideology and potentially class impinge on the narratives of statelessness and nationalism. While statelessness and citizenship are often juxtaposed as each other's negation, I will investigate how Kurdish and Palestinians diasporas conceive and value citizenship in the Middle East and European contexts, within which they are embedded. In order to illustrate the complexity of the political positioning of Kurdish and Palestinian diasporas, the study will look into the ways Kurdistan and Palestine are imagined within a nationalist and a non-nationalist framework in the context of military occupation and ethnic subordination. In other words, how they define or redefine the concept of community that reproduce or undo the reproduction of a nationalistic ontology that embraces statehood as vehicle of political freedom among other sovereign nations. In order to bring these two diasporas into a conversation about each other's political vulnerability and eligibility to statehood, I will explore how members of Kurdish and Palestinian diasporas politically relate to each other in the context of statelessness and establish hierarchies of statelessness in order to gain international recognition and situate themselves at the forefront of the queue to gain statehood and political sovereignty.

This introductory chapter orients the book toward scholarship on the importance of studying statelessness from sociological, political theory and legal perspectives. It does so by discussing the role of theory in relation to subjugated groups and surveying the theoretical and empirical field in relation to statelessness with a particular focus on Kurdish and Palestinian experiences. The chapter also discusses the role of diasporas as important international and transnational actors in endorsing status quo in the country of origin or politically struggling to alter the political situation of the countries of 'origin'. In this context, the chapter reviews the evolution of the Kurdish and Palestinian diasporas with regard to their statelessness and the political situation of their contested and occupied homelands. Moreover, I provide a brief methodological consideration in relation to Kurdish and Palestinian diasporas and the individuals that have been recruited to participate in the study and the analysis that guides the narrative accounts of the research participants.

The 'State' of Statelessness Studies

It is argued that "statelessness is a global phenomenon with causes that lie both outside the state and within it" (Blitz & Lynch, 2009, p. 95). Around the world, there are approximately between 12 and 15 million stateless people in the world, a number that leaves out many people who might hold formal citizenship but are prevented from enjoying citizenship rights (Redclift, 2013; Staples 2012). The concept of statelessness is predominantly informed by an idea that indicates "rightlessness" and "vulnerability" (Staples 2012) since it assumedly represents "a cold instrument of exclusion" (Redclift, 2013, p. 2). By large, the concept of statelessness is situated within a discursive field of negativity. For instance, statelessness has been viewed as an "expulsion from humanity altogether" (Arendt 1951, p. 297), "Kafaesaque legal vacuum" (UNHCR cited in Hayden, 2008, p. 249), "social death" (Castles 2005, p. 216), "the very definition of modern hell" (Ignatieff, 2009, p. 7), "bare life" (Agamben, 1998) and "a condition of infinite danger" (Walzer 1983, p. 32).

When statelessness is discussed by academics, policy makers and international organizations, it is mainly framed as a negation of citizenship that is assumed to allow individuals and groups to enjoy inclusion, freedom, rights and protection. Statelessness was famously described by Hannah Arendt (1951) as the loss of citizenship or the loss of the right to have rights. Consequently, from a legal or a right-based approach, the solution to statelessness is found in acquisition of a nationality that is often used interchangeably with the notion of citizenship (Blitz & Lynch, 2009;

Manly & van Waas, 2014; van Waas, 2008). According to the 1954 Geneva Convention, a stateless person is defined as 'a person who is not considered as national by any state under the operation of its law'. This approach to statelessness is permeated by a policy/institutional definition that views the solution to statelessness through granting a nationality. This is however not very surprising since "the study of statelessness emerged as the study of nationality law" (Manly & van Waas, 2014, p. 5). Staples (2012) argues that we should avoid referring to 'nationality' and 'citizenship' and instead interrogating the relations of inclusion and exclusion through the term 'membership'. In the same vein, Redclift (2013) points out that the legal anomaly that statelessness represents seems to be insufficient to grasp the complexity of statelessness as a lived experience and as an identity issue. This complexity requires an interdisciplinary approach that expands the notion of statelessness from a mere concern with nationality/citizenship to a question that also concerns sovereignty and the role of state power in excluding groups that are viewed as undesirable, disloyal or a political threat (Gibney 2011). Conklin (2014) contends that statelessness represents the enigma of the international community that claims "universal human rights and legal standards of humanitarian laws despite the exclusion of tens of millions of *de jure* and effectively stateless people" (2014, p. 302).

It is often difficult for those who possess and enjoy the rights of citizenship to understand and imagine a life permeated by conditions of statelessness. This might explain to some extent why statelessness is so understudied and marginalized in academic work but also why its occurrence is not limited or prevented (Bloom et al., 2017) since this would entail redefinition and reconfiguration of the state system and its citizenship regimes that have been structured by nationalist thoughts. Therefore, it is of paramount importance to sociologically investigate the voices and the experiences of stateless individuals and peoples in order to understand what statelessness means, and how statelessness is produced and experienced (Eliassi, 2013, 2016). It is equally important to examine how the creation of statelessness brings about deprivation (Bloom et al., 2017). It is not an overstatement to state that citizenship is viewed as the most desirable remedy to the collective sufferings and exclusion of stateless people (Eliassi, 2016) and this potential solution includes both the perspective of practitioners working with stateless people, prominent international agency like United Nations High Commissioners for

Refugees (UNHCR) and a large part of the scholarly work on statelessness (Bloom et al., 2017; Manly, 2012). There is however some call for more complex analysis of the lived conditions and experiences of statelessness that accord attention to historical and geographical realities (Bloom et al., 2017; Eliassi, 2016; Kingston 2017). Moreover, the question of statelessness cannot be separated from theorizations of rights and justice (Bloom et al., 2017).

The sources of statelessness cannot be reduced to one single reason since statelessness emerge in complex and multi-faceted way at different times and in different places (Bloom et al., 2017). For instance, the Kurds were rendered stateless after World War I following British and French division of the Middle East and as a consequence they were politically, economically and culturally minoritized and inferiorized within the nation-states of Turkey, Iran, Iraq and Syria (Eliassi, 2013; Vali 1998). The Palestinian statelessness emerged as a result of the decline of the Ottoman Empire enabled by the British colonial power and the establishment of Israel in 1948. Forced migration, dispossession and homelessness have come to shape the collective trajectory of the Palestinians (Khalidi 1997, 2006; Said 1992).

Statelessness can also emerge in societies whose citizenship regime is sharply patrimonial and this often affects children of couple who do not share the same citizenship status and become stateless. This is clearly a gendered form of statelessness that patrimonial citizenship regimes engender (see Bloom et al., 2017). States can also involve in denationalization of individuals and groups who are viewed as 'disloyal, 'treacherous' and 'the enemy of the state', whether they belong to an ethnic minority or engaged in activities that are defined as 'terror' by the state (Arendt 1951; Gibney 2019). Although it is true that totalitarian states have historically used denationalization as a powerful exclusionary weapon against their 'undesirable' others (Arendt 1951), revocation of citizenship as a form of discrimination is on rise in liberal democratic states. Denationalization often affects individuals who belong to groups whose citizenship status is insecure and imagined as not being a legitimate member of the nation. The target group of denationalization in contemporary Western Europe is European citizens with backgrounds from Muslim-majority countries (Gibney 2019).

Bloom et al. (2017) trace key moments in assessing how statelessness has been thought about. Statelessness was viewed as exception after the end of World War II. This notion of statelessness was changed at the beginning of the twenty-first century where statelessness came to be viewed as a phenomenon that needed some legal and political solutions. Contemporary discourse on statelessness considers statelessness as widespread and rooted in the formation of modernity. The way statelessness is theorized affects the way different solutions and remedy are stipulated to deal with statelessness as a condition of helplessness and vulnerability.

There are different approaches how to understand and solve statelessness. van Waas and de Chickera (2017) adopt a human rights and legal approach to statelessness that underline the importance of gaining nationality (citizenship) and strengthening their status. Moreover, they claim that "while those who have an ineffective nationality are not stateless, it makes little sense to provide stateless people with a nationality that is ineffective" (2017, p. 66). According to van Waas and de Chickera, approaches to and definitions of statelessness are surrounded by confusion and misapplication. For instance, by conflating the vulnerability of stateless people with refugees who become displaced and neglected within or across the boundary of states. While attempting to clarify the conceptual boundaries of stateless peoples/individuals and other vulnerable categories in the context of migration, van Waas and de Chickera maintain that it is important to distinguish between stateless refugees (Rohingya) and non-stateless refugees (Syrian refugees), stateless persons and irregular migrants. The Kurds are framed as a third category in their discussion and considered as one of the best-known nations without a state despite being formally recognized as belonging (not necessarily as Kurds) to the states in which they are governed. It is the absence of statehood that is viewed as central for the Kurdish struggle and not citizenship in itself. In order to confront the problems of statelessness, there is a need to construct a shared notion and definition of statelessness. A shared definition of a situation as a problem or as a vulnerable life condition often shapes the collective efforts of dealing with it (van Waas & de Chickera 2017). Likewise, Bradley asks for a more nuanced approaches to refugeehood and statelessness and cautions against uncritical conflation between refugees and stateless since such conflation "represents a potential disservice to the displaced, as it may perpetuate a mistaken impression of refugees as potentially impotent victims, and inadvertently undermine refugees' compelling claims against their states of origin for the redress of their rights as citizens" (Bradley, 2014, pp. 102–103).

In contrast to van Waas and de Chickera (2017), Kingston (2015) points to the experiences of Rohingya in Myanmar as a telling example of rightlessness, where the Rohingya are not only exposed to direct violence like rape, torture and murder but also structural violence that is expressed through statelessness and renunciation of nationality. Moreover, Kingston argues that the UNHCR as part of its global agenda has made the acquisition of citizenship/nationality to the definitive solution of statelessness. Although this legalistic approach is important for holding a legal status within a political community and can improve the life situation of stateless peoples, there is no political guarantee that it can undo the political, cultural and economic injustices that permeate the life-worlds of stateless peoples. While Kingston repeatedly underscores the importance of the legal strategies to undo the injustices and collective sufferings of stateless peoples, she insists that the legalistic/right-based approach (nationality) to statelessness is "a temporary bandage on widespread issues of structural inequality" (Kingston, 2017, p. 29). It is important to concomitantly address statelessness as a legal issue and eradicating the political and social forces that enable structural violence and inequalities that stateless people experience (Kingston 2017).

Rethinking Arendt's Conception of Statelessness

Until now, I have only briefly referred to the seminal work of Hannah Arendt (1951) on statelessness. As a result of the Nazi Germany's genocidal policies against the Jews, Arendt's personal experience of statelessness as a German Jew cannot be underestimated in producing one of the most sophisticated analysis of statelessness and the inherent exclusionary practices of the nation-state. It is a text that needs to be situated in a specific historical and political context where the Nazis formulated a 'final solution' to the Jews by liquidating them in extermination camps. At that time, Arendt was framing a theory about statelessness in relation to the lived experiences of Jewish subjects who were turned into an undesirable category of people, and as a consequence thrown out of the German citizenship regime where millions of them were exposed to genocide. Phillips (2015) argues that the deadly danger that was posed to Jews and Jewishness in Europe explain why Arendt despite her complex identity viewed 'Jew' as the only adequate response to the question, Who are you? In other words, persecution and violence against the Jews created a reactive identity among the Jewish diaspora and intensified their search for a political home, which resulted in Israel. Butler (2010) points out that Arendt was very engaged in the question of belonging and home, and how these two concepts could create the ground for making claims to rights and public appearance (Butler & Spivak 2010). Having a place and voice implies having some form of access to a shared world that enables political action.

Arendt's text engaged intensively with the Rights of Man and argued that they were not inalienable as declared in the Declaration of Rights but needed governments that citizens could rely on and can fall back on when they needed protection. This is what was exactly the Jews lacked when they were thrown out across frontiers and national borders. From the moment, the Jews lost their national rights in Germany, they lost their political home, government protection and political rights, in order to become following the wish of the Nazi leadership, "the scum of earth" (Arendt 1951, p. 267). While talking about the extermination camps, Arendt asserted that being merely a 'man' was a dangerous situation due to the "abstract nakedness of being nothing but human" (p. 301). This danger emerged in a context "where the existence of people forced to live outside the common world is that they are thrown back, in the midst of civilization, on their *natural givenness*, on their mere differentiation" (p. 302, my emphasis). Given this precarious situation, it was difficult for Arendt to understand the paradox and the irony due to the obstinate assertation of benevolent idealists who viewed human rights as inalienable or sacred, which were virtually rights mainly enjoyed by citizens and denied to stateless people. One of the most potent forms of retaining a recognized tie to humanity is through citizenship and belonging to a nation-state where one's actions and opinions matter (Arendt 1951). Yet, this is a dubious statement in our contemporary world of uneven nation-states where even those subjects who belong to a national community and are in possession of a sovereign state do not hold equal place and their voices, passport, mobilities and rights are not equally distributed (see Shachar 2009).

Being just a 'man' (a human) does not mean that people will treat you as equal, it is rather one's belonging or non-belonging to a political community and its place and value in the international comity that determines one's status. This position echoes the stance of Edmund Burke who repudiated the claims of the French Revolution's Declaration of the Rights of man and argued that he would rather embrace the rights of Englishmen than the rights of man. Arendt concurs with Burke's argument in the following way:

> The survivors of the extermination camps, the inmates of concentration and internment camps, and even the comparatively happy stateless people could see without Burke's arguments that the abstract nakedness of being nothing but human was their greatest danger. (Arendt, 1951, p. 300)

Despite this clear reference to Burke's ideas about the incoherence of human rights and national citizenship rights, Lacorix (2015) defends Arendt and argues that a large part of political philosophers in France have misunderstood Arendt's usage of Burke to mock human rights. Undoubtedly, the Nazis targeted the Jews both as particular ethnic or racial group and used a variety of de*human*izing strategies and rhetoric to place the Jews outside of the confines of humanity and legitimize their genocidal politics (see, for instance, Rancière 2004). Lacorix (2015) points out that Arendt's conceptualization of human rights and citizenship can be understood as an argumentative device to claim a cosmopolitan citizenship in our contemporary world. While cosmopolitanism might be an inclusionary project to pursue as Lacroix asserted above, it seems to be politically and practically remote to be realized in the contemporary world where national borders and identities are becoming more aggressive toward non-nationals and migrants. One explanation behind assigning a conservative interpretation to Arendt's conception of the human rights and the nation-state, as Lacorix (2015) earlier indicated, is the question of voice. Butler (2010) argues that Arendt's text on the *Decline of the Nation-state: End of Rights of Man* is characterized by different tones in relation to the subject and the political order that she engages with. In this text, the first part is dominated by a sardonic, skeptical and disillusioned voice that becomes more declarative, where Arendt "effectively *redeclares* the rights of man and tries to animate a discourse that she thinks will be politically efficacious" (Butler & Spivak, 2010, p. 46, emphasis in original). Butler concludes by stating that Arendt is looking for a polity and not a nation-state that can create non-national modes of belonging, where laws are not guided by nationalist principles (Butler & Spivak, 2010).

For Arendt, it was the citizenship that was the device by which people maintained and was recognized as having a tie with humanity. Lacking this tie with humanity via effective citizenship rights turned the stateless and the rightless into objects of charity and humanitarianism. In her analysis of Arendt, Phillips (2015) points out that human rights were rendered as empty words due to the persistent attachment to and investment in the nation-state as the sole and standard template of organizing a political community. In other words, it is the nation-state that creates such divisions between national citizenship and human rights. Arendt claimed that equality and justice are not given since "we are not born equal; we become equal as members of a group on the strength of our decision to guarantee ourselves mutually equal rights" (Arendt, 1951, p. 301). Institutions or organizations become central for a political life that aims to produce equality by bringing people together and a building a common equal world (Arendt 1951). Conversely, institutions can equally produce a divisive world that is built upon hierarchy rather than serving and representing diverse constituencies horizontally. In the same vein, Balibar (2014) reminds us that the nation-state as an institution conceals a deep antinomy. On the one hand, the nation-state is widely considered as cultivating rights and creating human subjects, and one the other hand, it has equally power to destroy rights or become a major obstacle to its realization. Arendt (1951) argues that from the moment the nation or more precisely agents of nationalism conquered the state, the state lost its power as an instrument of law. The state started to designate national interests as its primary concern and the will of the nation took over its legal institutions. This new political order made it clear for the majority of the world population that true freedom, popular sovereignty and emancipation could only be achieved by having a national government that could secure the human/national rights of its citizens.

Although critical of the Israeli treatment and expulsion of Palestinians from Palestine, Arendt (1951) made it clear that the experiences of statelessness showed that losing national rights entailed losing human rights and the creation of the State of Israel in 1948 was a form of achievement to restore and establish national rights that Jews were deprived from. This of course implied that the stateless Jews guided by Zionism achieved their national rights by turning Palestinians into a stateless nation dispersed around the world. While Arendt was highly critical of imperialism, Zionism and the nation-state, Spanos (2012) points out that Arendt was more concerned with the security threat against Israel by the neighboring Arab states than the well-being of the Arabs/Palestinians who were directly targeted, dispossessed and displaced by the foundation of Israel. This is a possible reading and interpretation of Arendt. It is worth mentioning that Arendt had expressed racist and Eurocentric views of African lives decimated by white colonial powers and condoned the unequal structural positions of the African Americans (see Dossa, 1980). Equally, Arendt clearly lamented the Jewish colonization and conquest of Palestinian lands, that enabled creation of Israel. Arendt maintained that Israel as a solution to the Jewish humiliation produced a new politically category of homeless and stateless people, namely the Palestinians (Arendt 1951, p. 290).

So how useful and valid is Arendt's conception of statelessness for our contemporary political order? In an attempt to reconsider the theoretical legacy of Arendt, Blitz (2017) maintains that Arendt's understanding of statelessness was not context-sensitive since statelessness arises differently in different geopolitical contexts and as such Arendt failed to provide a solution to the problems of statelessness and how rights can be restored. Moreover, Blitz continues, that stateless people are not always as helpless as Arendt wanted to depict them since there are many stateless peoples around the world that struggle for their rights. For Arendt, statelessness was equated with rightlessness and losses that entailed loss of home, loss of government/state protection and the loss of place in our world (Blitz 2017, p. 72). Arendt is also critiqued by Blitz to idealize the state and assuming the state as a universal source of protection. States differ from each other in regard to their ideological constructions and level of their popular democracy and institutional inclusion of different constituencies. If the state is weak, it can barely protect the rights of its subjects. In other cases, the state takes a predatory form as in the case of Myanmar that ferociously treats the stateless Rohingya. Thus, states are different and statelessness is experienced in varied and multiple ways and stateless individuals and peoples resort to different strategies to challenge the states and demand their rights (Blitz 2017).

Rancière is another vocal critic of Arendt's conceptualization of statelessness and the Rights of Man. For Rancière, the stateless people are not as powerless as Arendt want us to believe in regard to the totalizing power of the sovereign since the stateless can resist and even disrupt the naturalized order of domination that the sovereign and the superior identity have established. According to Rancière (2004), Arendt tends to create an ontological trap that resembles an "ontological destiny" (Rancière 2004, p. 301) when she creates a polarity of the Rights of Man (the stateless) and the Citizen (the state-bearing identity) and "from which only a God is likely to save us" (Rancière 2004, p. 302). For Rancière, Arendt's analysis and approach to human rights are paralyzing and makes it impossible to grasp the potentials of democracy and the modern rights declarations. While discussing the paradox of human rights, Rancière makes the insightful point that one becomes merely a human when one is deprived of those rights and states that "The Rights of Man are the rights of those who have not the rights that they have and have the rights that they have not" (ibid.). In other words, human rights are either the rights of jettisoned groups who do not have any rights or it is the rights of citizens who are already enjoying these rights.

Against this background, Gündoğdu (2011) provides a strong defense of Arendt's analysis of the Rights of Man and responds to Rancière's critique of Arendt for dooming human rights to a failing project. Gündoğdu maintains that the aporetic nature of Arendt's critique of human rights is to call into question how our conventional understandings of human rights are structured and distributed and create the possibilities of new thinking about the world and how it can be opened up for new forms of inclusionary projects. If we embark on a new project that aims to rearticulate human rights beyond the binaries of our conventional understanding of rights that divides the world into man/citizen or universal/particular, then an aporetic thinking that Arendt provides can become its condition of possibility (Gündoğdu, 2011, p. 7).

While Rancière seems to overstate the power of agency that is often attractive to scholars who engage with resistance of marginalized and inferiorized groups, Benhabib (2018) maintains that there are important limitations to how effectively excluded groups can assert and enact their rights. Focusing narrowly and excessively on the agency of deprived groups like refugees, migrants or stateless groups, "runs the risk of burdening the most vulnerable with their own defense as well as being voluntaristic in making the entitlement to rights dependent upon the capacity to assert them as well as to have them recognized" (Benhabib 2018, p. 120). According to Walzer (1970), stateless people are both helpless and enjoy some form of unaccountable freedom since they are not bound by citizen obligations and duties to the state (see also Arendt 1951, p. 296). The stateless figure as such lacks the protection that states are expected to provide their citizens due to their political membership in a particular nation-state. As statelessness is assumed to lead to impoverishment, insecurity and desperation, stateless individuals and peoples would readily exchange statelessness for a membership in a political community that provides them social safety and security (Gibney 2017; Walzer 1970). Statelessness for Walzer (1970, 1983) is thus situated between dangerous helplessness due to the political exclusion that the stateless faces and precariousness as a result of the non-citizenship and non-belonging that the stateless experience. Gibney (2017) underlines that statelessness is often an effect of ethnic discrimination, where ethnic and religious minorities are exposed to violence and rejection. It is within the context of the international nation-state system that they are facing this general injustice due to lack of effective citizenship and membership in a state. Without contending Walzer's approach to statelessness that primarily focuses on helplessness and danger, Gibney (2017) argues that stateless people attempt to do the best of this precarious and vulnerable situation and may even succeed in maintaining a strong collective identity across several generations. This collective identity is often communicated through articulated political claims and cultural activities and revival that challenge exclusionary state and citizenship regimes, where Kurds and Palestinians are highlighted as central examples in international politics.

Stateless peoples like Kurds and Palestinians have historically resisted the states in the Middle East in which they have been living and continue to do so, which shows that the stateless people as a politically conscious group is a force to be reckoned with. This is not to say that resistance does not have a limit both discursively and politically since the sovereign power can often repudiate the political claims or voices of the stateless people as 'noises', 'terrorism' and 'separatism' that allegedly disturb the political stability of national and regional/international orders. Both stateless and sovereign people are political subjects and these should not be viewed as definite collectivities but "names that set out a question or a dispute (*litige*) about who is included in their account" (Rancière, 2004, p. 303). It is evident that the sovereign and state-bearing identity can make itself present and representable through structural exclusion of what is conceived as superfluous and absent, namely the stateless (see Molavi, 2013, p. 36). For Gibney, it is important to empirically study the lived experiences of those who lack and/or possess citizenship in order to produce knowledge that can enable critiquing the international nation-state system and rethink the system that can "make membership more meaningful, secure and legitimate" (Gibney 2017, p. xxii), a task that this book will engage with. Violence and state oppression against Kurds and Palestinians are major reasons behind the forced migration, displacement and formation of Kurdish and Palestinian diasporas. These painful experiences and collective sufferings underpin their persistent struggle for political freedom and self-rule. In the following, I will discuss migratory experiences in an uneven world and discuss how the subordination of the Palestinians and the Kurds has been constructed and legitimized in the Middle East. Moreover, I will survey different studies that have discussed the emergence, meanings and experiences of Kurdish and Palestinian diasporas in different national contexts, with a particular focus on Sweden and the UK.

Migration, Exile and Otherness

People migrate due to different reasons. Although there might be some voluntarism in the decisions of people who leave their countries, there are significant structural conditions that make migration to a reality or an impossibility for certain groups who are targeted by state oppression or paramilitarily violence. In populist far-right discourses in the West, non-white migrants are often depicted as a category of dishonest people with calculated goals to abuse the welfare benefits of European and Western countries and undermine the cultural basis of the West. While migration is often portrayed in terms of 'crisis' if it is particularly related to the attempts of mobility by non-white subjects from the global south, the mobility of white subjects is interpreted as a sign of unboundedness, global citizenry and cosmopolitanism. White subjects that migrate to non-Western contexts are often characterized as 'expatriates', a euphemism for desired mobility and community-building opposed to the alienage and otherness that non-white migrant experience in general.

For the Kurds and Palestinians, political, economic, cultural and state violence are important underlying factors that make migration to an imperative in their lives. Forced migration is a central feature of statelessness characterized by loss and confusion. In this regard, Arendt (1951, p. 293) argued that statelessness entailed "the loss of the entire social texture into which they were born and in which they established for themselves a distinct place in the world". The notion of loss in is also apparent in the writings of Said, who defined exile as an "unhealable rift forced between a human being and a native place, between the self and its true home: its essential sadness can never be surmounted" (Said 2000, p. 173). This approach to exile and migration depicts a melancholic condition that shapes the lives of migrants who have escaped their homes. The search for home, purity and belonging is becoming more intense if not the dominate feature of what Malkki (1995) describes as 'a national order of things' with local and global significance. A group whose very status is insecure and precarious might delve into a search for purity and authenticity in order to strengthen communal bonds among its members against a threatening outer world. The exilic community or the diaspora can materialize itself as a home against exclusion and cultural degradation in the context of migration.

In the cases of the Kurds and Palestinians whose political status remain insecure and fragile in the Middle East and Western contexts due to ideological framework that view minority rights or national rights as a threat, members of Kurdish and Palestinian diasporas are not only adopting a victimhood discourse based on collective injury but also challenging the states and their dominant ethno-national others to become more democratic, transparent and justice-oriented. It is important to note that like all identities, diasporas are heterogeneous and pervaded by internal struggles and contestations about how political, religious, cultural, gender-based and linguistic differences can be negotiated and settled. All identities are based on narratives and have no existence outside of concrete and specific historical and political situations. If Kurdish and Palestinian identities were secure and established identities free from domination, its members would have adopted other narratives about who they are, who they want to be and who they do not want to be (see Yuval-Davis, 2011). Hence, there is an important epistemological and ontological difference between members of established and continuous nations and member of groups whose very status and existence is contested, devalued and rendered as irrelevant in the world of national identities (see Billig, 1995).

Dispersed Communities and the Ties that Bind Across Borders

Diasporas have a long history and they continue to be, with different levels of success, important transnational actors in shaping or influencing domestic politics both in the states where they currently live and the states or peoples that they have left due to migration. Many states are becoming increasingly aware that diasporas can be useful actors in endorsing their political and economic interests and relations with the states in which they inhabit. Therefore, states attempt to kindle the energy of diasporas and affect their patterns of identification, that make them see the world like the states that they have some emotional or political attachment to (see Adamson, 2016). The concept of diaspora has generally been used to describe the Jewish dispersion around the world and their continuous emotional, political and cultural ties with a Jewish homeland. Formation of diasporas like the Jewish and Armenian diasporas was historically situated within the context of statelessness and destruction of homeland (see Kenny, 2013). This is not to say that the Jewish diaspora should function as the immediate template for how a diaspora emerges and experiences displacement and otherness. It is often assumed that diaspora formation entails a triadic relationship among the country of origin, the country of settlement and the ethnic group dispersed within and across different states (Cohen, 2008; Safran, 2005). The concept of diaspora is contested particularly in relation to the way diasporas are conceived as concrete and bounded entities and expected to correspond to some typological criteria (Anthias, 1998; Betts & Jones, 2016; Brubaker, 2005; Ragazzi, 2017; Soysal, 2002). Anthias (1998) and Soysal (2002) insisted that the concept of diaspora is not a break with ethnicity and race since it tends to reproduce the essentialism of ethnic and racial boundaries and obstructing formation of transethnic identities and solidarities. Ragazzi (2017, p. 7) frames his contestation of diaspora uncompromisingly and declares that there is no such thing as diaspora and diasporas are neither mobile or transnational communities. His framing is highly informed by Brubaker's (2005) essay on diaspora, where Brubaker upheld that the concept of diaspora has lost its semantic, conceptual and analytical power since it is used in a nondiscriminatory way to embrace a wide range of identities. According to Brubaker, it is far more productive to talk about diasporic projects, claims, idioms and practices than ethnocultural fact. This implies a move from reification of group identities to historical and political contingency of diasporic projects and mobilizations. Diaspora as a normative category does not only intend to describe the world but also to remake it (Brubaker, 2005, pp. 12–13). Although Ragazzi (2017) represents a radical version of constructivist ontology, it is important to bear in mind that diasporas do have boundaries but "defined and highlighted situationally, dialectically and over time, in action, through performance and periodic mobilization" (Werbner, 2015, p. 51). To claim that a diaspora is imagined and politically contingent does not entail that diasporic identities lack content and will be less real in their effects and impacts, although there is a wide consensus around the social construction of states and nations, not all nations are equally subjected to contestation and controversy (Betts & Jones, 2016).

Being dispersed, resisting assimilation and retaining a continuous orientation toward the 'original' homeland are constitutive hallmarks of many diasporic identities (Brubaker, 2005). This minimal definition provided by Brubaker cannot be fixed across generations since younger generations who have not been or grown up in the 'original' homeland will experience their old and new homes differently, which in turn can lead to divided allegiances and belongings. Community, family, home, homeland and thus are often altered, renegotiated and redefined in light of historical rupture that immigration, dislocation and relocation create across different generations, temporalities and spaces (Alinia & Eliassi, 2014; Eliassi, 2013; Radhakrishnan 1996). Accordingly, diasporas cannot be reduced to a single experience but as a category in motion. Like all identities, diaspora does not have a life outside of history, representations and human agency with an unambiguous meaning rather constituted and reconstituted through the dynamics of historical challenges, political situations, crisis, interests and priorities both in the country of origin and the country of settlement. As Sökefeld (2006) argues, it is important to analyze and ask how, by whom and for which political purpose essentialist conceptions of identities are deployed by different actors. All essentialism attempts to achieve some political goals, whether they are emancipatory or exclusionary. If identity was a natural and transhistorical feature of human lives, then people would not fight for it, die for it, talk about it or seek recognition for it. It is the very negation and instability of identity that guide the identity discourse (Azar, 2001; Laclau, 1994, p. 3). Essentialist notions of identities are also historical when different groups attempt to politically and culturally fix identities with specific meanings. Authentication of identity claims is a response to political challenges that peoples and groups encounter in their lives (see Radhakrishnan 1996). Accordingly, diasporic claims can involve contestation, affirmation and negotiation of the naturalized political order and relations of inclusion and exclusion in the countries of origin and the sociopolitical setting in which they are situated.

Due to the political normativity of nationalist thoughts and the nation-state system, it is analytically helpful to distinguish between stateless diasporas and state-linked diasporas (Sheffer, 2003). Likewise, due to proliferation of different diasporas like victim diasporas, labor diasporas, trade diasporas, imperial diasporas and cultural diasporas (Cohen, 2008), it is theoretically urgent to make semantic and analytic distinction between different diasporas and their trajectories as the result of national contexts (authoritarian or democratic), and group positions (majority or minoritized), they have held prior to and after migration (Eliassi, 2013).

While state-linked diaspora like the Turkish diaspora tends to defend the territorial integrity and sovereignty of the Turkish state through reinforcing 'the ruling institutions, political practices and official history of the Turkish state' (Şenay, 2013, p. 377), the Kurdish and Palestinian diasporas are more aspirational and largely challenge the states, attempting to redefine and subvert the identity of the states and their citizenships. Whereas both state-linked and stateless diasporas are engaged in long-distance nationalism (see Anderson, 1992), there are significant asymmetrical political relationships that exists in a world of nation-states. As Werbner (2002, p. 129) indicates: "Pakistan, like Israel, is the nationalist fulfillment of a diasporic vision". By focusing on diasporic conceptualization of statelessness, we can develop a better understanding of how national consciousness emerges in the absence of a nation-state in diasporic contexts and how diasporic narratives can underpin political belonging and collective action that attempt to sustain or transform political imaginary as an answer to the political inequalities that nations without states experience.

The Ongoing Zionist Dispossession of Palestinians

Until 1917, the Ottoman Empire ruled most part of the Middle East, including Palestine which it lost to the British forces. The British rule signaled incongruous promises to the Arabs and the Zionists regarding the governance of Palestine. At that time, the Arabs constituted 90% of Palestine's population. The Jews who were living in Palestine were consisted of both long-time inhabitants of Palestine and Jews who had fled persecution in Russia and the wider Europe. When Hitler rose to power in Germany, the Jewish immigration increased to Palestine, which was facilitated by the British rule but resisted by the Palestinians (Beinin & Stein, 2006) sensing the looming danger of the Zionist project for the future of Palestine. The British Foreign Secretary, Lord Alfred Balfour, expressed a strong official support for the Zionist project to establish a Jewish state in Palestine. That resulted in the Balfour Declaration of 1917. Colonialism and Jewish nationalism collaborated in realizing this state and subordinating the Palestinians by political and military means (Falk, 2017). The UN approved a partition plan of Palestine in 1947 that would entail a Jewish state and a Palestinian/Arab state. The Arabs rejected the UN Partition Plan of Palestine in 1947 since they did not want a division of their homeland by putting a large number of Palestinian Arabs under

Israeli rule (Jabareen, 2014). Israel defeated the Arab countries in the wars of 1948 and 1967 and turned Palestinians into an occupied people and a predominantly 'landless' people. Following the Israeli-Palestinian conflict, around 89,000 Arabs and 23,000 Israelis have died (Hanafi, 2012, p. 191). Until 1967 war, the international community did not view the Palestinians as autonomous political actors but considered them narrowly as a humanitarian issue (Bunton, 2013). When the Palestine Liberation Organization (PLO) was founded in 1964, Palestinians gained the status of an autonomous people independent of the collective Arab identity that Palestinians shared with other Arab states (Said 1992).

Most studies on Palestinian exodus, forced migration and diasporas start with 1948, when the state of Israel was established. Depending on whose representation we look at, we arrive at different narratives about what this new Israeli state has entailed and accomplished for Jews and Palestinians. Consider, how in a historical book titled *The Making of Modern Israel* (1948–1967), Leslie Stein frames the achievement of the Israeli state and denounces the Palestinians as 'occupiers' of Jewish lands:

> By the late nineteenth century, the Jews, who had been in exile for almost two thousand years, found their ancestral homeland in Palestine largely *occupied by Arabs* and governed by the Turks. /…/ Many likened the rebirth of Israel to a modern miracle. (Stein, 2009, p. 1, emphasis added)

As soon as we leave the Zionist representation and celebration of Israel as a miracle, and arrive at Palestinian representations and narratives, miracle is substituted with *Al-nakba* (the catastrophe) where the beginning of a collective Palestinian journey toward suffering, loss, erasure and displacement begins. In this light, Sanbar writes:

> The contemporary history of the Palestinian turns on a key date: 1948. That year a country and a people disappeared from maps and dictionaries. /…/ 'The Palestinian people does not exist', said the new masters, and henceforth the Palestinians would be referred to by general, conveniently vague terms, as either 'refugees', or in the case of a small minority that had managed to escape the generalized expulsion, 'Israeli Arabs'. A long absence was beginning. (Sanbar, 2001, p. 87)

The very word Israel triggers a history of violence for many Palestinians. During one of my interviews, I was firmly told by a Palestinian male in Sweden: "Please do not use the word 'Israel' because by using it, we accept it. For us, Israel has meant suffering and homelessness and we cannot accept someone who violates our rights, lands and homes". Israel is a creation of a Zionist vision and project, where there is "room for one return and one exile" (Peteet 2017, p. 7). Israel welcomes the Jews of the world as its immediate citizens and deny Palestinians rights to return for those who were expelled and fled the war of 1948. As a national revival moment, Zionism was developed in the late 1880 by Jews in central and eastern parts of Europe. This national project was created to put an end to the systematic persecution and the increasing pressure on Jews to assimilate (Pappe, 2006). Despite false promises of inclusion, Jewish assimilation into the dominant ethnocultural identity did not save their lives in Europe, as the genocide of Jews in the Nazi Germany illustrated. In her book, *Exile, Statelessness, and Migration*, Benhabib depicts a painful and sorrowful story of Jewish life in diaspora, characterized by vulnerability, shame, weakness, impotence, humiliation and betrayal by their benefactors. Their subjugation and otherness reminded them of their "inability to stand up for themselves and take their fortunes in their own hands" (Benhabib 2018, p. 11). Zionism came with a recipe and a remedy that it is only by creating a Jewish national home, that the deep sense of humiliation and the tyranny of persecution can be ended. This is described by Cocks as a sovereign longing to escape subjugation (Cocks 2014, pp. 26–27).

It is widely argued that Zionism endorsed a settler colonialism of Palestine (see Al-Hardan, 2018; Matar, 2011; Pappe, 2006; Peteet 2005, 2017; Zureik, 2016), but contested by Benhabib (2018) who argues that Zionism did not initially aim to dispossess Palestinians and their land, but it was a direct effect of the Balfour Declaration (1917) and the Holocaust of Jews in Europe. These events might have influenced the Zionist vision and its uncompromising longing for a Jewish homeland. Hage (2015) agrees with Benhabib that Zionism cannot simply be equated with colonialism but it would not have been able to realize itself without mechanisms of colonialism. However, it is important to remember that the logic of settler colonialism is destruction, elimination and replacement (Wolfe, 2006). The founding father of Zionism, Theodor Herzl, noticed that "If I wish to substitute a new building for an old one, I must demolish before I construct" (cited in Wolfe, 2006, p. 388). When Israel was realized, the Zionist discourse asserted that it was making the desert bloom, which in reality has entailed among other things eradicating indigenous olive trees and replacing them with other trees. Renaming Palestinian territories and Judaizing them became also part of this Zionist state-building project (ibid.). Naming and renaming are central to state-building projects and regime change. They involve asserting presence and mastery of an identity or a regime, by erasing the defeated people and exempting them from claims to symbolic and historical presence, recognition and representation. However, this political project is not unchallenged by subordinated peoples, as the Palestinian struggle witnesses.

As Cocks (2014) argues, the foundational basis of the state is violence and erasure of peoples and cultures living on the same territory. This view is shared by Pappe (2006) who has depicted the Israeli policy against the Palestinians as designed ethnic cleansing by destroying Palestinians presence in Palestine/Israel. In dominant Israeli representations, 'ethnic cleansing' is substituted with 'transfer of population' as a voluntary act by Palestinians (Pappe, 2006). Similarly, Zureik (2016) shows that by violence Israel has been able to occupy Palestinian territories and control and displace its population. This policy is underpinned by a racialist discourse and practice that put Palestinian population under severe surveillance (Zureik, 2016). Thus, the dispossession of Palestinians goes hand in hand with "a complex regime of immobility, incarceration, surveillance, forced visibility and invisibility, and disciplinary order" (Peteet 2017, p. 201).

Place is central to arrangement of power, identities and meaning in the context of the nation-state and settler colonialism. Mobility through and across local, national and international spaces is relationally organized and unevenly allocated between different Palestinians and Israeli Jews, but also between different Palestinians who hold different legal status. Palestinian Arabs who hold Israeli citizenship are far more mobile than the Palestinians living in Gaza and the West Bank. Unlike the Palestinians in occupied territories, the Israeli citizens enjoy high-speed mobility as spatial masters of this land. While checkpoints have been central to the Israeli project to restrict Palestinian mobility and rights of movement, the erection of the wall through Palestinians lands have further marginalized and rendered the Palestinians lives vulnerable to economic deprivation. As Peteet (2017, p. 10) eloquently claims, the checkpoints are tangible and public declaration of Israeli domination and Palestinian submission. According to Palestinians, by erecting a wall in the name of security, Israel has created an open-air prison for Palestinians, in order to make the Palestinians leave their country. In other words, Israel has built a prison for the Palestinians not only to incarcerate them as political hostages but also to encourage them to escape, so the land can be devoid of Palestinians. But, the Palestinians have learnt a historical lesson from 1948 that by leaving their homes, dispossession becomes the order and return is postponed to an impossibility under Israeli occupation (Peteet 2017). While the Israelis call the 708 kilometers long wall (upon completion), that they started building in 1994 as a 'separation wall', the Palestinians view it as a 'wall of Apartheid'. This wall, according to Peteet (2017, p. 1) "separates and immobilizes, engender economic chaos, imposes discipline and punishment, appropriate Palestinian resources, and by ostensibly quelling resistance, gives the Israelis a sense of security". In reality, the wall deprives the Palestinian from having access to employment, education, health care and family relations. This 'calibrated chaos' fueled by Israeli occupation makes unpredictability to a norm in Palestinian lives in the occupied territories (ibid., p. 38).

Thus, it is mainly in relation to the state of Israel and its aftermaths, that Palestinian subjectivity, displacement and resistance have been shaped. Palestinian history is characterized by a struggle against forgetting and making memories of their lives, homes and homeland to a political tool against Israeli politics of erasure (see Al-Hardan, 2018; Blachnicka-Ciacke, 2018; Lindholm, 2019; Sa'di & Abu-Lughod, 2007; Saloul, 2012; Sayigh, 1979, 2013, 2015; Schwabe, 2018) and spatial erasure of Palestinian symbolic and territorial existence (Hanafi, 2012). For instance, as a part of the Israeli strategy to erase the memory of Al-Nakba and pre-Nakba Palestinian society, the Israeli state has created national parks and removed indigenous Palestinian almond, olive and fig trees and replaced them with imported trees from Europe (Pappe, 2006). Where Israel attempts to dismiss and disqualify Palestinian claims to land and ownership as irrelevant, Palestinian counter-narratives emerge to prove the opposite and delegitimize Israeli claims as fabricated. However, it is important to underline that Israel as a state has powerful institutions that can produce official and hegemonic histories and impose them on its own subjects but also exteriorize them to Europe and the US that have historically, militarily, politically and morally supported Israel. This spurs the Palestinians to work tenaciously to create rupture in the hegemonic Israeli discourse that aims to obliterate the Palestinians as an absent, non-existent and irrelevant people. The Zionist premise was that Palestine was a land without a people for a people without a land (Said 1992; Saloul, 2012).

The main battel between Palestinians and the Israeli state concerns three central issues: land, people and political sovereignty (Al-Hardan, 2018).

Between 1947 and 1948, more than 750,000 Palestinians were forced to leave their homes and homeland due to Israeli military assaults and negated returning to their homeland. More than half of the Palestinian population live outside of the Palestine. 400,000 of these refugees fled to Jordan and 150,000 migrated to Lebanon and Syria. The remaining 200,000 these refugees settled around the Gaza areas. In 1949, the UN General Assembly passed a resolution in which the refugees were recognized as having the right to return to their homes, a resolution that Israel has opposing since then. Israel not only denied them the right to return but also confiscated their homes and lands as absentees. The number of Palestinians refugees is estimated to be over 4 million, according to the United Nations Relief and Work Agency that was established in 1949 to provide service to Palestinian refugees. More than 160,000 Palestinians stayed inside the newly established state of Israel, which makes 20% of the Israeli population. Today, their number reaches two million out of Israel's 9 million citizens. These Palestinians are called by the Israeli government as Arab Israelis, an epithet that many Palestinians with Israeli citizenship reject. By adopting the appellation Arab Israelis, Palestinians of Israel view the peril of being depoliticized and disconnected from the highly political nature of Palestinian identity (Berger, 2019). Despite having formal access to Israeli citizenship, Palestinians are not enjoying equal status and rights. Jabareen (2014) disputes the claims that view Israel a 'normal' Westphalian state due to its colonial form of citizenship. Colonial citizenship is "based on ethnic hierarchy, which is built on institutional discrimination that leads to vulnerability, domination, and control on matters that make the citizens as citizen" (Jabareen, 2014, p. 192).

The exclusionary face and practices of Israeli citizenship do not only target the Palestinians citizens of Israel but also Arab or Oriental Jews, called Mizrachi Jews, who are dominated by Ashkenazi Jews (Shafir & Peled, 2002; Shohat, 2017). A widespread argument is that (white European) Ashkenazi Jews were the first Jewish settlers in Palestine and it was first after 1948 that Mizrachi Jews came to settle in the state of Israel. This framing is however contested by Shafir and Peled (2002) who argue that Mizrachi Jews have longer presence than generally assumed but it was Ashkenazi Jews who led the Zionist project, which in itself was a European movement. The Ashkenazi Jews hold Orientalist views about Mizrachi Jews as culturally 'backward' and this attitude has underpinned the cultural and economic subordination of Mizrachi Jews in Israel. Mamdani (2020) maintains that Ashkenazi Jews have been involved in a project of civilizing the Mizrachi Jews and de-Arabized them culturally. Ironically, the Mizrachi Jews are today one of Israeli's most devoted Zionists. This pattern of identification by the Mizrachi Jews is explained by Mamdani as related to modernity and internalization of its mentality, that lacks respect for non-dominant groups (Mamdani 2020, p. 19). While Mizrachi Jews are second-class citizens, Palestinian citizens are third-class citizens (Shafir & Peled, 2002). The Palestinian citizens of Israel have also been regarded as 'half-stateless' (Jamal & Kensicki, 2020) or as 'stateless citizens' (Molavi 2013). While the Jews in Israel have individual and collective rights, the rights of Palestinians citizens of Israel are limited to individual rights and do not enjoy collective goods like land, holidays, commemorations or land and water.

This division between Israeli Jews and Palestinians explains why Israel is conceived as an ethnocracy (Kimmerling, 2001, p. 230), despite its initial Declaration of Independence that its citizenship pledges equal citizenship and rights to all citizens regardless of gender, religion and race (see Jamal, 2007). As Ghanem (1998) has shown, Israel functions as an ethnic state and despite its invitation of Palestinians or Arab citizens to participate in its polity, they are not offered equality but maintains Jewish superiority in all societal fields. Moreover, Israel treats Palestinian citizens as a threat to its national security and Jewish majority in demographic terms (Ghanem & Khatib, 2017). This Jewish mastery is now conspicuously enshrined in law. In July 2018, the Israeli Knesset passed a Nation-State Bills that affirmed that Israel is the historical homeland of the Jewish people and only its Jewish citizens can afford the right to exercise political sovereignty. Moreover, this new Nation-State Law defined the state language as Hebrew and assigned the Arabic language a 'special status' (Jamal & Kensicki, 2020). It is worth mentioning that this Nation-State Law did not only consolidate the exclusion of Palestinian citizens but also the Druze minority who have fought for Israel and sought equality as citizens of Israel. This constitutional change in Israel was a public declaration of Israeli Jewish mastery and undid its own proclaimed democracy and pluralism, that have been used as a self-legitimating discursive weapon against critique of Israel as a highly exclusionary polity.

Palestinian Displacement and Dispersal

When it comes to Palestinians outside of the state of Israel, there are around 4.8 million Palestinians living in the West Bank, East Jerusalem and the Gaza Strip. Due to political and economic reasons, Lebanon, Syria and Jordan have responded differently to the plights of the Palestinian refugees when it comes to provision of economic, social and cultural rights. Syria and Jordan have enabled the integration of Palestinians refugees in a far more favorable way than other Arab states (Erakat, 2014; Gandolfo, 2012; Hanafi, 2003). Palestinian integration within the Jordanian society continues to be thorny due to exclusionary nationalist discourses in Jordan. According to Massad (2008), it is by producing the Palestinians as the other, that Jordanian national identity is shaped and reproduced. Palestinian Jordanians are aware that they are not viewed as legitimate citizens of the Jordanian society despite their economic and cultural contribution to the Jordanian society (Massad, 2008; Pérez, 2018). Achilli (2021) underlines that Jordanian authorities view expression of Palestinian identity as signs of disloyalty against the Jordanian state and its rule. Despite experiences of discrimination and hardship among Palestinian refugees in Jordan, they continue to struggle and integrate within the Jordanian society. In his conclusion, Achilli maintains that the Palestinians do not reject the Jordanian national identity but view it as complementary to their Palestinian identity (Achilli, 2015). Despite Jordanian efforts to contain the Palestinian nationalism, the idea and national symbols of Palestine continue to be present within the private spheres of home (Pérez, 2018). However, it is important to note that not all Palestinians hold equally the same subordinate position within the Jordanian society. Pérez (2021) demonstrates in his fieldwork among Gaza refugees based in Jordan, that there are both similarities and differences between Palestinians living in exile with regard to how they experience displacement and give meanings to their Palestinian identity. Refugees from Gaza are far more excluded than Palestinians refugees who hold and enjoy the privileges of Jordanian citizenship. This makes the Gaza refugees into a minority within a minority since it is often the experience of displaced Palestinian refugees from 1948 living in Jordan and the West Bank, that is highlighted and enjoys public recognition (Pérez, 2021).

While Jordan has provided many Palestinians with Jordanian citizenship, Palestinians refugees in Lebanon have restricted life opportunities.

The Lebanese state has not shown an interest in integrating the Palestinians into the Lebanese society due to the complex sectarian balance (Bunton, 2013). This clarifies why the Palestinians refugees based in camps in Lebanon consider themselves as 'the forgotten people' and after decades of living there, they are denied working in 20 professions including medicine, law, engineering and journalism. Moreover, the camps in which they live are overcrowded and unsanitary (Roberts, 2010). Unlike Lebanon, the Syrian regime provided the Palestinians with civil rights but was not interested in granting them Syrian citizenship due to political reasons and tensions with the Israeli state. Following the Syrian uprising in 2011, the Palestinian vulnerability became apparent since they were shuttled between the Syrian regime and the Sunni Arab opposition. Due to the divergent loyalties of the Palestinians, many of them were forced to leave the country and the Jordanian and Lebanese authorities did not show eagerness to accommodate these Palestinian refugees (see Erakat, 2014).

As Peteet (2005) has argued, the relationship between the 'host' society and the refugees is central to what kinds of rights the refugees are entitled to and make claim to, but also how they make sense of the past in their present time, and what future they envision. This relationship affects also the attitudes of Palestinian refugees in regard to the question of return. Lebanon has effectively tried to make the lives of Palestinians unbearable to so they can leave the country. In contrast to Lebanon, Jordan is experienced as a surrogate for a Palestinian state due to its immediate historical relationship with the Palestinians. This discourse has also been deployed by the Israelis to dismiss a Palestinian state and suggesting Jordan as their prospective homeland (see Karmi 2015). In Syria, Lebanon and Jordan, despite their disparate Palestinian policies, refugee camps have become a hallmark of Palestinians lives, as a persistent reminder of their dispossession and homelessness but also a continuous politicization of Palestinian identity. Palestinian refugees are living between the hope of liberation and the despair of suffering and rightlessness due to the ongoing Israeli occupation of Palestine (see Peteet 2005).

Hilal and Petti (2018) maintain that there is a continuous resistance to normalizing life and settlement in refugee camps and the surrounding states in the Middle East due to the fear of undermining the right of return to Palestine, which makes the authors wonder why the Palestinian refugees need to live in limbo and hardship in order to be qualified as having the right of return to their homeland. Palestinian refugees have experienced mass expulsion from Kuwait (1991), Libya (1996) and Iraq (2003), despite the formal rhetoric of these states that they champion Palestinian sovereignty and rights (see Erakat, 2014). What characterize the lives of Palestinian refugees in the camps is a contradictory condition of *permanent temporariness*, as a critique of being normalized as a citizen or perpetuated as a refugee. As a result of their expulsion from Palestine since 1948, the camps are not accepted by the Palestinian refugees as their final destinations or permanent homes. However, there is a risk that by highlighting the right of return, other rights such as citizenship rights can become sidelined in the countries in which they live their daily lives (Hilal & Petti, 2018, pp. 57–58).

The notion of diaspora has been contested and problematized in the context of Palestinian displacement and homelessness (Hanafi, 2003; Peteet 2007). Before the proliferation of diaspora studies, Sayiqh (1979) argued that integration into Arab societies were viewed by Palestinians living in the refugee camps as a continuation of the Zionist project to prevent the Palestinians from returning to their homeland. Against this background, Sayigh repudiated the idea of a Palestinian diaspora since it created a false parallel with the Jewish experience. For Sayiqh, the Palestinians are living in '*ghourba*', the Arabic word for a state of alienated exile (p. 96) and statelessness has made them to objects of oppression in Israel, Lebanon and Jordan. Sayigh's ideas echo partly in the work of Hanafi (2003), who argues that diasporization of Palestinians is viewed as a pretext for naturalization and normalization of Israeli occupation and erasure of Palestinian claims to lands and homes. Embracing diaspora is also viewed as inadequate to describe Palestinian experiences and weakening their defense and political cause. Moreover, many Palestinians are not allowed to visit or return to their countries of origin due to the Israeli law of return, forged to create a rupture between Palestinians and their territories, lands and homes. Palestine is not accessible to Palestinians due to occupation which makes it to a weak center of gravity (Hanafi, 2003). As the Palestinian poet Mahmoud Darwish has put it in relation to Palestinian exile: "We travel like other peoples, but we return to nowhere" (cited in Bowman, 1994, p. 138). By assuming a diasporic identity, the idea and the goal of returning to Palestine risks being suspended, which in itself constitute a potent danger to Palestinian resistance to Israeli occupation. Palestinian displacement is not just a relic of past but is viewed as ongoing and immediate due to the persistent violent subordination of Palestinians by the Israeli state (see Peteet 2007). Moreover, this Palestinian refusal to embrace the concept of diaspora can be understood as a resistance to putting down roots in other places and affirming their original collective identity and homeland that they are denied from returning to (see Malkki, 1995). Consequently, it is important to understand that by invoking uncritically the concept of diaspora, we risk "minimizing the range of traumatic conditions that fuel displacement and the way these shape sociocultural formations and subjectivity" (Peteet 2007, p. 630). However, Peteet (2007) suggests that the concept of diaspora is more useful for Palestinians living in the West than in the Arab countries where Palestinians are geographically much closer to their homeland but also due to common historical, linguistic and cultural references. Hanafi (2003) argues that it is the secure legal status that matters when Palestinians can be defined as diasporic or non-diasporic. In the Middle East, Palestinians refugees are not facing exclusion due to their cultural backgrounds, but it is mainly within the realm of economy that they are subordinated. This exclusion is intimately related to lack of legal work rights in the gulf states, Lebanon and Israel. Palestinians uphold a strong link to their homeland due to ongoing Israeli occupation and negative experiences of legal and economic rights in the majority of Arab countries. For example, Palestinians have chosen assimilation in order to escape popular racism in Egypt and institutional exclusion in France. By becoming citizens in the Arab countries, the Palestinian identity does not dissolve. It is often argued by Arab states that by giving citizenship to Palestinians, they will become assimilated and assimilation will entail political surrender to Israel. Another important reason why the Palestinian dispersion is not viewed as a 'classic' diaspora is that it lacks a self-evident center of gravity, due to fragmentation and occupation of Palestinian lands (Hanafi, 2003).

Palestinian history of migration has a longer history than the moment of Israel's foundation and the exclusions that it entailed. Those Palestinians who migrated before 1948 did so mainly to avoid doing Ottoman military service but also due to economic reasons. Latin America and North America became the destination of these migrants. These Palestinians could not return to Palestinians since they had left prior to the foundation of Israel in 1948. Israel erected various legal and administrative measures to dismiss their return. The second trend of Palestinian migration was due to their expulsion from Palestine by the Zionists in 1948 and the third trend was characterized by Palestinian migration to the gulf states and the West due to economic reasons (Hanafi, 2003). A variety of studies have investigated Palestinian experiences of dispossession, displacement and homeland politics in the West and Latin America. Schwabe (2018) in her ethnographic work among Palestinian diaspora in Chile has shown that remembrance and forgetting are central to the identity formation of Palestinians in relation to the ongoing Israeli occupation of Palestine. While Palestinians have direct experience of Chilean dictatorship under the rule of Pinochet, they tend to under-communicate the Chilean past and underscore the Palestinian dispossession and present politics of struggle. The Palestinian narratives tend to marginalize their collective experiences of discrimination in Chile where they were viewed as communists, *turcos* and terrorists since a leftist position was strongly tied to a pro-Palestinian stance (Schwabe, 2018). In the Australian context, Cox and Connell (2003) argue that statelessness continues to affect the lives of Palestinians in Sydney and push them to maintain their national identity and community formation. The ongoing political injustice that is inflicted on Palestine and Palestinians inform their continuous politicized Palestinian identity. In her work on a Palestinian community that was expelled from Kuwait as a result of 1990–1991 Gulf war, Mason (2007) maintains that the Palestinian experiences of anti-Arab sentiment have undermined their sense of home-making in Australia. However, this has not prevented them from creating intimate relationship with Australia and Palestine. While the generation of al-Nakba expresses a strong sense of estrangement, homesickness, isolation and non-belonging and loneliness, the generation of Palestinians which was born in exile diverges due to its hybrid identity and navigating between different identities. A hybrid Palestinian identity does not in itself entail abandoning the link to the occupied Palestine (Mason, 2007). Mavroudi (2007) has shown in her field work among Palestinians in Greece that Palestinians evoke strong experiences of injustices and statelessness. Unlike post-national deliberations about citizenship and membership, attaining Greek citizenship is viewed as pragmatic to realize and attain rights like mobility that Palestinians are deprived from. However, citizenship does not mean full inclusion or belonging to the Greek society.

In another study about Palestinian diaspora, Mavroudi (2018) points out that it is not self-evident that Palestinian feeling of injustices in times of crisis is translated into action, particularly when crisis becomes more a pattern than an exception in Palestinian lives. Frustration about lack of positive outcomes from Palestinian mobilization and inability to help the homeland can engender a Palestinian identity characterized by detachment and isolation. When it comes to the identity formation of second-generation Polish and British Palestinians, Blachnicka-Ciacke (2018) discusses that the younger generation of Palestinians are not passive recipients of intergenerational transmission of cultural identity, a conception that defies the work of Lindholm Schulz (2003, p. 172). It is largely due to the frequent violence that Palestinians are exposed to by the Israeli state, that underpins and activates their strong engagement with the Palestinian issue. Moreover, second-generations Palestinians are endorsing a long-distance post-nationalism than a primordial attachment to Palestine, that fosters justice and equality for Palestine in the context of occupation. When they return to Palestinian territories, they are reminded of the differences that exist between the Palestinians abroad and those living in Palestine. This is where they arrive to a conclusion that Palestine does not need to be the place in which they should live in order to be and claim a Palestinian identity. Some of the second-generation Palestinians challenge also their parents' way of expressing loyalty to Palestine, and being 'sofa activists', obsessed with the past (Blachnicka-Ciacke, 2018). Indeed, this result converges well with Hammer's study (2005), who demonstrated that Palestinians who returned to the West Bank and Gaza following the 1993 Oslo Peace Accords between PLO and Israel, realized the discrepancy between a lived Palestinian identity on Palestinian lands and transmission of memories, images and history of Palestine in diasporic contexts. 'Home-coming' became for many of these returnees a challenge and a disappointment for not having compatible lifeways and values with their Palestinian neighbors in the West Bank and Gaza (Hammer, 2005). When it comes to Sweden, which is home to more than 30,000 Palestinians with different legal status, Lindholm (2019) illustrates that Palestinians both appreciate Sweden as a country of welfare but at the same time experience exclusionary discourses of Swedishness that marginalize non-white migrants. Palestinians in Sweden express a strong emotional and political attachment the Palestinian identity, largely guided by a sense of homelessness. Similar to Blachnicka-Ciacke's study (2018), Palestinians are aware of the differences between being a Palestinian in Palestine and being a Palestinian in Sweden (Lindholm, 2019). When it comes to studies that have engaged with statelessness, Gabiam (2015) presents a convincing argument that statelessness among Palestinians in France need to be understood beyond the official discourse of UNHCR and the legal perspective, a conclusion that Fiddian-Qasmiyeh

(2016) adheres to in her work on Palestinian statelessness. Gabiam (2015) makes a clear distinction between stateless persons and stateless people. Palestinians might have citizenship as individuals but they are still member of a stateless people. Although considering themselves as stateless, some of the research participants in Gabiam's study did not view the state as necessarily emancipatory. In the context of Palestinians in France, Gabiam (2015) argues that while there is a variety of advantages with statehood and citizenship, statelessness cannot capture the dilemmas of Palestinians if its solely equated with lack of citizenship. Many Palestinians who hold American or European passports are not guaranteed access to places that are meaningful to them. Israel for instance can ban Palestinians with French passport from entering Israel if suspected of political activism. Similar harassments are also witnessed at Arab state borders (Gabiam, 2015).

The Political Encirclement of the Kurds in the Middle East

The Kurds are one of the largest nations without a sovereign state. Following the collapse of the Ottoman Empire, Britain and France took over the Middle East. As a result, Kurds were sidelined when the borders of new states were drawn and established in the Middle East. In light of nation-building processes in the Middle East, the Kurds have come to occupy a minoritized and inferiorized position within the states of Turkey, Iran, Iraq and Syria. The Kurds have either been viewed as a 'minority' or denied existence as a nation in the Middle East. This denial of Kurdish identity has informed Kurdish subjectivity, complicity and resistance against these states. The Kurdish population is estimated to be between 30 and 40 million, a number that is disputable due to reluctance of the states to acknowledge the Kurdish existence and the exaggeration of Kurdish nationalists to overestimate the number of the Kurdish population (see Hassanpour & Mojab, 2005). Kurdistan that many Kurds imagine as their homeland has been portrayed as an interstate colony (Besikci, 1988) and the situation of the Kurds in each state has been described as an internal colonialism due to the unequal center-periphery relations that inform sociopolitical, economic and cultural discrimination against the Kurdish population (Entessar, 2010; Kürt, 2018). If the Palestinians view the Zionist nationalists as their dominant other, the Kurds are embedded in a struggle against aggressive and expansionary Turkish,

Iranian, Iraqi and Syrian nationalisms, who all proclaim Islamic brotherhood but practice discrimination and ethno-national hierarchies where Kurds are placed at the bottom of their political orders (Ignatieff, 1994). These four states have adopted a variety of political strategies to exclude the Kurds or to include them on subordinated terms. In other words, the discursive field of Kurdish identity formation and resistance has been shaped by experiences of structural discrimination, physical and political violence, nonrecognition, misrepresentation, cultural inferiorization and denial. If there is one thing that unites these four states regardless of their ideological and historical antagonisms, it is their persistent and common efforts to prevent the Kurds from realizing sovereignty and statehood (see Ciment, 1996). In order to illustrate the deep Turkish aversion toward Kurdish autonomy and sovereignty, there are anecdotes about different Turkish leaders who have sworn to prevent the creation of a Kurdish state whether it is on the moon, in South Africa or Argentina. A central feature of the foreign policy of these four states is to destabilize Kurdish unity and deepen the divisions in order to keep them away from forming a common resistance front. Kurds are geopolitically trapped between four states who all have a considerable Kurdish population and these states are well aware that if a Kurdish region gains some form of autonomy, federalism or independence, it will send inspirational signal to other non-autonomous Kurdish regions about the possibility of not being subjected to political subordination, denial and erasure (Eliassi, 2013). A short description of each state is relevant in order to understand the sociopolitical context that has shaped Kurdish identity politics.

Turkey

Let us start with Turkey that has subsumed the largest part of the Kurdish population under its sovereignty. The Turkish republic was founded in 1923. While the Kurds were initially promised autonomy within the framework of this republic, the new Turkish republic dropped this promised policy and started asserting a politics of denial, assimilation and annihilation (Bozarslan, 2018; Yadirgi, 2017). The new Turkish state adopted the Kemalist notions of Turkish national liberation, modernization and secularism, in which there were no place for non-Turkish constituencies as legitimate political partners. Kurds who constitute the second-largest ethnopolitical group in Turkey were exposed to harsh assimilation policy. The main target of Turkish assimilation was the

Kurdish identity and language. While the Ottoman Empire, despite its limitations, cherished diversity, the new Turkish republic that replaced it has come to view diversity as a danger against its survival and national cohesion. School children in Turkey have been instilled with chauvinist slogans like: 'How happy is the one who says, I am a Turk', 'One Turk equals the whole world', and One language, one people, one flag'. This chauvinist rhetoric is not only endorsed by secular Turkish parties and governments but also by the current Islamist party, Justice and Development Party (AKP) led by the Turkish President Recep Tayyip Erdoğan. Kurds have historically been exempted from dominant Turkish representations and when they have resisted Turkish dominance and assimilation, they have been described as non-civilized, premodern, or as terrorists, crypto-Jews and pseudo-citizens (Yeğen, 1996, 2009).

For the Turkish state, there are broadly two kinds of Kurdish subjectivities, defined as 'good Kurds' and 'bad Kurds'. 'Good Kurds' are referred for those Kurds who declare their unequivocal loyalty to the Turkish state and express their readiness to serve Turkishness and even die for it. In contrast, the 'bad Kurds' are those individuals or movements who are viewed as anti-Turkish by expressing and investing in Kurdish identity politics. These Kurds are considered as undermining 'Islamic brotherhood' between the Turks and the Kurds by endorsing separatist politics and violence. Throughout history, Kurds have waged several rebellions against the Turkish state but have been defeated. The Kurdish region in Turkey are highly militarized, and cities and villages have been evacuated and destroyed as a result of the war between the Turkish state and Kurdistan Workers' Party (PKK) that started at the beginnings of the 1980s. Kurdish attempts to organize themselves politically and participate in Turkish politics have been limited by the ruling AKP.

There are strong Turkish ambitions to exclude the Kurds from political participation by banning the political parties that they establish. To further undermine the political organization of the Kurds in Turkey, in 2016 the Turkish state imprisoned the charismatic Selahattin Demirtaş due to baseless allegation of 'terror'. The pro-Kurdish Peoples' Democratic Party (HDP) that Demirtaş led before his imprisonment has been struggling as the first political party to endorse ethnic pluralism and political equality in Turkey's parliament. HDP's attempts have been harshly suppressed by the ruling AKP. In Turkey, it is mainly by depicting the Kurds or the Kurdish movement as a threat, that Turkish political parties can rally around a common politics. Turkey is waging a war on several fronts against the Kurds in Turkey, Iraq and Syria. This violence against the Kurds goes hand in hand with cultural denial and erasure. For Turkish nationalism, Kurds are not imagined as equals despite political rhetoric of brotherhood, but are urged to subsume themselves under the mastery of Turkishness or Turkish Islam. Under the Turkish leadership of Erdoğan, the Kurdish movement is not only depicted as a threat to the Turkish identity but it is also denigrated as anti-Islamic movement, in order to mobilize anti-Kurdish sentiment across the Muslim Middle East.

Iran

When it comes to Iran, Kurdish identity has been suppressed both violently and through cultural assimilation and economic deprivation. The Kurds are the third-largest ethnopolitical group in Iran after the Persians and the Azeris/Turks. But it is the Kurds as an ethnopolitical constituency that have been the main opponent of the central governments and involved in armed conflict with different Iranian regimes (Vali 1998). In 1941, Soviet and British forces occupied Iran and this created a political opportunity for the Kurds to gain some political power.

In 1946, Kurds established a short-lived Kurdish republic, which included certain parts of Kurdish territories. However, after less than one year, the republic was dismantled by the Iranian army and its leaders were hanged in 1947 on the same square where they had declared independence. Nevertheless, this republic has retained its symbolic and political value for Kurds of Iran but also other Kurdish regions in the neighboring countries. It is annually commemorated as a historical event in Kurdish history.

In 1979, When the Islamic revolution under the leadership of Ayatollah Khomeini succeeded in overthrowing the royalist regime of Iran, the Kurds like other groups in Iran were hoping that a new order would bring about structural changes that could foster equality between different ethnic and religious groups. But soon, the Kurds realized that this Islamic regime was not much different from the regime of Shah that endorsed Persian cultural supremacy. According to Khomeini, concepts like minority and nationalism were not part of Islam and should not be used since they supposedly stand in stark contrast to an Islamic doctrine (McDowall, 2004). Of course, this was just empty rhetoric since Iran under an Islamic regime was no less nationalist. Indeed, by adopting the notion of Islam as the unifying identity, the Islamic regime has tended to discard the claims of minoritized groups as 'foreign plots' endorsed by imperialist and Zionist powers.

Moreover, when the Islamic regime of Iran talk about Islamic or Muslim universalism, it practically and constitutionally denotes Shia Islam as the overarching identity that dictates the rules and constitutes the normative identity. As an example of this constitutionally endorsed inequality, Sunni Muslims, Christians, Jews or members of Ahl-Haq (Yaresanis) cannot be elected as president of Iran or entitled to powerful positions within the Iranian state. Many Kurds are exposed to discrimination on basis of ethnicity and religion and the Kurdish regions of Iran are securitized and highly impoverished. Following securitization and marginalization of the Kurds, economic investments are suspended in the Kurdish regions. In reality, the only non-Persian group that has benefited relatively from economic investment has been the Azeris/Turks (Shiites) who constitutes a numerical challenge to the Persian dominance.

The Islamic regime of Iran under Khomeini denied the Kurds their rights and declared a holy war against the (atheist) Kurds for opposing an 'Islamic' regime. This led to intense fighting in the Kurdish region between the Islamic regime and Kurdish forces led by Democratic Party of Iranian Kurdistan (PDKI) and Komala. As a result of these clashes, close to 55,000 people were killed and more than 300 villages were destroyed. Kurdistan has become a highly militarized zone with heavily mined areas. Both PDKI and Komala were militarily defeated due to the asymmetrical warfare power between the Iranian state and the Kurdish forces. Moreover, these two major political forces have lost important political figures due to political assassinations by the Iranian regime (Ciment, 1996; Wahlbeck, 1999).

The major demand of the Kurds in Iran has been 'Democracy for Iran, Autonomy for Kurdistan'. The Kurdish parties have understood well that it is only through a genuine democratization of the Iranian state and society, that pluralism and differences have a chance to survive, flourish and become institutionalized in a multiethnic society. This democratic demand has been fiercely rejected by the Iranian state and equated with separatism and foreign plots to undermine the territorial integrity of the Iranian state. Lately, the Kurds of Iran have shifted their autonomy discourse to federalism, similar to what Kurds have achieved in the neighboring Iraq.

The Kurdish region in Iran are subjected to both militarization and economic impoverishment, which force many Kurds to immigrate to major Iranian cities to earn a living. Immigration to western European countries is also a result of political and economic deprivation that Kurds suffer in Iran. In 2004, the Free Life Party of Kurdistan (PJAK) was founded and claimed itself to be the political alternative to PDKI and Komala for 'passively' sitting in Kurdistan of Iraq and watching the political situation of the Kurds in Iran. Contrariwise, PDKI and Komala have accused PJAK to be an extended arm of the PKK with no attachment to the political reality of the Kurds in Iran. Evidently, PJAK is a branch of the PKK but it has also strong support among Kurds, particularly in certain parts of the Kurdish region where PDKI and Komala have not been able to influence and recruit, as in Kermanshan and Ilam.

PDKI and Komala have split into several parties which in turn have created confusion among the Kurds of what and who they represent and fight for. These fragmentation and divisions have severely damaged their public image among the Kurds for lacking a united front to improve the political situation of the Kurds. Kurdish parties from Eastern Kurdistan/Iran have also become hostages of the Kurdistan Region and have not been able to carry out independent policy due to fear of retaliation mainly by the Patriotic Union of Kurdistan (PUK) and more recently Kurdistan Democratic Party (KDP). These two political parties which rule the Kurdistan Region of Iraq have warned the Kurds of Iran to not use 'their' territory to launch attacks against the Iranian state. Similar argument is continuously used against the PKK for using the Kurdistan Region and sparking Turkish aggression against Kurdish villages while bombing PKK inside the Kurdistan Region. Of course, this clearly shows how territorial fragmentation of the Kurds across four states has also led to political fragmentation and division among the Kurds themselves. In sum, Kurds in Iran are exposed to state-sponsored discrimination in the realms of culture, political representation, employment, education and housing.

Iraq

As a colonial construction, Iraq was established in 1918 by Britain, which had an immense interest in securing and monopolizing this oil-rich country. Britain occupied Kurdish cities and villages from 1918 to 1930. Unlike the common charge in the Middle East that Kurds constitute a colonial toy used by the West and Israel, the Kurds violently resisted the British occupation and was bombed fiercely by the British forces. In order to justify its ruthless aggression against the Kurds, the British administrators perceived the Kurds as 'primitive' tribesmen unqualified of governing themselves (Ciment, 1996).

Iraq was first ruled by the Pro-Hashemite monarchy but was overthrown by the mid-1950s. The leftist general Abdel al-Karim Qasim established the Republic of Iraq through a coup. Qasim initially adopted a friendly approach to the Kurds; however, this relationship did not last long and terminated in conflict. In 1963, the nationalist Baath Party took power through a coup and executed Qassim. This new regime promised autonomy to the Kurds and admitted the existence of the Kurds as a people with cultural rights, which resulted in a short peace-agreement in 1970 (Kirmanj, 2013). A central site of dispute between the Kurds and the Baath regime regarded the oil-refining city of Kirkuk, whether it should be put under Kurdish administration or not. This dispute could not be settled and engendered an armed conflict between the Kurds and the Iraqi army. At this time, Iran was supporting the Kurds with arms but soon dropped its support for the Kurds due an agreement with the Iraqi government. Iran and the US left the Kurds alone with no allies, which forced the Kurdish guerrillas to escape to Iran along with 150,000 civilian refugees (Ciment, 1996; Entessar, 2010).

Historically, no Iraqi government has been able to accommodate the political demands of the Kurds. Iraqi Arab nationalism has been the central framework through which Kurds have been viewed, treated and subjected to oppression. Warfare, mass execution, genocide, deportations and chemical attacks have at different times guided Iraqi politics against the Kurds (Kirmanj, 2013; Randal, 1999). In stark contrast to Turkey, Iran and Syria, Kurdish language was not oppressed and Kurds enjoyed a certain degree of cultural rights. When Iraq invaded Kuwait in 1990 and was defeated by the US and its allied, the Kurds took the opportunity to take control of many Kurdish cities. Due to fear of Iraqi retaliation against the Kurds, the UN established a no-fly zone to protect the Kurdish region. Ironically, Turkish and Iranian aggression was tolerated within these zones.

In 2003, a new opportunity emerged for the Kurds, when Saddam Hussein was ousted by the US and its allies. Kurdish forces took control of almost all areas that the Kurdish movements considered as Kurdish including Kirkuk, which they lost again to the Iraqi army and Shiite militias in 2017 following the independence referendum of Kurdistan Region. In 2005, a new Iraqi constitution was crafted in Iraq which provided the

Kurds with right to self-rule within a federal Iraq. However, many thorny issues remain unsettled between the Kurds and the Iraqi government, like the disputed areas, the Kurdish share of the Iraqi budget and the oil. Despite the article 140 of the Iraqi constitution, which maintains that the situation of Kirkuk and other disputed areas subjected to Arabization policy and demographic manipulation should be normalized through a referendum by its inhabitants, few steps have been taken to address this issue.

The Kurdish region which was considered to be a stable and prosperous is now facing huge economic crisis. This is due to the prolonged suspension of the Kurdish share from the Iraqi state budget and the widespread corruption by KDP and PUK, the two ruling political parties in Kurdistan Region. These two parties led by the families of Barzani and Talabani have monopolized the politics, economy, security and the armed forces of the Kurdish region. This has created a significant backlash for Kurdish nationalism as a unifying factor against the dominant Arab constituency, but also creating despair for Kurds in other parts of Kurdistan who have dreamt about Kurdish self-rule. The Iraqi government for its part has not been willing to create an inclusive and non-hierarchical Iraq where Kurds are not viewed as its other but included as legitimate co-partner of the Iraqi polity.

There are strong indications that the Shiite constituency has regretted the very idea of a federal Iraq in which Kurds have right to political autonomy. The Shiites who control the most sensitive positions of the Iraqi state are attempting to bring the Kurds under their authority with the help of the Iranian state. The future of Kurdistan Region remains highly insecure due to external threats by the neighboring states but also as a result of the widespread power abuse by the ruling political parties in Kurdistan. There is a potential risk that the Kurdistan Region becomes dissolved by dividing it into two autonomous regions, each led by KDP and PUK. If Kurdish leadership once was rhetorically aiming for independence, the peril of demise of Kurdish self-rule is not a groundless prediction. Turkey, Iran and Iraq are all politically, economically and militarily engaged in pressing the Kurds into a corner where they cannot aspire shared power, autonomy or independence. Geopolitical dynamics of the Middle East, the US presence and involvement in Iraq juxtaposed with domestic Kurdish politics and state policies vis-à-vis the Kurds will determine the future of the Kurdish self-rule in within the federal framework of Iraq.

Syria

Similar to Iraq, Syria as a colonial construction became an independent state in 1946. Compared to Turkey, Iran, Iraq and Syria have the smallest Kurdish population located mostly in northern parts of Syria. During the first years of this new Syrian republic, the relationship between the Kurds and Arabs was relatively good, but things started to change when Syria was monopolized by Arab nationalism and denied the Kurds as an ethnopolitical reality in Syria. When the French troops left Syria in 1946, Kurds were not directly excluded from the political life of the Syrian society. The army played a central role in the post-mandatory Syria, where Kurdish officers held an important place, but occupied a marginal position within the parliament. For instance, two of the three first dictators of Syria during 1949–1955 had Kurdish origin, namely Husni Za 'im and Adib al-Shishakli. These leaders did not have a political agenda to endorse Kurdish rights or autonomy for different minoritized groups in Syria. In contrast, al-Shishakli had a brutal stance toward minority rights and championed a unitary Syrian state based on chauvinistic conception of Arab nationalism. Although there were rumors and claims that these Kurdish leaders were planning to establish a Kurdish power in Syria, al-Shishakli not only refrained from admitting his Kurdish origin but also did not show any interest in accommodating Kurdish claims to autonomy in Syria. The rule for these two Kurdish leaders were too short-lived to have any significant effect on minority rights. In light of Arab nationalism, the processes of Arabization and anti-Kurdish politics and sentiments became salient in Syria (Tejel, 2009). In order to obstruct Kurds from realizing any demographic threat to the Arab Syria, a policy of Arabization of Kurdish areas and dispersion of Kurdish populated was carried out thoroughly. Kurds were deprived from having right to education in Kurdish and the names of Kurdish villages were Arabized. When the nationalist Baath Party took the power in Syria, it flagrantly asserted that Syria is the homeland of Arab. The new state was named as the Syrian *Arab* Republic and declaring the primacy of Arabs as its masters. Moreover, more than 300,000 Kurds have been denationalized and classified as stateless and foreigners (Lowe, 2006; Savelsberg & Hajo, 2011; Tejel, 2009).

Historically, the Kurds have been portrayed as an internal enemy of the Syrian state, with an allegedly Zionist agenda to create a Judistan. In this anti-Kurdish representation, the Kurds have been framed as 'malignant tumor' on the body of the Arab nation (Tejel, 2009; Vanly, 1992).

The Baath regime has used a variety of discourses and measures to deal with the Kurds. Dehumanization, exploitation, incorporation and co-optation have guided the Baath regime's policy vis-à-vis the Kurds. In 2004, following a clash between Kurdish and Arab supporters of two soccer teams (al-Jihad from Qamishli and Dayr al-Zur), both sides started chanting insulting slogans and exchanging derogatory ethnic slurs. The security forces along armed militias from Arab tribes sided with the Arab supporters and brutally treated the Kurds, which led to killings and arrests of Kurdish protestors against this brutality. Moreover, some forty students were expelled from Syrian universities (Savelsberg & Hajo, 2011; Tejel, 2009).

As other parts of the predominantly Arab world, at the end of 2010, the 'Arab Spring' knocked at the doors of Syria and its authoritarian regime. The Syrian regime brutally suppressed the protests and as a result of external support by Iran, (Lebanese) Hezbollah and Russia, the Syrian regime has managed to gain control over much of the territories it lost to the Sunni Arab opposition. The Sunni Arab opposition is now consisted of a variety of ideological groups. However, the fear of Islamists among the Sunni Arab opposition has discouraged many countries to stop supporting the Sunni Arab opposition. The Syrian regime despite its ruthless treatment of the Syrian opposition has used the intolerance of these armed religious groups as an argument to solidify its position as the guardian of ethnic and religious pluralism. The Syrian regime is no less sectarian than the Islamists that fight for ousting the Baath regime. While the Kurds have not engaged militarily with the Assad regime of Syria, they have been viewed by the Sunni Arab opposition as infidels in alliance with the enemies of the 'Syrian revolution', including the Syrian regime and the US. At the beginning of the Syrian uprisings, the Syrian regime promised the Kurds citizenship rights, not only to dissuade them from fighting the regime but also to create a rupture between the Sunni Kurds and Sunni Arabs. The overall goal of the Syrian regime was to prevent creation of a united resistance front. The Syrian regime abandoned the predominantly Kurdish regions of Syria and Kurdish forces took over them. This was of course a tactical retreat by the regime in order to first focus on the fierce Sunni Arab opposition. After militarily defeating more or less the armed Sunni Arab opposition, the Syrian *Arab* army has returned to certain parts of the Kurdish region on the border with Turkey in 2019.

Between 2014 and 2015, the Islamic State of Iraq and the Levant (ISIL) besieged the Kurds in the city of Kobane, which draw international responses and sympathies. The US started bombing ISIL, and the Kurdish fighters on the grounds expelled ISIL from Kobane. It was in this context that the image of female Kurdish fighters started circulating in Western press, in opposition to ISIL's misogynic ideals and practices. This US intervention in the Syrian conflict engendered a military relationship between the US and the Kurds, led by the Democratic Union of Party. Initially, the Kurds named their region as *Rojava* (West Kurdistan), which they have renamed to the Democratic Federation of Northern Syria (DFNS), to create a more inclusive polity based on the existing ethnoreligious constituencies in the region. The US helped the Kurds to form the Syrian Democratic Forces (SDF) which is dominated by People's Protection Units (YPG). The Kurds have lost several thousand fighters in their armed struggle against ISIL and indeed managed to a large extent with American support neutralize ISIL, but they have been betrayed by both the US and major European powers despite claims that Kurds are fighting for humanity against the ruthless ISIL.

Turkey views the overall project of Rojava as a project of 'terror' to create a Kurdish state led by PKK given that PYD has a strong link to PKK. It is however not a coincidence since many Kurds of Syria have lost their lives while fighting for PKK against the Turkish state. Ironically, while Turkey was an easy corridor for recruitment of ISIL fighters, the Turkish President Erdoğan has on many occasions argued that there is no difference between ISIL and the Kurdish movement in Syria, led by PYD. Despite the Kurdish insistence that they are not posing a threat to Turkey, the Kurds have been attacked and dispossessed by the Turkish army and Islamist groups. Turkey has ironically justified its invasion of the majority-Kurdish Afrin District in northwest Syria as the 'Operation Olive Branch' in 2018, which has led to displacement of hundreds of thousand Kurds, demographic engineering and erasure of Kurdish symbols, all endorsed and implemented by Turkish support. Predictably, every time Turkey launches an attack against the Kurds, it claims that it is not targeting the Kurds but 'terrorists'. The Turkish state's aggression against the Kurds did not stop here. In 2019, Turkey launched a new invasion against the Kurds of Syria which was branded by Erdoğan as 'peace corridor', which in practice entails that Kurds should be removed and replaced with Syrian Arab refugees. This Turkish formula in practice entails that Turkey aims to address the displacement of Syrian Arab refugees in Turkey by displacing the Kurds. The concept of 'peace' in Turkish state's conception has come to entail dispossession, denial and displacement of Kurds as not belonging to the geography in which they live or want to rule themselves.

Although the Turkish state poses a threat to the ethnopolitical rights of the Kurds inside Turkey and outside Turkish borders, it is also important to note that the embattled Syrian regime under the leadership of Bashar al-Assad has not demonstrated a genuine interest or understanding for the plights of the Kurds seeking ethnopolitical rights. In contrast, it has shown clear aversion and denial of the Kurds as having legitimate political claims. In 2020, Bashar al-Assad called the Kurdish issue in Syria as 'illusive and a lie'. In the same interview, al-Assad lamented that some 'Kurdish separatists' supported by the US have betrayed the 'hospitality' of the Syrian state when they sought safety and security in Syria. Throughout his talk, the 'We' is used by al-Assad to depict the Arabs as the host and the master of the state and the Kurds as refugees and guests. Al-Assad goes so far to announce that the Arabs are the majority and they are the one that could dictate the rule, as though they have not done so by criminalizing, Arabizing and de-nationalizing and dispossessing hundreds of thousands of Kurds in Syria. Al-Assad has made it clear that federalism is not an option for the Kurds given that the Arabs are the majority of the state, implicitly with the right to be the spatial managers of the state and rule the Kurds.

The Sunni Arab opposition that challenges al-Assad is not much different from the ruling regime in Damascus given that it rejects the very basis of ethnopolitical realities of the Kurds, but ask them to subsume themselves under an imposed (Arab dominated) Syrian identity. For the Kurds in the region, the situation is gloomy and their political survival and rights will be highly dependent on the American and Russian interests in endorsing the right of Kurds to self-rule. With respect to the Kurdish leadership, it becomes important to maintain a balanced and positive relationship with the Russians, due to the fragile American protection and supports of the Kurds in Syria and Iraq. The greatest threat comes from the Turkish state that seems determined to neutralize the Kurds in the Middle East by invasion of Kurdish-majority regions and demographic manipulation.

Moreover, the Kurds are internally fragmented and there is no serious attempt among the Kurdish parties to establish a common front against the oppressive states that harass and threaten Kurdish lives and rights. The geopolitical situation of the Kurds encircled by four states with historical anti-Kurdish sentiments and policies makes it difficult to predict a democratized and pluralist approach to settling the relationship between the states and the Kurdish movements. Historical experiences of violence, political oppression and economic deprivation continue to be the major factors behind Kurdish migration to the West, that I will engage with in the following section.

Kurdish Diaspora Formations in Sweden and the UK

Kurdish migration to Western countries is a relatively new phenomenon. There are no accurate data about the number of the Kurds in the West since the Kurds lack a unified nation-state and are often officially registered as Turkish, Iranian, Iraqi and Syrian nationals. However, the size of the Kurdish diaspora is increasing due to the continuous armed conflicts in the Middle East and particularly in Syria and Iraq, where many Kurds of Syria and Yezidis have left their homes. The emergence of the extremist Islamic State of Iraq and the Levant (ISIL) in 2014 left many Yezidis homeless and traumatized. Many young Yezidi women were also sexually abused and raped by ISIL. According to Wahlbeck (2018), Kurdish organizations tend to exaggerate the number of Kurdish diasporas in the West. The number of Kurds during the 1990s was estimated to be 660,000 in Germany, 120,000 in France, 80,000 in the Netherlands, 60,000 in Austria, 50,000 in the UK, 70,000 in Switzerland, 40,000 in Sweden, 60,000 in Belgium and some several thousands in Greece, Italy, Denmark, and Finland. There is also around a 75,000-strong Kurdish community in the US and 50,000 Kurdish migrants in Canada. Despite its recent history in the West, the size of the Kurdish diaspora is modestly estimated to exceed 1 million (Wahlbeck, 2018; see also Hashemi, 2014). Of course, this is just an estimation and some numbers might be much higher than indicated above. Close to 85 percent of all Kurdish diaspora comes from the Kurdish regions of Turkey (Hashemi, 2014).

In order to understand the formation of Kurdish diasporas in the West in the latter part of the twentieth century, we need to consider two major reasons. The first is connected to the continuing suppressive assimilation policy and structural discrimination that Kurds are exposed to in the Middle East, which has elicited Kurdish resistance, guerrilla wars and political activism. The Kurdish regions are not only economically underdeveloped but they have also been continuous sites of armed conflicts and subjected to militarization as a result of state violence and guerrilla activities. Middle Eastern states have not historically viewed Kurds as legitimate constituents and citizens of their societies and continue to view them as marked citizens and politically framed as a national security issue. The Kurdish diaspora can thus be described as a conflict-generated diaspora. The second development that engendered mass Kurdish emigration, mainly from Kurdistan of Turkey, was related to the economic boom in Western Europe that stimulated recruitment of a large number of Kurdish guest workers (Hassanpour & Mojab, 2005).

During the 1960s, the Kurdish immigrants to Europe were principally consisted of young intellectuals pursuing their education. It was in Europe that Kurds from different parts of Kurdistan could meet and articulate the ground for a shared politicized Kurdish identity. Many of them were involved in establishing student associations and supporting Kurdish plights in the Middle East. Kurdish immigrants who were defined as guest workers from Turkey mainly arrived during the 1970s. These immigrants considered themselves and were identified by the receiving societies as Turkish. This pattern of identification came to a change under the influence of Kurdish students and the PKK who started 'a reawakening' of Kurdish identity among these 'economic' immigrants. Following the state violence and clashes between Kurdish guerrilla movements in Iran, Iraq and Turkey, many Kurdish refugees fled their homes from 1980 to 2000 (Sheikhmous, 2000).

The experiences of the Kurdish diaspora have been examined through a number of empirical studies in Sweden (Alinia, 2004; Eliassi, 2013; Galip, 2014; Khayati, 2008; Mahmod, 2011; Zetterval, 2013) and the UK (Demir, 2012; Eliassi, 2016; Fernandes, 2018; Griffiths, 2002; Uguris, 2004; Wahlbeck, 1999). The focus of these studies has generally engaged with the migratory experiences of Kurdish migrants across different generations, their political involvement in the country of origin, gender relation in diasporic contexts, language use and preservation in transnational contexts, development of Kurdish literature and novels, experiences of social inclusion and exclusion in the Western Europe and politics of statelessness and home. Following migration, gender relations become sites of a battlefield between patriarchal order of the Kurdish community across different generations and racist representations of Kurdish masculinity and families in European contexts (Eliassi, 2013).

Following migration, many Kurdish intellectuals, artists, writers and political activists created a politicized ground for the Kurdish diaspora in countries like Sweden that is functioning as the center of gravity for the diaspora and transnational political activism (Khayati, 2008). For instance, Kurdish literature and novels have been partly developed in diasporic contexts where Sweden takes a leading role in supporting the Kurdish language (see Ahmadzadeh, 2003; Galip, 2014). Sweden hosts also *Dalkurd FF*, which is a successful Kurdish-Swedish football club in the diaspora. Dalkurd FF was founded in 2004 and played a season in *Allsvenskan*, the highest professional football league in Sweden and currently playing in the third top football leagues in Sweden. Kurdish associations are important in diasporic contexts since influential figures and animators can create and sustain discourses of Kurdish identity and organize demonstrations and conventions in support of the Kurds (see Sökefeld, 2006). These animators are central in constructing a politicized Kurdish identity and bringing into existence a Kurdish diaspora by using ideas, network and money. Political animators have an important role in paving the ground for the emergence, evolution and impact of the diaspora in the country of settlement and the country of origin and the dispersed population (Betts & Jones, 2016). For instance, they have had an important role in disseminating the idea of an oppressed Kurdish identity that cuts across different national boundaries and are involved in lobbying for recognition of Kurdish language and rights, through a variety of mobilizing practices such as associational activities, satellite and radio channels and activities in cyberspace among different Kurdish generations in different community forums. As a result of these political activities, the Kurdish 'question' can no longer be viewed as an internal question to those Middle Eastern states that subject Kurds to structural discrimination and political violence but has gained an important transnational character (see McDowall, 2004; van Bruinessen, 2000).

An important site for the construction of a politicized Kurdish identity is cyberspace where a virtual *Kurdistani* identity has been created through online activities, such as personal and political websites, blogs, news sites, talk forums, Facebook and YouTube (Mahmod, 2011; Sheyholislami, 2010). Likewise, online activities not only offer Kurds with an important political and social space to articulate a trans-border Kurdish identity worldwide but can also enable them to communicate, contest and negotiate their differences and heterogeneous formation of Kurdish identities. This is of course not done consistently in Kurdish but a variety of languages that are accessible and intelligible to them. In the context of globalization and communication technologies, the Kurdish diaspora and stateless nations have particularly found a way to challenge the official state discourses and circumventing its sovereignty, although in a restricted way.

Transnational activism among the Kurds is not free of surveillance and repression in Europe. In the context of European complicity with repressive Turkish long-distance nationalism and diplomacy, the UK takes a front role against Kurdish activism targeting the Turkish state. Despite the more favorable political contexts in the UK, compared to Turkey, Kurds of Turkey tend to be more surveilled, targeted and exposed to a securitization process in the UK since the PKK is labeled as a 'terrorist organization' by the US, the European Union and Turkey. This UK policy under the banner of fighting terror is also complicit with the Turkish government's policy and its intelligence agency that turns Kurds into a suspect community and frames transnational Kurdish struggle for political rights, gender equality and pluralism in the ethnocratic and authoritarian Turkey as an expression of 'terror' (Fernandes, 2018).

It is notable that migration can have a transformative impact on Kurdish identity formation in diasporic contexts. Immigration has enabled Kurds from all four parts of Kurdistan with a democratic political space in the West where they can negotiate, overcome and integrate their differences. Yet, this is not to say that political antagonism among different Kurdish political parties evaporates in the diaspora. In effect, many of the political and ideological differences are often strengthened in the diaspora. Based on my fieldwork, the PKK is viewed as a disrupting political force by members KDP, led by Masoud Barzani, and Kurdish parties from Eastern/Iranian Kurdistan. This antagonism is best expressed on social media where PKK members or supporters expose the KDP to harsh critique for being led by a tribal, patrimonial and corrupted elite that endorses the oppressive policies of the Turkish state in order to weaken the PKK's sphere of influence in Kurdistan. In contrast, KDP members view the PKK as an anti-Kurdish force through abandoning the claims of Kurds to political sovereignty and statehood and accepting an insignificant autonomy under the banner of democratic autonomy.

These divisions are often reflected in diasporic contexts and segregating association activities that endorse loyalty to party politics. The question of which Kurdish flag diasporic Kurds should use during demonstrations that support Kurdish demands and collective pain is one of the most infected intra-Kurdish issues. During the many demonstrations that I have participated in and observed, several PKK supporters view the official flag of the Kurdistan Region of Iraq as a 'Barzani flag' and reject it as the universal flag of all Kurds. In contrast, one Kurdish interviewee in Sweden told me that he did not understand where the PKK have got this new flag from, which is waved in Northern Kurdistan/Turkey and Rojava/Syria, since, 'it looks more like an African flag than a Kurdish one'. Notwithstanding this ideological antagonism, partisans of different political parties and associations tend to reach a compromise and use both flags in order to avoid further fragmentation of the Kurdish diaspora communities. This becomes particularly evident when Kurds experience critical events that need a united front. There is an awareness among influential Kurdish figures that for a Kurdish identity politics to succeed, they need to underscore their collective sufferings and common bonds instead of stressing their political and ideological differences. Thus, diasporic animators often ask for unity and downplay intra-Kurdish differences when Kurds are facing political and lethal violence in the Middle East. The activism and financial and moral support of diaspora to Kurdish movements make them into important key players in shaping and influencing Kurdish party politics.

While diaspora is often discussed in relation to endorsing or wrecking peace (Brinkerhoff, 2011; Koinova & Tsourapas, 2018), I find the vulnerable position of the Kurds in the Middle East as complicating this dichotomous conception of diasporic mobilization practices. While the Kurdish diaspora, for instance, fights for recognition and acknowledgment of Kurdish identity, the Turkish diaspora is generally pursuing to retain its master position. For example, in April 2017, the Turkish diaspora in Germany, Austria, the Netherlands, Belgium, France and Norway supported the constitutional referendum in Turkey that paved the way for presidential powers that Erdoğan pursued and achieved, which created both divisions in Turkey and in diasporic contexts (Koinova & Tsourapas, 2018).

Crises, critical events and wars are central to diasporic political mobilization. Critical events trigger "emotional response for those in diaspora who feel attached to the homeland" (Mavroudi, 2018, p. 1310). Moreover, critical events are important since they provide the condition for the materialization of an imagined transnational community among dispersed immigrant communities (Sökefeld, 2006). This is not to say that all putative members of the Kurdish diaspora can be counted on to mobilize and support Kurdistan at times of crisis, especially in the context of protracted conflicts where a crisis is often the rule than the exception. Yet, within the Kurdish diaspora, there are core members, academics and influential figures who can appeal to passive and silent members of the Kurdish diaspora at times of crisis and existential threat that Kurds face in the wider Middle East (see Shain & Barth, 2003, p. 452). Critical events like the Siege of Kobane by ISIL between 2014 and 2015 showed how Kurdish identity was organized globally to win support for the Kurdish women and men fighting against ISIL. While the city of Kobane was largely destroyed, it became nevertheless an important victory for the Kurds in general and a turning point in the war against ISIL. Two other contemporary events created huge distress for the Kurdish diaspora: the loss of Kirkuk to the Iraqi army and Shiite militias and the invasion of Rojava by the Turkish army and Islamist militias. When the people of the Kurdistan Region of Iraq and the disputed area voted in September 2017, the vast majority of the voters supported the Kurdish referendum on independence. However, this referendum brought together Iran, Iraq and Turkey to avert Kurdish independence.

In October 2017, the Iraqi army along with Shiite militias took over approximately half of the areas under Kurdish control without much resistance from the Kurdish peshmergas (armed forces of Kurdistan Region, which in effect belongs to KDP and PUK). The ruling KDP and PUK started immediately a media war and exchanging accusation of treason. The loss of the multi-ethnic city of Kirkuk with a Kurdish majority which was supposed to be the engine of Kurdish independence created a huge sense of despair, humiliation and defeat among Kurdish diasporans. The Rudaw Media Network that is affiliated with the KDP succeeded in turning the son (Bafel Talabani) and the family of the late PUK leader Jalal Talabani into traitors and collaborators for their collaboration with the Iraqi Shiite militias. Nonetheless, the KDP did not explain why it gave up the territories to Shiite militias and the Iraqi army that were under its own military control. Turning a certain fraction of the PUK into traitors and collaborators provided the KDP with two discursive weapons, to explain why the referendum 'failed' and intensifying the already division within PUK.

During the Turkish invasion of Afrin in 2018, Kurdish diasporas clashed with pro-Erdoğan supporters at Hannover Airport in Germany and Kurdish protestors blocked railway stations in London and Manchester in order to gain support for Afrin and in condemning the Turkish military invasion of Afrin. Rallies were held around the world in support of Afrin without affecting the outcome of the invasion. The British position was complicit in that Turkey was protecting its national security and as such criminalizing Kurdish right to political autonomy and justifying Turkish aggression and violence against Afrin. Once again, many Kurds in diaspora felt that they have been sold out by the major powers despite being celebrated as fighting on behalf of the world and humanity against ISIL. This shows that Kurdish diaspora has a limited role in affecting homeland politics and gaining international support despite its fervent transnational political activism. Moreover, the continuous violence against the Kurds and normalization of crisis facing the Kurds in the Middle East might lead to a politically indifferent subjectivity in light of hopelessness and lack of radical change in Kurdistan.

Narrating Experiences of Statelessness and Political Otherness

The empirical data of this book is grounded on the narratives of 50 Kurdish interviewees living in Sweden and the UK and 20 Palestinian interviewees based in Sweden. All the interviews with the Kurdish interviews in the UK have been carried out in England. As argued earlier, this book engages primarily with Kurdish experiences in Sweden and the UK. Although Sweden and Britain have different immigration patterns and ethnic relations, both countries represent multicultural integration models. The selection of these two sites has impact on the narratives of the interviewees and the line of questioning. For instance, Kurdish immigrants in Italy or Greece might offer a different perspective due to these states' lack of multicultural policies, social welfare and recognition of differences, which Kurdish and Palestinian immigrants enjoy in Sweden and the UK. In fact, many Kurdish immigrants use the experiences of British and Swedish multiculturalism to strike back against the states in the Middle East for suppressing and repressing ethnic differences. The interview guide included similar questions posed to the interviewees in both countries. For example, I asked the interviewees questions about how they conceived the absence of a Kurdish/Palestinian state; how statelessness impinge on their identities and political belonging; how statelessness affect their voice and security as well as the ways they look at themselves and their places in the world. I have endeavored to create an interpretative framework to make sense of statelessness through a micro-perspective and illustrate the place of nations without states in a world of the nation-states.

While the Swedish sample is consisted of 26 interviewees (twelve women and fourteen men), the British sample includes 24 interviewees (fourteen men and ten women). The study involves Kurds from all four parts of the Kurdish region in Iran, Iraq, Turkey and Syria. I conducted the interviews in *Sorani*-Kurdish, *Kurmanji*-Kurdish, English and Swedish depending on the interviewee's preferences. The interviews include individuals with diverse political, class and educational trajectories as well as different migratory histories and positions, such as irregular immigrants, asylum seekers, marriage migration, family reunification and quota refugees. Among the 26 Kurds interviewed in Sweden (Göteborg, Kalmar, Lund, Malmö, Uppsala, Stockholm) twenty-four hold Swedish citizenship, while two of them hold permanent residence permit. In turn, the 24 interviewed Kurds in England (London, Manchester and Oxford), eighteen of the interviewees are British citizens, three interviewees are EU citizens (two from the Netherlands and one from Belgium), two interviewees have permanent residence permit and one interviewee is an irregular immigrant. The interviewees include predominantly 'ordinary' Kurdish immigrants but also five Kurdish migrants (three in England and two in Sweden) who described themselves as political activists. When it comes to the Palestinian interviewees, they include Palestinians who have experienced migration in the Middle East prior to migration to Sweden. The interviewees include Palestinians who have lived in Gaza, Jordan, Syria, Lebanon and Germany. Furthermore, this study comprises Palestinians who have fled the war in Syria while living there as refugees. The majority of the Palestinian interviewees hold Swedish citizenship and use it to gain access to Palestine despite Israeli restrictions and severe interrogation process at Jordanian, Egyptian and Israeli borders. I have carried out the interviews in Swedish and Arabic following the preferences of the research participants. The interviews with Palestinian migrants were carried out in Sweden and took place in the cities of Malmö, Gothenburg, Stockholm, Lund and Kalmar.

Whereas Sweden and the UK represent liberal democracy with different immigration patterns and histories of ethnic relations, both countries represent progressive multicultural integration models although changing noticeably toward exclusionary notions of Swedishness and Britishness. This study includes individuals with diverse political, generational, class and educational trajectories as well as migratory histories and positions, such as labor migration, political asylum, marriage migration and family reunification. Moreover, the interviewees include mostly 'ordinary' Kurdish and Palestinian immigrants but also a few individuals who defined themselves politically in relation to nationalism and feminism. Focus on ordinary Kurdish and Palestinian immigrants are informed by the conception that if spokespersons and elites speak in the name of a diaspora, they can monopolize the legitimate representation of the group through resorting to essentialist grand narratives about the diaspora that they make claim to (see Ragazzi, 2012). By according attention to the voices of 'ordinary' people, it is possible "to go beyond a rigid approach to the binary distinction between public and private, and to analyse everyday practices of individuals as social sites for the transformation of social hierarchies. Choices made in everyday life form the politics of small things" (Lamont & Mizrachi, 2012, p. 367). Moreover, the voices of marginalized groups can both challenge and reinforce group boundaries often sanctioned by the state as the legitimate political order. Examining these voices is also important to explore how group boundaries are made and unmade (Lamont & Mizrachi, 2012) in relation to politics of nation-building.

The notion of narrative is of paramount importance for the accounts of the interviewees in relation to their experiences of statelessness and the ways they imagine the political structures and the world in which they inhabit and what alternative worlds they envision. Narrative is a central vehicle through which people experience the world. For instance, social actors do locate themselves in different story-lines from which they gain knowledge about the world. Narratives are not only personal but also public and they can guide our behavior (Somers & Gibson, 1994). This implies that narratives can do political work since individuals and groups use stories to mobilize, promote and strengthen sense of belonging. Furthermore, stories are also told to persuade, justify, argue and remember but also mislead the people that we are exposing to our narratives (Reissman, 2008). Focusing on the narratives of the Kurds and Palestinians can allow us to "understand their contributions as important and necessary to the dialogue for change, rather than as problematic to stability" (Johnson, 2014, p. 23). This is particularly important in the context of stateless peoples who have been denied effective agency and voice in national and international forums. By emphasizing the narratives and voices of members of stateless constituencies, it is possible to challenge silences and exclusion of their representations of how they experience and imagine the existing world order both in relation to temporality and the importance of place and territory for political power.

The questions of temporality and place affect how narratives are constructed. Narratives equip the individuals with the possibility to attain some form of unity, purpose and meaning by reconstructing the past and imagining the future (McAdams & Mclean, 2013). Memory is an important repertoire for identity construction among traumatized nations since memories are inscribed on our bodies and minds (Treacher, 2005). In the same context, Bhabha makes the point that remembering cannot be reduced to "a quite act of introspection or retrospection. It is a painful re-membering, a putting together of the dismembered past to make sense of the trauma of the present" (Bhabha, 1994, p. 121). When it comes to narrating physical, political and cultural suffering, episodic memories by individuals are often deployed to justify present political interpretations and goals. As Reissman (2008) puts it, the relationship between narrative, time and memory is complicated since individuals tend to adjust the remembered past in order to sustain, challenge or transform present realities. By focusing on narratives, individuals can "interpret their lives in their social and political complexity" (Hammack, 2011, p. 312). The 'small stories' that interviewees frame are often performative in the sense that they aim to accomplish social and political effects (Bamberg, 2006). Moreover, individual narrative can "produce knowledge that might challenge a status quo of inequality, cultural or political subordination, or other forms of injustice for groups" (Hammack, 2011, p. 313). It is important to remember that the narratives that are presented in this book about how Kurdish and Palestinian migrants experience and talk about statelessness, belonging, citizenship, home and otherness do not need to be fixed but can change or reframed across generations given that identity and belonging are categories of practice and sensitive to the dynamics of structural and political changes in the countries of settlement and the countries from which they have migrated.

Organization of the Book

In the next chapter, I examine the political value of the nation-state and those perils and promises that follow such a political organization. The question of sovereignty holds a central role in relation to the nation-state and it is embraced globally as the political template for organizing human life. In the context of the nation-state, peoples are constructed according to a logic of majority and minority that stipulates relations of dominance and subordination. The chapter engages with the ways nationalist ideas produce groups who are viewed as masters and enjoying ethnocultural primacy and groups who are assigned to the margins of the political home that the nation-states rule.

In Chapter 3, I move to the empirical material. This chapter engages with the narratives of Kurdish and Palestinian migrants regarding what statelessness entail to them and affect their identity formation, voice, status, visibility and presence in the world in the context of sovereign and non-sovereign identities. It also discusses commonality and differences between these two groups in relation to statelessness and how they relate to each other as members of two nations without states. While the Kurds generally regard statelessness as a political device to gain international recognition and support, the Palestinians view statelessness as a dangerous appellation since it is interpreted as turning the Palestinians into a 'landless' people and legitimizing Israeli mastery. The question of resistance to statelessness is also highlighted. An important focus of this chapter is to discuss hierarchy of statelessness and suffering that certain Palestinian and Kurdish individuals either endorse or challenge. Chapter 4 aims to illuminate that while most non-white migrants have a complicated relationship with issues of home and belonging, statelessness as an ascribed status and as a lived experience adds a further dimension to the sense of alienation, aloneness and political otherness in a nation-state-centric world. Likewise, the chapter discusses the perils and promises of the search for a fixed and exclusive political home in an uneven world. While estrangement is a central feature of migration, the question of home has become the central device of inclusion and exclusion in contemporary Europe in the context of migration and multiculturalism. Although it is important to feel at home and belong, it is equally dangerous to make a home to a fetish and turn it into an exclusionary symbolic object, which is denied people who are not viewed as organic members of the political community. Stateless peoples often view themselves as lacking a homeland or mastery over a political entity, that is conceived as being 'stolen' or taken over by other groups. This conception and lived experiences of homelessness make the search for a political home to a political imperative in the collective project of many members of stateless diaspora. Attention shifts in Chapter 5 toward the processes of ethnic inclusion and exclusion in multiethnic societies in the Middle East and Western Europe. The chapter examines specifically how citizenship, mobility and belonging across different nation-states are conceived, valued and experienced and how ethno-national and ethnoreligious hierarchies of citizenship and belongings are constructed.

Chapter 6 assesses how migration can become a transformative experience for Kurdish migrants in Sweden and the UK who have fled Turkey and attempt to shake of their imposed Turkish identity and/or alter their pattern of identification with the Turkish. In this regard, the chapter engages with the ways Kurdish migrants have experienced Turkish assimilation policies and practices and the meanings they assign to these experiences in diasporic contexts. Moreover, the chapter explores the politics and limits of resistance that attempt to destabilize Turkish assimilation discourses and reclaim Kurdish identity and language in the context of ongoing political violence and denial of Kurdish identity in Turkey. In Chapter 7, I move to discuss the way members of Kurdish diasporas in Sweden and the UK conceive the political value and the symbolic importance of the Kurdistan Region of Iraq in the context of Kurdish statelessness and political subjugation in the Middle East. By analyzing their narratives, we can gain an understanding of diverse, dominating and oppositional political voices that exist within the Kurdish diaspora. Many postcolonial states have used the discourse of national security/cohesion/unity to quell dissent and this issue becomes more urgent in the cases of ethnic groups who are operating in a vulnerable geopolitical context surrounded by nation-states that are unforgivingly inimical to Kurdish self-determination. Therefore, it is important to investigate how members of Kurdish diasporas juxtapose the urgent issue of democracy in their imagined homeland with maintaining stability and unity notwithstanding external threat by the neighboring countries and dominant ethno-national constituencies. Furthermore, the chapter problematizes the notion of political freedom and sovereignty when the 'homeland' is monopolized by those political leaders and parties that promised justice and Kurdish freedom from 'foreign invaders'. Finally, I conclude with a reflection about the role of critique in diaspora and obstruction of authoritarianism that often makes societal institutions weak through consolidating personal or family hold on power. Lastly, Chapter 8 revises the results and the theoretical arguments of this study and how statelessness is conceived, valued and experienced in a world of nation-states and why decolonization of the nation-state as a political template is needed to create more inclusive and pluralistic societies beyond permanent majorities and minorities with disparate power relations. This chapter will also focus on the questions of universality, difference, sameness and equality in the context of the nation-state.

References

Achilli, L. (2015). *Palestinian refugees and identity: Nationalism, politics and the everyday*. I.B. Tauris.

Achilli, L. (2021). The Deep Play: Ethnicity, the Hashemite monarchy and the Arab Spring in Jordan. In Paolo, M. & Idir, O. (eds.), *Minorities and state-building in the Middle East: The case of Jordan* (pp. 151–173). Palgrave Macmillan.

Adamson, F. (2016). The growing importance of diaspora politics. *Current History, 115*(784), 291–297.

Agamben, G. (1998). *Homo sacer. Sovereign power and bare life*. California University Press.

Ahmadzadeh, H. (2003). *Nation and novel: A study of Persian and Kurdish narrative discourse*. Uppsala University.

Al-Hardan, A. (2018). *Palestinians in Syria: Nakba memories of shattered communities*. Columbia University Press.

Alinia, M. (2004). *Spaces of diasporas: Kurdish identities, experiences of otherness and politics of belonging* (PhD dissertation). Göteborg University.

Alinia, M., & Eliassi, B. (2014). Temporal and generational impact on identity, home(land) and politics of belonging among the Kurdish diaspora. *Nordic Journal of Migration Research, 4*(2), 73–81.

Anderson, B. (1992). *Long-distance nationalism: World capitalism and the rise of identity politics*. Center for Asian Studies.

Anthias, F. (1998). Evaluating diaspora: Beyond ethnicity. *Sociology, 32*(3), 557–580.

Arendt, H. (1951). *The origins of totalitarianism*. Shocken Books.

Azar, M. (2001). *Frihet, Jämlikhet, Brodermord: Revolution och colonialism hos Albert Camus och Frantz Fanon*. Symposion.

Balibar, E. (2014). *Equaliberty*. Duke University Press.

Bamberg, M. (2006). Stories: Big or small: Why do we care? *Narrative Inquiry, 16*(1), 139–147.

Beinin, J., & Stein, R. L. (Eds.). (2006). *The struggle for sovereignty. Palestine and Israel 1993–2005*. Stanford University Press.

Benhabib, S. (2018). *Exile, statelessness and migration: Playing chess with history from Hannah Arendt to Isiah Berlin*. Princeton University Press.

Berger, M. (2019). *Palestinians in Israel*. Foreign Policy. https://foreignpolicy.com/2019/01/18/palestinian-in-israel/. Accessed 30 June 2020.

Besikci, I. (1988). *Kurdistan: An interstate colony*. Australian Association.

Betts, A., & Jones, W. (2016). *Mobilising the diaspora: How refugees challenge authoritarianism*. Cambridge University Press.
Bhabha, H. (1994). Remembering Fanon: Self, psyche and the colonial condition. In W. Patrick & C. Larua (Eds.), *Colonial discourse and post-colonial theory* (pp. 112–124). Columbia University Press.
Billig, M. (1995). *Banal nationalism*. Sage.
Blachnicka-Ciacke, D. (2018). Palestine as a 'state of mind': Second-generation Polish and British Palestinians' search for home and belonging. *Journal of Ethnic and Migration Studies, 44*(11), 1915–1931.
Blitz, B.K. & Lynch, M. (2009). *Statelessness and the benefits of citizenship: A comparative study*. Swiss Initiative to Commemorate the 60th Anniversary of the UDHR.
Blitz, B. K. (2017). The state and the stateless: The legacy of Hannah Arendt reconsidered. In B. Tendayi, T. Katherine, & C. Phillip (Eds.), *Understanding statelessness* (pp. 70–84). Routledge.
Bloom, T., Tonkiss, K., & Cole, P. (Eds.). (2017). *Understanding statelessness*. Routledge.
Bowman, G. (1994). 'A country of words': Conceiving the Palestinian nation from the position of exile. In L. Ernesto (Ed.), *The making of political identities* (pp. 138–170). Verso.
Bozarslan, H. (2018). When the present sends back to the past: Reading the Kurdish issue in the 2010s. *Middle East Critique, 27*(1), 7–24.
Bradley, M. (2014). Rethinking refugeehood: Statelessness, repatriation, and refugee agency. *Review of International Studies, 40*, 101–123.
Brinkerhoff, J. M. (2011). Diasporas and conflict societies: Conflict entrepreneurs, competing interests or contributors to stability and development? *Conflict, Security & Development, 11*(2), 115–143.
Brubaker, R. (2005). The "diaspora" diaspora. *Ethnic and Racial Studies, 28*(1), 1–19.
Bunton, M. (2013). *The Palestinian-Israeli conflict: A very short introduction*. Oxford University Press.
Butler, J., & Spivak, G. C. (2010). *Who sings the nation-state?* Seagull Books.
Butler, J. (2012). *Parting ways: Jewishness and the critique of Zionism*. Columbia University Press.
Castles, S. (2005). Nation and empire: hierarchies of citizenship in the new global order. *International Politics, 42*, 203–224.
Ciment, J. (1996). *The Kurds: State and minority in Turkey, Iraq and Iran*. Facts on File.
Cocks, J. (2014). *On sovereignty and other political delusions*. Bloomsbury.
Cohen, R. (2008). *Global diasporas: An introduction*. Routledge.
Conklin, W. E. (2014). *Statelessness: The engima of the international community*. Hart Publishing.

Cox, J., & Connell, J. (2003). Place, exile and identity: The contemporary experiences of Palestinian in Sydney. *Australian Geographer, 34*(3), 329–343.

Demir, I. (2012). Battling with Memleket in London: The Kurdish diaspora's engagement with Turkey. *Journal of Ethnic and Migration Studies, 38*(5), 815–831.

Dossa, S. (1980). Human status and politics: Hannah Arendt on the Holocaust. *Canadian Journal of Political Science*, 13(2): 309–323.

Eliassi, B. (2013). *Contesting Kurdish identities in Sweden: Quest for belonging among Middle Eastern youth*. Palgrave Macmillan.

Eliassi, B. (2016). Statelessness in a word of nation-states: The cases of Kurdish diasporas in Sweden and the UK. *Journal of Ethnic and Migration Studies, 42*(9), 1403–1419.

Entessar, N. (2010). *Kurdish politics in the Middle East*. Lexington Books.

Erakat, N. (2014). Palestinian refugees and the Syrian uprising: Failing the protection gap during secondary forced displacement. *International Journal of Refugee Law, 26*(4), 581–621.

Falk, R. (2017). *Palestine's horizon toward a just peace*. Pluto Press.

Fernandes, D. (2018). The Kurdish diaspora in the UK. In G. Michael (Ed.), *Routledge handbook on the Kurds* (pp. 451–464). Routledge.

Fiddian-Qasmiyeh, E. (2016). On the thresholds of statelessness: Palestinian narratives of loss and erasure. *Ethnic and Racial Studies, 39*(2), 301–321.

Gabiam, N. (2015). Citizenship and development: Palestinian in France and the multiple meanings of statelessness. *St Comp Int Dev, 50*, 479–499.

Galip, O. (2014). Where is home? Re-visioning 'Kurdistan' and 'diaspora' in Kurdish novelistic discourse in Sweden. *Nordic Journal of Migration Research, 4*(2), 82–90.

Gandolfo, L. (2012). *Palestinians in Jordan: The politics of identity*. London: I.B.Tauris.

Ghanem, A. (1998). State and minority in Israel: The case of ethnic state and the predicament of its minority. *Ethnic and Racial Studies, 21*(3), 428–448.

Ghanem, A., & Khatib, I. (2017). The nationalization of the Israeli ethnocratic regime and the Palestinian minority's shrinking citizenship. *Citizenship Studies, 21*(8), 889–902.

Gibney, M. J. (2011). The rights of non-citizens to membership. In S. Caroline & K. B. Brad (Eds.), *Statelessness in the European Union: Displaced, undocumented, unwanted* (pp. 41–68). Cambridge University Press.

Gibney, M. J. (2017). Foreword. In B. Tendayi, K. Tonkiss, & P. Cole (Eds.), *Understanding statelessness* (pp. xx–xxii). London: Routledge.

Gibney, M. J. (2019). Denationalisation and discrimination. *Journal of Ethnic and Migration Studies*. https://doi.org/10.1080/1369183X.2018.1561065

Griffiths, D. J. (2002). *Somali and Kurdish refugees in London: New identities in the diaspora*. Ashgate.

Gündoğdu, A. (2011). 'Perplexities of the rights of man': Arendt on the aporias of human rights. *European Journal of Political Theory, 11*(1), 4–24.
Hage, G. (2015). *Alter-politics: Critical Anthropology and their radical imagination*. Melbourne University Press.
Hammack, P. L. (2011). Narrative and the politics of meaning. *Narrative Inquiry, 21*(2), 311–318.
Hammer, J. (2005). *Palestinians Born in Exile*. Texas: University of Texas Press.
Hanafi, S. (2003). Rethinking the Palestinian abroad as a diaspora: The relationships between the diaspora and the Palestinian territories. *International Social Science Review, 4*(1–2), 157–182.
Hanafi, S. (2012). Explaining spacio-cide in the Palestinian territory: Colonization, separation, and state of exception. *Current Sociology, 61*(2), 190–205.
Hashemi, M. (2014). Contemporary Kurdish diaspora in Europe: A driving force toward peace and democracy in the Middle East. In G. Galia & S. Walid (Eds.), *Non-state actors in the Middle East: Factors for peace and democracy* (pp. 117–145). Routledge.
Hassanpour, A., & Mojab, S. (2005). Kurdish diaspora. In E. Melvin, R. E. Carol, & S. Ian (Eds.), *Encyclopedia of diasporas: Immigrant and refugee cultures around the world* (Vol 1, pp. 214–225). Springer.
Hayden, P. (2008). From exclusion to containment: Arendt, sovereign power, and statelessness. *Societies without Borders, 3*(2), 248–269.
Hilal, S. & Petti, A. (2018). *Permanent temporariness*. Art and Theory Publishing.
Ignatieff, M. (1994). *Blood and belonging: Journeys into the new nationalism*. Vintage.
Ignatieff, M. (2009). *True Patriot Love: Four generations in search of Canada*. Viking Canada.
Jabareen, H. (2014). Hobbesian citizenship: How the Palestinians became a minority in Israel. In K. Will & P. Eva (Eds.), *Multiculturalism and minority rights in the Arab world* (pp. 189–217). Oxford University Press.
Jamal, A. (2007). Nationalizing states and the constitution of 'hollow citizenship': Israel and Its Palestinian citizens. *Ethnopolitics, 6*(4), 471–493.
Jamal, A., & Kensicki, A. (2020). Theorizing half-statelessness: A case study of the Nation-State Law in Israel. *Citizenship Studies*. https://doi.org/10.1080/13621025.2020.1745152
Johnson, H. L. (2014). *Borders, Asylum and global non-citizenship: The other side of the fence*. Cambridge University Press.
Karmi, G. (2015). *Return: A Palestinian memoir*. Verso Books.
Khalidi, R. (1997). *Palestinian identity: The construction of modern national consciousness*. Columbia University Press.
Khalidi, R. (2006). *The Iron Cage: The story of the Palestinian struggle for statehood*. Beacon Press.

Khayati, K. (2008). *From victim diaspora to transborder citizenship? Diaspora formation and transnational relations among Kurds in France and Sweden* (PhD Dissertation). Linköping University.

Kenny, K. (2013). *Diaspora: A very short introduction*. Oxford University Press.

Kimmerling, B. (2001). *The invention and decline of Israeliness: State, Society, and the military*. University of California Press.

Kingston, L. N. (2015). Protecting the world's most persecuted: The responsibility to protect and Burma's Rohingya minority. *The International Journal of Human Rights, 19*(8), 1163–1175.

Kingston, L. N. (2017). Worthy of rights: Statelessness as a cause and symptom of marginalisation. In B. Tendayi, T. Katherine, & C. Phillip (Eds.), *Understanding Statelessness* (pp. 17–34). Routledge.

Kirmanj, S. (2013). *Identity and nation in Iraq*. Lynne Rienner Publishers.

Koinova, M., & Tsourapas, G. (2018). How do countries of origin engage migrants and diasporas? Multiple actors and comparative perspectives. *International Political Science Review, 39*(3), 311–321.

Kürt, M. (2018). "My Muslim Kurdish brother": Colonial Rule and Islamist governmentality in the Kurdish region of Turkey. *Journal of Balkan and near Eastern Studies, 21*(3), 350–365.

Laclau, E. (1994). Introduction. In L. Ernesto (Ed.), *The making of political identities* (pp. 1–8). Verso.

Lacorix, J. (2015). The 'right to have rights' in French political philosophy: Conceptualising a cosmopolitan citizenship with Arendt. *Constellations, 22*(1), 79–90.

Lamont, M., & Mizrachi, N. (2012). Ordinary people doing extraordinary things: Responses to stigmatization in comparative perspective. *Ethnic and Racial Studies, 35*(3), 365–381.

Lindholm, S. H. (2003). *The Palestinian diaspora: Formation of identities and politics of homeland*. Routledge.

Lindholm, H. (2019). Emotional identity and pragmatic citizenship: Being Palestinian in Sweden. *Diaspora Studies*. https://doi.org/10.1080/09739572.2019.170815

Lowe, R. (2006). The Syrian Kurds: A people discovered. *Middle East Programme Briefing Paper, 6*(1), 1–17.

Mahmod, J. (2011). Designing scripts and performing Kurdishness in diaspora: The online-offline nexus. *Cultural Policy, Criticism, and Management Research, 5*, 72–90.

Malkki, L. (1995). Refugee and exile: 'Refugee studies' to the national order of things. *Annual Review of Anthropology, 24*, 495–523.

Mamdani, M. (2020). *Neither settler nor native: The making and unmaking permanent minorities* . The Belknap Press of Harvard University Press.

Manly, M. (2012). UNHCR's mandate and activities to address statelessness in Europe. *European Journal of Migration and Law, 14*, 261–277.

Manly, M., & van Waas, L. (2014). The state of statelessness research: A human rights imperative. *Tilburg Law Review, 19*, 3–10.

Markell, P. (2003). *Bound by recognition*. Princeton University Press.

Mason, V. (2007). Children of the "idea of Palestine": Negotiating identity, belonging and home in the Palestinian diaspora. *Journal of Intercultural Studies, 28*(3), 271–285.

Massad, J. (2008). Producing the Palestinian as other: Jordan and the Palestinians. In H. Roger (Ed.), *Temps et espaces en Palestine: Flux et résistances identitaires* (pp. 273–292). Liban.

Matar, D. (2011). *What it means to be Palestinian: Stories of Palestinian peoplehood*. I. B. Tauris.

Matin, K. (2019). Democratic confederalism and societal multiplicity: A sympathetic critique of Abdullah Öcalan's state theory. *Geopolitics*. https://doi.org/10.1080/14650045.2019.1688785

Matin, K. (2020). Liminal lineages of the "Kurdish question". *Middle East Report* 295. https://merip.org/2020/08/liminal-lineages-of-the-kurdish-question/ Accessed 7 April 2021.

Mavroudi, E. (2007). Palestinians and pragmatic citizenship: Negotiating relationships between citizenship and national identity in diaspora. *Geoforum, 39*, 307–318.

Mavroudi, E. (2018). Deconstructing diasporic mobilization at a time of crisis: Perspectives from the Palestinian and Greek diasporas. *Ethnic and Migration Studies, 44*(8), 1309–1324.

McAdams, D. P., & McLean, K. C. (2013). Narrative identity. *Current Directions in Psychological Science, 22*(3), 233–238.

McDowall, D. (2004). *A modern history of the Kurds*. I.B. Tauris.

Molavi, S. C. (2013). *Stateless citizenship: The Palestinian-Arab citizens of Israel*. Brill.

Öcalan, A. (2017). *The political thought of Abdullah Öcalan: Kurdistan, Woman's revolution and democratic confederalism*. Pluto Press.

Pappe, I. (2006). *The ethnic cleansing of Palestine*. Oneworld.

Pérez, M. V. (2018). Materializing the nation in everyday life: On symbols and objects in the Palestinian refugee diaspora. *Dialectical Anthropology, 42*, 409–427.

Pérez, M. V. (2021). Minoritizing Gaza refugees in Jordan. In M. In Paolo & O. Idir (Eds.), *Minorities and state-building in the Middle East: The case of Jordan* (pp. 131–150). Palgrave Macmillan.

Peteet, J. (2005). *Landscape of hope and despair: Palestinian refugee camps*. University of Pennsylvania Press.

Peteet, J. (2007). Problematizing a Palestinian diaspora. *International Journal of Middle East Studies, 39*(4), 627–646.
Peteet, J. (2017). *Space and mobility in Palestine*. Indiana University Press.
Phillips, A. (2015). *The politics of the human*. Cambridge University Press.
Radhakrishnan, R. (1996). *Diasporic mediations: Between home and location*. University of Minnesota Press.
Ragazzi, F. (2012). Diaspora: The politics of its meanings. *International Political Sociology, 6*(1), 107–111.
Ragazzi, F. (2017). *Governing diaspora in international relations: The transnational politics of Croatia and former Yugoslavia*. Routledge.
Rancière, J. (2004). Who is the subject of the Rights of Man? *The South Atlantic Quarterly, 103*(2/3), 297–310.
Randal, J. (1999). *After such knowledge, what forgiveness?* Westview Press.
Redclift, V. (2013). *Statelessness and citizenship: Camps and the creation of political space*. Routledge.
Reissman, C. K. (2008). *Narrative methods for the human sciences*. Sage.
Roberts, R. (2010). *Palestinians in Lebanon: Refugees living with long-term displacement*. I.B. Tauris.
Safran, W. (2005). The Jewish diaspora in a comparative and theoretical perspective. *Israel Studies, 10*(1), 36–60.
Sa'di, A. & Abu-Lughod, L. (Ed.). (2007). *Nakba: Palestine 1948 and the claims of memory*. Columbia University Press.
Said, E. W. (1992). *The question of Palestine*. Vintage Books.
Said, E. W. (2000). *Reflections on exile and other literary and cultural essay*. Granta.
Saloul, I. (2012). *Catastrophe and exile in the modern Palestinian imagination: Telling memories*. Palgrave Macmillan.
Sanbar, E. (2001). Out of place, out of time. *Mediterranean Historical Review, 16*(1), 87–94.
Savelsberg, E., & Hajo, S. (2011). Ten years of Bashar Al-Asad and no compromise with the Kurds. *Syrian Studies Association Newsletter, 16*(1), 1–3.
Schwabe, S. (2018). Paradoxes of erasure: Palestinian memory and the politics of forgetting in post-dictatorship Chile. *Interventions: International Journal of Postcolonial Studies, 20*(5), 651–665.
Şenay, B. (2013). Seeing for the state: Kemalist long-distance nationalism in Australia. *Nations and Nationalism, 19*(2), 376–394.
Shachar, A. (2009). *The Birthright lottery: citizenship and global inequality*. Harvard University Press.
Shain, Y., & Barth, A. (2003). Diaspora and international relations theory. *International Organization, 57*(3), 449–479.
Shafir, G., & Peled, Y. (2002). *Being Israeli: The dynamics of multiple citizenship*. Cambridge University Press.

Sheffer, G. (2003). *Diaspora politics: A home abroad*. Cambridge University Press.
Sheikhmous, O. (2000). *Crystalisation of a new diaspora: Migration and political culture among the Kurds in Europe*. Center for Research in International Migration and Ethnic Relations.
Sheyholislami, J. (2010). Identity, language, and new media: The Kurdish case. *Language Policy, 9*(4): 289–312.
Shohat, E. (2017). *On the Arab-Jew, Palestine, and other displacements*. Pluto Press.
Sökefeld, M. (2006). Mobilizing in transnational space: A social movement approach to the formation of diaspora. *Global Network, 6*(3), 265–284.
Somers, M. R., & Gibson, G. D. (1994). Reclaiming the epistemological 'other': Narrative and the social constitution of identity. In C. Craig (Ed.), *Social theory and the politics of identity* (pp. 35–99). Blackwell.
Soysal, Y. (2002). Citizenship and identity: Living in diaspora in post-war Europe? *Ethnic and Racial Studies, 23*(1), 1–15.
Spanos, W. V. (2012). *Exiles in the city: Hannah Arendt & Edward W. Said in counterpoint*. The Ohio State University Press.
Staples, K. (2012). *Retheorising statelessness. A background theory of membership in world politics*. Edinburgh University Press.
Stein, L. (2009). *The making of modern Israel 1948–1967*. Polity.
Sayigh, R. (1979). The Palestinian experience: Integration and non-integration in the Arab Ghourba. *Arab Studies Quarterly, 1*(2), 96–112.
Sayigh, R. (2013). On the exclusion of the Palestinian Nakba from the 'trauma genre.' *Journal of Palestinian Studies, 43*(1), 51–60.
Sayigh, R. (2015). Silenced suffering. *Borderlands, 14*(1), 1–20.
Tejel, J. (2009). *Syria's Kurds: History, politics and society*. Routledge.
Treacher, A. (2005). On postcolonial subjectivity. *Group Analysis, 38*(1), 43–57.
Uguris, T. (2004). Diaspora and citizenship: Kurdish women in London. *Studies in Culture, Policy and Identities, 5*(1), 137–157.
Vali, A. (1998). The Kurds and their "others": Fragmented identity and fragmented politics. *Comparative Studies of South Asia, Africa and the Middle East, 18*(2), 82–95.
van Bruinessen, M. (2000). *Transnational aspects of the Kurdish question*. Working paper presented at Robert Schuman Centre for Advanced Studies. Florence: European University Institute.
van Waas, L. (2008). *Nationality matters: Statelessness under international law*. Intersentia.
van Waas, L., & De Chickera, A. (2017). Unpacking statelessness. In B. Tendayi, T. Katherine, & C. Phillip (Eds.), *Understanding statelessness* (pp. 53–69). Routledge.

Vanly, I. C. (1992). The Kurds in Syria and Lebanon. In G. K. Philip (Ed.), *The Kurds: A contemporary overview* (pp. 112–134). Routledge.

Wahlbeck, Ö. (1999). *Kurdish diasporas: A comparative study of Kurdish refugee communities*. Palgrave Macmillan.

Wahlbeck, Ö. (2018). The future of the Kurdish Diaspora. In G. Michael (Ed.), *Routledge Handbook on the Kurds* (pp. 413–424). Routledge.

Walzer, M. (1970). *Obligations: Essays on disobedience, war and citizenship*. Harvard University Press.

Walzer, M. (1983). *Spheres of justice: A defense of pluralism and equality*. Basic Books.

Werbner, P. (2002). The place which is diaspora: Citizenship, religion and gender in the making of chaordic transnationalism. *Journal of Ethnic and Migration Studies, 28*(1), 119–133.

Werbner, P. (2015). The boundaries of diaspora: A critical response to Brubaker. In K. Florian & S. Klaus (Eds.), *Diasporic constructions of home and belonging* (pp. 35–51). De Gruyter.

Wolfe, P. (2006). Settler colonialism and the elimination of the native. *Journal of Genocide Research, 8*(4), 387–409.

Yadirgi, V. (2017). *The political economy of the Kurds of Turkey: From the Ottoman Empire to the Turkish Republic*. Cambridge University Press.

Yeğen, M. (1996). The Turkish state discourse and the exclusion of Kurdish identity. *Middle Eastern Studies, 3*(2), 216–229.

Yeğen, M. (2009). "Prospective-Turks" or "Pseudo-citizens": Kurds in Turkey. *Middle East Journal, 63*(4), 597–615.

Yuval-Davis, N. (2011). *The politics of belonging: Intersectional contestations*. Sage.

Zetterval, C. (2013). *Reluctant victims into challengers: Narratives of a Kurdish political generation in diaspora in Sweden* (PhD Dissertation). Lund University.

Zureik, E. (2016). *Israel's colonial project in Palestine: Brutal pursuit*. Routledge.

CHAPTER 2

The Nation-State Crafting of Majorities and Minorities

In order to understand the political value of the nation-state, it is pertinent to discuss the perils, benefits, possibilities and limits that sovereign states can represent in a world where the nation-state is viewed and cherished as the political standard of organizing human life. It is also equally important to look into the modes that states construct majorities and minorities and justify relations of dominance and subordination, ethnocultural primacy and cultural otherness. In other words, how state with the help of nationalist ideas produces a *master identity* and *marked constituencies* whose lives, legal, political, cultural, economic status remain insecure and precarious. Due to the dominance and the persistence of the nation-state, stateless subjects continue to invest in nationalism with an aspiration to achieve some form of autonomy, federalism or sovereignty. In other words, the antidote to the status injury of stateless nations continues to be located in the nation-state as a political bandage to alleviate or end their sufferings and vulnerabilities. Statehood can be envisaged as vehicle to achieve and sustain peace and security from outsiders and internal unrest; it can also be viewed as home for one's national community. For those who are at the margins of the state, the governing state is viewed as a means of ethnic oppression and an obstacle to one's political aspiration to achieve independence (Grzybowski & Koskenniemi, 2015) and mastery over one's land, natural resources, identity, culture, religion and language.

B. Eliassi, *Narratives of Statelessness and Political Otherness*, Minorities in West Asia and North Africa,
https://doi.org/10.1007/978-3-030-76698-6_2

Sovereignty and the State

Sovereignty and state, two mutually constituting concepts, are widely contested but enduring in International Relation and Political Theory. By and large, there is an understanding that the very idea of sovereignty or nation-state obstructs us from achieving a world community in which bounded states and nationalized communities are not the normative reference point for establishing a shared human identity (see Bartelson, 2009).

So what does sovereignty entail and what does it aim to achieve as a supreme form of authority? Sovereignty is one of the central constituting ideas of post-medieval order and stands for a particular form of state authority. A state is conventionally consisted of a delimited population with a permanent population, ruled by a government (Jackson, 2007). It is in such context that Skinner (2013) equates a state with a government. Following the Treaty of Westphalia (1648), sovereignty became intimately linked to the nation-state which often entails a population, a territory and an authority. This indeed make the whole idea of the modern nation-state to a European invention. The diverse forms of political organization in human history were reduced to the form of the nation-state (Holsti, 1996; see also Malešević, 2013). However, Mamdani (2020) argues that the Treaty of Westphalia is not the true biography of the modern state that promised religious toleration and mutual recognition of sovereignty. The biography of the modern state, according to Mamdani, should be traced back to 1492, the year in which the Castilian monarchy attempted to create a homogenous political home for Christians Spaniards by either expelling or forcibly making the Muslim Moors and Jews to convert to Christianity. For Mamdani, the biography of the modern state does not start with tolerance but with ethnic cleansing and colonialism (ibid., pp. 1–2). A central effect of the Westphalian order is that the state is viewed by people around the world and aspired (by those who lack it) as "the highest form of political manifestation of peoples or any other close-knit groups of whatever ethnicity or shared sentiments" (Schuett, 2015, p. 224). However, a central ideology that guides the principle of inclusion and exclusion is nationalism that glorifies possession of a state as a necessary condition for a people's existence in a world of nation-states and nations (see Schuett, 2015). It is virtually impossible to be a member of the international community without being in charge of a recognized sovereignty, statehood and territory. Lack of a recognized statehood entails lacking a political standing in public international law. However, this formal designation of state sovereignty conceals major differences between how different states are constructed, ruled and organized (Holsti, 1996).

What makes the sovereign state a desirable entity is due to the fact that states are central right holders under international law and they are the major authorities with legal responsibility to protect human rights in the world. This makes the sovereign state to a permanent legal subject of international relations (Jackson, 2007, pp. 123–124). Concurrently, Jackson (2007) argues that those people who enjoy sovereign states are also the people that are mostly heard and listened to when talking from position of authority. This privileged position can illuminate why pursuing statehood and independence is viewed as a necessary condition for political survival in a world of nation-states. Sovereignty is neatly attached to modernity since one of the core ideas of modernity was the notion of independence. Following such notion of sovereignty as promising independence, statehood was pursued in order to repudiate and prohibit unwanted interference from foreign powers and actors. Sovereignty as such became a vehicle of political freedom from foreign interference in a state's internal affairs (Jackson, 2007; see Cocks, 2014 for a critique).

Historically, despite having different ethico-political legitimacy, many actors and subjects have made and asserted their claims to sovereignty; the kings, dictators, colonial powers and nationalist anti-colonial movements (Jackson, 2007). What is central to sovereignty is its relational constitution. In our contemporary world, Palestinians, Kurds, Catalans and Scots are all making claims to sovereignty in order to represent their peoples effectively and impose their ownership over territories and natural resources by defying the states and the titular nations that subdue them. For Jackson (2007), in order to have a place on the political map of the world, a government must have sovereign authority. It has been argued that it is nearly impossible to think of the world without taking the state into consideration. An exclusion of the state, "would be like thinking of a fleet at sea only by reference to a lot of sailors acting - without any reference to the performance of ships" (Manning cited in Grzybowski & Koskenniemi, 2015, p. 27). The sovereign state is expected to provide both security and peace and at the same time use violence to defend its people, territory and authority. It is in this regard that Hobbes talks about 'sword of justice' in context of domestic threats and 'sword of war' against foreign aggression and threats. Without these 'swords', the state is viewed as useless and powerless (Jackson, 2007, p. 17). This leads to the question of violence as a central constituting feature of state. Following Weber (1994), violence is a central means for politics when the political order is challenged and threatened outside of defined parameters that the political order stipulates. Against this background, a central definition of the state is based on its monopoly over the legitimate violence or use of force inside its territorial jurisdiction (Weber, 1994), but also outside of its borders when it allegedly targets 'terror' or 'separatism', as for instance in the Middle East where Turkey targets Kurds in Syria and Iraq. Indeed, many states betray the very principle of sovereignty of non-interference and respect for the territorial borders of each nation-state, which is often viewed as sacrosanct.

It is often argued that the nation-state is a dominant war-prone social organization (Appadurai, 2006; Giddens, 1987; Malešević, 2010; Pandey, 2006). In this context, Malešević (2010) argues that it is possible to replace a despotic government or split an entity into two or several formations, but it is much more difficult to undo the nation-state as a social organization. Empirically speaking, this is not something that most people would aspire to undo. When a nation-state breaks down, different actors tend to engage in bloody and violent attempts to impose their monopoly over the legitimate use of violence, as contemporary examples of Somali and Democratic Republic of Congo have illustrated (Malešević, 2010, pp. 332–333). An important feature of the state is its proneness to wage war. By making wars, the state in Europe managed to create political, administrative and fiscal unity. Tilly memorably made the famous statement that "war made states and states made wars" (1985, p. 170). A striking example is the case of Israel that fought at least four major wars with different Arab countries; the 1948 War, the 1956 War, the 1967 Six-Day War and the 1973 Yom Kippur War. These wars militarized Israel as a state and created a strong political unity among its Jewish population due to the existential threat that Arab states could pose to Israel. However, Tilly's statement about wars as a central feature of state-making cannot be universalized to political contexts like the Arab Middle East. Schwarz (2012) argues that Arab states carried out 'wrong wars' to support their state-making projects. While in Europe, the states were either defending their territories against foreign invaders or waging war to expand their territories, the Arab states carried out wars that seriously damaged their state's survival. Iraq and Syria are two striking examples. For Schwarz (2012), it does not suffice to have a state and exercise sovereign authority over its territory. The function of the modern state should also include security, welfare and representation (p. 1). While the states in the Middle East can be securitized to maintain the power of the regime, welfare and representation are far from being institutionalized since many of the ruler lack legitimacy to rule the country despite making claims to democracy. The states in the Middle East can hardly make claim to popular sovereignty if "the authority of the final words resides in the political will or consent of the people of an independent state" (Jackson, 2007, p. 78). It is important to remember that pseudo-democratic 'general' elections are performed in the Middle East, but it is questionable whether the people have the final say about how the state should be run. White (2012) argues that democracy cannot be reduced to representative democracy. On the contrary, rulers claim to be representative of the population and use this representativeness to foreclose the emergence of a genuine democratic and pluralistic representation. What is conspicuous in the Middle East is that non-democratic regimes are also aware about the rhetorical power of representation and use it frequently to quell dissent from oppositional groups that might want to transform the state into a more plural and representative political entity (see White, 2012). Although states and governments are viewed as synonymous, the political order matters whether the state and the government correspond to each other. In a liberal democracy, governments can be voted and be re-elected or replaced, but the institutions of a democratic state can remain more or less intact if not illiberal political parties capture the institutions of the state and appropriate them to serve their narrow benefits and agenda, as we see a tendency across Eastern Europe and the US under Trump administration and his legacy. When it comes to the authoritarian state contexts of the Middle East, the state is largely corrupted and hijacked by a political party that views itself as the guardian of the state, the nation and in some cases even God's interests as in Iran. There is a pattern across the Middle East, where a family captures the armed and security forces, the media and the economy, in order to monopolize the power and transfer the power from a generation to another (see Sasson, 2016). In authoritarian states, welfare policy is not primarily used as a vehicle of distributive justice, but deployed to contain and punish the dissent of the population against undemocratic rule, lack of rule of law and widespread corruption. Access to welfare in authoritarian states requires affirmed and continuous loyalty to the rulers by obeying and enchanting the social order and its leaders.

The risk of being labeled and stigmatized as a 'quisling' or 'anti-national' becomes rife in context of opposition to authoritarian regimes.

It makes sense when Jackson (2007) declares that the state can be both a source of suffering and human flourishing, like upholding freedom, safety and dignity of its citizens. Jackson confidently maintains that it is true that chaotic and despotic states can be abusive and violate human rights, but it is not by abandoning the state that injustices and human rights violations can be addressed. However, this claim by Jackson (2007) is contestable since it deflects attention from exclusionary faces of Western democracies. Many of the democratic states of the West that are so glorified in Jackson's book (2007) on sovereignty are not exempted from violating human and minority rights directly or indirectly. The case of Syrian refugees knocking at the gates of Europe is an illustrating example that people who really escape violence and war from the bloody war in Syria are not given the right to seek asylum. Instead, these vulnerable Syrian refugees are becoming pawns in a geopolitical game between Turkey, Russia and the European Union. While the EU pays Turkey to contain these refugees, Turkey uses them to gain political and economic benefits from the EU. Those who come to suffer are those subjects called 'the Syrian people' who are shuttled between bombs, borders and walls of aggressive sovereign states. Even in a highly democratic state like Sweden, major political parties are involved in a political race to show who is harboring the most restrictive and exclusionary refugee policy by slogans like 'Sweden is full', 'close the border', 'Strengthen the border!' Migration is indeed one of the most telling examples of how inequalities and geopolitical relations of power between the sovereign Western states in the global north and the global south are established when it comes to disparate distribution of political voice, mobility, legal protection and economic rights.

Hierarchies of Nation-States and Contesting Globalization

Although all internationally recognized states regardless of their territorial and population size hold a seat in United Nations, they are in practice hierarchically and relationally constituted according to a colonial logic. Bartelson (2014) suggests that it is within the framework of bounded communities that sovereignty makes sense in our world and the main ideological function of the concept of sovereignty is to legitimize the international system/state system within which the sovereignty proves to be meaningful. Moreover, Bartelson (2014) points out that the very practice of recognition or nonrecognition of non-European states and peoples as sovereign has been a central vehicle to maintain and create a hierarchical relationship between European and non-Europeans. For instance, non-Europeans were often denied inclusion in the international society due to beliefs that they were 'uncivilized' and lacked proper political institutions similar to European and Western states. Such processes of othering paved the ground for European domination and subordination of non-Europeans. Even when non-Europeans managed to enter the international society formally, they were not viewed as equals but given conditional sovereignty (Bartelson, 2014, p. 29). It is in this light that Agnew (2009) distinguishes between nominal and effective sovereignty. Due to differences in military, economic and political power, the recognized states of the world enjoy 'independence' and 'sovereignty' in different ways. Many of the Arab states in the Gulf region cannot make claim to effective sovereignty since they are ***dependent*** on the military support of the US to 'protect' them against each other or against rival states like Iran. Qatar might be a tiny state, but it possesses large natural gas reserve and enjoys the media network of Aljazeera Arabic and Aljazeera English to endorse its political agenda across the world. In addition to the soft power of its media networks and economic power, Qatar hosts the largest US military base in the Middle East. Of course, it might not be in the interest of the US to assist a Middle East where arms are silent and peace can prevail, given that the Gulf states continue to take a leading position in purchasing American weapons. This is an example of the fact that these states are existentially dependent on Western power to survive due to unequal and volatile geopolitical order in the region. And this leads to the question of suitability of Westphalian state model in non-Western contexts and the discourse of globalization.

The discourse of sovereignty was appropriated by colonial projects to discard native claims to equality and justifying territorial dispossession of the indigenous peoples in Australia, the US, South American, Canada (see Cocks, 2014; Moreton-Robinson, 2015). This implies that the global order is primarily structured by Western states, citizenship regimes and values, where Western and European bodies are valued highly and treated as more equal than non-Europeans (Castles, 2005), even when non-Europeans share the same citizenship status and rights at formal basis

(Eliassi, 2013). While the Westphalian model took hundreds of years in Europe to take shape and become institutionalized in context of lengthy experiences of bloody conflicts and wars (see Agnew, 2009, p. 60), there is a belief that the same state model is "gift-wrapped and ready to be shipped across the oceans in order to provide the framework for the liberal peace-building mission" (Jütersonke & Kartas, 2015, p. 109) in the global south. There is a paradox that permeates how sovereignty has been used against non-Europeans and how it has been adopted in local contexts. It is conspicuous that the ethnic and religious diversity of the Middle East or Africa is not compatible with the Westphalian model despite decades of attempts to reconcile state-building projects with ideas of "the Euro-American-style territorial state of sharp borders" (Agnew, 2009, p. 212). Those ethno-national constituencies in the Middle East that have managed to secure and monopolize the states tend to dismiss alternative voices, experiences and non-sovereign identities as 'anti-national', 'foreign plots' and 'internal enemies'. In addition, as Jackson (2007) shows, the international comity of sovereign states is a conservative club that neither encourage creations of new states nor show willingness to recognize claims by stateless peoples who consider themselves as having legitimate claims to statehood. Rejection of statehood claims is often justified in the name of 'peace' and 'stability' and serves to sanctify the territorial integrity of the existing state regardless of how ill-fit and contradictory their borders might be. Many of the existing borders of global south have been established by European imperial powers and since then the political map of the world has been largely unchanging. Jackson deploys the metaphor of an ill-fit shoe to depict the difficult reality on the ground between territory and population that established and recognized states made claim to:

> Even though the territorial shoe did not come anywhere near to fitting the population foot in the greater number of cases, the prospects of changing the shoe was more daunting and disturbing than the problem of retaining it. That was particularly so when viewed from the international angle. Those inherited borders became sacrosanct and border change correspondingly difficult. (Jackson, 2007, p. 107)

It is worth mentioning that no state has a transcendental and transhistorical existence since the state is a human construction, yet with real consequences for those peoples who are subsumed under its universality. Despite fixation of territorial borders of the state and claims of its unchangeability, there are diverging claims about how processes and market forces of globalization have altered and complicated the role and the power of the state in the world. Globalization is often discussed in relation to the decreasing importance of space and distance that global financial markets, communication technologies and rapid transportation have produced (Agnew, 2009). Following globalization, the decline or the retreat of state sovereignty has been deliberated and underlined (see Levy & Sznaider, 2006; Sassen, 1996; Strange, 1996). However, the effects of globalization have been interpreted in different ways. It has been viewed as an emancipatory political force by creating the political grounds for non-national forms of belongings, rights and membership. While those on the left tend to consider the eroding power of globalization on the welfare state, the ethno-nationalist right-wing parties across the West consider globalization as a force that undermines national identity and endorses a multiculturalist doctrine that allegedly divides and undermines the national cohesion (see Eliassi, 2013). Hobson (2015) states that globalization has been appropriated by Western powers to remake the world that endorses Western civilizational logics and interests, although facing fierce resistance from China and Russia. Moreover, a widely embraced global discourse primarily originated in Western contexts tends to construct non-Western identities as constituting a threat to democracy, gender equality and tolerance that West supposedly embodies and nurtures (see also Brown, 2006). Relatedly, the global othering of Muslims as inherently fanatical, misogynic, violent and intolerant tend to have violent and bloody consequences for Muslim populations in states like India, Israel, China and Russia.

In the context of the continuous or the declining power of the states, there are two contrasting but not mutually exclusive positions. For instance, Skinner (2013) argues that the international stage is still dominated by leading states in context of war, economy and humanitarian interventions. Domestically, the states continue to have a significant political role shaping politics and laws. Moreover, the states have become more aggressive by guarding their borders intensively against foreigners and putting their citizens under unrivalled surveillance. The states also tend to lend money when the bank system encounters economic collapse as the Financial Crisis of 2008 witnessed. We can also add how the outbreak of the COVID-19 pandemic in 2020 led to a strong resurgence of the nation-state. As a response to contain the spread of the COVID-19, many states started closing their borders and limiting freedom of mobility domestically and internationally. These actions included also the member states of the European Union that have built a common doctrine around open border and a strong European identity, flow of people, goods and capital. It became apparent that the European Union lacked a common mechanism to counter the outbreak of pandemic. On the contrary, the states started selfishly guarding their national borders and emphasized the danger as a primarily national concern despite the globality of the pandemic. Moreover, due to the massive destabilizing effects of pandemic on the economy, many states have promised to provide state aid and economically support domestic private companies that are at risk of bankruptcy. Accordingly, the state has not fallen or faded in the shadow of a globalized word that allegedly has buried the state (see Skinner, 2013).

By the same token, Cohen (2001) maintains that globalization did not mean transcendence and irrelevance of states and sovereignty since states and particularly the powerful Western ones were key protagonists in taming and shaping the globalized world economy. However, this is not to state that nothing has changed but the change is rather about reconfigurations than the death of states. States still maintain power over their territorial borders and exercise a flexible sovereignty to pursue their interests in a global context. Moreover, there are those who argue for a Leviathan calling and view the state as "the major vehicle of human liberty, of social peace and security, and paradoxically provides sanctuary for the political critics who attack it" (du Gay, 2012, p. 397). Unlike Skinner (2013) and du Gay (2012) who emphasize the significance and the necessity of the state, Brown (2014) argues that the walled states of the world cannot be understood as a muscular strength of a state but as a sign of its waning sovereignty. A central feature of our contemporary globalized world is the tension between the practices of state in relation to opening and fortifying their borders, global networks and local nationalisms. It is not due to invading armies that the states fortify their borders, but it is mainly in relation to non-state actors. The states tend to legitimize their walls or fortresses by reference to 'threat of terror', 'unwanted migration' and 'smuggling'. Regardless of how rich or poor the states are, there is a strong desire to build walls in the name of ensuring the security of the state and its subjects. Brown (2014) refers to Israel and the US as two striking examples of how these states legitimize their walls. While Israel evokes a discourse of victimization and vulnerability due to threats of terror from Palestinians, the Latino migrants have been portrayed in the work of Samuel Huntington as a cultural threat to the Anglo-Saxon cultural dominance and infamously labeled as an 'invasion' by President Donald Trump. As a potent response to block these 'intruding' forces, these states view hostility as a legitimate line of action to stop the 'barbarian' Muslims or Latinos from crossing their borders by containing, expelling or sometimes even killing them. By doing so, the state sends signals to its citizens and the outer world of being sovereign, righteous and powerful to secure the security of its citizens by erecting walls and militarizing their borders. The state is both victimized and regarded as a powerful vehicle to neutralize potential enemies inside and outside its borders in order to safeguard a civilized world that imagined 'barbarians' supposedly aspire to dissolve. Since the state is viewed as representing sovereignty and as the supreme power to protect its citizens from domestic and foreign threats, it needs to undo whatever signs of weakness, vulnerability, dubiousness and instability. By erecting walls as a compensation of lost or weakened sovereignty, and aggressively guarding its borders, the state spectacularizes its power and contributes to production of political subjectivity of those subjects it defends and those it aspires to exclude. The state not only aims to constitute social subjects as member of the nation but also attempts to monopolize their sense of identification with the state (Brown, 2014). In their discussion about the subject of the political, Edkins and Pin-Fat (1999) maintain that the social order and subjectivity are co-constituted and their existence is dependent on each other. More concretely, national identity as a form of political subjectivity is often placed within the social order of an existing nation-state or a future nation-state. This explains why members of the dominant group consider the perils of loss, decline of state power and national identity as their own losses and vulnerabilities, and support closing and securing national borders that supposedly foster their physical security, psychic and economic well-being (Brown, 2014). This line of argument does not entail that Brown denounces the importance of the state but underlines their weakened sovereignty. As Brown emphasizes, despite postnational constellations, governance and arguments, the state continues to remain as the:

> crucial emblem of political belonging and political protection. The plight of refugees and other stateless peoples is a reminder of the extent to which

> states remain the only meaningful sites of political citizenship and rights guarantees, as well as the most enduring emblems of security, however thin practices of citizenship have become, however compromised and unevenly distributed rights may be. (Brown 2014, pp. 67–68)

In the same light, Malešević (2013) argues that the idea that globalization has challenged the power of the nation-state and undermined its political legitimacy is highly dubious and misperceived (see also Agnew, 2009). Malešević maintains that cosmopolitanism and consumerism have not eroded or replaced the nation-state and nationalism as predicted by Ulrich Beck and Zygmunt Bauman. Likewise, religious insurgencies and belonging despite its transnational character have not been able to undo the power of the nation-state and function as a surrogate for nationalism. Despite his overall critical approach to nationalism, Malešević emphasizes that globalization has not undermined nationalism but reinforced the nation-states and increased the spread of nationalist ideology and popularity of self-identification in national terms. It is largely due to the long-lasting ideological investments that have made the nation-state as the standard mode of organizing a polity in the world where people continue to place their identity, identification and belonging within the framework of the nation-state and nationalism. Contrary to the idea that globalization has brought the importance of geography or place to an end, territorial belonging and geography in the context of nationalism continue to matter in relation to processes of belonging and non-belonging, inclusion and exclusion (Malešević, 2013). In the next section, I will engage with the relationship between the nation-state and constitution of majorities, minorities and nations without states.

The Nation-State, Minority/majority and Statelessness

The nation-state functions as a central reference point for the ways people understand their identities and the world (see, for instance, Anderson, 1991; Gellner, 1983; Hobsbawm, 1990). There are over 190 nation-states around the world. All of them make claim to and assert jurisdiction over a particular territory and a population; some subjects of these nation-states are qualified and cherished as citizens, others are viewed and treated as pseudo-citizens and marked groups while inhabiting the same nation-state (see Pandey, 2006; Yeğen, 2009). Despite the rhetoric of horizontal comradeship that nationalism promises (Anderson, 1991), the unevenness of the nation-state is constituted through its hierarchical citizenship order at national and global levels (Bosniak, 2006; Castles 2005; Shachar, 2009). In this context, nations without states in the global south are found at the bottom of the international hierarchy of citizens and identities (Castles, 2005). For instance, it is ethico-politically perfidious to put the extreme vulnerability and rightlessness of Rohingya in the same basket as the Catalans in Spain. Irrespective of the democratic or authoritarian order of the state in which they live, both nations are denied claims to statehood and encounter suppression and oppression at different scales. In the case of Rohingya, the state of Myanmar largely views the Rohingya population as 'Muslim foreigners' and as such excluded, dispossessed and deprived from basic human rights (see Kingston, 2015). When it comes to the Catalans, the Spanish state endorses the idea of a unitary Spaniard identity across all regions and the Catalans are at its best viewed as a minority and not as a distinct nation with right to self-determination (Guibernau, 2004).

One of the main reasons for states to reject claims of minorities to be recognized as a distinct nation is based on the idea that claiming nationhood and gaining recognition as a nation increase the validity of aspiration to statehood and political divorce from the existing state. Many states around the world are suspicious of constitutionally granting the status of minority to groups who are numerically inferior and ethno-culturally distinct since they fear that such status can underpin tendency to 'division', 'separatism' and 'secession'. One way for the state to contain the power of such putative nations that either seeks full citizenship rights or aspire some form of self-rule such as autonomy, federalism or independence is to deny the existence of this people and bring them coercively under its universality by banning its symbolic and cultural existence or to assign this constituency a minoritized position from which they cannot claim mastery over their political fate but encompassed as subordinated to the dominant group's political and cultural grammar. The very usage of the terms 'stateless', 'stateless nations' or 'nations without states' indicates that they are not in hold of a state that can represent their identities, languages and religions and effectively protect their rights and security. These terms also indicate the political normativity of the state in the world as the standard template for organizing human life (see Chouinard, 2016).

There is a strong relationship between how the nation-state forms majority and minority populations and assigns them different status and values within the ethno-national or ethno-religious hierarchies of the nation (Maggiolini & Ouahes, 2021). Being a member of numerically inferior group or belonging to a non-dominant group often constitute the standard definition of a minority (see Castellino & Cavanaugh, 2013). Due to power abuse by majorities, minorities are often culturally otherized and face legal, political, economic and social disadvantages (White, 2012). Although it is more common that the numerically superior group controls the state and universalizes its identity, culture, religion as the master identity of the state, there are cases where a numerically minor group have or continue to assert themselves as the dominant group; Sunni Arabs of Iraq prior to 2003, Alawites in Syria, white settlers in South Africa and Sunni Arabs in Bahrain. In contrast to the rest of the Middle East, Alawites in Syria and Sunni Arabs in Bahrain are numerically a minority and they control central political institutions and dominate security institutions. Moreover, they implement policies that privilege their groups and obstruct the majority (numerically) to achieve political power. One of the main discursive strategies of these two ruling minorities is informed by the idea that the majority group constitutes an existential threat to the state and minorities if they control the state. The excluded majorities of Bahrain and Syria are also accused of sectarianism endorsed by foreign powers (Dajani, 2015). In this light, Chakrabarty (2000) argues that majority and minority should not be conceived as natural entities or primarily as statistical terms. For instance, while the Europeans who numerically are a minority in the world have "assumed that their histories contained the majority instances of norms that every other human society should aspire to; compared to them, others were still the 'minors' for whom they, the 'adults' of the world, had to take charge" (Chakrabarty, 2000, p. 100). This shows how power relation is central to construction of majorities by inferiorizing and marginalizing certain constituencies as minorities within the historiographies of titular nations. Alcoff and Mohanty (2006) emphasize the aspect of power than the issue of number, since power is not equally shared between the dominant and the minoritized groups. In this light, they approach the concept of minority in conceptual, political, and institutional senses. Conceptually, a minority entails occupying a nonhegemonic and nondominant position that "has to be explained rather than assumed, or the identity that is not taken for granted but is *on trial*. Politically, minority signifies a struggle, a position that is under contestation or actually embattled, that does not enjoy equality of status, of power, or of respect. Institutionally, minority studies have been made up by necessity of whatever has been excluded from the canon and the mainstream work of the disciplines, if though at all" (Alcoff & Mohanty, 2006, p. 6, emphasis added). However, I do think that issue of number is important in context of majority and minority relations, especially when it is politicized. One of the major fears of the Israeli state is the high rate of child birth among Palestinians who can outnumber the Israeli Jews in a near future. Similar concerns are also found in Turkey about the Kurds and in the US about the white constituency as losing their numerical primacy.

In regard to Kurdish and Palestinian experiences in the Middle East, Kurds are viewed as a trapped minority (Castellino & Cavanaugh, 2013) divided between the states of Iran, Iraq, Syria and Turkey, while it is often and mainly the Palestinian citizens of Israel that are defined as a minority. Those Palestinians who are living in Gaza, the West Bank and East Jerusalem are rarely discussed in terms of being a minority but as a people subjugated to illegal Israeli occupation following the Six-Day-War of 1967 when Israel occupied the remaining Palestinian territories (see Ghanem, 1998; Heins, 2012; Jamal & Kensicki, 2020). The concept of minority might also be used sometimes to describe Palestinian refugees and migrants living in Arab countries, South America and Western countries. Before the emergence of the modern nation-states, the concept of minority was barely used (Robson, 2016; White, 2012). In the context of the Ottoman Empire, it was rather millets or communities that were used to depict its diverse and confessional-communal constellation. Christians and Jews as non-Muslim communities were also viewed as millets. The Ottoman Empire is often cherished as being the original enactor of tolerance and diversity in light of ethnic and religious differences. However, this is not to say that Jews, Christians or Shia Muslims enjoyed full equality in relation to the dominant Sunni Muslim constituency (Castellino & Cavanaugh, 2013). Tas (2014) argues that the Ottoman millet-system endorsed both territorial and non-territorial recognition and autonomy of different ethnic and religious groups and become a source of inspiration for contemporary nation-states that are facing the political challenges of ethnic and religious minorities. In contrast to the violent assimilation policies of modern Turkish nationalism vis-à-vis the Kurds of, the Ottoman millet-system provided from the sixteenth century political and cultural space for Kurds to enjoy autonomy and run their affairs. The

Ottoman Empire used the Kurds to safeguard its border and Kurds were obliged to provide the Sultan with soldiers and taxes (see also Arakon, 2014; Matin, 2020; Nimni, 2015).

However, things started to change dramatically when Turkish nationalism hijacked the pluralistic constellation of the millet-system and established Turkishness as the master identity of Turkey (Tas, 2014). Although Kymlicka and Pföstl (2014) underline the impressive and constructive role of the millet-system in endorsing tolerance and co-existence, they assert that the Sunni Muslims were treated and conceived as the owner of the Ottoman state. The inclusion of non-Sunni Muslims was based on submission and subordinated terms since it was the Sunni Muslims who were extending their protection and tolerance of non-Muslim groups which indicate the uneven power relations between those who tolerate and those who are tolerated. As such, the millet-system endorsed inclusion but it also justified creation of second-class status for those groups that did not enjoy normative primacy. When the Ottoman Empire officially ended in 1922, and the colonial power of Britain and France monopolized the political scene of the Middle East, notions of majority and minority in national terms became salient in stipulating conditions of inclusion and belonging to the newly established nation-states in the region.

Minorities need to be conceived in relational terms since they are constituted in relation to a state and the titular nation that controls the political, cultural and economic and administrative unity of the state (see Nimni, 2015). While it is the minorities that are often problematized in political and academic discourses and majorities are assumed as unproblematic entities (White, 2012), it is vital to any liberatory and inclusive political project to destabilize the category and political normativity of groups that hegemonize themselves as majorities. As with nationalisms of dominant groups and dominated groups, it is more common to project the exclusionary forces of nationalism on ethnic minorities that fight for creating their own states and challenging the status quo of established nation-states. The nationalism of the dominant group is often denied and escapes being an object of problematization and investigation since it has managed to politically assert itself as invisible, natural and banal (Billig, 1995, p. 179).

In his book, *The emergence of minorities in the Middle East*, White (2012) argues that we should return to the formation of the nation-state in order to trace and understand the emergence of the categories of majorities and minorities and the sociopolitical context in which they have become meaningful for the way people think of themselves or others in terms of majorities and minorities. The nation-state creates a framework for nationalization of territory and assertion of state authority across the national territory. From the moment the nation-state is recognized as an objective entity, it starts spreading its authority across the territory it is assigned and attempts to bind the diverse populations under a single unit and common institutions like educational system, the media and the army. Within these structures, certain groups become minorities or minoritized, while others are endorsed as belonging to the dominant cultural constituency (White, 2012). While the international nation-state system can recognize a state and its territorial borders, it is not given that the state automatically gains internal recognition by different constituencies it wants to subject to its rule. Many of the states in the Middle East are suffering from the fact that the ultimate political loyalty of the diverse populations does not lie with the state. It is not by consent, but often by coercion, emergency laws and the continuous presence of violence as a tool to reinforce its rule and power. The case of the Kurds in the Middle East is illustrative that the states have not been able to gain the loyalty of the Kurdish people and preventing them from dreaming about a sovereign homeland where Kurds can run their own affairs. Although the states in the Middle East want to display themselves as muscular in maintaining state sovereignty and its territorial 'integrity', history has shown that as soon as they become weak and suffer from political crisis and instability, they become more accommodating to diversity and less assertive about state sovereignty. White (2012) maintains that the states often claim that they derive "their legitimacy from some version of the principle of representativity expressed in the claim to share a cultural identity with a numerical majority of their population" (White, 2012, p. 2). From the moment, a majority is constituted and takes power, minorities are created and pushed to the margins of the state, where the majority asserts itself as the head of the state and minorities as its tail. There is an important political convergence between the emergence of statelessness and minorities, since they are both effects of exclusionary state- and nation-buildings and hierarchical citizenship regimes. It is the nation-state form that "creates the objective conditions in which people begin to consider themselves as majorities and minorities; however, these remain subjective categories" (White, 2012, p. 209). Since the state establishes a relationship with the populations it wants to subject to its rule, it is imperative for the state to define this relationship since it clarifies which group or groups it claims to represent (White, 2012). It is under such conditions that the state endorses and institutionalizes a cultural identity that reflects the interests, experiences and perspectives of the numerically dominant group. This entails that the dominant group universalizes its identity and values across the state border, whereas the minoritized group is geographically ghettoized and contained within their particular geography.

Citizenship is the central instrument of the states to tie a population to their polity. While citizenship often promises horizontal inclusion within the boundary of the state, it is often marked and tainted by the cultural identity of the dominant group. This hierarchical citizenship contributes to a division between majority subjects and minoritized subjects in relation to power, rights and cultural and political primacy. Minoritized are rarely included or asked about how to formulate the citizenship of the state in order to create a multilateral universalism where rights and interests of different constituencies can be guaranteed and institutionalized. Since dominant groups control the power of interpellations and means of violence, the state and the majority are viewed as active political subjects by 'giving' rights to minorities. Of course, this is far from truth, since minorities have not just waited to be generously given their rights, but it is due to their persistent political and armed struggle, that they push the state to respond to their political, cultural and economic grievances and recognize their ethnopolitical reality. What is central to the White's arguments (2007) is that by looking at how minorities are created we can learn about the formation of majority power and identities. Accordingly, we can understand how cultural insiders and aliens are constructed within the realms of the nation-state. As I stated earlier, one of the strategies of the state as representative of a majority identity is to discard the claims of minority to equal participation, cultural recognition and political parity as divisive and expression of separatism or foreign plots to undermine the state. White (2007) illustrates how minorities become the necessary others to produce majority nationalism:

> Nationalist responses to separatism are not really aimed at separatists: they intend, rather, to promote a sense of territorial nationalism among the mainstream, *assuming* the existence of a majority and its right to impose its authority. The emergence of such a 'majority' consciousness might easily

> stimulate a 'minority' consciousness in communities outside the mainstream, which, in circular process, would create its own impression on majority attitudes. (White, 2007, pp. 76–77, emphasis in original)

Although White is right about this state strategy to produce mainstream nationalism, I am not sure if state responses to minorities *are not really* aimed at minorities, since they are the ones who often pay with their lives and homes when the state targets them, put them outside of law and vilify them as internal enemies. Hence, minorities are not marginal to the modern nation-state although they tend to be marginalized by a majority view when the history of the nation-state is narrated and formed. The response to a majority view is not a minority view that can produce a self-marginalization. Instead, it is more important for minorities to not take for granted the idea and the political position or status that they have always been a minority and the dominant group has always been a majority. The history of the majorities and the minorities is historically and politically imbricated and co-constitutive (White, 2007).

Predatory Majorities and the Struggle Over (Re)definition of the Political Home

While discussing how categories of majorities and minorities are constructed and the conditions that bring them about, Pandey (2006) contends that *routine violence* "is written into the making and continuation of contemporary political arrangements, and into the production and reproduction of majorities and minorities" (p. 1). Routine violence is not reduced to the spectacular and visible violence that states use against minorities to secure their power and naturalize majoritarian identity but it also includes our daily behavior vis-à-vis strangers, how we construct, imagine and relate to our neighbors, but also what we read about them and get to see when they become visible to the majority view. It is equally about how we talk about them and the silences we are involved in, when they are targeted by words and arms (ibid., p. 8). It is under the political arrangement and conditions of nationalist idea and violence that minorities are produced and viewed as 'marked' while the dominant group remain 'unmarked' and naturalized. Nationalism is often oriented toward constructing political and social hierarchies and creating relations of privilege and oppression, dominance and subordination outside and within the realms of the nation-state (ibid., p. 13). In a similar context,

Appadurai (2006) formulates an alarming narrative about the dangerous idea of the nation-state and its construction of minorities. According to Appadurai, "No modern nation-state, however benign its political system and however eloquent its public voices may be about the virtues of tolerance, multiculturalism, and inclusion, is free of the idea that its national sovereignty is built on some sort of ethnic genius" (ibid., p. 3). If wars have historically been used to build states, the nation-state have used violence against minorities to build national community and strong attachment between the dominant group and the state (see Mamdani, 2020). Appadurai makes the points that majorities are in greater need of minorities for their existence since they become central in the process of a 'we-making' by setting boundaries and creating ethnic others who do not fit or serve the general national interest. Since it is within the context of the nation-state that categories of majority and minority become meaningful, it is also in this respect that the majority can suffer from an anxiety of incompleteness and due to the remaining gap (minorities as obstacle) to achieve a pure and untainted national wholeness. This sense of anxiety and incompleteness push the majority toward violence against minorities (ibid.) who claim equality, representation, autonomy and rights as members of distinct ethnocultural constituencies. Minorities per se become political rivals and obstacle to 'complete' visions and goals of nation-building that majority groups aspire. Appadurai (2006) maintains that this sense of insecurity by the dominant group can pave the ground for genocidal acts against minorities. In a globalized world characterized by differences and blurred boundaries and identities, the majorities are becoming more predatory to contain their sense of uncertainty and incompleteness that minorities are blamed to produce. Minorities are also becoming important objects of aversion for states and majorities who are displacing their anxieties "about their own minority or marginality (real or imagined) in a world of few megastates, of unruly economic flows and compromised sovereignties" (ibid., p. 43).

Majorities have no interest in trading their place with minorities since they as member of dominant group know that minorities often hold a position of marginality and otherness. This sense of insecurity often leads to construction of predatory majorities (see Appadurai 2006) that view minorities as an existential threat to their security, welfare and power within the state. Obviously, it is political discourses that mobilize majorities to view themselves as besieged on the edge of dissolution. By political mobilization, majorities are encouraged to actively carry out politics that privilege their dominance and primacy. Let me give two examples of how this resentment against minorities are expressed and felt in Iraq and the US. Despite political optimism that the Kurds of Iraq can gain their constitutional rights and autonomy within the federal state of Iraq, representatives of Iraqi-Arab nationalism view the Kurdistan Region as a danger to the Arab nation. Consider how the Iraqi-Arab commentator Samir Ubayd frames his understanding of the Kurdistan Region:

> Have you ever heard of a region that swallowed the original homeland, trampled its identity and changed it into that of a region? The answer is no, we have not heard nor have we read that a region and small nation could become so domineering as to obliterate the unique history of the big homeland and nation, except in Iraq. Arab Iraq, whose civilization is seven thousand years old, has become the Kurdish region's tail, while the Arab nation has turned into a mere servant of the Kurdish nation. (cited in Bengio, 2012, p. 4)

The account above indicates that the Kurds do not deserve an equal position within the republic of Iraq that should first and foremost be an Arab republic since it has 'always' been so but interrupted by the ascending Kurdish identity and political power in the Kurdish Region of Iraq. After the Kurdish referendum for independence in September 2017 that gained over 90% of the votes, Arab nationalism in Iraq became more assertive about sovereignty and the Iraqi government in Baghdad continue to cut the Kurdish share of the Iraqi budget and weaponize it against the Kurdistan Region. Of course, this is not to condone the widespread corruption within the oil sector in the Kurdistan Region monopolized by the two ruling Kurdish parties, KDP and PUK. Economic and political corruption is no less pervasive but higher in the non-Kurdish parts of Iraq where Shia or Sunni Arabs rule. Iraq as a country belongs to one of the most corrupted states in the world. In 2012, the former Iraqi Prime Minister Nouri al-Maliki complained about the rising power of Kurdistan Region and told a Kurdish TV channel that the Kurdistan Region acts as though Iraq was a part of Kurdistan and not vice versa (Eliassi, 2013). Indeed, it does not seem to matter who holds the position as the Iraqi Prime Minister since the very idea of Kurdish right to autonomy and self-rule is not embraced by the ruling Shia Arabs in Iraq even if it is enshrined in the current Iraqi constitution. The example above was more concerned with the territorial autonomy of Kurds who constitutes a majority in their region but are numerically inferior to the Arabs in the context of Iraq.

Now let us move to another example that illustrates how *a white majority* in Louisiana considers itself as a *besieged minority* due to the presence of non-white groups who wants their share of the American welfare or dream (Hochschild, 2016). According to Hochschild, these non-white groups are viewed by member of the white community as 'cutting ahead in the line' and postponing the achievement of American dream for the white majority. The alleged political correctness of multiculturalism in the US, blamed on the liberal media, has created a situation in which the white majority cannot express their 'true' feeling about their plagues, blacks, women, immigrants, gays. Interestingly, it is the historically and contemporary disenfranchised groups that are objects of aversion and viewed as 'stealing' their place in line that leads to the rights and benefits. Members of this white community consider themselves as culturally marginalized and ridiculed by the liberal media due to their conservative views about marriage, guns, gender roles, race and the Confederate flag. Hochschild depicts their worldviews and experiences in the following way:

> Strangers step ahead of you in line, making you anxious, resentful, and afraid. A president allies with the line cutters, making you feel distrustful, betrayed. A person ahead of you in line insults you as an ignorant redneck, making you feel humiliated and mad. Economically, culturally, demographically, politically, you are suddenly a stranger in your own land. (Hochschild, 2016, p. 222)

By feeling besieged, minoritized, ridiculed, marginalized, the so-called silent white majority resorts to President Donald Trump as a supposed white savior who can make America Great Again. By electing Trump, the silent white majority can become the spatial manager of their homeland and no longer feel as strangers in their own homeland, that ethnocultural pluralism has allegedly induced (ibid.; see also Hage, 1998). This is not something unique for Iraq or the US regarding how majorities are expressing fear and anxiety about being suspended as spatial managers of the country. On the contrary, this is a political pattern that permeates the discursive field of anti-immigration forces in Europe that are warning white Europeans that Muslim migrants will soon demographically and culturally besiege Europe and making Europeans into a minority in *their own homelands* (see Eliassi, 2013).

It is of paramount importance to underline that states use a range of different policies to accommodate, include or exclude minorities.

The demographic weight of minorities along with their ethnic and religious identities affect the way states responds to their grievances. For instance, Christians in the Middle East are numerically inferior than the Muslims and often found themselves between authoritarian promises of state protection and risks of marginalization by the majority groups that defines the state as a Muslim state. Ironically, many of the states in the Middle East including the Kurds view their alleged or real protection of Christians and other minorities as a certificate to gain Western recognition and support for their forms of governance. According to the Zabad (2017), there are three major political and social factors that can explain the dilemma and political behavior of minorities in the Middle East. First, there is a continuous nationhood crisis that had haunted the region since the Sykes-Picot agreement in 1916 between Great Britain and France. The states that were created by these two colonial powers did not reflect the aspirations, loyalties or sentiments of the population inhabiting these newly formed states. The legacy of these fault lines between different ethnic and religious group are still vibrant in the region. Moreover, the states in the Middle East have not been able to create an all-inclusive political entity that cherishes and embraces diversity and difference. This had put the minorities in a constant vulnerable situation. Second, liberal forces are either absent or weak, secular nationalism has entailed political suffering and economic impoverishment, Islamism whether in its moderate or extreme forms have all entailed despotic majoritarian rules where minorities cannot expect other than subordination, oppression and violence. Of course, these forces might use conspicuously inclusive terms like 'brotherhood' (rarely sisterhood), 'coexistence' and 'equality', but few of these have been translated into real politics. Third, the dynamics of majority and minority and the institutional contexts that they are embedded in have generated mutual distrust and political distance. Majorities often blame the minorities for obstructing social cohesion by collaborating with foreign forces to split up the country. While minorities often support multiculturalism, majorities tend to view multiculturalism as undermining the power of majority and unity of the nation (Zabad, 2017, pp. 2–3). The rights of minorities are equated with endorsing separatism and diversity is interpreted the antithesis of national identity and cohesion.

In a similar context about the failure of the nation-states of the Middle East to create an inclusive political framework for diversity and ethnic and religious differences, Kymlicka and Pföstl (Kymlicka & Pföstl, 2014, pp. 9–16) point equally to three important factors. First, the legacy of Ottoman millet-system created grounds for legal vulnerability, political marginalization and social subordination for groups who were not viewed as Sunni-Muslims. Second, the colonial legacy is still widespread in the Middle East where minorities are viewed as unreliable and mercenaries of foreign and Western power that aim to rule and divide the Muslim world. Of course, this does not only need to be a question of Western manipulation. For instance, while Iran empowers politically and militarily Shia minorities or majorities in the Arab world, Saudi-Arabia is working hard to contain Persian and Shiite power in the region, although less successful. The cases of Syria, Iraq, Lebanon, Bahrain and Yemen are illustrative of these force measurements. Third, Arab states and I would also add Iran and Turkey have been ruled by authoritarian leaders and arrangements of nation-building, which in turn created alienation and suffering both for the majorities but most of all for minorities who are suspiciously viewed as a fifth column. The states in the Middle East have been involved in aggressive forms of homogenization policies and exclusion of minority language, identity and cultures from public spaces. Kymlicka and Pföstl (2014, p. 15) refer to Khaddar (2012) who distinguishes between the colonial nationalism that dominated the Arab world where different and diverse ethnic and religious groups fought side by side against colonial power, and state nationalism that have adopted authoritarian and homogenizing discourses and considering minority and diversity claims as a national security issue (Kymlicka & Pföstl, 2014). When the national movements in the global south achieved some form of political independence from the Western colonial powers, they did not manage to create a citizenship based on social equality and how to distribute the wealth equally between different members of their newly established political communities. In contrast, they started following a colonial logic to endorse belonging based on ethno-national hierarchies that depicted minoritized groups primarily as a threat to the dominant community's survival (Mamdani, 2020).

Viewing Minority Rights Through the Lenses of Securitization

Securitization of minorities is widespread in the Middle East. For instance, many parts of Kurdistan are militarized by the states that rule the Kurds, which often entail displacement and continuous violence as a state pretext for fighting 'terrorism'. It is not only the Kurds as a people who are securitized but also the geography in which they live. Kurdish geography is viewed as unruly and 'bad lands' by the states that want to subject Kurds to its dominance. Securitization is often used to suspend economic investments in the Kurdish region and maintain the Kurdish regions as impoverished and neglected. The same applies to Palestinians who are viewed as a security threat to the very existence of Israel. The checkpoints, security fences and surveillances that the Israeli military deploys against the Palestinians indicate the level of securitization targeting and disabling Palestinian mobility and rights. In other words, Palestinian and Kurdish claims to rights, equality and lands are viewed through a security lens. Nimni (2015) argues that securitization has been central to nation-buildings. By conflating nations with popular sovereignty and territorial states, minorities are turned into cultural aliens when minorities respond politically and violently to state policies. The history of securitization of non-dominant ethnic groups goes back to more than 200 hundred years and could be found in the discourse of French republicanism and English liberalism that viewed diversity and heterogeneity as a danger to national unity and democracy (Nimni, 2015). When a state securitizes a minority group as a peril for state security, the state can suspend laws and enforce emergency measures, in order to justify whatever action it takes against the securitized minorities (Dajani, 2015). According to Kymlicka, securitization of minorities occurs when states do not view minority claims "through the lens of fairness and justice" but "through the lens of security and loyalty" (Kymlicka, 2004, p. 134). This implies that securitization takes the antecedence over justice for minorities with the belief that a strong state can only be established if minorities are politically weak so they cannot threaten the territorial integrity of the state. Croft (2012, p. 219) adopts the concept of insecuritization in order to describe the process "through which the dominant power can decide who should be protected and who should be designated as those to be controlled, objectified, and feared". Kymlicka (2004) contends that the West has avoided securitization of minority nationalism and allowed secessionist politics in normal politics where different actors can contest, challenge or defend the very existence of the state. This democratic approach is viewed as an antidote to illiberal and violent forms of identity politics that non-democratic states pursue and nurture. In a democracy, it is important to not view secession as:

> a crime against humanity, and that the goal of a democratic political system shouldn't be to make it unthinkable. States and state borders are not sacred. The first goal of a state should be to promote democracy, human rights, justice, and the well-being of citizens, not to somehow insist that every citizen view themselves as bound to the existing state 'in perpetuity' – a goal which can only be achieved through undemocratic and unjust means in a multination state. A state can only fully enjoy the benefits of democracy and federalism if it is willing to live with the risk of secession. (Kymlicka, 2004, p. 166)

Indeed, this democratic approach that Kymlicka represents is not only utopian in a Middle Eastern context where authoritarian regimes are subjecting minorities to harsh treatments, violence and exclusionary practices but even in European liberal democracies like Spain. For instance, when the Kurdistan Region of Iraq and Catalonia voted for independence in 2017, both were suppressed and condemned for destabilizing the states in which they inhabit. Both Iraq and Spain suspended the results of these referendums and carried out actions that undermined the very basis of democracy and right to self-determination. Europe could not tell the Kurds: you deserve independence but the Catalans must remain under Spanish jurisdiction. To show the discursive consensus, in 2017 the German Foreign Minister Frank-Walter Steinmeier denounced Kurdish independence as further destabilizing the Middle East, a discursive rhetoric that did not differ much from the authoritarian regimes and leaders of the Middle East that equate minority rights with political instability.

To sum up, as minorities, their legal status, language, life-style, prosperity or poverty, and most of all their politics are factors that reminds the majority about the incompleteness of the nation-state as a site of singularity and ethnic purity (Appadurai, 2006). Likewise, minorities function as key witnesses to the atrocities of the nation-states and holder of memories that the states want to expel from its history and self-legitimation practices (see Butler, 2004). By asserting the social construction of minorities, I am not assuming minorities as non-peoples but interested in the processes of minoritization that the nation-state establishes, by privileging majorities and putting the minorities on the receiving end of oppression. This is where minority politics and movements come in and shoulder the struggle to alter and refashion the existing unequal political conditions, formula or arrangements that have been established to serve the interest of the dominant ethnicity. When the state is monopolized by a particular ethnicity, it tends to seize and shape societal institutions and hegemonizes itself as the national identity of all. Any radical or insurgent resistance against this hegemonic order tends to be repudiated as acts of 'terror' and 'separatism'. Obviously, this is a discourse that states use to justify violent repression of minorities who are pursuing their rights to act as legitimate constituents of the society and not as marked citizens whose culture, identity and language are on trial when they encounter dominant institutions and members of the dominant ethnicities.

References

Agnew, J. (2009). *Globalization & sovereignty*. Rowman & Littlefield.

Alcoff, L. M., & Mohanty, S. P. (2006). Reconsidering identity politics: An introduction. In M. A. Linda, H.-G. Michael, P. M. Satya, & M. L. M. Paula (Eds.), *Identity politics reconsidered* (pp. 1–9). Palgrave Macmillan.

Anderson, B. (1991). *Imagined communities*. Verso.

Appadurai, A. (2006). *Fear of small numbers: An essay on the geography of anger*. Duke University Press.

Arakon, M. (2014). Kurds at the transition from the Ottoman Empire to the Turkish Republic. *Turkish Policy Quarterly, 13*(1), 139–148.

Bartelson, J. (2009). *Visions of world community*. Cambridge University Press.

Bartelson, J. (2014). *Sovereignty as symbolic form*. Routledge.

Bengio, O. (2012). *The Kurds of Iraq: Building a state within a state*. Lynne Rienner.

Billig, M. (1995). *Banal Nationalism*. Sage.

Bosniak, L. (2006). *The citizen and the other: Dilemmas of contemporary membership*. Princeton University Press.

Brown, W. (2006). *Regulating aversion: tolerance in the age of identity and empire*. Princeton University Press.

Brown, W. (2014). *Walled states, waning sovereignty*. Zed Books.

Butler, J. (2004). *Precarious life: The powers of mourning and violence*. Verso.

Castellino, J., & Cavanaugh, K. A. (2013). *Minority rights in the Middle East*. Oxford University Press.

Castles, S. (2005). Nation and empire: Hierarchies of citizenship in the new global order. *International Politics, 42*, 203–224.

Chakrabarty, D. (2000). *Provincializing Europe: Postcolonial thought and historical difference*. Princeton University Press.

Chouinard, S. (2016). Stateless nations. In C. Karl & W. Stefan (Eds.), *The Routledge handbook of ethnic conflict* (pp. 54–66). Routledge.

Cocks, J. (2014). *On sovereignty and other political delusions*. Bloomsbury.

Cohen, E. S. (2001). Globalization and the boundaries of the state: A Framework for analyzing the changing practice of sovereignty. *Governance: An International Journal of Policy and Administration, 14*(1), 75–97.
Croft, S. (2012). Constructing ontological insecurity: The insecuritization of Britain's Muslims. *Contemporary Security Policy, 33*(2), 219–235.
Dajani, O. M. (2015). The Middle East's majority problems: Minoritarian regimes and the threat of democracy. *Ethnic and Racial Studies, 38*(14), 2516–2533.
Du Gay, P. (2012). Leviathan calling: Some notes on sociological anti-statism and its consequences. *Journal of Sociology, 48*(4), 397–409.
Edkins, J., & Pin-Fat, V. (1999). The subject of the political. In E. Jenny, P. Nalini, & P.-F. Véronique (Eds.), *Sovereignty and subjectivity* (pp. 1–10). Lynne Rienner Publishers.
Eliassi, B. (2013). *Contesting Kurdish identities in Sweden: Quest for belonging among Middle Eastern youth*. Palgrave Macmillan.
Gellner, E. (1983). *Nations and nationalism*. Cornell University Press.
Ghanem, A. (1998). State and minority in Israel: The case of ethnic state and the predicament of its minority. *Ethnic and Racial Studies, 21*(3), 428–448.
Giddens, A. (1987). *The nation-state and violence: Volume two of a contemprary critique of historical materialism*. University of California Press.
Grzybowski, J., & Koskenniemi, M. (2015). International law and statehood: A performative view. In S. Robert & M. R. S. Peter (Eds.), *The concept of the state in international relations: Philosophy, sovereignty, cosmopolitanism* (pp. 23–47). Edinburgh University Press.
Hobsbawm, E. J. (1990). *Nations and nationalism since 1780: Program, myth, reality*. Cambridge University Press.
Guibernau, M. (2004). *Catalan nationalism: Froncoism, transition and democracy*. Routledge.
Hage, G. (1998). *White nation: Fantasies of white supremacy in multicultural society*. Routledge.
Heins, V. (2012). Three meanings of equality: The 'Arab problem" in Israel. *Res Publica, 18*, 79–91.
Hobson, J. M. (2015). Decolonising sovereignty: Globalisation and the return of hyper-sovereignty. In S. Robert & M. R. S. Peter (Eds.), *The concept of the state in international relations: Philosophy, sovereignty, cosmopolitanism* (pp. 135–162). Edinburgh University Press.
Hochschild, A. R. (2016). *Strangers in their own land: Anger and mourning on the American right*. The New Press.
Holsti, K. J. (1996). *The state, war, and the state of war*. Cambridge University Press.
Jackson, R. (2007). *Sovereignty*. Polity Press.

Jamal, A., & Kensicki, A. (2020). Theorizing half-statelessness: A case study of the nation-state law in Israel. *Citizenship Studies*. https://doi.org/10.1080/13621025.2020.1745152

Jütersonke, O. & Kartas, M. (2015). The state as urban myth: Governance without government in the global south. In R. Schuett & M. R. S. Peter (Eds.), *The concept of the state in international relations: Philosophy, sovereignty and cosmopolitanism* (pp. 108–134). Edinburgh University Press.

Kingston, L. N. (2015). Protecting the world's most persecuted: The responsibility to protect and Burma's Rohingya minority. *The International Journal of Human Rights, 19*(8), 1163–1175.

Kymlicka, W. (2004). Justice and security in the accommodation of minority nationalism. In M. Stephen, M. Tariq, & S. Judith (Eds.), *Ethnicity, nationalism, and minority rights* (pp. 144–175). Cambridge University Press.

Kymlicka, W., & Pföstl, E. (2014). Introduction. In K. Will & P. Eva (Eds.), *Multiculturalism and minority rights in the Arab world* (pp. 1–24). Oxford University Press.

Levy, D., & Sznaider, N. (2006). Sovereignty transformed: A sociology of human rights. *The British Journal of Sociology, 57*(4), 657–676.

Malešević, S. (2010). *The sociology of war and violence*. Cambridge University Press.

Malešević, S. (2013). *Nation-state and nationalisms*. Polity.

Mamdani, M. (2020). *Neither settler nor native: The making and unmaking permanent minorities*. The Belknap Press of Harvard University Press.

Matin, K. (2020). Liminal lineages of the "Kurdish Question". *Middle East Report* 295. https://merip.org/2020/08/liminal-lineages-of-the-kurdish-question/ Accessed 7 April 2021.

Moreton-Robinson, A. (2015). *The white possessive: Property, Power, and indigenous sovereignty*. University of Minnesota Press.

Nimni, E. (2015). Minorities and the limits of liberal democracy: Demoicracy and non-territorial autonomy. In H. M. Tove & P. Francesco (Eds.), *Minority accommodation through territorial and non-territorial autonomy* (pp. 57–82). Oxford University Press.

Maggiolini, P., & Ouahes, I. (Eds.). (2021). *Minorities and state-building in the Middle East: The case of Jordan*. Palgrave Macmillan.

Pandey, G. (2006). *Routine violence: Nations, fragments, histories*. Standford University Press.

Robson, L. (Ed.). (2016). *Minorities and the modern Arab world*. Syracuse University Press.

Sassen, S. (1996). *Losing control? Sovereignty in an age of globalization*. Columbia University Press.

Sasson, J. (2016). *Anatomy of authoritarianism in the Arab Republics*. Cambridge University Press.

Shachar, A. (2009). *The birthright lottery: Citizenship and global inequality*. Harvard University Press.
Schuett, R. (2015). Open societies, cosmopolitanism and the Kelsonian state as a safeguard against nationalism. In S. Robert & M. R. S. Peter (Eds.), *The concept of the state in international relations: Philosophy, sovereignty, cosmopolitanism* (pp. 221–243). Edinburgh University Press.
Schwarz, R. (2012). *War and state building in the Middle East*. University Press of Florida.
Skinner, Q. (2013). The sovereign state: A genealogy. In K. Hent & S. Quentin (Eds.), *Sovereignty in Fragments: The past, present and future of a contested concept* (pp. 26–46). Cambridge University Press.
Strange, S. (1996). *The retreat of the state*. Cambridge University Press.
Tas, L. (2014). The myth of the Ottoman millet system: Its treatment of Kurds and a discussion of territorial and non-territorial autonomy. *International Journal of Minority and Group Rights, 21*(4), 497–526.
Weber, M. (1994). *Weber: Political writings*. Cambridge University Press.
White, B. T. (2007). The nation-state form and the emergence of 'minorities' in Syria. *Studies in Ethnicity and Nationalism, 7*(1), 64–85.
White, B. T. (2012). *The emergence of minorities in the Middle East: The politics of community in French Mandate Syria*. Edinburgh University Press.
Yeğen, M. (2009). "Prospective-Turks" or "Pseudo-citizens": Kurds in Turkey. *Middle East Journal, 63*(4), 597–615.
Zabad, I. (2017). *Middle Eastern minorities: The impact of the Arab spring*. Routledge.

CHAPTER 3

Defining, Embracing and Resisting (State)lessness

After the collapse of the multinational Ottoman Empire during World War I and redrawing of the borders of the Middle East, Kurds and Palestinians were denied statehood. Despite the absence of their nation-states, Kurds and Palestinians have reached and developed national consciousness and a sense of shared national identity (Khalidi, 1997). What characterizes their political situation in the Middle East is that the Kurds and Palestinians "live in disputed homelands that overlap with those of other people, and the territory they claim has ambiguous and indeterminate boundaries" (Khalidi, 1997, p. 11). Kurds currently live under the national jurisdiction of Iran, Iraq, Syria and Turkey. These four states have used different political strategies to deal with what is often called the 'Kurdish question'. These strategies have entailed assimilation, subordinated inclusion, denial, mass murder campaigns, forced displacement and destruction of Kurdish villages. The sovereign identity of Iran, Iraq, Syria and Turkey has historically reflected the identity of the dominant ethnic groups (Turkish, Arabs and Persians) and triggered a reactive political identity among Kurds, which "continue to occupy the forefront of opposition to the sovereign" (Vali, 1998, p. 88). The national identities of these states were partly constructed through suppression of Kurdish identity. Accordingly, political and cultural othering of the Kurds explain the resilient Kurdish identity formation in relation to the states in which

B. Eliassi, *Narratives of Statelessness and Political Otherness*, Minorities in West Asia and North Africa,
https://doi.org/10.1007/978-3-030-76698-6_3

they are living, but also among the members of the Kurdish diaspora who have migrated to Western countries. Following the establishment of Israel in 1948, Palestinians have faced mass expulsion, violence, destruction of their homes and cities, trees. It is not an exaggeration to state that Israel has attempted and succeeded to a certain extent, to make Palestinians into 'foreigners' or 'strangers' in their own homelands, by displacing Palestinians and settling Jewish migrants in Palestine.

The majority of Kurds holds the citizenship of Iran, Iraq, Syria and Turkey and do not qualify for the position of stateless if statelessness is delimited to lack of formal citizenship. Different studies indicate that there are people who are internally stateless without leaving the place they belong to, like the Kurds in the Middle East (Vali, 1998), Arab citizens of Israel (Molavi, 2013) and African Americans following the tragedy of Hurricane Katrina in New Orleans (Somers, 2008). This shows the political vulnerability of non-sovereign identities within the framework of the international state system, where sovereign states play a principal role in determining conditions of belonging to the state, and the distribution of rights and resources. Although it is important to not make superheroes of stateless peoples by demanding them to make resistance regardless of the hardship and sufferings that they experience, it is equally important to not undervalue their resistance to power abuse by the states. Following Krause's (2011), reading of Arendt, the stateless people hold a position where they are subjected to domination but also occupying a position as political actors, through attempting to appear in public light and resisting the oppression that they are experiencing. For instance, the sovereign powers in Iran, Iraq, Syria and Turkey strive to not allow the Kurds to claim a position of statelessness because from the moment the Kurds make claim to statelessness, they are asserting themselves as political and a challenge to the sovereign identities in a refusal to be subsumed under their universalities. In a paternalist fashion, Kurds are often told by the leaders of these states that they do not need a Kurdish state since they allegedly enjoy equal rights within the existing states. Equally, Palestinians are either denied statehood or told by Israelis that they should blame themselves for their own political fate by not accepting the UN plan for partition of Palestine into a Jewish and Palestinian state. Moreover, the Palestinians are prevented from returning to their homelands and are spatially under erasure due to Israeli settlement policies that encourage Jewish mastery over Palestinian lands. It is in relation to the persistence of political and structural violence, that Kurds and Palestinians are resisting the states in which they have been subordinated and exiled from power. This shows that stateless peoples as politically conscious groups are a major force to be reckoned with. Although statelessness is invoked by the research participants as informing their grievances, sufferings and hardship, it is worth noting that "neither statehood nor citizenship, by themselves, can fully promote their human development" (Gabiam, 2015, p. 497).

As argued in the first chapter of this book, it is important to not limit our understanding and notion of statelessness to a strict legal definition statelessness. As Gabiam (2015) correctly argues, we have stateless persons and stateless peoples, since "it is difficult, if not impossible, to completely disentangle statelessness as an individual issue from statelessness as a collective issue" (p. 486). There are both Palestinian and Kurdish individuals who are not legally stateless but experience statelessness as a member of a collectivity with regard to questions of land, language, identity and belonging. Accordingly, this chapter engages with the narrative accounts of Kurdish and Palestinian migrants about what statelessness entail to them and affect their identity formation, voice, status, visibility and presence in the world in the context of sovereign and non-sovereign identities. It also discusses commonality and differences between these two group in relation to statelessness. While the Kurds generally regard statelessness as a political device to gain international recognition and support, the Palestinians view statelessness as a dangerous appellation since it is interpreted as turning the Palestinians into a 'landless' people in light of Israeli spaciocide of Palestinian presence, culture and history (Hanafi, 2012). This resistance toward the concept of statelessness can be understood as a spatial resistance toward Israeli occupation and mastery of lands perceived as historically belonging to Palestinians.

Statelessness as a Status Injury

In the following, I will present the narratives of the Kurdish and Palestinian research participants and the ways they define, critique, embrace and resist identities based on belonging to states and non-belonging as a stateless. All identities are constituted through an interplay and dialectic of internal and external identification and categorization (Jenkins, 1996). Although many immigrants encounter problem of self-ascription when they are asked and interrogated about their identities, the position of statelessness further complicates pattern of identification and self-ascription. Lara, who is a young woman from Kurdistan Region of Iraq, grew up in the Netherlands and moved to England to study, illustrates the problem of self-ascription and self-presentation that she, as a stateless person, encounters in her everyday life:

> We Kurds cannot have a comfortable life because our identity is always a question mark. When you do not have a state, your identity and responses about your identity lack legitimacy. Because you cannot easily point to a place and say that I am from here and we have this and that. You lack a coherent response because your reality lacks a clear structure. You feel deficiency as a person when you see that everybody has their flags recognized. You also feel having a deficient identity when you fill in forms where you need to fill in the name of the country you are from or you were born. I often write that I am from the Netherlands but when it is written where you were born, I become obliged to write Iraq and I do not feel at all as an Iraqi. Statelessness means many questions and no easy answers about your identity. You have a lot of self-doubt about your identity. I mean if you get the question where are you from once, then it would not have been a problem but this is a question that I have to encounter many times now and in future. As a stateless person, you feel alone with a difficult question. (24 years old woman, Kurdistan Region-Iraq, UK)

Thus, the stateless needs to clarify himself/herself in an excessive way in order to arrive at a point of an intelligible identity, which is often a national identity or a state identity. This 'intelligible' identity privileges those groups who have attained and monopolized nationhood since their identities have been exteriorized and achieved universal objectivity. It is not only that the stateless persons cannot provide an intelligible response but are often obliged indirectly to subsume themselves under a national identity or within a state, that they might not, or feel reluctant to, identify with. Due to the recurring nature of the question 'where are you from', the interviewees avoided occasionally to delve into lengthy self-clarification with their interlocutors, and occasionally identified themselves as from Iran, Iraq, Syria and Turkey. As Lara indicates above, the identity of the stateless lacks legitimacy in a world of nation-state and cannot easily opt out of nationhood. Furthermore, the stateless person faces both difficulty in defining himself/herself in everyday life but also within bureaucratic frameworks where people are defined following the country of birth and not necessarily how they wish or want to define themselves. We live in a world where having or belonging to a nation is a naturalized order. If you say in response to the question 'where are you from' that you do not have a nation, "your answer would not be taken as a serious response. Instead you would be seen as either a joker, a naïve utopian or a nuisance" (Malešević, 2013, pp. 156–157). Several of the interviewees underlined that question about one's identity becomes an insult to an injury. This suggests that political status matters for inequality since people care about the status they are ascribed and how that status impinges on the ways they are valued and treated by other groups (Ridgeway, 2014). In the same vein, Masoud underlined that statelessness implies global invisibility and neglect when stateless people face political violence:

> Statelessness has obstructed Kurds from maintaining their identity, culture and history. As a stateless person you are not represented. The world does not see you. Nobody protects you when you face cultural and human disaster. When Kurds were gassed in Halabja by the Iraqi state, who could protect you? There are still many people who do not know that hundreds of thousands of Kurds were killed in Iraq due to genocide campaigns by the Iraqi state during 1980s. I am reading Peace and Conflict Studies and I have read books about genocide that are 800 pages and they mention the name of the Kurds only twice. As a stateless person you do not exist anywhere. Your existence is just a question mark. When I think about statelessness, I think about a people thrown out from the international community. (31 years old man, Kurdistan-Iran, Sweden)

Statelessness is thus not only a question of political marginalization, but it is also about vulnerability and exposure to political and physical violence by the sovereign state. The stateless runs the risk to be both a political outcast and an object of atrocity. Moreover, the sovereign state denies the stateless right to claim a political identity that differs from the sovereign identity and defines the stateless people as 'its own people' in order to legitimate political authority and violence in the name of state order. Consequently, the state uses states of exception (Agamben, 1998) to exceptionally punish people who are viewed as a threat to state identity and its territorial and political unity. For instance, during the mass murder campaigns against the Kurds in the 1980s, it was often claimed that Saddam Hussein killed 'his own people' and thus subsuming the Kurds under his jurisdiction and denying them the right to claim autonomous peoplehood and international protection. When I posed the question whether Masoud had read Hannah Arendt, he replied no. Despite this, he framed statelessness in the same way as Arendt (1951, p. 297) who defined stateless people as expelled from the international community. This suggests how valuable it is to take into consideration the point of view of people who define themselves as stateless and consider them as a site of an epistemic orientation and social positioning that can provide useful insights into the way the world is structured as well as how the social institutions privilege the epistemology of dominant and powerful groups who have attained statehood. Kurdish *voices* have historically been ignored, pre-empted and discredited as *noises* by the dominant regimes in the Middle East. Kurdish claims to shared sovereignty and equality are often viewed as a destabilizing force. The interviewees in this study used their lived experiences to claim an alternative knowledge about the fates of Kurds who are often denied the right to claim an autonomous nationhood and represent their tormented experiences engendered by statelessness. As Harding (1993, p. 59) points out, the grounds for knowledge production are intimately linked to history and social life and "marginalized lives are better places from which to start asking causal and critical questions about the social order". Hence, there is a strong nexus between empowering "oppressed groups and the development and distribution of knowledge" (Hartman, 2000, p. 22).

For the Palestinian research participants, the question of statelessness is both framed and experienced differently than the Kurdish interviewees. However, there are common experiences of not having a recognized and established homeland where they can fully realize their identities (see Bowman, 1994, p. 139). When I asked about statelessness, they either rejected the idea that they are stateless or pointed to the fact that they have a state that Israel has occupied and renamed it as Israel. Statelessness becomes a status injury that affects everyday encounters with groups that can give a relatively or confident answer to the question 'where are you from?' For instance, for a dominant group like the English constituency that has been at the forefront of ruling and establishing hierarchies in the world, it is not surprising that they might be unwilling to define themselves in national terms or articulate their Englishness, because they have historically not needed to engage with the mystery of identity. This is due to the fact that "they're so certain of their own. The notion of belonging is alien to them because they belong" (Kenny, 2014, p. 7). However, this has changed since the English have politically and economically lost their global power, and challenged by Scottish nationalism and the striking presence of non-white migrants in Britain (Kumar, 2000). The Kurds and Palestinians are in contrast much more insistent that they need to articulate themselves and declare their existence to the outer world since denial, misrecognition and nonrecognition encircle their political subjectivity. Their political residency in the world is insecure and questioned (see Ahmed, 2017). Dalia provides an example how difficult it is to not exist on the political map in the contemporary world:

> Since state borders are so important, to be stateless means that you are less important. You need to possess a place and a territory because borders are important for people. And people ask you often where are you from and who are you. You cannot just say that I am myself since you need to come from a place. When you do not have this place, you become nobody. Palestinians in Lebanon are for example nobodies. (23 years old Palestinian woman, Sweden)

Statelessness was also strongly associated with political invisibility and perceived as a stigmatized social position. It was argued that an English or a French person can claim his/her identity with confidence, while a Kurd has not the same self-confidence to speak about his/her identity as worthy of attention:

> As a stateless you realize that you are different when you encounter other people. They say with such confidence where they are from but you as a Kurd have to sit down and tell the history of the Kurds during a century so they can understand who you are and why you do not have a state. (Aras, a 51 years old Kurdish man, Kurdistan Region-Iraq, UK)

Palestinian and Kurdish insistence and self-promotion as autonomous nations or entitled to sovereignty confirm the unfitting nature of their residence in a nation-state-centric world. This indicates how problematic it is for members of stateless groups to embrace a new identity outside of the nationalist order that nationalizes borders, territories and belongings. The importance of place-based identity among Palestinian diasporas in France (Gabiam, 2015) converges with Palestinian realities in Sweden. The idea that territorialized or place-based identities lack importance in constructing individual and collective belongings and identities has shown to be empirically flawed. Despite the qualified potency of post-national and cosmopolitan perspectives to undo the exclusionary mechanisms of the national citizenship and the nation-state, the tendency in Western Europe and in the US has been more about reinforcing state sovereignty than abolishing it (Eliassi, 2013). Shachar (2014, p. 117) underlines that 'Like the rumors of Mark Twain's death, vogue predictions about the ultimate demise of borders and membership boundaries have been greatly exaggerated'. Diasporic identities might have ambivalent and multiple relationships to places, but they do not create a rupture between territory/place and identity formation, but complicate patterns of identification. Thus, the very orientation of the concept of statelessness suggests a territorial account of belonging (McNevin, 2007; Redclift, 2013), where nationhood can be realized. As McNevin (2007) points out, political belonging is mainly represented through the lens of the Westphalian state system, where territory, state and identity are intimately linked to each other. Those who are situated outside of these categories will face difficulty to assert their presence on the international scene but also encounter difficulty to prove their existence as a people among other peoples. According to Said (1999), it is hard a task to maintain a Palestinian identity in exile regarding what Palestinians are, where they have come from and what constitutes Palestinian identity. Palestinians cannot take the issues of identity for granted and are often required to show evidence of their identity and existence in a constant manner. Indeed, this is a reality that Kurds might encounter more than the Palestinians in the Muslim Middle East that views politicized Kurdish identity as a threat to Muslim brotherhood and cohesion in the region. For the stateless who lacks confidence due to non-recognition, there is a need to act as a historian to explain for the outer world about one's origin and legitimate political struggle and presence in the world. In this context, Said underlines that the Palestinians feel that:

> they have been excluded and denied the right to have a history of their own. When you continually hear people say: "Well, who are you?" you have to keep asserting the fact that you do have a history, however uninteresting it may appear in the very sophisticated world. (p. 126)

In effect, the Kurdish and Palestinians are not only questioned about their identity and place of origin, but they are also viewed as questionable constituencies with destabilizing claims about right to statehood. The question 'where are you from?' becomes a painful reminder of their non-normative political presence in the world shaped by nation-state-territory. Recent studies have shown that despite postmodern discourses about the demise or the weakening effects of globalization on nation-state and territorialized identities, geography continues to shape national identities and people continue to have emotional and political attachments to political space such as the nation-state (Kaplan & Herb, 2011; Rembold & Carrier, 2011). Accordingly, the very question of place-based identity is a question of presence that Palestinians are denied by the Israeli occupation, since place "stabilizes and gives durability to social structural categories, differences and hierarchies, arranges patterns of face-to-face interaction" (Gieryn, 2000, p. 473). When a dominant group achieves statehood, it tends to create a nationalist attachment between the people and the place, by which it can define the boundary of the nation and stabilize its memory (see Gieryn, 2000). Karim who was born three years after the foundation of Israel, and spent parts of his life in Jordan and Lebanon before fleeing to Sweden, defined statelessness in relation to respect and dignity:

> When you are stateless, you are lost, you do not have an identity, a personality, and an existence. Look at us Palestinians, we are lost and dispersed around the world. If you have a state, the first thing people do is respecting you. Everyone belongs to a specific state. But we are not recognized. Statelessness means deficiency in a human being's life. We are chasing after this state because we need it. We are running after it. (70 years old Palestinian man, Sweden)

The centrality of the state is evident in the account above. For Karim, statelessness entails subordination at the level of intersubjective domain of the definition of the self and the other. Following Axel Honneth, Staples (2012) maintains, it is only by having rights, that respect can be attained and one way to attain this respect is by being a member of a recognized and legitimate political community. Those groups who are misrecognized or non-recognized at structural level run the risk of being denied right and respect in everyday life. Arendt (1951) in this regard equated statelessness with exclusion from humanity, a domain reserved for superfluous and non-normative political identities. As Staples (2012, p. 102) correctly claims, statelessness affects the individual at two levels, it deprives him/her from an effective citizenship status, and deprive him/her from having a legitimate status and presence in the international political community. There is however a political dilemma facing the stateless regarding the role of the state in relation to providing or suspending rights. One the one hand, it is the state that produces statelessness and denies the stateless subjects respect and recognition. On the other hand, the solution as framed by the interviewee above is founded in creating a state that can provide these rights. This illustrates that the stateless is bound by the state regardless of its societal condition and position.

For both Palestinians and particularly the Kurds, statelessness was not just a question about not having a recognized culture or language but it also included cultural dispossession that only statehood could assumedly prevent from occurring:

> When you do not have your own state, you lose your history and culture. Others can make claim to your history and make it their own. For example, they deny you the right to claim a certain dance as Kurdish. You become like a stolen people. But if you have your own state, the state becomes like a library where you can preserve the belongings of your nation in it. In that library, you know what your identity is and what your rights are. (Alan, a 45 years old man Kurdistan-Syria, UK)

It is thus presumed that the state is the institutional framework within which a group can flourish and preserve their cultural identity. This explains why the nation-state is often perceived as a political home. The stateless people are denied a place in history and their contribution to humanity is also rendered invisible or inferior, something that the same interviewee above pointed out. The official state ideologies in Iran, Iraq, Syria and Turkey have subsumed Kurds under the national identities and deprived them from being legitimate constituents of territories and geographies that Kurds make claim to as their historical homeland. Naming becomes a central instrument in asserting presence and absence, dominance and marginalization, recognition and non-recognition in relation to structurally unequal positioned identities that make claim to political and cultural existence. Since the stateless people assumedly lack a sovereign position, it cannot make claim to rights in the name of its identity and as such are deprived from having a normative and material presence in society and the wider international contexts. For the international community, the stateless often tends to become object of charity and framed as a humanitarian issue when its rights are violated (Vali, 1998). Regardless of their political belonging and ideological framework, leftist/internationalist or nationalist, the Kurdish interviewees expressed their awareness of the vulnerability, status injury, inaudibility, dispossession, invisibility and marginalization of stateless people due to the political and ideological dominance of the nation-state model. One of the interviewees, a 46-year-old Kurdish man from Rojava (Syria) living in Oxford asserted that being stateless sounds: 'like something that does not have to do with humanity'. The Kurdish migrants underlined the centrality of having a recognized territory that could provide them with a political framework to defend themselves against misrecognition and non-recognition:

> When you have your own state, you can have rights, you can freely live your culture and language. When you do not have a state, your existence is questioned. In this world, when you are a part of a nation, people place you in a certain country. That is exactly what Turks tell me when I say that I am Kurdish. They tell me, is there any place called Kurdistan that you say that you are Kurdish. Having a state is about having an identity. (Aram, a 48 years old man, Kurdistan-Turkey, Sweden)

This elucidates that statelessness is interpreted as a basis of cultural and political denial. It is not a coincidence that the interviewee above refers to the 'Turks' with a sovereign subject position that denies the Kurds right to political existence, not only on predominantly Kurdish lands but also in the virtual world. The Kurds as a nation without a state are often repudiated at micro- and macro-level for not having a recognized existence on the world map. Even when they try to assert their presence in the virtual world, they are resisted, outlawed and exiled from existence. For instance, in 2018, the map of the Greater Kurdistan existed for a short period on Google My Map, but Turkey used its diplomatic and economic power to remove that map. The Turkish lawmaker that complained to Google depicted the Kurdistan map as a 'terrorist propaganda'. Several of the Kurdish interviewees referred to the dilemmas that they faced to explain for their children about Kurdistan particularly in relation to its flag and map that they could not find in the atlas. Based in Sweden, Memo, a 50-year-old man who works as a teacher in Kurdish language argued that his Kurdish pupils have asked him many times why they cannot find the Kurds on the world map and he has explained to them that they should struggle to achieve that goal if they want to exist in the world. In a similar vein, Rubar who is a 37-year-old Kurdish woman from Northern Kurdistan (Turkey) recalled a walk in Stockholm that turned out to witness the invisibility of the Kurds in public spaces:

> I am walking in Södermalm with my daughter Jian and her friend Bahar who is of the same age. We found a place where we could eat lunch. Suddenly Bahar shines up and says: "Look, there is a Turkish flag there!" The flag was hanging in the middle of other flag pennants. Jian asks: "Why do all flags hang there except the Kurdish one?" At that moment, I wanted to be silent and did not want to start a political discussion with my daughter in a pedagogical way. But Jian continues: "Is it because Kurdistan is a secret country?" Bahar intervenes and says: "No, Kurdistan is not secret and exists but there was not enough space for the Kurdish flag among the flag pennants" Jian insists and declares: "No, there is a lot of space for the Kurdish flag". Bahar sees the Italian flag and tells Jian: "The Italian flag is almost like the Kurdish flag". Jian agrees and says: "Yes, it does. We just need to add a sun in the middle of the Italian flag".

The conversation above between members of two Kurdish generations in Sweden indicates how invisibility affects the identity formation of both adult and younger generations of Kurds who are struggling to confirm their existence in a nation-state-centric world order. As long as recognition and representation are informed by the ideals and markers of the nation-state, stateless nations will face stigmatization and invisibility, which in turn can lead to an inferiorized subject position.

The metaphors that the Kurdish and Palestinian interviewees used to describe statelessness were numerous and situated within a negative discursive field. The interviewees deployed metaphors like 'injury', 'refugees' 'orphan', 'hopelessness', 'lack of character', 'less valued' 'living in the air and not on earth', 'homelessness', 'lost', 'beggar' 'confused', 'ignored', 'isolated', 'outlawed', 'animals', 'emptiness', 'prostitute' 'nothing', 'zero', 'non-existence' and 'thrown out on the street' to describe what they thought about when they described their own experiences of statelessness. This shows that there is a danger in romanticizing the experiences of statelessness in order to imagine an unbounded or a cosmopolitan world order beyond the mighty organization of the nation-state. Treating stateless people as superheroes and deny the hardship, depression and oppression that they experience at individual and structural levels can lead to mystification and normalization of power and domination (see Pyke, 2010). According to the Kurdish research participants, statehood might not solve all political problems of the Kurds but its lack has not either produced a constructive mode of governance in the Middle East where Kurds can enjoy their political, cultural and economic rights. For Palestinians, they could not make compromises regarding the ownership and identity of Palestine, since Israel is an illegitimate state created on Palestinian lands.

Resisting Statelessness, Otherness and Invisibilization

It is by making categories that hierarchies and ordering are established (Anthias, 2021). The stateless as a category is not only object of violence and oppression but it can also become a "source of agency and collective struggle, either in terms of their contestation and through disidentification, or through their refashioning" (pp. 30–31). While the stateless peoples can be subjected to processes of othering and invisibility, they can nonetheless use a variety of strategies and campaigning to assert their presence in the countries in which they live. The majority of the Kurdish individuals interviewed defined themselves as belonging to a stateless people, despite holding Swedish and British citizenship that can provide them with safety, rights and mobility. The Swedish authority responsible for the registration of the population in that country—*Skatteverket*—categorizes and registers Kurdish migrants as citizens of Iran, Iraq, Syria and Turkey, despite the reluctance of many Kurds to identify themselves as citizens of these states. In the British context, Kurds have challenged the British bureaucracy and have asked for a space of recognition of the Kurdish identity through outlining different forms and applications, where Kurdish identity is recognized. Likewise, when Kurds apply for asylum, they do not in general claim statelessness as the reason behind seeking asylum but assert their Kurdish background along with their political and religious belonging. This implies that they downplay the overarching national identities of the states they come from and communicate their Kurdish identity as politically repressed. In contrast to the Palestinians, the majority of the Kurds still live in the regions that they call Kurdistan and did not feel territorially dispossessed but ethnically, economically and culturally subjugated in 'their own homeland'. It should be emphasized that the processes of Arabization and Turkification through demographic manipulation exist in Iraq, Syria and Turkey. While the Palestinian interviewees saw a peril in defining themselves as stateless (understood as landless), the Kurds saw it as a possibility to gain a sovereign identity by breaking with the domination that they are subjected to in the states they are inhabited. For the Kurds, the main focus was on altering the political situation in the Middle East in order to gain a sovereign identity that could enjoy universal recognition and protection from predatory states in the region.

In the British bureaucratic contexts, where people do enjoy more rights to define themselves in ethnic terms, the Kurdish migrants have pursued different campaigns to gain more recognition of their Kurdish ethnicity detached from the dominant ethnicities in the Middle East. Lana, who is a 32-year-old woman from Northern Kurdistan (Turkey), described how the diasporic political activism of the Kurds could be transformative:

> For example, when you go to the city council and fill in the forms and there it stands Turkish or Other. I usually tick the box where it is written Other and I add Kurdish and I love to do that. Then I told them at the city council: Do you know that there are more than 200,000 Kurds in the UK? Couldn't you find a space for the name *Kurdish* in the forms? Why do you oblige them to indirectly tick in the box where it says Turkish? I told them: You are unconsciously reinforcing the oppression and denial of Kurdish identity. So we had a campaign in 2004 and 2005 and we went many times to the city council. We also asked members of the Kurdish community that whenever they found a form in which they could not find the name Kurdish, they could bring it to us so we could contact the responsible authority and ask them to change it. The campaign was very successful and now many types of councils have Kurdish in their application forms.

The British multiculturalism empowers ethnic groups who have historically been denied the right to claim political existence. The interviewee above shows that the stateless figure is not only a victim to total domination but also a political actor (Krause, 2011) who can enact equality within conditions of structural inequalities by challenging and interrupting the naturalized order of domination that exclude stateless groups from the right to define themselves and their place in the world (see Rancière, 2004). In contrast to the Kurdish research participants, the Palestinian interviewees did not embrace the concept of statelessness as a resource to define their identity. There was a widespread understanding among the Palestinians that statelessness is another word for homelessness, landlessness and rootlessness, an issue that I will come back to in Chapter 4. By and large, Palestinians have not given up their attachment to Palestine despite the fact that Israel has erased traces of Palestinian presence in many parts of the historical Palestine. Samira who was born in Jordan and migrated to Sweden points out that she cannot accept the concept of statelessness for the Palestinians since this will entail approval of Israel as the legitimate possessor of their homeland. Samira asserts why she is not comfortable with the notion of statelessness:

> When I hear the word stateless, I think about not having the right to live in my country and being obliged to leave my country. Being without rights and deprived from homeland come to my mind when I think about statelessness. I understand that we Palestinians are stateless because we are thrown out from our homeland but that is different from saying that I do not have any homeland at all since we still have Palestine. I am both stateless and not stateless. They have taken the country from us but Palestine still exists. If I say that I am stateless, it sounds to people that I have given up my home and do not want to get back my homeland or that Palestine does not exist anymore and it does not belong to us anymore. (18 years old Palestinian woman, Sweden)

For Samira and other Palestinian interviewees, to accept the concept of statelessness would be an act of surrender to Israeli mastery over the Palestinian homeland. It was assumed that by embracing statelessness as marker of one's position in the world, acts of resistance and the hope of return among Palestinians would be suspended. Thus, it is the fear of political erasure that guides Palestinian resistance toward the term statelessness as marker of identity. Unlike the Kurds, it is not viewed as discursive resource to claim their rights. Politics of naming is a central part of their daily resistance in order to secure their political and cultural survival in a place where Zionism claimed nativeness in the already inhabited Palestine. As Peteet (2017) argues, the Zionist project "made it necessary to erase the indigenous population narratively and physically, and the Palestinians who remained had to be controlled to ensure their exclusion from the state" (p. 8). Dina who was born in Sweden belongs to a family that is a vocal proponent of Palestinian rights. For Dina, history of dispossession is not a relic of the past but haunts the Palestinian in the present and this history defines how she embraces her Palestinian identity:

> We Palestinian are very careful to stress our Palestinian identity due to our tragic history. Therefore, we stress our Palestinian much more and we want to be clearer about that. If we do not identify ourselves as Palestinians, we will disappear as Palestinians. It is important to maintain the Palestinian identity. The Israelis take and occupy our land and they build more and more settlements day by day. This is done because they want us to disappear as a people. They take your land because they do not want

> you to have a place on this land. When you do not have a land, you do not have an identity. Therefore, we should define ourselves strongly. As long as you define yourself as Palestinian, you will exist. (23 years old Palestinian woman, Sweden)

Zionism as a political project has entailed territorial dispossession of Palestinian lands and the Palestinians who refuse to leave their lands are manifesting acts of resistance against their erasure (see Butler & Athanasiou, 2013). Dina went on and declared that she will never accept to be stateless even if whole Palestine becomes occupied by the Israelis. She argued that by defining herself as stateless, she will create a painful emptiness within herself. This sense of political erasure was not equally felt among the Kurdish research participants. In order to prevent political annihilation, the Kurds and Palestinians engage with politics of naming as "a symbolic intervention and a performative act" (Peteet, 2017, p. 147). By naming their homelands as Kurdistan and Palestine, they make claim "to sovereignty and attempts to confirm the meanings of place" (ibid.). Hence, for the Kurdish and Palestinian research participants, self-definitions are acts of resistance against their political and spatial erasure on the political geography of the Middle East. It is only by repetition of 'who we are' and 'who we are not', and 'where we belong' that Kurds and Palestinians affirm their continuous existence in the world, despite hegemonic state narratives that aim to disqualify and contest their definitions and representations as illegitimate and destabilizing. It is not only in Israel that Palestinians experience denial of Palestine as their legitimate political home, but also in institutional contexts like school in Sweden. Samira provides an example of how she challenges this denial in her classroom:

> In the classroom, there have been some fights between me and the teachers in Sweden, because the teachers say all the time Israel, Israel, and Israel. Once I become so infuriated that I stood up and hit on the table and told the teacher: respect me as a Palestinian and do not say Israel because its name is Palestine. And the teacher said: 'oh my god, but it is written Israel on the map!' I said that I do not give a shit about what is written on that map, because it is still Palestine. I am Palestinian and you should respect that. Now, the teacher says Israel backslash Palestine. And I say hello, it is Palestine and do not irritate me. Once she wanted to say *Isra* and then she said Palestine. I do not care if it is written Israel on that map because

> it is still Palestine and will remain as Palestine. (18 years old Palestinian woman, Sweden)

This narrative illustrates that the stateless figure can contest the hegemonic definitions of world map as a supposedly natural and objective portrayal of how the world is ordered and divided into different states. Also, it is true that Israel is formally recognized as a state by major powers; there has been strong aversion among many predominantly Muslim countries to recognize Israel as a normal state but viewed largely as a colonial and occupying power. This Palestinian resistance and sensitivity to Israel needs to be understood in the context of Israeli spatial and cultural erasure of Palestinians. Israel started already in 1948 to erase Arabic names of villages and towns and replaced them with Hebrew names in order to politically eliminate traces of Palestinian presence and create a disconnection between the Palestinians and their memories of these places (Peteet, 2017). One can say, this is an attempt to foreignize the Palestinians in their own homeland by restructuring and re-designing the space to fit Zionist imagination of Israel as a Jewish land. The nativization of Israeli Jews has occurred at the expense of foreignization of Palestinians in their homelands. As Peteet (2017) poignantly puts it:

> To erase and rename is a relational undertaking, an act of simultaneous appropriation and denial. In short, naming is an act of intervention, a way of organizing and giving meaning to place that draw lines of exclusion and inclusion. (p. 147)

Despite continuous Israeli renaming and erasure of Palestinian presence, Palestinians continue to use Arabic names for these renamed places and contest the validity of these names and the constituency that stands behind its implementation. As the writer Milan Kundera has underlined: "A name means continuity with the past and people without a past are people without a name" (cited in Rushdie, 2012, p. 30). Words and names are sites of contestation for both sides since they attempt to determine the ownership and primacy of one group over the other and gain legitimacy as spatial manager of this contested territory. For the late Palestinian poet Mahmoud Darwish, the struggle over words is central to maintaining a Palestinian identity in light of dispossession. In his poem, *One Traveller Said to Another: We Won't Return As*, Darwish (2006, p. 126) writes:

> We won't return…even secretly
> I do not know the desert
> However often it's haunted me
> In the desert absence said to me
> Write!
> I said: There is another writing on the mirage
> It said: Write and the mirage will become green
> I said: I lack absence
> I said: I still have not learned the words
> It said to me: Write and you'll know them
> And where you came, and who you will be tomorrow
> Put your name in my hand and write
> So you'll know who I am and will go, a cloud into the open…
> So I wrote: Whoever writes his story will inherit the land of words, and possess meaning, entirely!

This poem highlights the role of writing as a form of claim making to the land that Palestinians have been exiled and deprived from. Since the Israeli state has invested immense energy and resources to Judaize Palestine, Palestinians feel the pressure to counteract and collect their stories, songs, narratives, memories and experiences of this land and its loss so future generations of Palestinians can use them as a discursive weapon and living testimonies against the Israeli state's politics of erasure. Karim who invited me to his home to carry out the interview was very proud to show how he had managed to inculcate a Palestinian identity in his children and grandchildren:

> I tell my children and grandchildren that they are Palestinians and not Swedes or Jordanians. I have made a Palestinian military ID card so they remember their Palestinian identity. The military ID card on which it is written Palestine is better than all ID cards in the world. Because this ID is mine and proves that I am Palestinian. That Palestinian ID proves that I have right to Palestine and to returning. When I die, I want my children to remember that they are Palestinians. (70 years old Palestinian man, Sweden)

And consider how this project of retaining Palestinian identity alive is reflected among younger generation of Palestinian living outside of Palestine:

> I am proud to belong to the Palestinian identity and its struggle without giving up I am proud that I am 30 years old and yet have safeguarded my

> Palestinian identity without being in Palestine and having left Syria when I was 6,5 years old. Although I have grown up in Sweden, I still have a Palestinian identity. I am thankful to my parents for giving us this identity. (Mona, a 30 years old Palestinian woman, Sweden)

In Karim's account above, there is not only an assertion about how important it is to transmit the idea of Palestine to future generations but also the fear that this might fail, which in itself can be a victory for the Israeli state. In Mona's case, it is one thing to maintain Palestinian identity in Palestine but a much difficult issue to do so in exile and diaspora. Invocation of pride by Palestinians needs to be situated within the negative discursive field that Palestinian identity is situated in relation to 'terror' and 'violence' that Israel propagates for. As Kundera has argued, one of the main struggles against the power "is the struggle of memory against forgetting" (cited in Rushdie, 2012, p. 38). For instance, Israeli's first Prime Minister David Ben-Gurion was hopeful that the Palestinians will forget their past when the old generation Palestinians will die and the younger generation forget. Bowman (1994, p. 140) with reference to the poet Darwish maintains that people who suffer from national and territorial dispossession are communities of words. As Saloul (2012) rightly argues, the main battle between the Palestinians and the Israelis is over land, "but when it comes to questions of who owns the land, who has the right to settle and work on it, who cultivates it, and who plants its future, all of these issues are effectively reflected, contested, and decided in and through narrative" (p. 4). Israel as an established state wants to exteriorize itself as 'real' and those forces and voices that challenge its givenness and realization "are muted or marked as criminal, alien or insane" (Bowman, 1994, p. 142). In this respect, the persistent Palestinian acts of self-definition function as a source of inspiration for the Kurdish diaspora:

> We should stop saying that we are Iraqis, Turkish, Iranians and Syrians or saying that we are Iraqi Kurds, Iranian Kurds, Turkish Kurds and Syrian Kurds. We should not accept the definitions from the occupying states and should instead say that we are Kueirdistanis, that our homeland is Kurdistan and that it is Kurdistan that unites all Kurds. This will make it easier for us Kurds to identify with each other and feel closer to each other. Look at the Palestinians, they never say that they are Israelis, they always say that they are Palestinians and want to remain Palestinians. But we Kurd do adopt the definitions from our enemy states and forget our

> Kurdish identity. (Marivan, a 28 years old man, Kurdistan Region-Iraq, Sweden)

While it is presumed that a Kurdish identity is not attached to a particular territory or geography, a Kurdistani identity is used to create a national imaginary within specific geographical borders in the Middle East. Geography is central to creating a national identity because national identities are generally anchored in territories. For Kurds, territorial identity has been an important part of the struggle for recognition, autonomy and even independence. Many Kurds are well aware that in a world of nation-states, they need to locate their identity on the world map because it is where it is displayed, recognized and represented to the outer world. The Facebook campaign 'I am Kurdistani' that Marivan contributed to its initiation clearly shows that naming is important in the construction of a new national imaginary but it is also central to reclaiming and renaming territories that have been Turkified, Arabized and Persianized and where Kurdish presence has been given a marginal position. This framing can be understood as a discursive attempt to produce new forms of solidarities among Kurds across Iran, Iraq, Turkey and Syria.

Since the Israelis possess strong state institutions, they can produce hegemonic histories to promote their own narratives as official and objective regarding different events that have shaped the current Israeli state and the precarious Palestinian situation, that is mainly reduced to a security issue for Israel. Certainly, this problematic securitization of Palestinians is not only limited to Israeli representation but also widely present in Western and European representations. Mona, a 30-year-old Palestinian woman who was born in Syria and came to Sweden at the age of six, pointed to the problematic Swedish representations of the Palestinians as 'terrorists' while also shouldering the responsibility of defending Palestinian rights. She provides an example of a Swedish schoolbook titled Religion and Life (2014), and how it distorts the conflict between the Israeli state and the Palestinians. The schoolbook illustrates an everyday situation with an image of Israeli civilian men, women and children and a soldier, standing in a queue to board a bus. In this image, there is also a young Palestinian woman with an explosive belt who allegedly intends to commit a suicide attack against the passengers on the bus. The schoolbook asks the Swedish students:

> Imagine if you would ask a Jew and an Arab about who has the right to the country that is presently called Israel. Write down what you think they will respond and how they will motivate their opinions. Why do you think the young Palestinian woman want to blow herself up with the rest of the passengers? (my translation from Swedish)

For Mona, this representation illustrates a widespread idea that Palestinians are inclined to terror and violence without even explaining the political context of the violence, misery and dispossession that Palestinians have faced since the creation of Israel. Mona along with other Palestinian debaters in Sweden protested against this schoolbook and asked the publisher to immediately remove this racist depiction of Arabs as prone to violence. The Swedish publisher *Natur och Kultur* declared in an announcement that they deeply apologize for this material and asked all schools to change this schoolbook and replace it with an updated one. This shows that the stateless diaspora is not a passive actor but actively engage in the public debate and can challenge representations that endorse official Israeli narratives about the nature of the conflict. Until now, I have engaged with the narratives of the Palestinian and Kurdish research participants and the ways they define, embrace and resist statelessness and the effects of statelessness in a world pervaded by the nation-state. In the next section, I will discuss how different groups view their statelessness in relation to each other and why the Roma is invoked as a central metaphor for statelessness due to their vulnerable conditions in an uneven world structured by the nation-state.

(De)stabilizing Hierarchies of Statelessness and Suffering

When I asked the Kurdish and Palestinian research participants if they could name other putative stateless groups than themselves, the Roma emerged particularly for the Kurds as a central category and as a metaphor for statelessness. As soon as we started discussing the nature of statelessness among Kurds and Palestinians, the interviewees started to delve into a competition about whose suffering should be accorded more attention and whose right to statehood was more legitimate or should be given more priority. Although it is not my intention to put these two vulnerable groups in competition with each other, I think it is important to discern those existing perspectives within both groups and how antagonism or bonds of solidarity are endorsed or undermined. Moreover, I will discuss why the Kurdish struggle is provincialized as not serving the 'general Muslim interest' in contrast to the Palestinian battle for statehood, endorsed by Islamist and a large part of the left as a global struggle for social justice. This question is highly contentious since there are both Kurdish and Palestinian individuals who blame each other for enchanting the oppressors as 'liberators' or as 'supporters' of their grievances. When I asked Sherzad about stateless peoples, he talked about those ties that bind them together:

> I think of Berbers. Wounded people do usually have sympathy for other wounded people. You feel that Berbers have also been discriminated and oppressed because of their identity. We have Roma who are the most group in the world. The Roma do not belong to anywhere. Palestinians are also stateless and they do not feel belonging to any states except their country. The Palestinians are before the Kurds when it comes to the queue of getting their own state. Since they have been forced to migrate and disperse around the world, their mental status is not really good. You can see the suffering in their faces. (Sherzad, a 49 years old man, Kurdistan region-Iraq, Sweden)

Common experiences of sufferings can endorse bonds of solidarity between different groups. In Sherzad's account, the Roma is identified as the group that is ranked at the bottom of the international hierarchies of identities and oppressed groups. While discussing the experiences of statelessness, a Kurdish interviewee referred to the advices of his father to identify with the Roma and endorse a bond of solidarity with them. He also frames his strong support for solidarity with the Palestinians:

> We lived in a refugee camp where there were a lot of Palestinians and Roma. My father told me that: "we Kurds are like Roma and we are brothers and I love them". Our common experience is our statelessness. My father told me: "Never treat a Roma in a negative way. Be kind to them". I have talked with my best friend who is a Palestinian about statelessness. We usually say that we are Roma. We usually back up each other when we are told that we don't have a state. We are like two stones that cannot be detached from each other when it comes to the question of statelessness. We share similar experiences of statelessness and living under poverty and in refugee camp. Just saying the word Roma is enough to

> say that something is not desirable and something that you do not want to be. Roma means to be a vagrant people. You do not have a place to belong to. They do not have a fixed place and wherever they go, they are treated as less valued than those people who live there. To be stateless, means to be less valued. When you have a fixed place and territory, you can show the world where you roots and culture are. You become proud. Whenever you achieve something, you can say that you are Kurdish, but for us Kurds if we achieve something, it becomes Turkish, Syrian, Iranian and Iraqi. (Heval, a 30 years old man, Kurdistan-Turkey, Sweden)

This account proves that Palestinian and Kurds do not need to invest in antagonism by undermining each other's claim to rights and recognition as stateless people. Moreover, they are not involved in a competition about whose suffering should be given priority. Interestingly, both the Kurd and the Palestinian deploy the figure of the Roma to illustrate the vulnerability of the stateless. The Roma figure works here as a category and a lived experience of unlimited otherness in our world. The question of belonging, place-based identity, territory, roots and culture is interweaved in creation of what statehood and statelessness entail for different groups. Although the Kurds, Palestinians and Roma share the same space as refugees, the account above seems to be informed by the idea that Roma run much higher risk to be subjected to maltreatment and discrimination. Bhopal and Myers (2008) have shown in their empirical work among 'Gypsies' in the UK that the Roma is both exoticized and romanticized and at the same time linked with being dirty, lazy and disruptive. These images guide the widespread negative treatment of the Roma. The Roma is also believed to be situated within another temporality and belong to another age and economy, distant from the 'civilized world'. Unlike other groups, the racism against the Roma is more blatant and impolite and it is expressed in such a way in the public sphere that it "would be considered entirely unacceptable if it was directed at other ethnic minority groups" (Bhopal & Myers, p. 203). The notion of solidarity was also evident in the accounts of Muhammad, a 37-year-old Palestinian man, who underlined that both Kurds and Palestinians are stateless because they do not or are not allowed to belong to any place on this planet. He points out what Kurds and Palestinians are different from other migrant groups in Sweden:

> We are not like the Turks and Iranians. They have their own states. It is fascinating that Turks live in Sweden when they have their own country.

> People go there and spend their vacation. What are they doing in Sweden? The same applies to the Lebanese.

This stance was also evident among several Kurdish interviewees who did not understand what Turks, Arabs and Persians were doing here in Sweden when they had their own states and defend their authoritarian states when you criticize their treatment of minorities. In this framing, the stateless is viewed as the one with legitimate claim and right to migrate in order to escape persecution. Masoud, a 31-year-old Kurdish interviewee, forcefully argued: 'why do they come to a democracy like Sweden when they support dictatorship and oppression of minorities in their homelands'. The same interviewee went on and talked about having Persian and Turkish students in his class at the university level who were studying Peace and Conflict, but lacked the understanding for the Kurdish struggle and the reasons behind Kurdish reluctance to identify and define themselves as Iranians, Iraqis, Turkish or Syrian. He added: 'they want to dominate and assimilate you even in Sweden'.

One of the most recurring ways to define the lifestyle of the Roma was based on the reference to Roma nomadism as epitomizing statelessness and homelessness. In this regard, a Sweden-based Kurdish interviewee drew this connection with the Roma further:

> We Kurds are like Roma carrying our home on our backs because we do not have an identity. Statelessness means lacking an identity. When you live like Roma, you do not have a home because you move from one place to another and nobody respects you. That is not what I call a life because you are not attached to a soil and a place. Roma are known for not having a country. (Sherzad, a 49 years old man, Kurdistan Region-Iraq, Sweden)

In contrast to some academic insistence on deterritorialization and unboundedness of identity (see Malkki, 1995), lacking a stable, rooted and territorialized identity is not celebrated as a liberating force in the life of the stateless. On the contrary, this lack is perceived to inform the disrespectful encounters that the stateless peoples face in their everyday life. Although the Roma is strongly associated with nomadism, this assumption is believed to be misplaced (Bhopal & Myers, 2008) since it tends to inform the idea that the Roma do not want to be part of the world as a settled community and their 'vagrant' lifestyle does not fit the administrative and bureaucratic order of the nation-state in terms of governing its subject and creating a bond between the place and rooted citizens. Within political theory, the Roma identity is viewed as disrupting the dominant discourse of international politics due to the idea that the Roma lacks an attachment to place and political hierarchy. Consequently, the Roma challenge the Westphalian order that categorizes people and fix them in static groups and territories. It should be underlined that the Roma existed in Europe long before the states came into being in Europe. Due to widespread experiences of discrimination and racism, the Roma are pushed toward ideas of unity and homogeneity as a political strategy to defend and represent Roma rights (Haughey, 1999).

Whereas both Palestinian and Kurdish research participants did not identify with vulnerable positions of the Roma as a desirable condition, there were clearly some efforts to have more understanding for their conditions and experiences of insecurity and harassment. This was reflected in the words of a 28-year- old man from the Kurdistan Region-Iraq, who presented the Roma as the archetypal metaphor for statelessness:

> We can take the Roma as an example. Roma are a people without a state. The insecurity makes them feel that they can never settle down in a place. The majority of Roma move from a place to another all the time. I have encountered many Roma and I identify with them as a Kurd. I have asked many Roma why they move so much. They move and move until they find a fixed place where they can feel at home and protected. They have accepted that they do not have a state. The only thing that is common to the experiences of the Kurds and the Roma is a sense of solidarity. (Marivan, a 28 years old man, Kurdistan-Region-Iraq, Sweden)

In the first of these two above interview excerpts pertaining to the quintessential nature of Roma's statelessness, mobility is framed as the cause of their statelessness; however, although the first quotation conveys the view that the Roma's statelessness has developed as the result of their chosen lifestyle—'When you live like Roma, you do not have a home because you move from one place to another'—in the following extract, it is the very absence of a place where they feel protected and secure that has caused their ongoing mobility. However, it should be noted that the dominant images and ideas about Roma as a "problematic, parasitic and dangerous community" (McGarry, 2014, p. 770) are mainly constructed, owned and reproduced by non-Roma. The Roma are often prevented access to formal local, national and international channels to represent themselves and "articulate their voice, make demands and control dominant images of themselves" (ibid., p. 757). Due to power abuse of the majority, the Roma often lack the means to dispute the negative images and representations that remain in the hand of the dominant constituency (Sigona, 2005). Kofman (2005) maintains that the idea of the cosmopolitan figure as mobile with no need for bounded identity functions as a new orthodoxy to privilege the experience of the already privileged figure in relation mobility. If we posit that the Roma identity endorses mobility as part of their lifestyle, one can wonder why is the nonconforming mobility of the Roma so defamed and undesired in many countries around the world. The Roma figure in Sweden is highly associated with an 'elusive beggar identity' that violates Swedish norms and creating discomforts for the Swedes when faced with Roma at the entrances of Swedish shopping malls. It should not come as a surprise that racism and otherness tend to reinforce the boundary of the Roma identity in the context of everyday and institutional racism. Although the Kurdish interviewees used the Roma condition to underline the importance of a rooted identity and statehood, it was also viewed as important to distance themselves from the stigmatized Roma position:

> I had a discussion with my English teacher about identity and homeland in the classroom. He said that Kurds are originally Gypsies. I never forget those words until the day I die. He would not have called us Gypsies if we have had our own state. People do not know where are we from. Gypsies are those people who not have a place and roots. Nobody knows where they are from and where they come from. (Rozhgar, a 19 years old man, Kurdistan-Region-Iraq, UK)

> The situation of the Roma is a good example because they belong nowhere. They have a much tougher situation than us Kurds. There are so many prejudices against them. It is not an ugly thing to be Kurdish but to be a Roma it is not a compliment. I remember my parents telling me in Kurdistan: "Do not speak with a Roma, they will kidnap you and take you to another country". We were manipulated and you get influenced by this. (Sheno, a 26 years old woman, Kurdistan-Iran, Sweden)

I have discussed elsewhere how Roma are demonized by the Kurds through racist representations (see Eliassi, 2013, pp. 91–94). The term 'Roma' is also used by some Arabs, Persian and Turkish migrants as an ethnic slur to name the Kurds as rootless and landless; a discursive weapon to denounce the rights and claims of Kurds to statehood and a territorialized identity in the Middle East. The reference to the Roma as a people without a homeland or a state situates the stateless beyond the moral and political order of the world. It is only by attaining statehood or being recognized as belonging to a political geography, that the stateless people is believed to inscribe themselves in the normative order of humanity, which involves among other things, possession of a nation-state.

When it comes to how Kurdish and Palestinian research participants viewed their statelessness and their place in the 'hierarchy' of statelessness, some Kurdish interviewees strongly rejected the privileged position of the Palestinians and the international attention that it attracts. For this Kurdish interviewee, it is no longer valid to designate the Palestinians as stateless since they have their own state:

> I have always wondered why Palestinians are regarded as stateless while we Kurds are not viewed as such. They have almost their independence and many countries recognize them and treat them as a state. The Palestinian case is endorsed internationally that is not comparable to the Kurdish question. I do not understand why they do not call the Kurds stateless. (Masoud, a 31 years old man, Kurdistan-Iran, Sweden)

Many Kurdish interviewees identified the political privilege of being defined as stateless by the international community and viewed this label as granting international legitimacy to claim the right to have a state. It was a widely held idea by the Kurdish interviewees that the Palestinians were at the forefront of the queue of stateless people to gain statehood while they felt that they were denied the same right because they are categorized as Iraqis, Iranians, Turkish and Syrian regardless of their sense of non-belonging, self-categorization and self-identification. We can argue that members of the Kurdish and Palestinian communities are involved in what Angela Davis has aptly termed as "an Olympics of suffering" (cited in Radhakrishnan, 2003, p. 98): a process through which they can strive to gain an epistemic privilege to create hierarchies of suffering, gain political precedence and achieve international recognition for one's political cause. Authoritarian or ethnocratic states like Turkey, Iran and Israel are involved in intensifying the antagonism between the Kurds and the Palestinians. For instance, both Hamas and Fatah as representatives of the Palestinians movements have been supportive of Turkish invasion of Kurdish regions in Syria for allegedly defending Islam and the territorial integrity of the Syrian state. In a similar vein, the Palestinian representative in the Kurdistan Region opposed the Kurdish referendum for independence in 2017 and called for preserving the territorial integrity of the Iraqi state. During our discussion about Kurdish statelessness, a Palestinian interviewee argued:

> I do not understand why Kurds do not like Saddam. He was a great fighter. He did a lot of things for Palestinians. (Mahmoud, a 28 years old Palestinian man, Sweden)

When I provided Mahmoud with some information and images about what Saddam Hussein did to the Kurds in Iraq during his era, he became silent and did not want to continue the discussion. It is notable that a huge moment of Saddam Hussein is erected on Palestinian lands by Palestinian activists, which has to do with Saddam Hussein's support for the Palestinians against the Israelis. There is also a strong yearning for a figure like Saddam Hussein in the Sunni Arab world, to counter the expansion of Iranian/Persian clout in the Arab world. For many Kurds, this Palestinian support for Saddam Hussein is like adding insult to an injury that Kurds have experienced during Saddam Hussein's political power. Another Palestinian interviewee endorsed the current President of Syria, Bashar al-Assad and argued that 'if Syria does not exist, the Palestinian case will die'. When I was in Oxford in 2014, I encountered a Palestinian teacher in Arabic who expressed that 'Syria is a true multicultural society and nobody is discriminated'. When I tried to nuance what multiculturalism entails in authoritarian contexts and raised the question of stateless Kurds, he was too assertive and denounced it as a fabrication by the enemies (read Israel) of Syria. It might not come as a surprise given that Palestinians in Syria were much better treated than in Lebanon and such a positive contrast might endorse Palestinian support for the Syrian regime despite its brutality. During the Kurdish referendum for independence in 2017, there were a few Kurds waving the Israelis flags alongside the Kurdish flag and this event made it to the headlines of Arab and Iranian news that Kurds are potentially 'crypto-Jews', endorsing a Zionist project in the region. While discussing Kurdish statelessness, Huda, a 55-year-old Palestinian lawyer, who lived in Syria and came to Sweden as a political refugee, argued that she did not understand 'why Kurds were waving the Israeli flag in Iraqi Kurdistan and why do the Kurds want to break up with Iraq as a Muslim state'. Their situation according to Huda was not equal to the Palestinians since 'Kurds are not discriminated as Palestinians and their lands have not been taken by Iraq'. Ava, a 46-year-old Kurdish woman Kurdistan Region-Iraq, who works as a teacher in a large Swedish municipality underlined the threat and the hatred that she felt as a Kurd from Arabs and particularly Palestinian students:

> I always say that I am Kurdish when a Swede asks me. But I do not say that I am a Kurd when an Arab asks me because when I worked in a suburb in Malmö, a lot of problem emerged when I said to Arab students that I was Kurdish. I found out that Arabs, Shiites, Palestinians hate the Kurds. Palestinians hate the Kurds because Saddam supported them and they see Saddam as an Arab hero and they view the Kurds as traitors. I have stopped talking politics with Arabs, Persians and Turks. They arrive at a point that they swear at me and even call me an agent of Israel or a Jew. For them being Kurdish means being a Jew. They say that we Kurds have brought Israel to Iraqi Kurdistan. Unlike their claims, I can prove and show that the Israeli flag is flying proudly in Arab capitals. And why should I be loyal to Arabs? We Kurds do not owe them anything. Their contribution to our lives has been oppression and mass murder.

Ava was so mad at the Palestinians that she cursed Saladin for liberating Jerusalem from the Crusaders and pointed out that Palestinians cannot be considered as a stateless people. When the Kurdish issue and rights are framed as a tool of the Zionist agenda, there is a risk that Kurds are denied agency and political subjectivity to define their own grievances caused primarily by the widespread structural discrimination in Iran, Iraq, Syria and Turkey. Ava also made the point that unlike the Kurdish and Balkan students in Sweden, the Palestinian and Arab parents did not want their children to make study visits to synagogues since they were afraid that they would 'make their children into Jews'. The Jews are according to Ava 'really misrepresented in the Muslim world'. Interestingly, Ava makes an important point about that Kurds cannot be expected to show loyalty to states and dominant constituencies that expose Kurdish lives and homes to violence and destruction. Ava's account about 'Palestinians hating Kurds' is a sweeping generalization and was contradicted by some of the Palestinian interviewees due to their passionate support for the Kurdish struggle. Ahmad, who is a 33-year-old Palestinian man living in Malmö, attacked those Palestinians and Arabs that chant anti-Jewish slurs during pro-Palestinian demonstrations. This is for him 'playing in the hand of the Israeli state that Palestinians hate the Jews'. According to him, Palestinian rights cannot be secured through anti-Semitic sentiments:

> I have stopped going to pro-Palestinian demonstrations. For some years ago, I used to go to all demonstrations in Malmö but it is no longer attractive to participate in these demonstrations. I think if an ordinary Swede who does not have any connection to Palestine and Israel see 500 persons demonstrate and many of them are hateful against the Jews and chant anti-Semitic slogans. They shout: "Death to the Jews!" They equate Jews with Israel.

For Ahmad, such behavior undermines international sympathy for the Palestinian rights when 'bearded men are shouting and frightening the Swedes'. If contrasted with 'Israeli politicians, men and women, they are well-dressed and talk eloquently and behave in a civilized way. People in Sweden identify more with the Israelis'. The very attempt to homogenize the Jews as all supporters of Israel reinforces the legitimacy of Israel in the eyes of the international community. In this context, Butler (2012, p. 2) laments the fact that while Israel claims to represent the Jewish constituency, "popular opinion tends to assume that Jews 'support' Israel without taking into account Jewish traditions of anti-Zionism and the presence of Jews in coalition that oppose the Israeli colonial subjugation of Palestinians". Ahmad was puzzled that Kurds can socialize with the Arabs, Turks and Persians in Sweden, even if the states of these groups oppress and kill the Kurds. To contradict what Ava pointed out earlier regarding the Palestinian attitude vis-à-vis the Kurds, Ahmad provides a rationale why he is 'angry at the Kurds':

> Sometimes, I get really angry at the Kurds because they have accepted the idea of autonomy in Iraq. I tell my Kurdish friends that Kurdistan in Iraq might be flourishing now but you cannot know what can happen if the government in Iraq changes its attitude toward the Kurds. I have Kurdish friends who can socialize with the Arabs without problems. I think that it is fantastic that they can put aside hatred and can distinguish between the state and the people. The Arab states have not apologized to the Kurds and have not admitted that they have wrongly treated the Kurds.

As we see, Ahmad's anger regards the potential vulnerability of the Kurds in Iraq, which he correctly frames as a question of time before the central Iraqi government turns its weapon against the Kurds. In reality, the Shiite

Iraqis who have gradually monopolized Iraq after 2003 and neutralized the Sunni Arab with the help of the Americans are threatening the Kurdistan Region and its autonomous position by political, military and economic pressures. Shiite political parties are competing about having the harshest policies vis-à-vis the Kurdish region in regard to its share of the Iraqi budget but also security issues related to border control and the disputed areas between the Iraqi state and the Kurdistan Region. Ahmad who was well aware of the political otherness that Kurds experience in Turkey talked about his strategy to champion Kurdish identity when encountering the members of the Turkish constituency:

> When I encounter Turks, I usually use the word Kurdistan although there is no state called Kurdistan. For me saying Kurdistan is about freedom of political expression and that there should be a Kurdistan. It sounds provocative to Turks when you say Kurdistan. I had a Turkish colleague at the same workplace. Once I said Kurdistan and he said that there is no Kurdistan and every time I said Kurdistan, he became angry. The reason behind this reaction is because many Turks are nationalists and look down on Kurds. Amnesty International and Human Right Watch all witness this oppression. I find it problematic when many Palestinians praise Turkey and Saddam Hussein. If our Palestinian question is about Israel's violation of human rights, we cannot at the same time support leaders like Saddam or the Turks who discriminate and murder people who are not Arabs and Turks. The Palestinian movement loses credibility when you support these regimes. Supporting a dictator is wrong regardless of this support or non-support for our Palestinian case. We blame the Israelis for killing Palestinian children, men and women but do not see that Turkey does the same thing toward the Kurds. We Palestinians can go to Morocco on vocation and support its state but we forget about West Sahara. We say boycott Israel because it has occupied our homeland, nobody says boycott Morocco! This double standard is wrong.

Ahmad provides a fierce critique of how an oppressed people can become complicit in oppression and domination of other oppressed groups. This sophisticated formulation by Ahmad indicates that oppression needs to be resisted wherever it is. The humanism and universalism that Ahmad represents were not championed by major part of the Palestinian and Kurdish interviewees due to polarized discourses about alleged Kurdish alliances with Zionism and Palestinian complicity in Arab, Turkish and Persian oppression of the Kurds. It is of paramount importance to uncover important historical connections between the Kurdish and the Palestinian movement. Akkaya (2015) argues that the leftist Kurdish movement was highly inspired by the Palestinian Fedayeen movement. The relationship between the Kurdish and the Palestinian movement goes back to 1960s. The Kurds were received both military training in camps and economic support from the Palestinian movement in Lebanon. It is partly thanks to the Palestinian movement that PKK became influential in Kurdish politics in terms of its armed struggle. Members of the leftist Kurdish movement fought side by side against the Israeli army during 1980s. The Kurdish guerrillas in Lebanon suffered both causalities and some were taken as prisoners of war by the Israeli army. However, this relationship came to the end when the Palestinian movement lost military ground in Lebanon (Akkaya, 2015). In 2018, Leila Khaled who is a leading member of the People's Front for the Liberation of Palestine participated in the Third Congress of the People's Democratic Party (HDP) in Ankara. During her participation in the Congress, she condemned the Turkish invasion of Afrin and underlined the similarities between what Kurds and Palestinians experience as two oppressed nations:

> Today in Ankara I saw two different scenes. On the one hand all the policemen who surrounded the congress hall and filled the street. The same picture we see in Palestine. /.../ Wherever there is colonialism, oppression and violence, resistance will gain strength. You are resisting. You are the voices of those who resist colonialism. I greet you on behalf of the fighting Palestinian people. (Leila Khaled cited in ANF News, 2018)

It belongs to a rarity to hear scholars and debaters in the Middle East to talk about the political situation of the Kurds as a colonial relation. This entails that the transnationality of the Kurdish suffering is silenced when their identity, language, culture and lands are targeted by colonial practices and hierarchical relations of dominance and subjugation. In contrast, colonialism and racism are often used in the context of the Israeli occupation of Palestinian lands.

Turkey, Iran and Israel contribute intentionally or unwittingly to polarization between the Kurds and Palestinians by either taking side or minimizing the collective suffering of these two groups. Although Turkey was the first Muslim majority country to recognize Israel as a state in 1949 and having considerable economic and military cooperation, it has under Erdoğan's leadership turned itself into the champion of Palestinian rights.

Whereas Erdoğan has emphasized that the creation of a Palestinian state is not an obligation but a necessity, he rejects the very idea of a Kurdish state in any parts of the Middle East. For Erdoğan, Kurds do not need to look for a Kurdish state in Turkey since "the Republic of Turkey is the state of all of us. Kurds' state is the state of the Republic of Turkey". He also added: "We don't say 'there are no Kurds', we say 'there is no Kurdish problem'" (Hurriyet, 2018). This claim can be equated with the same discursive arsenal of the Turkish state; we do not have a problem with the Kurds but with 'terrorism' that the Kurdish movement supposedly represents and endorses. In order to thwart Erdoğan's pro-Palestinian stance, the Israelis have used the Kurdish card and the sufferings of the Kurds in Syria to dismiss critique of Israeli oppression of the Palestinian community. In fact, every time the Israeli government rhetorically expresses its alleged support for Kurdish independence, it reinforces the widespread image of the 'Kurdish issue' as a Zionist fabrication to divide the Muslim world and underpins popular aversion against the Kurds in the Muslim world.

The Palestinians and the Kurds are both two subjugated nations in the Middle East. However, there is a major difference between these two groups. Whereas Palestinians are viewed by the majority of the nation-states in the world as a sovereign people with a legitimate right to statehood and sovereignty, the Kurds are viewed as an ethnic group or a minority that should be subsumed under the universalities of the nation-state in which they inhabit and 'given' some minority rights like receiving education in Kurdish language. One can also say that while the Palestinian struggle is viewed as a global struggle for political freedom, recognition and statehood, the Kurdish struggle is at best viewed as a domestic question to be solved within the existing state boundaries. Such ranking and qualification as a recognized nation matters when statehood is strived. For instance, while Palestinian statehood is viewed as fostering stability in the Middle East, Kurdish claims are viewed as generating instability, fragmentation and undermining the general interests of the nations in the Middle East. In contrast to a potential Palestinian state that allegedly brings stability to the Middle East, establishment of a Kurdish state is mainly viewed as bringing chaos and instability to the Muslim world. Prior to the Kurdish referendum for independence in Iraq, a BBC reporter asked the former president of Kurdistan Region that "many say that this referendum will bring incredible instability, is not that the last thing the region needs?" In response to this, Barzani underlined: "When have we ever had stability and security that we should be concerned about losing it? When was Iraq so united that we should be worried about breaking its unity? Those who are saying this are just looking for excuses to stop us" (BBC, 2017a). The Turkish and Iranian reactions to the Kurdish referendum was unsurprisingly harsh and uncompromising. For instance, Erdoğan described the referendum as "a threat to national security", and a "treachery", and if the Kurdish leadership does not retreat from this referendum, "they will go down in history with the shame of having dragged the region into ethnic and sectarian war". Erdoğan threatened with sanctions that would make the Iraqi Kurds go hungry by closing the oil taps and stopping Turkish food trucks to enter the Kurdistan Region (BBC, 2017b). Similarly, the Iranian newspaper *Ettela'at* considered the Kurdish referendum for independence in 2017 as a Zionist project for 'creating a new Israel in the region'. Another major Iranian newspaper *Kayhan* labeled the referendum as "a treachery and a threat to the future of the region". A senior advisor to the leader of the Islamic Revolution Ayatollah Seyyed Ali Khamanei regarded the Kurdish referendum as a "new US-Israeli plot in the Middle East to partition Iran, warning that the Kurds will suffer as a result of the plan" (Kayhan, 2017). Khamaeni was assertive that this Zionist plot in Iraqi Kurdistan must be stopped since Israel/Zionism is a 'virus' that needs to be eradicated, a framing that was declared through a Tweet:

> Some argue that the Zionist regime is a reality that the region must come to terms with. Today, the Covid-19 is a reality; should it be accepted or fought?! The long-lasting virus of Zionism will be uprooted thanks to the determination and faith of the youth. (Khamenei, 2020, May 22)

If the dominant perception in Iran and the wider Middle East identify Israel or Zionism as a 'virus', then Kurdish aspiration for independence, autonomy or federalism will not be interpreted in light of human and minority rights discourses but as an expression of an alleged 'Zionist pandemic' that needs to be dealt with and uprooted. In racist Arab imaginations, the Kurds have been equated with a 'tumor' planted on Arab bodies with ambitions to create a Kurdish state that implements Zionist agenda in the Muslim world. For some of the Palestinian interviewees, the Palestinian struggle is not only a struggle that concerns the Palestinians. In this respect, Mahmoud underlined that "Palestine is not only my homeland but the homeland of all Muslims. All Arabs want Palestine to be given back to Palestinians". Indeed, this is where the Kurdish frustration comes in why the Palestinians are given such a privileged position as 'Muslims': Heval who consider himself both as a Kurd and as a Muslim cannot understand why Mosques have become sites of hierarchization of sufferings and lives:

> When I visit the mosques and the Imam starts praying loudly for those people who are sufferings. "Oh God, may Somali, Chechens and Palestinians have a better life". Usually he prays a lot for Palestinians. But I have never heard him praying for the Kurds and Kurdistan. Sometimes, the Imam can ironically be a Kurd. I do not mind these peoples to have their states and have a good life, but why not talking about Kurdish sufferings too. (Heval, a 30 years old man, Kurdistan-Turkey, Sweden)

Such differentiation and hierarchization illustrate how the alleged universalism of Islam is particularized to represent certain Muslim constituencies and their sufferings as more important and grievable. Furthermore, this affirms that the Palestinian issue and struggle are not only a viewed as a question that regards the Palestinians but also constitute a central component of the global Muslim struggle against Zionism and imperialism. Among Muslims in Western Europe, there are for instance many campaigns and fundraisings for Palestinians. Ghada Karmi (2015) who is a famous Palestinian writer and doctor, based in the UK, underscores the global Muslim solidarity with the Palestinians. Karmi points out that Muslim migrants from the Indian subcontinent in Britain are passionately engaged in the Palestinian issue and regularly raise funds in support of the Palestine and its Arab inhabitants (Karmi, 2015). Sayyid (2014) in his work about decolonization of images of Muslims and Islam refers to anti-Zionism as a unifying bond for Muslims across the world. In this light, Sayyid argues that if the American narratives about Palestine are primarily told and repeated through a Zionist lens, invocation of a global Islamic *ummah* (community) has become a counter-narrative to Zionism. Furthermore, Sayyid maintains how transnational Muslim solidarity works and can be fashioned to champion Muslim rights and struggles in the world:

> Muslims thousands of miles from Palestine are able to see in the plight of the Palestinian people something that they have empathy for. The spread of the anti-Zionist narrative has become one of the threads that connects the *ummah*. There is no reason why the struggles of Muslims

in Kashmir, Burma and Chechnya could not become another common thread connecting and binding an ummatic culture. Harnessing cultural output to the production of the Islamicate rather than the policing of the Muslim would support the conditions for the articulation of a global Muslim counterpublic. (Sayyid, 2014, pp. 186–187)

The political vision that Sayyid depicts as decolonial by disrupting Western representation and power tends to reproduce another hierarchical order regarding which lives and sufferings can and should matter for the Muslim community across the world: It is *only* those sufferings that are inflicted on Muslim by non-Muslims that seem to be the "common thread connecting and binding an ummatic culture", that Sayyid seems to view as a legitimate case for the Muslim world to endorse. This position illustrates how the existing ethnic and religious hierarchies and inequalities within the majority Muslim states are brushed under the carpet in the name of anti-imperialism.

However, it is not only Islamists or imams in Mosques who champion the Palestinian struggle to establish their state and undo Israel as a state through the lens of religious affiliation. The global left has also had a partisan role in endorsing the Palestinian struggle as part of the global struggle against imperialism and colonialism, while downplaying the atrocities committed against the Kurds or the Christians by the states in the Middle East. Although it is true that the West has exploited the Kurds on many occasions for their own political and economic goals, it is not clear with whom and which states the Kurds can build strategic alliances with, in order to politically survive in a region where the ethnopolitical reality of the Kurds is often perceived as a threat to the 'security', 'national cohesion' or 'Islamic brotherhood' in the Middle East. Consider for instance Edward Said who was a champion of Palestinian nationalism and a seminal writer on imperialism and postcolonialism, and the way he denied the Iraqi government's gassing of the Kurds in 1988, while writing in the *London Review of Books*:

The claim that Iraq gassed its own citizens has often been repeated. At best, this is uncertain. There is at least one War College report, done while Iraq was a US ally, which claims that the gassings of the Kurds in Halabja was done by Iran. (Said cited in Najmabadi, 1991, p. 2)

When the feminist scholar Afsaneh Najmabadi (1991) countered Said on the role of the intellectuals and how he tends to blame all the ills of the Middle East on the US and Israel, and acting as an apologist to the sufferings of the Shia and Kurds in Iraq, Said degraded Najmabadi's critique to be consisted of a "wacky and rather obtuse political views" (Said, 1991, p. 43). One can really wonder if Said himself was not endorsing an academic authoritarianism that rejected his opponents as 'ignorant' and 'crazy', not worth listening to, and as such justifying their exclusion from the debates, even when he was apparently wrong. It needs to be emphasized that Western imperialism has cultivated many political ills in the Middle East and prevented democratization process in the Middle East. As a strategy to dismiss American imperialism and military intervention in the Arab world, Said denied more or less the genocidal campaigns and suffering of the Kurds in the Arab Iraq. If we consider the role of the intellectuals that Said (1996) has framed as speaking the truth to power and challenging oppressive political orders, then it would be important to attack the unequal relationship between dominant and subordinate groups at local, national and global levels. Since Postcolonial Studies is highly influenced by the work of Said, it might not be surprising that most students of Postcolonial Studies focus mainly on Palestinian suffering and express much more sympathy for the Palestinian case, than for instance the Kurds, Tamils, Assyrians, Tibetans or Kashmiris. Such partial focus on suffering of one people as the chosen people of Postcolonial Studies and objects of racist colonial policies prevent the suffering of many disenfranchised peoples to be noticed and challenged through intellectual work and moral support.

In 2017, when the Kurdish leadership in Iraqi Kurdistan decided to carry out a referendum for independence, the Iranian scholar Hamid Dabashi (2017) wrote a column for Aljazeera English in which he framed his position discursively as a progressive voice that can understand the vulnerability and grievances of the Kurds in Iran, Iraq, Syria and Turkey. Although he as an ethnic Persian points out that "No Iranian, Turk, or Arab can or should even try to pontificate to Kurds about Kurdish independence", he himself does so with regard to Kurdish aspiration for independence in a paternalist and conspiratorial fashion. It makes sense that ethnic nationalism does not solve the problem of oppression based on ethnic oppression, that Kurds have been experiencing for almost a century. Yet, what is striking about Dabashi is how he discursively connects Kurdish desire for statehood to the Israeli settler colony as an alarming political path for the region. Dabashi seems to make a political argument of empty promises by Israel as supporting Kurdish independence. Conversely, it would be dishonest to blame Israel for all the political ills that face the Middle East in general when it comes to how minorities are abused and discarded as outcasts. The inter-subaltern colonialism or hierarchies, to paraphrase Matin (forthcoming), are rooted in the state structures and dominant historiography of the majority Muslim states that rule the Kurds and subject them to "politico-cultural destruction, assimilation or subordination as well as economic exploitation, resources extraction and environmental degradation" (Matin, forthcoming). Dabashi reduces flagrantly the Kurdish desire for independence to a predominantly Zionist attempt to Israelify the Arab and the Muslim world:

> The Israeli settler colony is constitutionally discomforted by any pluralistic nation in the region for it exposes the ethnic racism at the roots of Zionism. The more ethnically fragmented the region in which they live the paler will appear the European settler colony in their midst. Let the entire Arab and Muslim world break down and fracture into tiny ethnic, xenophobic, racist colonies, so "Israel" feels perfectly at home in Palestine. Divide them to their tiniest racialized denominators so you can rule them better. (Dabashi, 2017)

In effect, what Dabashi frames above is more and less what the non-democratic and authoritarian Islamic regime of Iran is preaching about the Kurdish desire for statehood, that a Kurdish state is equal to a "new" or the 'second Israel' in the Middle East. This testifies that the Islamic nationalism of the Iranian regime and the postcolonial leftism that Dabashi represents are not competing but completing each other in relation to the ways the Kurdish struggle is conceived and condemned. Dabashi warns that the creation of a Kurdish state will lead to ethnic cleansing and turn into a "nightmare" (Dabashi, 2007, pp. 259–260) and "would be disastrous for all peoples of the region, including the Kurds themselves" (Dabashi, 2017). Using metaphors like 'nightmare' and 'disaster' function as warrants to justify resistance and denouncement of Kurdish aspiration for sovereignty. Such conceptualization of Kurdish rights and freedom tend to vilify the Kurds within the Muslim world. Dabashi (2017) alerts that the nation-state that Kurds aspire for will lead the Kurds "further down the drain of retrograde parochialism, racism, nativism, ethnic nationalism, and hateful jingoism". However, except a vague reference to democratic pluralism, Dabashi does not provide an answer to what Kurds should do when their lives and homes are continuously destructed by these states. Accordingly, Dabashi deploys a deconstructive rhetoric that he spouts in the face of the Kurds in relation to their nationalism and requiring from them to demonstrate a new humanism beyond nationalism, while Persian, Arab and Turkish nationalism with religious undertones continue to violently dominate the political scenes of the Middle East. It is widely assumed that nationalism is considered both inevitable and desirable in our world. However, not all nationalisms can be put in the same basket as equally reactionary or radical in its emancipatory sense (Davidson, 2016). It is important to pay attention to who is using nationalism as part of oppression and who is using it in something like a liberation struggle, but more important, we need accord attention to which groups have access to state power to endorse their national agendas and which groups lack such power. Hence, it is due to this absence that Kurds embrace nationalism as a vehicle to protect their existence as an ethno-national constituency and realize their political dreams, although this might not lead to realization of freedom and democracy.

The Palestinian experience has been defined as "perhaps the most persistent popular and intricate case of contested statehood" (Grzybowski & Koskenniemi, 2015, p. 39). Concurrently, the Kurdish aspiration for statehood is considered as a utopian project due to the fact that Kurds are surrounded by four states that might differ on many political issues and have fought each other but agree that Kurds should be contained and prevented from achieving autonomy or independence. Moreover, Kurds lack an international patron that can secure their national rights (Bajalan, 2019). The Palestinian scholar Khalidi (1997) points out that the Palestinians, the Kurds and the Armenians were the three major peoples who were denied statehood after the World War I in the Middle East. Although the Kurds and the Armenians have suffered, Khalidi maintains that they are "freer than the Palestinians, and less subject to domination by others" (p. 11). Khalidi also maintains that it is true that the Kurds are denied statehood but they enjoy an internationally protected autonomous region in the Northern Iraq. Whether intentionally or unwittingly, Khalidi creates a hierarchy of sufferings among oppressed nations where Palestinians take the leading position as the most oppressed one. Of course, such a claim to the suffering of Palestinians is a political strategy to prioritize their voices, perspectives and collective pain in order to gain some form of rights, recognition and sovereignty that they have been denied by the Israeli state. It is also logical that Khalidi writes first and foremost from a Palestinian perspective and representing their voices and grievances. As Butler (2004) has argued, vulnerability is experienced differently and allocated differently across the world. There is also a need to maintain caution in making vulnerability to a competitive sport that can lead to hierarchization and prioritization of the political struggles of oppressed nations that pursue international attention, recognition and solution to their suffering. However, this is not to say that by not hierarchizing sufferings, we should equalize vulnerabilities (Schueller, 2009) with the belief that all vulnerable constituencies embarking the same boat and sharing the similar political fate. Hence, it is analytical and ethico-politically more apt to understand the vulnerability of different groups in their specific geopolitical and historical contexts. And of course, some of these histories are politically imbricated. The Jewish humiliation and the persistent European anti-Semitism pushed the Jews to the extreme that the only solution to their vulnerability was a Jewish homeland, which in its turn created a new highly vulnerable group of Palestinian Arabs who paid a high price with their lives, homes and lands for the monstrous atrocities committed against the Jews in Europe. Benhabib (2018, p. 97) provides a critique of Butler and argues that Butler does not accord attention to "the lingering collective psychosis of many Jews, whether in Israel or not, namely their fear of annihilation in the hands of a hostile world as well as the post-1945 persecution of the Jews of the Middle East". It was mainly by making use of Jewish vulnerability (see Schueller, 2009, p. 249) that Palestinians were displaced and dispossessed by the Zionists and made into undesired foreigners in their own country.

As Said (1992) points out, the Palestinian voices were by large absent and preempted on the international scene until sixties and seventies. The Zionist project had monopolized the scene by asserting itself as the mouthpiece of a suffering Jewish people. One of the greatest achievements of Zionism was the "international legitimization for its own accomplishments, thereby making the Palestinian cost of these accomplishments seem to be irrelevant" (Said, 1992, p. 71). Said continues and asserts that Zionism as a Jewish movement nurturing colonial settlements in Palestine cannot be embraced by the Palestinians as representing the Jewish victims of European anti-Semitism but consistently viewed as a movement that oppresses, discriminates and excludes Palestinians and occupy their lands. Following the hierarchical logic of Zionism, Palestinian Arabs were framed as inferior, irrelevant, backward, and living on a land that they did not deserve to inhabit but should be removed so the Jews could reclaim it as their historical land, which they could cultivate and develop. Accordingly, Zionism is theoretically based on imperialism and practically endorsing a settler colonial project (Said, 1992, p. 69). It is argued by prominent scholars of Palestinian studies like Sayigh (2015) that international media and academia continue to silence the sufferings of the Palestinians that the creation of the Israeli state has contributed to. In this light, Sayigh (2013) contends that Palestinian experiences and sufferings are by large excluded from the vast literature on trauma, social suffering, memory and loss. This marginalization of Palestinian sufferings from the literature and politics is based on the idea that Palestinians do not belong to the comity of moral communities (see the work of Morris, 1996). The question of power is important in relation to what moral communities can do in relation to validating and invalidating the experiences of sufferings. Although the majority states in the Middle East support the Palestinian cause at popular and state level, it is not the attention, the gaze and the sympathy of Muslims and their states that are the main object of Palestinian discourse. In contrast, in search of recognition and compensation for their suffering, it is primarily the Western states which enjoy global political power that Palestinians seek to convince with regard to their suffering and grievances.

Although it is true that Palestinian sufferings have not received the same attention and recognition as the Jewish suffering in the West, it is important to note that Palestinian suffering is increasingly enjoying more legitimacy among certain European and American political circles. In this respect, many European countries have started to support Palestinian statehood and continue to criticize the settlement policies of the Israeli state as an obstacle to enduring peace in the region. In addition, many seminal Jewish writers and scholars like Noam Chomsky and Judith Butler openly support the Palestinians struggle, even if it entails undoing Israel as a state and its military force (Butler, 2012, p. 217). In contrast to the Palestinians, Kurds do not enjoy the attention of powerful media like Aljazeera English by shedding light on their narratives and sufferings. Likewise, most Turkish, Persian and Arabic media outlets endorse and reproduce the states' dominant narratives of the Kurdish struggle as a question of 'separatism' and 'instability'. As long as the Kurdish predicaments are interpreted through the dominant lenses of the states in the Middle East as a security problem, Kurds cannot expect national and international solidarity. This securitized notion of Kurdish rights and claims that the Middle Eastern states endorse and popularize can explain why Kurdish suffering do not fall within the border of moral communities of the Muslim world and their losses are deemed as irrelevant. It was mainly after the emergence of ISIL and the bloody sacrifices of Kurds against this fanatic group that Kurds gained some form of international recognition to exist as a people. And it was also in this context that the Turkish President Erdoğan lamented in 2014 that the West is making a big fuss over the vulnerability of the Kurds in the besieged city of Kobane due to the assaults of ISIL and not paying similar attention to the Sunni-Arab Muslim vulnerability in Syria. This illustrates how important it is for the Middle Eastern states that rule the Kurds to preempt Kurdish suffering to gain universal recognition and rendered it as politically and morally irrelevant.

Certainly, the discourse of suffering is central to the narratives of most disenfranchised peoples, who look for a better political order in which they can escape being targets of violence and oppression. The position of victimhood relies on memories of suffering as a framework for political self-legitimation of different groups who view themselves as objects of violence, oppression and indifference. According to Bauman, "a successful victimhood is a prospective call to share power, to slice the cake of global attention, and to grant access to realpolitik and the established political vocabulary" (Bauman and Donkis, 2013, p. 124). It might not be a coincidence that different marginalized groups imitate each other, with regard to appropriating the narratives and concepts of victimhood that have enabled some form of productive results in improving the life situation of a marginalized group and gaining international recognition and sympathy for their suffering. In the context of Jewish suffering and genocide, there is a strong tendency among Jewish elites in Israel to denounce other sufferings that equally can be described as genocide, like the fate of Armenians in Turkey. Hence, there is a danger that the uniqueness and specificity of suffering are not merely deployed to gain recognition and compensation but also utilized to claim moral superiority (Benbassa, 2010).

Nonetheless, the discourse of suffering can either be used to endorse a more equal world, or politically abused to legitimize power abuse and implement a politics of revenge against peoples who are viewed as constituting a threat to one's existence. Competition between different memories and sufferings often aim to create a hierarchy of suffering (see Robins, 2018). For instance, the Jewish suffering in the West is much more recognized than the suffering of Roma, Native Americans, Aboriginals and African Americans. Finkelstein (2000), who has written a highly debated book about the 'Holocaust industry', maintains that memories of Holocaust are often used to exploit Jewish suffering in order to gain financial support and political legitimacy, and justify the Zionist oppression of Palestinians. In a similar vein, Benbassa (2010) provides a strong critique of suffering as identity in relation to the Jewish experience and challenges the view that Jews are eternal victims of oppression and passively watching their history. Benbassa defies the lachrymose approach to Jewish history and maintains that the entire Jewish history and past cannot be reduced to a single story of suffering and tears. For Benbassa, "Victimhood is not part of any group's genetic code: it is always a question of a latent possibility that circumstances can actualize" (p. 179). Benbassa laments that the lessons that have been extracted from the Holocaust have not entailed championing minority rights and the fight against racism across the globe. According to Bauman and Donkis (2013, p. 34), political memory can be used either to "serve the cause of improvement and learning from mistakes" or evil acts. In line with Benbassa's arguments above, Bauman and Donkis (2013) draw a similar conclusion in relation to the usage of Jewish suffering, that it can be deployed to "assist in the salvation of our jointly inhabited world from another catastrophe of a potentially similar character and magnitude" (p. 34). With respect to Palestinian suffering and the Israeli oppression, Bauman bemoans that Israel and many states around the world have not learnt from history and offered "Hitler – whether intentionally or inadvertently – such a posthumous victory of sorts" (p. 35).

Against this background, it is important for stateless peoples to understand that the inability to see beyond their immediate concerns and an excessive preoccupation with their own sufferings might prevent them from developing sympathy, alliances, understanding and knowledge about other groups than their own constituencies. This political vision is important in order to avoid falling into the traps of 'narcissistic victimhood and nationalism' in search of empowering their identities and interests even if it occurs at the expense of other groups (see Hage, 2015). By endorsing oppressive state structures that support their movement but subjugate other minoritized groups, they undermine the ethico-political basis of their struggle as emancipatory in the name of realpolitik.

References

Agamben, G. (1998). *Homo Sacer. Sovereign power and bare life*. California University Press.

Ahmed, S. (2017). *Living a feminist life*. London: Duke University Press.

Akkaya, A. H. (2015). The "Palestinian Dream" in the Kurdish context. *Kurdish Studies, 3*(1), 47–63.

ANF News. (2018). *Leila Khaled: We also raise our voices for Afrin*.

Anthias, F. (2021). *Translocational belongings: Intersectional dilemmas and social inequalities*. Routledge.

Arendt, H. (1951). *The origins of totalitarianism*. Shocken Books.

Bajalan, D. R. (2019). The First World War; the end of the Ottoman Empire, and the question of Kurdish Statehood: A "missed" opportunity? *Ethnopolitics, 18*(1), 13–28.

BBC. (2017a). *Iraqi Kurdish leader: 'Our right to seek independence'*. https://www.bbc.com/news/av/world-middle-east-41222094. Accessed 15 March 2021.

BBC. (2017b). *Iraqi Kurds must give up on independence or go hungry—Erdogan*. https://www.bbc.com/news/world-middle-east-41398199 Accessed 15 March 2021.

Bauman, Z., & Donkis, L. (2013). *Moral blindness: The loss of sensitivity in liquid modernity*. Polity.

Benbassa, E. (2010). *Suffering as identity: The Jewish paradigm*. Verso.

Benhabib, S. (2018). *Exile, statelessness and migration: Playing chess with history from Hannah Arendt to Isiah Berlin*. Princeton University Press.

Bhopal, K., & Myers, M. (2008). *Insiders, outsiders and others: Gypsies and identity*. University of Hertfordshire Press.

Bowman, G. (1994). 'A country of words': Conceiving the Palestinian nation from the position of exile. In L. Ernesto (Ed.), *The making of political identities* (pp. 138–170). Verso.

Butler, J. (2004). *Precarious life: The powers of mourning and violence*. Verso.

Butler, J. (2012). *Parting ways: Jewishness and the critique of Zionism*. Columbia University Press.

Butler, J., & Athanasiou, A. (2013). *Dispossession: The performative in the political*. Cambridge: Polity.

Dabashi, H. (2007). *Iran: A people interrupted*. The New Press.

Dabashi, H. (2017). *On the Kurdish Question*. Aljazeera English. https://www.aljazeera.com/opinions/2017/11/27/on-the-kurdish-question. Accessed 15 February 2021.

Darwish, M. (2006). *Why did you leave the horse alone?* Archipelago Books.

Davidson, N. (2016). *Nation-State: Consciousness and competition*. Haymarket Books.

Eliassi, B. (2013). *Contesting Kurdish identities in Sweden: Quest for belonging among Middle Eastern Youth*. Palgrave Macmillan.

Finkelstein, N. (2000). *Holocaust Industry: Reflections on the exploitation of Jewish suffering*. Verso.

Gabiam, N. (2015). Citizenship and development: Palestinian in France and the multiple meanings of statelessness. *Studies in Comparative International Development, 50*, 479–499.

Gieryn, T. F. (2000). A space for place in sociology. *Annual Review of Sociology, 26*(1), 463–496.

Grzybowski, J., & Koskenniemi, M. (2015). International law and statehood: A performative view. In S. Robert & M. R. S. Peter (Eds.), *The concept of the state in international relations: Philosophy, sovereignty, cosmopolitanism* (pp. 23–47). Edinburgh University Press.

Hage, G. (2015). *Alter-politics: Critical Anthropology and their radical imagination*. Melbourne University Press.

Hanafi, S. (2012). Explaining spacio-cide in the Palestinian territory: Colonization, separation, and state of exception. *Current Sociology, 61*(2), 190–205.

Harding, S. (1993). Rethinking standpoint epistemology: What is "strong objectivity"? *The Centennial Review, 36*(3), 437–470.

Hartman, A. (2000). In search of subjugated knowledge. *Journal of Feminist Family Therapy, 11*(4), 19–23.

Haughey, É. (1999). Gypsy identity and political theory. In E. Jenny, P. Nalini, & P.-F. Véronique (Eds.), *Sovereignty and subjectivity* (pp. 141–151). Lynne Rienner Publishers.

Hürriyet Daily News. (2018). *Kurds in Turkey need no other state, says Erdoğan*. https://www.hurriyetdailynews.com/kurds-in-turkey-need-no-other-state-says-erdogan-132748. Acessed 9 February 2021.

Jenkins, R. (1996). *Identity*. Routledge.

Kaplan, D. H., & Herb, G. H. (2011). How geography shapes National Identities. *National Identities, 13*(4), 349–360.

Kayhan. (2017). *Iran: Iraqi Kurdistan referendum 'illegitimate'*. http://kayhan.ir/en/news/44613/iran-iraqi-kurdistan-referendum-'illegitimate' Accessed 25 September 2017.

Karmi, G. (2015). *Return: A Palestinian Memoir*. Verso Books.

Kenny, M. (2014). *The politics of English nationhood*. Oxford University Press.

Khalidi, R. (1997). *Palestinian identity: The construction of modern national consciousness*. Columbia University Press.

Khamenei, S. A. (2020). https://twitter.com/khamenei_ir/status/1263750159890079745. Accessed 1 July 2021.

Kofman, E. (2005). Figures of cosmopolitan: Privileged nationals and national outsiders. *Innovation, 18*(1), 83–97.

Kumar, K. (2000). Nation and empire: English and British national identity in comparative perspective. *Theory and Society, 29*(5), 575–608.
Krause, M. (2011). Stateless people and undocumented migrants: An Arendtian perspective. In S. Caroline & K. B. Brad (Eds.), *Statelessness in the European Union: Displaced, undocumented, unwanted* (pp. 22–40). Cambridge University Press.
Malešević, S. (2013). *Nation-state and nationalisms*. Polity.
Malkki, L. (1995). Refugee and exile: 'Refugee studies' to the national order of things. *Annual Review of Anthropology, 24*, 495–523.
Matin, K. (Forthcoming). Decolonising Iran: A Tentative Note on Inter-Subaltern Colonialism. *Current Anthropology.*
McGarry, A. (2014). Roma as a political identity: Exploring representations of Roma in Europe. *Ethnicities, 14*(6), 756–774.
McNevin, A. (2007). Irregular migrants, neoliberal geographies and spatial frontiers of the 'political.' *Review of International Studies, 33*(4), 655–574.
Molavi, S. C. (2013). *Stateless citizenship: The Palestinian-Arab citizens of Israel*. Brill.
Morris, D. B. (1996). About suffering, voice, genre, and moral community. *Daedalus, 125*(1), 25–45.
Najmabadi, A. (1991). Said's war on the intellectuals. *Middle East Report, 173*, 2+42.
Peteet, J. (2017). *Space and mobility in Palestine*. Indiana University Press.
Pyke, K. (2010). What is internalized oppression and why don't we study it? Acknowledging racism's hidden injuries. *Sociological Perspective, 53*(4), 551–572.
Radhakrishnan, R. (2003). *Theory in an uneven world*. Blackwell.
Rancière, J. (2004). Who is the subject of the Rights of Man? *The South Atlantic Quarterly, 103*(2/3), 297–310.
Redclift, V. (2013). *Statelessness and Citizenship: Camps and the creation of political space*. Routledge.
Rembold, E., & Carrier, P. (2011). Space and identity: Constructions of national identities in the age of globalization. *National Identities, 13*(4), 361–377.
Ridgeway, C. (2014). Why status matters for inequality. *American Sociological Review, 79*(1), 1–16.
Robins, S. (2018). Thinking through and beyond "Competitive Memory" and Hierarchies of Suffering. *Cambridge Journal of Postcolonial Literary Inquiry., 5*(1), 98–105.
Rushdie, S. (2012). *Home*. Vintage Minis.
Said, E. W. (1991). Edward Said responds. *Middle East Report, 173*, 43.
Said, E. W. (1992). *The question of Palestine*. Vintage Books.
Said, E. W. (1996). *Representations of the Intellectual: The 1993 Reith Lectures*. Vintage Books.

Said, E. W. (1999). *After the last sky: Palestinian lives*. Columbia University Press.
Saloul, I. (2012). *Catastrophe and exile in the modern Palestinian imagination: Telling memories*. Palgrave Macmillan.
Sayigh, R. (2013). On the exclusion of the Palestinian Nakba from the "Trauma Genre", *Journal of Palestine Studies, 43*(1): 51–56.
Sayigh, R. (2015). Silenced suffering. *Borderlands, 14*(1): 1–20.
Sayyid, S. (2014). *Recalling the Caliphate: Decolonisation and world order*. Hurst & Company.
Shachar, A. (2014). Introduction: Citizenshop and the 'Right to Have Rights.' *Citizenship Studies, 18*(2), 114–124.
Schueller, M. J. (2009). Decolonizing global theories today. *Interventions: International Journal of Postcolonial Studies, 11*(2): 235–254.
Sigona, N. (2005). Locating the 'the gypsy problem'. The Roma in Italy: Stereotyping, labelling and 'nomad camps. *Journal of Ethnic and Migration Studies, 31*(4): 741–756.
Somers, M. R. (2008). *Genealogies of citizenship: Markets, statelessness, and the right to have rights*. Cambridge University Press.
Staples, K. (2012). Statelessness and the politics of misrecognition. *Res Publica, 18*, 93–106.
Vali, A. (1998). The Kurds and their "others": Fragmented identity and fragmented politics. *Comparative Studies of South Asia, Africa and the Middle East, 18*(2), 82–95.

CHAPTER 4

Politics of Home and 'Statesickness': Perils and Promises

What kind of world are we inhabiting? Are we living in a world where thick attachment to place is passé as proponents of cosmopolitanism and globalization argue? What does this condition mean to people who voluntarily and unproblematically choose thin attachment to places called home and people who are forcibly thrown out of their homes and their returns to homeland are suspended and securitized? It is often argued that globalization has led to an increased mobility of people and goods across national borders. Moreover, it is frequently assumed that mobility is opposed to attachment to places (Gustafson, 2014). In this respect, Duyvendak (2011) distinguishes between two approaches to place-attachment and home in the context of globalization. The first position is represented by the *universalists* who argue that people are less inclined to be attached to places and homelands. In contrast, the particularist position maintains that due to the uncertainty that globalization engenders, the meanings and value of attachment to places become more acute. Geschiere (2009) points out that despite the fact that we are believed to live in a globalized world, people across the world are investing energy and resources in their local identities as deeply rooted and the nation-state still matters as site of spatial and symbolic inclusion and exclusion. Concretely, by deploying 'claims of autochtony'—to be born from the soil, powerful groups aim to establish themselves as

B. Eliassi, *Narratives of Statelessness and Political Otherness*, Minorities in West Asia and North Africa,
https://doi.org/10.1007/978-3-030-76698-6_4

embodying primordial and naturalized rights to belong and having the power to exclude other peoples as outsiders. While 'autochtony' was mocked by the Europeans in colonial contexts as standing for the non-white and 'uncivilized natives', it has been appropriated more and more by the Europeans to determine who belong to Europe and who are its outsiders. Consequently, obsession with belonging and exclusion of foreigners and strangers are becoming hallmark of politics in the world (Ceuppens & Geschiere, 2005; Geschiere, 2009).

Like most scholarship on globalization, the figure of European and Western subject functions as an immediate point of reference for cosmopolitan belonging, while the harsh empirical reality of our bordered world is demoted (see Ahmed, 1999; Kofman, 2005). Ahmed (1999) has challenged those theoretical deliberations that celebrate nomadism by choosing homelessness. It would be naïve to assume that all subjects can equally choose to be homeless given that there are external circumstances or better put structural constraints that privilege and enable certain subjects to have or not having home without affecting their place in the society and the world. Those subjects that can embrace homelessness or can adopt a nomadic way of thinking can do that "*because the world is already constituted as their home*" (ibid., p. 335, emphasis in original). While to be rooted or grounded does not mean that one is fixed, choosing mobility or being mobile does not automatically imply that one is homeless or lacks attachment to a place (Ahmed et al., 2003, p. 1). This implies that it might be a less adventurous project for members of dominant nation-states with powerful citizenship regimes, to enjoy the privileges of nomadism and alleged homelessness, and at the same time, engage in a deconstructive rhetoric about the suspension of home. For people from the global south, they can hardly choose homelessness in the name of nomadism given that there are numerous structural constraints that encounter them both when they want to enter European territories and/or when they are inside and want to live their lives there as legitimate members of European societies. This indicates that both leaving and arriving, uprootings and regroundings for non-white migrants become a risky journey in a world of unequal citizenship regimes. In this respect, Duyvendak (2011) points out that the question of home has become highly politicized. Dominant groups view their home as endangered by the arrival of the non-white migrants and ask for policies that endorse the home-feelings and belongingness of the white constituency, which often entails constructing ethno-racial hierarchies and creation of national homes at the expense of racialized and minoritized groups (see also Geschiere, 2009). It is in such settings that both Kurds and Palestinians have been expelled from nation-building processes and formation of political power in the Middle East. Experiences of otherness and displacement often inform their trajectories as racialized diasporas in Western contexts. Moreover, as stateless diasporas, both Kurds and Palestinian deploy a discourse of 'autochtony' in order to make claim to places from which they are deprived of establishing their political homes and states.

The notion of diaspora has to do with dislocation and leaving specific places and living somewhere else (Sökefeld, 2006). It also provides us with an important perspective on migratory experiences of dislocation, estrangement, uprootings and regroundings that links together "three dimensions of movement, connectivity, return" (Kenny, 2013, p. 105). The aim of this chapter is to illuminate theoretically and empirically that while most migrants following forced migration have a complicated relationship with issues of home(land) and belonging, statelessness as an ascribed status and a lived experience adds a further dimension to the sense of alienation, aloneness and political otherness. However, due to the political standard of nationalist thoughts and the nation-state system in our contemporary world, stateless peoples are asymmetrically positioned in a world that empowers national belonging and discards stateless peoples as political outcasts and homeless. Likewise, the chapter aims to theoretically discuss the promises and perils of the search for political home, statehood and belonging among stateless diasporas in an uneven world. Drawing upon the experiences of Kurdish and Palestinians diasporas in Sweden and the UK, I will illustrate how narratives and experiences of homelessness, statelessness and belonging are framed across different generations and national contexts both at individual and collective levels.

Belonging and Home-Making in an Uneven World

The questions of home and belonging are widely discussed in the context of migration and dislocation (Brah, 1996; Butter, 2015; George, 1996). For diaspora studies, it seems inevitable to engage with the concept of home in the context of dispersal, resettlements and homesickness. Exile and diaspora are often viewed as domains of creativity but they can also become a place characterized by racism, discrimination and destructive group relations (see Cohen, 2008). For example, experiences of ethnic and religious discrimination can underpin reactive identities among diasporic groups and trigger search for alternative modes and places of belonging (Eliassi, 2013). Home as an idea or as a place is a central basis for construction of belonging and security but it is also a powerful ideological device to construct exclusionary discourses against people who are not perceived as members of the 'core group' that forms the nation. Generally, home is equated with one's place of origin and roots. Yet, there is a need to conceptualize home and belonging at multidimensional and multiple scales. While home can include dwelling places like the private home, the local neighborhood, the city, the region, the nation-state, the continent, the earth, belonging can also take a multidimensional form where one can feel belonging to a range of placed-based identities (Antonsich, 2010).

The sense of belonging to a place, a state or a group often underpins shared collective identity and social solidarity. Guibernau (2013) views belonging as a key antidote to experiences of alienation and loneliness in context of existential anxiety and political powerlessness. Anthias (2006) points out that in our globalized world, people feel destabilized and seek to cope with experiences of uncertainty, disconnection and invisibility, that lead to obsession with finding and asserting a particular social space as home, where 'we' as a group, family and nation belong. Moreover, people are often aware that there are a wide range of places, locales and identities, to which they do not want or are not allowed to belong to. In the same vein, Antonsich (2010, p. 644) inspired by Nira Yuval-Davis provides an analytical framework, where belonging can be analyzed both "as a personal, intimate, feeling of being 'at home' in a place (place-belongingness) and as discursive resource that constructs, claims, justifies, or resist forms of socio-spatial inclusion/exclusion (politics of belonging)". What is conspicuous in this analytical framework provided above by Antonsich is the focus on territoriality of belonging since feelings, practices and discourses of belonging are mainly located in geographical contexts (Antonsich, 2010, p. 647). This contextualization that Antonsich posits becomes more tangible in everyday negotiation of place-belongingness and challenges the postmodern discourses about the demise or the weakening effects of globalization on nation-states and territorialized identities. Few of us escape the recurrent question in everyday life: 'where are you from?' Although this question might appear as innocent or a sign of curiosity about one's personal history, it is often interpreted and conceived as an act of othering by non-white immigrants, where the immigrant *background* becomes the *foreground* (Eliassi, 2016). Tellingly, a young Kurdish woman talks about her experiences of being interrogated about where she belongs and where she originally is assumed to belong:

> Homeland means where you belong. It is your home. Home is when I am in Norrköping (a town in Sweden) at my parents. That is my home. I was not born here in Sweden but in Kurdistan so my first experiences in life were in Kurdistan and those memories do not just go away by moving to a new country. Even if you were born here in Sweden, you do not feel at home here because you encounter prejudices all the time. You become reminded all the time that you are not Swedish. You are asked all the time: where you are from? I usually say Norrköping. I find this as a good answer. Then the Swedes feel a little bit disappointed for not telling them the answer they like to hear. I want to finish the conversation with some Swedes about my belonging through saying Norrköping. But they continue and say: where are you parents from? For me being from Norrköping is more important than being from Sweden. When I talk about Norrköping, I become warm in my heart. I feel safe in Norrköping. But Sweden does not give me the same feeling and does not make me warm in my heart. For me belonging means to be safe. (Sheno, a 26 years old woman, Kurdistan-Iran, Sweden)

Sheno does not reduce home and homeland to a nation-state but to a city where she has her primary attachments, namely her family and friends. However, this is not considered as a satisfactory response and declaration, since she is interrogated about her belonging and reminded that she needs to explain herself and her roots to ethnic Swedes who view themselves as governors and true inheritors of the Swedish nation-state. When racialized people contest the exclusionary effects of the question 'where are you from?' 'originally?', 'from beginning?', certain members of dominant group quell this contestation and explain that their questions are not guided by the desire to exclude non-dominant groups but informed by sheer curiosity. In contrast, for racialized groups, when the question 'where are you from?' is repeated over and over again, they cannot be reduced merely to a matter of curiosity but increasing the experiences of discomfort and non-belonging among racialized groups (see Noble, 2005). The dominant and racialized groups apparently have incompatible descriptions of the world they inhabit in an uneven way. To be a full-edged member of the core group is to belong without follow-up questions (Skey, 2011) and stipulate the conditions of belonging and distribution of rights and obligation. As Ceuppens and Geschiere (2005) argue that while belonging is often assumed to entail safety, the flipside of belonging implies "fierce disagreement over who 'really' belongs – over whose claims are authentic and whose are not" (p. 3879). This indicates that belonging is relational and cannot be reduced to an individual issue since it often concerns boundaries that define 'us' and 'them', privilege and discrimination, inclusion and otherness. These boundaries are not only constituted between members of different nation-states but also within the territorial framework of the same nation-states, where there is an ethno-national hierarchy of belonging and non-belonging. Nationalist discourse sets limit to who can belong and not belong and excludes certain marked constituencies from sharing and making claim to the same social space equally (see Sharma, 2014). As a result, the dominant group perceives itself and acts as the governor and the master of the nation and creating a strong nexus between entitlement and belonging (Hage, 1998). Although citizenship is the formal framework of belonging to a nation-state, it is often in the everyday life and encounters that people can translate their citizenship into rights and are made aware whether they belong or not belong (Eliassi, 2013). Interestingly, it was not only Sheno who viewed the city as a central site of belonging and home. For Berin, it is not Britain or England that is her home but London:

> In London there is an accepting environment because it is such a multicultural town but once you are out of London, you experience a lot of racism like for instance in Hartford which is on the outskirt of London. I spoke to my (white) English workmate who is from Hartford and she said that "where I live there are no problems and it is so clean and we have not yet any trouble". I asked her where she does live. She said: "I live in Hartford and it is only white English people living there". I was quite surprised and I was kind of thinking just because there are white English people, there are no trouble. Because she wanted to say that it is other ethnic groups that cause trouble. (Berin, a 25 years old woman, Kurdistan-Turkey, the UK)

While multiculturalism was welcomed during 1960s as a device to create more inclusionary societies, it has gradually come to be seen as a threat to national cohesion and social integration (see Amin, 2012) and the ontological security of the dominant white group (Noble, 2005). It should be underlined despite the progressive claims and ambitions of liberal multiculturalism to level the political power between the dominant white constituencies and racialized groups, western forms of multiculturalism were not enough radical to destabilize white primacy and privilege. In racist representations, the very presence of racialized people is equated with undesirable and disruptive attributes. This reflects a white identity politics that endorses the absence of racialized groups from sharing the same living spaces. The aim of this identity politics is to prioritize white concerns and interests and marginalize the racialized others in what is defined and valued as home(land). In societal debates across Western world, the identity politics of non-white migrants to endorse their equal right to participation, representation and justice is discarded as undermining the universalism of national identity and encouraging a 'parallel society'. This is however far from truth since the very 'universalism' that the critics of racialized groups' identity politics defends as the solution to a cohesive society is corrupted and tainted by white primacy and perspectives, since it neglects the existing political, cultural and economic distances between the dominant and the dominated groups. In this light, Gilroy (2005) argues that we need a new value based on convivial culture where people are able to "live with alterity without becoming anxious, fearful, or violent" (p. xv). Gilroy introduces the idea of conviviality that involves "processes of cohabitation and interaction that have made multiculture an ordinary feature of social life in Britain's urban areas and in postcolonial cities elsewhere" (ibid.). This is not to say that by introducing the idea of conviviality, racism and intolerance are no longer important lived experiences in the lives of racialized peoples, but to challenge fixed social categories and reification of identity that structure ethnic and religious divisions (ibid.). This deliberation is also important for inclusive political projects that support the ideas of home and belonging without hierarchy and exclusion.

So, while the literature suggests that belonging is central to our comfort, well-being and security (Anthias, 2006; hooks, 2009; Guibernau, 2013), it is viewed as equally important to create inclusive ways of imagining and constructing home and belonging that do not create new forms of exclusion (Duyvendak, 2011). There is a suspicion that the ideals of home and nostalgia often turn into a politically conservative project (see Bonnett, 2016). This political project according to Iris Young Marion longs for "an impossible security and comfort, a longing bought at the expense of women and of those constructed as

Others, strangers, not-home, in order to secure their fantasy of a unified identity" (Young cited in Bonnett, 2016, p. 143). Accordingly, home is not always a cosy dwelling place since it can be a space permeated by gender-based violence, sexual abuse and child abuse across all societies and groups. Moreover, home for stateless diasporas are often dangerous places characterized by lethal violence and destruction due to militarization and authoritarian political rules, as the cases of the Kurds, Palestinian, Assyrians/Syriacs and Tamils illustrate. Second, dislocation and experiences of otherness strengthen a homing desire where the diasporic subject yearns for social inclusion and feeling at home. Salman Rushdie represents a voice that is highly critical of diasporic obsession with home. He argues that longing for a home can become a dangerous and pathological process of fetishization and monopolization that will involve rejections of different subjects and groups and obstruct creating intimate social relationship with the surrounding individuals and societies (Butter, 2015, p. 355). Consequently, when home becomes a fetish, it contributes to alienation and counteracts processes of home-making in the present place and time. Rushdie (2012) also warns that it is important to avoid a 'ghetto mentality' by believing that there is not a world beyond one's immediate community and restrict ourselves within parochial cultural frontiers. For diasporic and exiled peoples, the question of home and returning is often interlinked. The identity of displaced people is haunted by discourses of loss that underpin claims to restore and reclaim what have been lost. Returning is viewed as a symbolic act to compensate that loss by being physically present in the place hailed as home. Rushdie correctly alerts with reference to Indian migrants that "if we do look back, we must do so in our knowledge – which gives rise to profound uncertainties – that our physical alienation from India almost inevitably means that we will not be capable of reclaiming precisely the thing that was lost; that we will, in short, create fictions, not actual cities or villages, but invisible ones, imaginary homelands, Indias of the mind" (pp. 32–33). Thus, the present ills of racism, rootlessness alienation from one's culture, are understood to be cured by acts of returning to the country of origin. The recurrent racist and exclusionary interpellation that targets non-white migrants are often framed in relation to place and homeland: "Bloody wog, go back home to your homeland!" Hence, the process of authentication (Radhakrishnan, 1996) deployed by migrants regarding home and belonging is a strategy to cope with exclusive nationalist and racist structures. However, most of the Kurdish and Palestinians despite feeling that they were reminded of their otherness and non-belonging to the Swedish and British identity did not fall into a Manichean logic by categorically dismissing Sweden or the UK as their prospective home(lands).

The Swedish-Kurdish writer, Mustafa Can (2006) has captured this issue in a book about his mother's life and death following displacement. Can who came to Sweden at the age of six narrates his family's migration from a deprived village in Kurdistan of Turkey to Sweden and how the question of home has visited and plagued his parents' lives and relationship with their children and grandchildren. Consider the following passage from Can's book (2006, p. 247, my translation from Swedish) about the (im)possibility of home and belonging in a diasporic context, while being back in the village:

> After three weeks in the village I am missing the Western life-style because I have lived in it during 30 years. I am thirty years Western and six years Eastern. Thirty years of satiation and freedom of expression, six years of hunger and lack of freedom of opinion. Despite this, I still feel more Eastern than Western, regardless of how long I live in Sweden, how much and fast I am spinning in the tumble of integration. Wherever, I find myself, I feel more Kurdish than Swedish, East before West.
>
> No, I know that this equation rhymes badly. I cannot solve this equation. Maybe I do not want to solve it.
>
> Yes! I am Swedish.
> No! I am a Kurd.
> Yes! I want to live here.
> No! I do not want to live here.
> Yes! I can live here.
> No! I cannot live here.
> Yes, no, yes, no, yes, no...
>
> Home is away, away is home. In Sweden, I say home in the village. And in the village, I say home in Sweden. I cannot make these countries to change their places. I want to move the social security, the free and the open society of Sweden to the village, or to move the people of the village, its traditions and fragrances to Sweden.
>
> These contradictions are having meeting inside me and I am carrying their blisters. 'Yes' and 'no', 'home' and 'away' are hammering in my head, and increasing my consciousness of guilt for not being able to choose a home.

Can vividly describes narratives about home across different generations within the same family. When his father asked the grandchildren whether it was not time to go back home, they responded:

> - 'Home to the village?' What home? We were born and grown up in Sweden – we are already at home. (Can, 2006, p. 234, my translation from Swedish)

While Can's parents are strongly attached to the village as the place of origin, Can admits that it happens that he and his sisters think about the village and miss it, but it would not come to the mind of the grandchildren to be awake during nights and think about the neighbors and relatives in the village and yearning for the sounds, the fragrances, tastes and the long and warm seasons of the home village. These tensions and ambivalences create dilemmas for the first generation of diasporas who feel that they live in a social and cultural vacuum and become a nameless stranger in a foreign country. Regular visits to the village by Can's father become a device of homecoming where people understand and respect him, where he has a name and not treated as a 'wog' ('*svartskalle*'), as he experiences in Sweden. Returning becomes thus a strategy of momentarily escaping otherness, homelessness and homesickness. For Can's father, the longer he and his children stay in diaspora, the less, they feel attached to the Kurdish culture. His father's nightmare is the day when his grandchildren are given Swedish names, which he views as the final dissolution of his family's link to the village. Through encouraging regular visits to the home village, he initiates a strategy of counteracting the process of assimilation that absorbs the younger generation and detaches them from their 'original' cultural identity. 'Loosing' one's culture is equated with leaving one's place in the cultural order and complicating the dream of future homecoming to the village.

The younger generations of Kurdish migrants in diaspora and particularly the young women constitute a transformative force in defying parts of the cultural order of the Kurdish society that underpins patriarchy, strict social codes and gender oppression. In order to create a safe and an inclusive home, Kurdish women are at the forefront of the struggle for democracy, gender equity and rule of law in the Middle East (Eliassi, 2016). Experiences of return are not always rosy but can be "marked by confrontations with the social and cultural institutions in the place of origin; these institutions, together with wider behavioural norms and practices of the home society (which for the second-generation resettler becomes a host society), obstruct the political project of homecoming, to the frustration and annoyance of the returnee" (King & Christou, 2010, p. 112). For Kurdish migrants, returning home is a highly complicated issue due to the political situation of the Kurds where Kurdish identity is systematically oppressed and Kurdistan has continuously become a zone of war, permeated by political, economic and cultural inequalities. Despite their ambivalence toward the Sweden and the UK as their 'homes', many Kurdish and Palestinian migrants are aware that the current democratic order, social security and rule of law they experience in Sweden or the UK cannot be delivered by the precarious political conditions of the Kurdish society in the shadow of the political oppression and militarization in the predominantly Kurdish regions. Since homecoming becomes a postponed mission, life in diaspora for the first generation continues to be held in suspension (see Maxey, 2006). Generally, the younger generations of Kurdish and Palestinian diasporas do not view Kurdistan or Palestine as their final destination where they can finally rest and undo the existential anxiety they experience as a result of their in-betweenness and non-belonging (Blachnicka-Ciacek, 2018; Eliassi, 2013; King & Christou, 2010, p. 210). Similar experiences and attitudes toward homeland and returning were evident among Palestinian interviewees who appreciated the existing social security in Sweden, but they were not sure that this can endure due to anti-immigrant discourses in Sweden: Consider for instance Muhammad and the dilemma that he faces regarding the issues of belonging, returning and homeland in the context of statelessness.

> I usually say that I am from Palestine. Because when we people ask me where I am from, that question is often directed toward my origin. Sometimes, I have said that I am from Lund. But the subsequent question was 'where are you from?' 'originally?' because they see that you are dark-haired. Then I say Palestine if that is what pleases you. This question is really difficult for Palestinians. When I was in Palestine, they told me that I was too Swedish because I put on my security belt in the car and I stood at the queue waiting for my turn. This is a concrete example that whatever you do, you do not really belong. You are either too Palestinian or too Swedish. This is why I am stateless even when I have Swedish passport. I do not have a homeland to go to. If Sweden suddenly says: "Expel all wogs!" Where should I go? I cannot go to Palestine because it does not exist. There is the West Bank and Gaza and I am not from these places because my family is from Haifa and Haifa is now part of Israel. We cannot

> return there. I cannot go to Lebanon because I am an immigrant there too. It is tragic when you think about this. You belong neither here nor there. (Muhammad, a 27 years old Palestinian man, Sweden)

The possibility of being evicted was raised by several interviews giving that anti-Muslim political parties are gaining power in the West. For Palestinians, the idea of returning is deeply complicated given that many cities and villages that were once Palestinians are in Israeli custody and have been reshaped by Israeli Jewish presence. It is conspicuous that Palestinians like the Kurds are shuttled between exclusionary nation-building projects in the Middle East and Western Europe. The Palestinian condition of homelessness and statelessness is permeated by an ontological insecurity (see Noble, 2005) where they do not feel that they are allowed to develop attachments and invest emotions and energy in peoples and places outside of Palestine as their homes. Mona explains this situation metaphorically:

> As soon as I hear the word stateless I think about myself. Because the word is part of my background and identity. It is a difficult situation because my grandparents left Palestine and they left Lebanon and lived in Syria where my father and my mother were born. They grow up there and I was born there, then we left Syria and now I am in Sweden and wonder what next destination will be. Because you are never safe whether you will live here or are allowed to live here. I might be obliged to leave one day. This is like as you have been in a love relationship and you have been hurt, abandoned, humiliated and violated. After this relationship you will meet a new person that might appear as the perfect one but then you get reminded that you have already experienced this situation and can be once more abandoned. What can I do to trust this new person? Statelessness is like a relationship that you experience with every person that you fall in love with and get abandoned and treated badly. The fear becomes part of your identity because whenever you go, you are not fully accepted. Sweden can today be the perfect partner but still there is a fear that this relationship can change and end. If I have a state, then I will not be so afraid because I have a place where I can seek refuge. You can make a choice to stay or leave, as many immigrants can do when they have their own states. There is no Palestine to return to now and Syria is not an option due to the war there. (Mona, a 30 years old Palestinian woman, Sweden)

In Mona's account, there is not much romantic or celebratory about being a stateless in a world where certain people enjoy nationalism and feeling at home, while stateless peoples are exposed to violence and expulsion. The experience of the stateless differs dramatically from self-appointed cosmopolitan figures who can choose mobility and claim the world as their homes, and having the privilege to enjoy embracement by a nation-state with its citizenship and belonging (see Ahmed, 1999). Statelessness as a form of vulnerability also informs Mona's desire that it is mainly by attaining a Palestinian state with an effective sovereignty that a non-alienated Palestinian identity and presence in the world can be secured. However, this sovereign longing becomes difficult in a world where nation-state asserts the idea of ethno-national homogeneity and unitary notions of homeland, as I will discuss below.

'Statelessness Means a Grave Without an Address'

We live in a world ordered by what Connor (2001, p. 53) defines as "homelands in a world of states". This entails that different peoples have given names to geographical places and call them their primordial place of being. For instance, the name Turkey indicates that it is the land or country of the Turks, despite the fact that there are other constituencies like Kurds, Assyrians and Armenians who are living within that political space. Despite not being a state, this applies also to Kurdistan, which literally means the land of the Kurds, while in reality it is also a political space that is home and homeland to Assyrians, Turkmens and Arabs. According to Connor (2001), the notion of homeland is deeply linked to the idea of ancestry and family. While majority of the states in the world are multi-ethnic or multinational, they are also multihomelands. This needs to be taken into consideration when we assess political instability and ethnic conflicts in the world. Different ethno-national movements have some form of ambitions to become masters of their homes or homelands. When a dominant group reduces the multihomelands to a uni-homeland, minoritized groups initiate political and armed struggle to assert their presence and create a homeland for themselves. Homeland psychology is important to understand why different groups contest or affirm where they belong and where they do not, and what they should do, in order to achieve the lack of this homeland or defend the existing homeland (ibid.). Homeland construction is often linked with exclusive ownership:

> As a consequence of the sense of primal ownership that an ethno-national group harbours toward its homeland, non-members of the ethnic group

> within the homeland are viewed as aliens ('outsiders'), *even if they are compatriots*. They may be endured, even treated equitably. Their stay may be multigenerational. But they remain outsiders or settlers in the eye of the homeland people, who reserve what they deem their inalienable right to execute their primary and exclusive claims to the homeland whenever they desire. (ibid., p. 64, emphasis in original)

This idea of primal ownership is constitutive to how ethno-national hierarchies are constructed and justified, when the 'core' group assumes itself as having the privileged status to dictate the rule of belonging and non-belonging, privilege and disadvantage. Certainly, for members of stateless group, the questions of belonging and homelessness are both lived and embodied. It is in this context that statelessness becomes a status injury in a world of nation-states (Eliassi, 2016; Said, 1999). For stateless peoples; "The struggle for the homeland becomes the struggle to constitute a ground on which human beings can have their integrity" (Bowman, 1994, p. 149). The Jewish desire for becoming a nation was deeply rooted in the experience of disrespect and lacking self-respect as a people among other peoples (see Baron, 2018). Although most migrants can experience estrangement, alienation and homesickness when they live far from their homelands, for members of stateless peoples who have been violently displaced and expelled, there is also a sense of '*statesickness*', that entails a strong longing for a sovereign state as a central solution to their sense of non-belonging in the world. Consider the following quote by a 70-year-old Palestinian refugee in Sweden about statelessness:

> Nothing, you are zero. A people without a state are nothing. Nothing. We are struggling daily to survive because we do not have a state. It is a catastrophe that we do not have a state. Everybody puts you in jail, kills you and nobody care about you. If a Palestinian is killed, nobody asks about him because he does not have a state to protect him. Many people have their states that care about them. But for you as Palestinian, who cares about you? Israel? An orphan is better than a stateless because you do not exist if you do not have a state. An orphan might have relatives that can take of him/her but we do not have that and nobody embraces us. A human being without a homeland is nothing. Your homeland is one of the most intimate issues you talk about in your life. If you are stateless, it is like when nobody asks you if you are sick, hungry or thirsty. But when you have a state, you belong to a state that can care about you. Just look at Israel, it can start a war over an Israeli citizen, hundreds of Palestinians are

> killed, nobody cares. You feel that you are weak. In Sweden, I am nobody but in Palestine I have my roots there and when people pass by my grave, they know that I belong to a rooted Palestinian family and not a rootless person that nobody knows about him. My family is rooted in Palestine. Our flesh and blood are part of Palestinian soil now. Statelessness means a grave without an address. You are gone. (Karim, a 70 years old Palestinian man, Sweden)

Thus, statelessness adds a further dimension to the sense of alienation, aloneness and political otherness in the context of migration. This framing of statelessness provided above by the interviewee is best understood as a response to the political oppression and powerlessness that Palestinians experience as a stateless people in the context of the Israeli occupation but also in relation to the experiences of ethnic exclusion and otherness in West European contexts. Moreover, Karim adopted a 'Bismarckian terminology' (see Connor, 2001, p. 53) when he talked about the mixture of Palestinian blood with Palestinian soil. While the interviewee above appreciated the Swedish passport and expressed his gratitude toward the Swedish state for its hospitality toward the Palestinians refugees, he was not convinced that Sweden was his homeland due to his degraded immigrant background. He has been told on several occasions that if he does not like Sweden, he can leave, and that immigrants have destroyed Sweden. It is in this context that Connor (2001, p. 65) maintains that dominant groups do not need to use physical violence to expel migrants, but they can create "a generally unfriendly atmosphere or policies favouring the homeland people". This is also what Israel has done to the Palestinians by degrading their citizenship rights, identity and history and institutionalizing the Jewish primal ownership of Israel. This political tendency is conspicuously striking in Western Europe, where Muslim and non-white migrants are problematized as causing disintegration and undermining national cohesion. For instance, a central discursive rhetoric used by the anti-immigrant political party *Sweden Democrats* is based on the idea that 'real Swedes' do not longer recognize their own homeland due to uncontrolled and irresponsible migration policies from the Middle East. This is based on the idea that the 'strangers' have made their homes in a country where the natives should feel at home but no longer feel that they are its master. This is a politics of resentment that is shaping many Western societies (see Connor, 2001; Duyvendak, 2011; Hochschild, 2016). According to Amin (2012), across

Europe, a nostalgic identity politics is coupled with exclusionary politics against non-white migrants. It is assumed that by excluding the non-white migrants from being and having an equal place in Europe, that the collective well-being of the white European nationals can be secured. Expert and opinion formers warn if this does not happen, Europe will face a catastrophic future.

If we return to Karim, the Palestinian interviewee above, the state is viewed as a protective 'father' that provides safety and defends its citizens against external danger and violence. To illustrate this, Israel is invoked as an example that disproportionately compensates the losses of Israeli/Jewish lives, when it targets Palestinians. Relatedly, a Kurdish interviewee in Sweden viewed the muscular and militarized Israel as the model for the Kurds to adopt in order to defend themselves against the predatory states in the Middle East. After many years of exile, the same interviewee talks about his return to his village in Kurdistan, a village that was exposed to the genocidal campaign of the Iraqi state in 1980s:

> In 1995, When I entered Kurdistan for the first time after my migration, I could not believe that human beings can commit such crimes against humanity. It was a full-scale destruction of Kurdistan by Saddam's regime. I could not see a village that was not destructed by that regime. I was witnessing this through the windows of the car that was taking us to my village. When I arrived there, it was empty. All memories that I had with the trees and the stones in my village were gone. I cried and cried when I saw that destruction. Tears cannot heal the pain. Witnessing such human disaster cannot be healed by tears. Those who did this cannot be regarded as human beings. This hatred cannot disappear and remains eternal against Iraq. I will never forget the Arabs of Iraq. Never never. If all Kurds forgive them, I will not forgive them. I am not saying that I want to kill Arabs but that crime has to be remembered and embodied in the same way as the Jews remember the experiences of Holocaust. You cannot forgive those enemies that want to eradicate you. We should do like Israel, to chase the killers of the Kurds and execute them so our enemies do not dare to take a Kurdish life. Is there anyone who dares to take the life of a Jewish person? Israel will demolish the killers of its people. If Palestinians kill a Jew, Israel will kill 100 Palestinians. I am not asking for revenge but we should not forget our enemies and the innocent Kurds who were killed by the Iraqi army. (Rezgar, a 63 years old man, Kurdistan Region-Iraq, Sweden)

This illuminates how destruction of homeland and sites of belonging can produce a tormented Kurdish identity that views militarization of Kurdish identity as an antidote against the state oppression that targets the Kurds in the Middle East. Although the interviewee points out that he is not after killing Arabs or taking revenge, there is a strong resentment against the atrocities that the Arab constituency has carried out against the Kurds in Iraq. His assumption is based on the idea that it is only a creating a muscular Kurdish state, that Kurdish lives and homeland can be defended and secured. It is not a coincidence that Rezgar underlines the role of remembering as a tool of resistance against injustices. Before envisioning an egalitarian future, the past must be taken into consideration and states need to address and resolve political injustices and past histories of atrocities against minoritized groups (see Eliassi, 2013). Rezgar added that "there is no day that I do not think about Kurdistan's independence and every time I put my head on the pillow, that idea can come to my head. I will live with that hope until that day I die". In 2019, I was informed that he had passed away and his body was sent back to Kurdistan in order to be buried in his home village. This act of burial in one's 'original' homeland is supposed to create a naturalized bond between the body and the soil. But it is also about being able to make claim to it and have the right to be there. In contrast to Rezgar, the Palestinian interviewee Karim was so frustrated that he could not get buried in his homeland if he dies and wondered why a 'rootles Zionist Jew' can monopolize that right: "Ariel Sharon is buried in our soil and who allowed him to be buried there. He is an invader. Occupation forces have to leave soon or later. This soil is too sacred for us. Palestine is not just a word but everything for us Palestinians. Palestine will return". Geopolitics, ethno-national conflicts and nation-building processes impinge highly on the narratives of the Kurdish and Palestinian interviewee when it comes to what homeland is and how it can be restored. For both Kurds and particularly the Palestinians, a defiant nostalgia plays an important role in creating "a sense that longing and loss must be maintained, consciously hung onto, across the years and across the generations, in the teeth of attempts to smooth over the past, because to do otherwise would be to allow the occupiers to win" (Bonnett, 2016, p. 104).

Despite the political difficulty and the legal hurdles that many Palestinians experience in regard to returning to Palestine, there is also a widespread fear of facing the unpleasant realities of Palestine, even if the possibility of returning exists. A 30-year old Palestinian woman illustrates this condition:

> My Swedish and Palestinian friends often tell me that I speak so beautifully about Palestine although I have never been there. They have told me: 'We give you the advice to never visit Palestine because you will be destroyed after being there'. I tell them that they frighten me and ask them why they say like that. They tell me: 'When you go down there, you will see how dirty it is there, you see the corruption, you see the division among Palestinians, you see all the nasty things that you do not want to see in Palestine'. This creates a lot of frustration and these experiences demolish one's worldview of Palestine. I am still living and dreaming about Palestine through my grandparents' words that there is a community; everybody cares about each other, the old Palestinian woman who is preparing Za'atar, an old man who is picking olives from the olive tree and produces olive oil. I have a very romantic image of Palestine. I do not know if it is the correct image but it is this image that makes Palestine to be alive within me. (Mona, a 30 years old Palestinian woman, Sweden)

Acts of forgetting and remembering (Ahmed, 1999) characterize the life narratives of many migrants in relation to what they have left behind and what they yearn for. Although Palestine is viewed as the 'true home' by many Palestinians, it is not certain that they are acquainted with the reality of their ancestral homeland due to the political transformations of the Palestinians society in the context of Israeli occupation and intra-Palestinian political rivalry represented by the political parties Fatah and Hamas. Relatedly, despite nostalgic representation of the homeland by some of the Kurdish interviewees, Lara was not sure that Kurdish diaspora was so romantic about their homeland but depicted it largely in negative terms due to the power abuse of the ruling elites:

> Home is imaginary and it is the place where you are comfortable and you do not need to legitimize yourself all the time why you are here. I feel that the Kurds are not always so romantic about the Kurdistan Region because they do not point to the positive things all the time but the negative things like corruption in Kurdistan. (Lara, a 24 years old woman, Kurdistan-Region-Iraq, the UK)

In effect, this negative representation of Kurdistan Region dominates the political discourse of Kurdish diasporas, since many Kurds viewed this Kurdish rule as a historical moment to establish a political order based on equality and not patrimonial power abuse that the ruling political parties are contributing to. Obviously, this critique against Kurdistan Region is often refuted by the ruling elites as complicit with foreign plots to undermine the Kurdish rule.

If Mona expressed her dreams and anxiety about visiting and returning to Palestine, Karmi who had spent most of her life in Britain critically engages with her encounter with Palestine after leaving it, when Israel was founded. Tellingly, the title of her book is: *Return: A Palestinian Memoir*:

> What on earth did I ever come to this place, I asked myself again? What made me imagine that there was anything here for someone like me? I looked back on my whole assignment in 'Palestine' and realized that I have achieved none of my aims because it would never have been possible in the Palestine that I found. I had travelled to the land of my birth with a sense of return, but it was a return to the past, to the Palestine of distant memory, not to the place that is now. The people who lived in this Palestine were nothing to do with the past I was seeking nor were they part of some historical tableau frozen in time that I could reconnect with. This Palestinian world I had briefly joined was different: a new-old place, whose people have moved on from where I had them fixed in my memory, had made of their lives what they could, and found ways to deal with the enemy who ruled them. (Karmi, 2015, p. 313)

In Karmi's account, her images and memories of Palestine did not match the reality of the present Palestine. Prior to their return, many displaced migrants are enthusiastic about "the great magic of the return" (Kundera, 2002, p. 5) but when encountered with the reality of their nostalgic homeland, they experience what Kundera aptly calls "the pain of ignorance" (ibid., p. 6). However, it would naïve to assume that all migrants have the same structural conditions and constraints when they decide to return or visit their homelands. Palestinians are exiled from their homeland and their private homes are besieged by people who have expelled Palestinians and claim themselves to be natives of this land. Literally, Palestinian homes and lives are in "alien custody" (ibid., p. 267). This experience is reflected in Karmi's encounter with those people who now control Palestinian homes and streets and assert themselves as the natives:

> The streets and villas we passed had different inhabitants now, people from faraway places we have never heard of in those innocent days of 1940s Palestine: Kiev, Minsk, Pinsk, Byelostok, Riga, Vilna, Lodz – all towns and

> cities in Lithuania, Ukraine or Poland that could have been from Mars for all the connection they had with us Palestinians. (ibid., pp. 116–117)

One can argue what is wrong with Ukrainian or Lithuanian Jews to live in Palestine and share the same political space as their homes? The problem is that these Jews did not move to Palestine to live there as its residents but aggressively asserted themselves, according to the logic of Zionism, as settlers and turned its Palestinians inhabitants into undesired aliens and 'terrorists'. The exclusivity of Zionist claims and suppression of Palestinians presence are central to foundation of Israel (see Said, 1999, p. 62). This is very similar to what happened in the US when white migration asserted itself as the true owners of a territory that was inhabited by native Indians. The US is *par excellence* a settler state and not an immigrant state as it is euphemistically called (see Mamdani, 2020). This applies also to Canada, Australia and New Zealand. Despite her disappointment upon her return to Palestine, Karmi views the return at the heart of the Palestinian issue since "Without it, the injustices that had blighted our lives for generations would never cease" (ibid., pp. 314–315). The older generation transmit romanticized narratives about Palestine to the younger generations of Palestinian migrants that can function as a motivational device to kindle the energy of the subsequent generations of Palestinians to not give up the idea of Palestine and continue their struggle against Israeli occupation. Undoubtedly, place holds a central place in the memory of Palestinians since place functions as an immediate reference and a symbol for what they have lost and long for, a return that is criminalized (Matar, 2011). According to some of the Palestinian interviewees, the existence of refugee camps was a central reminder to the Palestinians, that they lacked a home and need to keep to the idea of return:

> As long as there are refugee camps, Palestinians will continue dreaming about returning to Palestine. Palestinians have suffered a lot in refugee camps in the Middle East. We are discriminated on daily basis because of our identity. This treatment reminds the Palestinians about the heavy price that they pay due to their statelessness. Oppression and statelessness strengthen the will of Palestinians to return to Palestine. The refugee camps are like a symbol for our statelessness and the struggle for Palestinians and the need of Palestinians to create a Palestinian state. The refugee camps stand for a dream of returning to Palestine. (Karim, 70 years old Palestinian man, Sweden)

According to Hilal et al. (2018, p. 170), the lives of Palestinian refugees are characterized by extraterritoriality and return. While extraterritoriality points to the "endless present of homelessness", return concerns nostalgic yearning for a utopia. Likewise, the extraterritoriality of Palestinian lives in refugee camps is an extension of marginalization and exclusion engendered by the foundation of Israel. It is difficult to detach the question of return from decolonization and it would be implausible for Palestinians to return to Palestine without decolonizing Israel. However, Hilal et al. (2018) suggest that it is difficult to reverse time and there is also a need to go beyond pathologization of refugees in need of cure, that can only occur through returning. Accordingly, "during the sixty-five years of exile, conditions have changed not only in the cities, towns, and villages that were cleansed, but also in the places of refugee, where a new political culture has gradually started to articulate itself" (ibid., p. 171). Karim might be right that the existence of refugee camps and Palestinian refugees and their desire of return challenge the sovereign power of Israel. However, containing Palestinian refugees in refugee camps under severe life conditions is ethico-politically questionable, that some Arab states endorse. It is also not a coincidence that Israel resists the return of Palestinian refugees, that can undermine Israel's demographic and ethno-symbolic power based on Jewish supremacy. Despite their precarious condition, Israel does not view the Palestinian refugees as a vulnerable group, but consider them largely as enemies from which to be protected. This securitized notion of Palestinian refugees explains why Israel has violently targeted Palestinian refugee camps as sites of struggle (ibid., p. 173). In this same context, Sayigh (2015) points out the importance of the Palestinians living in the refugee camps since they:

> offer fora of resistance to both Israeli hegemony and late liberalism's vision of the future 'development' of the Arab region. Though not currently in a state of militancy, Palestinian refugee camps form nonetheless 'communities of memory' in that they incorporate stateless people who trace their origin back to Palestine. The very existence of camps commemorates the 1948 Nakba and the 'bad life' they enfold pushes their memories to struggle for restoration, as such camps form an evident obstacle to the disappearance of self-identified Palestinians. (pp. 2–3)

Several studies have pointed to the importance of the camp Palestinians as the quintessential figure of Palestinian identity and resistance. It is by enduring suffering in exile and in the refugee camps, that they maintain their will to continue the resistance against the Israeli state (Achilli, 2021; Sayigh, 1979). Although Palestinian migrants in Sweden are aware that a 'pre-Israel' Palestine is virtually impossible, they tend to assert Palestine as a necessity to be included in individual and collective life projects of Palestinians in order to avoid territorial obliteration of their national home. This self-assertion by Palestinians and the process of authentication of Palestinian identity in diasporic contexts need to be situated within the context of Israeli denial and inferiorization of Palestinian existence and identity.

(Un)imagining Statehood

While attaining Kurdish statehood was a desirable goal by a majority of the Kurdish research participants, there were also anti-state positions that challenged the hegemony of state in the world. This perspective came predominantly from interviewees who adhered to leftist and feminist ideologies. It should be underlined that leftism and nationalism do not necessarily stand in opposition to each other but my choice of highlighting these voices is due to the fact that Kurdish national movements in different parts of Kurdistan are shuttled between ideas of national liberation, nationalism, statehood, federalism and democratic autonomy. In this respect, Hana who actively supports Rojava underlined that her struggle is mainly about socialism, feminism and national rights without the need to create a new state:

> We Kurds do not need more borders but we need more rights. Border means both a system and a jail. We Kurds have so many borders, Turkey, Iraq, Iran and Syria. We want our rights as Kurds. Kurds want a democratic autonomy in Syria. I would like to have a Kurdish state but it is not my priority now. My main goal is to be able to speak my language and express my identity and having Kurdish schools whenever I want it without being afraid of an Arab regime. (29 years old woman, Kurdistan-Syria, UK)

The account above refers to Kurdistan Workers' Party's (PKK) rhetorical move from nationalism toward democratic autonomy that asserts feminism, socialism, ethnic and religious pluralism and highly decentralized self-governance (see Matin, 2020). Likewise, Dilar, who is a young woman from Kurdistan of Turkey was very critical of the idea of the nation-state and deconstructed the idea of the statehood in the following way:

> It is both important and not important to have a nation-state. In order to exist as a nation or as a people you should have a nation-state. *The idea of nation-state immediately entails an attack on Kurdish identity since it excluded Kurds from its definition.* Absence of a Kurdish nation-state is automatically defined as non-existence of the Kurds. In order to exist in this world, you need to have a nation-state. Kurds want recognition as a people and not a state. But if the idea of the nation-state is a modern phenomenon from eighteenth century and does not have a long history, which means that we human beings should not need to have a nation-state or belong to a state. (28 years old woman, Kurdistan-Turkey, Sweden, emphasis added)

Dilar's deconstructive rhetoric shows that we are both captive of a world order dominated by the nation-state but at the same time she rejects the idea that it is natural for human beings to possess or belong to nation-state. This perspective was mainly dominant among the Kurds with leftist inclination who were ambivalent about how to reconcile leftist ideas with Kurdish national rights. Nevertheless, even the leftist could not neglect the hegemony of states and borders in the world, which is illustrated by Lana who defines herself as a "hardcore Kurdish Alevi and feminist activist":

> I know that we Kurds do not have a state and a country of our own. Obviously, that hurts because we live in a world where there are borders, territories, states and governments. If these things did not exist in this world, everybody would be living a free life. I am saying this because I am a Kurd without a state. I do not think that people who have their states would say what I am saying. A Turkish, an English or a French person would not say this because they have that and want to keep that. But as a person without a state, it would have been a perfect world if there were not borders and territories. But because we live in world like that, I know this will never change. (32 years old woman, Kurdistan-Turkey, UK)

The political and ideological power of the nation-state has attained such universality that is now seen as inevitable part of human life. Lana's position illustrates that the world order does not benefit the stateless people even if stateless people give up the idea of statehood and imagine a non-state-centric world community. For some of the Kurdish interviewees, there was nothing radical about having a state since this is how the world is structured, divided, experienced and governed:

> We live in a system in this world where everybody has its own state. There are tribes who have their own states. South Sudan became independent. I have also this right to have my own state. It is my decision to have it and I do not want to hear people telling me that I am a nationalist because I want to have my own state. This world is nationalist so why should not I be nationalist? United Nations also agree that every nation has right to their national self-determination. *We are not asking for something new but for something the whole world is enjoying and knows well.* Kurds will always be in trouble if they do not have their own state. (Sherko, a 46 years old man from Kurdistan-Syria, UK, emphasis added)

The perspective above is based on careful political calculation of the world order as dominated by nation-states. In this view, creation of a Kurdish state is seen as solution to escape ethnic oppression in the Middle East. It also raises the ethico-political legitimacy of the Kurds to claim statehood since members of stateful groups can simultaneously enjoy nationalism and engage with deconstructive rhetoric about nationalism (Radhakrishnan, 1996, p. 165). As Calhoun (2007) argues in relation to those groups who are denied collective autonomy and self-determination: "Solidarity need not always be national, and need not always develop from traditional roots. But for many of those treated most unfairly in the world, nations and traditions are potentially important resources" (p. 302). The same interviewee above suggested that when he had his Kurdish state, then he could sit down with Arabs, Turks and Persians and determine together a new future for the Middle East where they could dismantle the borders between the nations and create a Middle East that resembles the European Union. Moreover, Sherko added that this is, for the moment, not his first priority which is the national rights of the oppressed Kurds in the Middle East where statehood is central to attain these rights. Concurrently, Aras, who is a 58-year-old man from the Kurdistan Region of Iraq and lives in the UK talked about the danger of normalizing and naturalizing statelessness as the fate of the Kurds, whereas the Arabs, Turks and Persians can continue and behave as masters in the states where Kurds live as an inferiorized people. Aras added that since these groups control the states, they become also its representatives to the outer world, while the

Kurds "have to sit down and tell the history of the Kurds during a century so people can understand who you are and why you do not have a state". In the same context, Sherzad underlined that although it is important for the Kurds to have a state in order to protect themselves against the states that have dominated the Kurds, it was far more important to him to have a state that is democratic:

> There are couples who cannot have children and there are couples who have many children. The couple without children might wish to have a child whether he or she is disabled, blind or deaf just to enjoying the joy of having a child. We Kurds tend to be like that because we do not have a state. That is why we should be careful and not create a state that kills people in the name of the state. Saddam killed hundred thousand people in Iraq in the name of Iraqi identity because Iraq was a state that served the interest of the Sunni Arabs. We Kurds should strive to have a state but not a state by name, it has to be democratic and not ruled by a family or a political party. (49 years old man, Kurdistan-Iraq, Sweden)

This diasporic vision illustrates that Kurds in diaspora do not necessarily or uncritically embrace the idea of Kurdish statehood when the state cannot guarantee democracy, rule of law and effective citizenship. Thus, statehood is not only perceived as a liberating or an opportunity-enhancing vehicle but it can also play a destructive role in relation to individual and groups that do not comply with the ethnopolitical identity of the state and its mode of political governance. Against this background, Walzer (2001) has argued that nationalism as an ideology engages significantly with the question of place. Since agents of nationalism make claim to places contested by different ethno-religious groups, state borders are often insecure, disputed and can become enacted in blood. Walzer adds that the "critical test of any nationalism comes when it has to cope with the surprise of a new nation, or more accurately, of a new liberation movement laying claim to nationhood" (ibid., p. 211). In this respect, I asked Alan, that his strong desire for a Kurdish state can entail creating new minorities which oppose a Kurdish state that hierarchizes Kurdishness as its main building block. Alan and Hassan provided their positions in relation to this thorny question in the following way:

> I want to have a Kurdish state but I do not want a Kurdish state that is fascist like the Turkish state, the Arab states of Iraq and Syria, and the Persian state. Because in Kurdistan we have different groups like Yazidis

> and Christians and they should be protected and have their rights. I talked to my Christian friends and tell them you Christians have right to your own state inside Kurdistan like the Vatican. I cannot allow myself as a Kurd to claim statehood but deprive Christians from that right. We cannot go on and continue with a fascist face. (a 45 years old man, Kurdistan-Syria, the UK)

> I think that a potential Kurdish state should protect first and foremost the minorities in Kurdistan. If you want to be different from the neighbouring states, then you have to treat minorities better. The Kurdish state should be different and I do not want a Kurdistan that says 'on language', 'one culture' and 'one identity'. It is not fair to groups who are not Kurdish and we should not repeat the mistakes of our Arab, Persian and Turkish neighbours. (a 53 years old man, Kurdistan-Turkey, the UK)

A dominant narrative that exists among the Kurd is informed by the idea that unlike their Arab, Turkish and Persian neighbors, they are less religious and more tolerant toward diversity. In this respect, Mustafa, a Kurd of Syria referred to the Kurdistan Region of Iraq, where thousands of Arabs live under Kurdish rule without being oppressed. For him, this shows that "Kurds are better than their neighbours since they can forgive the same people that committed genocide against the Kurds". Violence and harassment against Kurds (in Arab cities) or Arabs (in Kurdish cities) are undoubtedly exploited by Kurdish and Arab politicians to mobilize national and racial sentiments, often calling for some form of revenge. Elite discourse matters and affects the salience of racism and vicious nationalism in the Middle East. There are no political guarantees that Kurds cannot become oppressive in relation to minorities and national groups that seek full recognition and representation of their national identities, but it would be equally dangerous to claim that Kurds cannot choose a political template that endorses heterogeneity and avoiding the predatory routes of ethno-nationalism. In this vein, Kardo argued that there is no need to have a new nation-state but can create a new union for the peoples of the Middle East:

> We can create a union where everybody has their identity recognized with open borders. A union where no group should be oppressed because of their ethnicity, culture, language and religion. We can blame a lot of the problem on the nation-states. If we create a united Kurdistan, we should

> know that there are other peoples living inside Kurdistan. We cannot subordinate them and tell them to become Kurdish. I think about Syriac and Assyrians who live in Kurdistan. We do not have right to oppress them as we have been oppressed. They should be equally involved in governing the region and should have right to their culture, religion, and language. They should also receive education in their own language. We might call this state for Mesopotamia and not Kurdistan in order to not associate it with a certain people. (a 34 years old man, Kurdistan-Turkey, Sweden)

Although diaspora and exile can be hotbeds of nationalism, there are also diasporic voices and perspectives that can envision a political order beyond ethno-national hierarchy by championing diversity and equality. A few Kurdish interviewees also emphasized that there are many Kurdish dialects and all these dialects have to be recognized and respected. The response to Kurdish statelessness is not the Turkish model where everybody has to become Turkish and speak Turkish. Kardo seems to be aware that when a people monopolize a state and asserts its identity as the overarching identity, the path to exclusion of different constituencies is not remote. It is in this regard that he even proposes the suspension of the name 'Kurdistan' in order to create a polity that does not solely or mainly serve the interest of a specific ethno-national constituency. This line of argument converges with the political rhetoric of PKK that views the nation-state model as site of colonial, ethnic and capitalist oppression. As Dirlik (2002) has argued, the nation-building is in itself a colonial practice since nations establish boundaries and promote homogenous national identities and cultures at the expense of local cultures and identities. It is with respect to this political erasure, that there are vocal Kurdish voices that highlight the internal diversity of the Kurdish constituency and challenge those attempts that aim to impose one language on the Kurds as a putative nation. Against this background, Casier (2011) has shown that the Kurdish movement in Kurdistan of Turkey seeks to ideologically appropriate and re-imagine Mesopotamia as a form of break with the classical nation-state model that underpins ethnic and racist oppression. This ideological shift by the Kurdish movement points to the importance of the Kurds to democratize themselves in order to help the democratization process in the Middle East (ibid.). Equally, Baris (2020) maintains that the major Kurdish movements in Turkey and Syria are aversive toward state-building and aim to create a political community that differs from the nation-state. According to Baris (2020), the Kurdish conflict in these two countries is no longer based on a competition between the Kurdish nationalism and the nationalism of the states of Turkey and Syria, but rather a competing vision of a political community that endorse strong local autonomy for different constituencies beyond the divisive politics of nationalism (Baris, 2020). However, the geopolitical situation of the Kurds is far from favorable for such a political vision, where the states violently target every Kurdish attempt to refashion the principle of inclusion and exclusion in the states in which they are subjected to colonial and nationalist oppression. What further complicates this political vision is that there is no single Kurdish movement but a variety of Kurdish political parties with disparate ideological and often divergent political agendas.

Pluralizing Claims to Home(Land)

It is often difficult for migrants to fully feel at home, whether they are 'here/home' or 'there/away'. Home and away are often interchangeable in diasporic narratives since they are not dichotomous (Radhakrishnan, 1996). In the same vein, Ahmed (1999) argues that "Interestingly, it is the 'real' home, the very space from which one imagines oneself to have originated, and in which one projects the self as both homely and original, that is the most unfamiliar: it is there that one is guest, relying on the hospitality of others. It is this home which, in the end, becomes Home through the very *failure* of memory" (Ahmed, 1999, p. 330, emphasis in original). While non-white migrants are often assumed to homesick, there is also a tendency among 'white natives' across Western Europe to delve into nostalgia about how their homes looked like before the arrival of the Others. The question of home has become the central device of inclusion and exclusion in contemporary Europe (see Duyvendak, 2011). Homeland can be experienced in different ways. For racialized groups, the idea of 'original' homeland can be embraced as a place where ethnic and religious discrimination do not shape one's life. Homeland is a marker of belonging where people can live their culture and identities without being stigmatized in public and everyday life. For people living far away from the assumed homeland, it can be imagined as a magical space that can solve the conundrums of alienation and non-belonging. The idea of the 'original' homeland can also be imposed by dominant groups who view racialized migrants as invaders and undesired, and urge them to return to places they are believed to essentially belong. For those who view the 'original' homeland and returning as the solution to their experienced non-belonging, it can turn into a disappointment and further deepen the sense of confusion and otherness. It is not uncommon for migrants to claim that they feel like 'strangers' when they return to their 'original' homeland.

Estrangement is a central feature of migration. Whereas it is important to feel at home and belong, it is equally dangerous to make home to a fetish and turn into an exclusionary symbolic object, which is denied people who are not viewed as legitimate constituents of the society. Stateless diasporas often view themselves as lacking a homeland or assert that their homelands have been 'stolen' or taken over by other groups. This makes search for a political home to a political imperative in the collective identity projects of many members of stateless diasporas. According to Cocks (2006), stateless people who are injured and oppressed by national sovereign power often reproduce a nationalistic ontology through their struggle for sovereign power, which assumedly leads to political freedom. Even when they attain sovereign power, there is no political guarantee that the dynamic of majority/minority or oppressor/oppressed will come to an end. By becoming a majority in the new nation-state that one has achieved, there is a historical tendency that a new group becomes ethnic strangers and a potentially politically threatened and oppressed minority. This makes the nation-state to an inherently problematic form of social organization (Cocks, 2006). Departing from the Israeli-Palestinian experiences, Cocks (2006) provides a compelling account of how the search for national sovereignty by minorities is understood by the majority who has left a minority position and achieved sovereignty. In order to escape subjugation, the minority:

> embraces the institutional ground of its plight as the antidote for it, hammering itself into a sovereign national majority while shifting the costs of minority status to an even more vulnerable population in its way. The latter's predictable reaction to that shift – anger, indignation, violent antagonism – is interpreted by the former as evidence of the continuation of its own threatened minority plight. Such an interpretation leads the new majority to make greater effort to entrench its sovereign mastery, which multiplies the hostile reaction against it, producing another version of the precarious situation that mastery was meant to end. (Cocks, 2006, p. 28)

While Cocks uses this deconstructive rhetoric to create more inclusive forms of social organization than the nation-state, authoritarian regimes as in the case of the Middle East often use this discourse to quell the dissent of stateless people who struggle for parity of participation in the political, social and economic life (Eliassi, 2016). It is worth mentioning that Jewish longing for sovereignty was due to the fact that Jews lacked a secure home to reside (Baron, 2018). However, despite the realization of a Jewish nation and the creation of Israel, these achievements did not entail an end to the Jewish diaspora, although the ultimate political goal of that state was to bring an end to the suffering of the Jewish diaspora and create a political home and safe haven for the Jewish people. In a similar and imbricated context, Radhakrishnan (2012) argues that in the case of Palestinians who lack a sovereign state, it is difficult to valorize exile when "exile is the very political ill that has been plaguing the Palestinian people ever since the founding of the state of Israel in 1948". Since expulsion was imposed on the Palestinians, they are looking to "sovereign nationalization as an answer to their political homelessness" (pp. 40–41).

Statelessness as a form of political homelessness is based on a territorial notion of belonging. As I argued in Chapter 3, members of the Palestinian and Kurdish diasporas view statelessness in different ways. While the Kurdish diaspora describes themselves as stateless to gain political recognition in the international community as an autonomous nation and partly detach themselves from the dominant identities of Iran, Iraq, Syria and Turkey, the Palestinian diaspora considers statelessness as a perilous appellation since it assumedly legitimizes their absence and denies them the right to claim Palestinian territories as their national home. However, this does not entail that Palestinians are not experiencing statelessness:

> Each Palestinian is by definition 'without a state', even if they possess some form of citizenship within the nation in which they currently reside. They continue to feel that they belong to a singular community. They are men and women tied to a human experience, to a memory, to a dream to be realized. A nation without a state, without a right to citizenship; a people rooted in absence of place. The traces of this absence are found in the documents which should represent them: passes from the Lebanese Government, special identity cards for those living in Jerusalem, Egyptian travel documents, a passport with no state, travel documents from the Palestinian authority, Jordanian, European, or American passports. (Hilal & Petti, 2018, p. 75)

The Kurdish and Palestinian interviewees talked about their differences from migrant groups who had their 'own states'. They asserted that they do not have secure national homes to which they could return and live their identities free from ethnic oppression. Relatedly, Kurdish and Palestinian migrants viewed the rise of populist right-wing movements in Western Europe as a threat to their social safety and citizenship rights in Sweden and the UK. They pondered where to go, if these groups gain power, undermine these liberal democracies and decide to evict them from Sweden and the UK. Palestinians have long experiences of evictions in the Middle East, not only from Israel but also from Arab countries. Experiences of otherness in the Middle East and Western Europe strengthened their desire for a national sovereignty, which is ironically the source of their collective suffering and banishment. According to Cocks (2006), collective identities are often hardened as a result of ethnonationalism. The question is how to create new pluralistic political forms where the unequal relations between the sovereign and non-sovereign are not reproduced. Without excusing the political oppression of non-sovereign groups, national identity and the search of a national home constitute a major obstacle to liberation of non-sovereign constituencies. Although this vision seems adventurous and might be interpreted as utopian, it is imperative to create a political form that nurtures equality and heterogeneity where different constituencies can live their lives and identities non-hierarchically. Both stateless and state-linked diasporas have an important political responsibility to "create a political home for a beleaguered people, now humanly enriched and enlarged" (Cocks, 2006, p. 38) than the present choking confines that create destructive political division and undermine social solidarity in our world. Although ideal of home or homeland runs the risk of becoming a politically conservative project with exclusionary effects, "the appropriate response...is not to reject the values of home, but instead to claim those values for everyone" (Young, 2005, p. 151). In order to achieve this goal, there is a need for critical and intellectual engagement with the very idea of home and how we can avoid to provide it with a transhistorical immunity against critique even if it would entail its reconfiguration or suspension. Concurrently, Radhakrishnan (forthcoming) has argued that as soon as we "step out of our domestic ghettos, all we encounter are other such homes, other such domestic enclaves and enclosures each with its own built in walls of intended inclusion and exclusion". When home is conceived as mystical and sacred, intellectual and critical engagements with the very constitution of home are discouraged and at times muted, in the name of the nation, religion or the homeland. To illustrate this position in the context of nationalism and its relation to 'truth', Renan argued that "One cannot feel bitterness towards one's homeland. Better to be mistaken along with the nation than to be too right with those who tell it hard truths" (cited in Said, 2003, p. 148). Criminalization of critique and gratification of home are often "disarmed in the name of piety and loyalty: my dad/mom/family right or wrong" where "Familiarity turns into legitimacy without the benefit of critique" (Radhakrishnan, forthcoming). This is noticeable in the context of ethnonational struggles for justice where critique against the state is interpreted as a 'threat against Islamic brotherhood', 'the Islamic revolution', 'separatism' (in Iran) or as expression of 'anti-Semitism' (in Israel). One important way to make home more inclusionary is to destabilize categories of majority and minority and adopt a non-nationalist template, that does not end up in political hierarchy and exclusive home-making and belonging. Consider for instance, how Mahmoud al-Zahhar who co-founded Hamas and acts a leading member of Hamas envisions a post-Zionist Palestine and the fate of the Israeli Jews:

> They will not be expelled or made to suffer as they fear and as the world accuses us of aiming for. But they have to *learn their place* and understand *they are in our region*, not the other way around. They will live *under our rule* and find peace and contentment, never fear. Islam is a religion of tolerance and justice. (Karmi, 2015, p. 201, emphasis added)

This illustrates that Hamas as a representative of a considerable section of the Palestinian constituency clearly envisions a hierarchical order where putative Muslims are at the top and the Jews included on subordinated terms. The tolerance that Hamas dictates is clearly based on a hierarchical order, where Jews "have to learn their place" because "they are in our region". The Hamas representative is clearly deploying a discourse of autochtony that automatically reproduces inclusion and otherness, hierarchy and subordination. This hierarchical order that Hamas envisions does not only target the Jews, but equally Palestinian Christians, who are putatively co-nationals. According to Pérez (2014), the political imagining of the Palestinian nation that Hamas endorses has the potential to cultivate inequality between Palestinian Muslims and Christians. Offering a *place* to the Christians and the Jews within a prospective Palestinian state does not explain whether these non-Muslim groups will hold an equal role in governing this prospective state (Pérez, 2014), or assigned a position as marked citizens.

Tolerance is not enough to ensure unconditional equality in multi-ethnic and multi-religious societies. As Brown (2006, p. 178) has taught us, "Tolerance as a political practice is always conferred by the dominant, it is always a certain expression of domination even as it offers protection or incorporation to the less powerful". Hence, tolerance is not the same as unconditional equality, recognition and respect of communal differences that the dominant and the secured group can deliver to the marginalized and insecure groups (Brown, 2006). Despite decades of experienced oppression and otherness, by adopting a nationalist template of home-making, there are no political guarantees that Kurds and Palestinians will not deploy exclusionary discourses of home-making in order to restore what they have been deprived from, namely the legitimate right to belong, live their differences and feel at home. This is however not the same thing as suggesting a muffling or an erasure of the very differences of Kurds and Palestinians, that the states have based their oppression on. It might be perfidious to demand a post-national humanism from the Palestinians and Kurds who are continuously exposed to destructive forms of ethno-religious nationalism in the region and putting the claims of the dominant and the subordinated constituencies in the same ethico-political basket. Therefore, it is primarily the responsibility of the dominant constituency as the crucial gatekeeper to undo its societal privileges, dismantle state-sanctioned and routine violence as a means of producing loyalty and communities. As long as the rights and differences of the *others* are viewed as a threat to the dominant group's ethnocultural existence, peace and conviviality will not prevail, and minoritized groups will carry out their political and armed struggle to reshape the society and alter its hierarchical order. What I suggest, is that the affirmation of ethnic and religious differences should not entail hegemonization of Kurdishness or Palestinianness at the expense of other ethno-religious constituencies that are sharing the same political space or prospective residents who want to live their lives and identities there. It is only by pluralizing and democratizing the notion of home(land) that we can avoid falling into the elephant traps of parochialism and protracted ethno-national and religious conflicts that haunt the Middle East and the wider world.

References

Achilli, L. (2021). The deep play: Ethnicity, the Hashemite Monarchy and the Arab Spring in Jordan. In M. Paolo & O. Idir (Eds.), *Minorities and state-building in the Middle East: The case of Jordan* (pp. 151–173). Palgrave Macmillan.

Ahmed, S. (1999). Home and away: Narratives of migration and estrangement. *International Journal of Cultural Studies, 2*(3), 329–347.

Ahmed, S., Castañeda, C., Fortier, A.-M., & Sheller, M. (2003). Introduction: uprootings/regroundings: Questions of home and migration. In A. Sara, C. Claudia, F. Anne-Marie, & S. Mimi (Eds.), *Uprootings/regroundings: Questions of home and migration* (pp. 1–19). Berg.

Amin, A. (2012). *Land of strangers*. Polity.

Anthias, F. (2006). Belonging in a globalizing and unequal world: Rethinking translocations: In Y.-D. Nira, K. Kalpana, & V. Ulrike (Eds.), *The situated politics of belonging* (pp. 17–31). Sage.

Antonsich, M. (2010). Searching for belonging—An analytical framework. *Geography Compass, 4*(6), 644–659.

Baris, H. (2020). *The Kurdish model of political community: A vision of national liberation defiant of the nation-state*. Lexington Books.

Baron, I. Z. (2018). The contradictions of diaspora: A reflexive critique of the Jewish Diaspora's relationship with Israel. *Journal of International Political Theory, 14*(1), 85–106.

Blachnicka-Ciacek, D. (2018). Palestine as 'a state of mind': Second-generation polish and British Palestinians' search for home and belonging. *Journal of Ethnic and Migration Studies, 44*(11): 1915–1931.

Bonnett, A. (2016). *The geography of Nostalgia: Global and local perspectives on modernity and loss*. Routledge.

Bowman, G. (1994). 'A country of words': Conceiving the Palestinian nation from the position of exile. In L. Ernesto (Ed.), *The making of political identities* (pp. 138–170). Verso.

Brah, A. (1996). *Cartographies of diaspora: Contesting identities*. Routledge.

Brown, W. (2006). *Regulating aversion: Tolerance in the age of identity and empire*. Princeton University Press.

Butter, S. (2015). No place like home? Conceptualizations of "home" in Salman Rushdie's "At the Auction of the Ruby Slippers" and Roshi Fernando's *Homesick*. In K. Florian & S. Klaus (Eds.), *Diasporic constructions of home and belonging* (pp. 349–365). De Gruyter.

Calhoun, C. (2007). Social solidarity as a problem for cosmopolitan democracy. In B. Seyla, S. Ian, & P. Danilo (Eds.), *Identities, affiliations, and allegiances* (pp. 285–302). Cambridge University Press.

Can, M. (2006). *Tätt intill dagarna: berättelsen om min mor*. Nordstedts.

Casier, M. (2011). Beyond Kurdistan? The Mesopotamia Social Forum and the appropriation and re-imagination of Mesopotamia by the Kurdish movement. *Journal of Balkan and near Eastern Studies, 13*(4), 417–432.

Ceuppens, B., & Geschiere, P. (2005). Autochtony: Local or global? New modes in the struggle over citizenship and belonging in Africa and Europe. *Annual Review of Anthropology, 34*, 385–407.

Cocks, J. (2006). Jewish nationalism and the question of Palestine. *Interventions: International Journal of Postcolonial Studies, 8*(1), 24–39.

Cohen, R. (2008). *Global Diasporas: An introduction*. Routledge.

Connor, W. (2001). Homelands in a world of states. In G. Montserrat & H. John (Eds.), *Understanding Nationalism* (pp. 53–73). Polity Press.

Dirlik, A. (2002). Rethinking colonialism: Globalization, postcolonialism, and the nation. *Interventions: International Journal of Postcolonial Studies, 4*(3), 428–448.

Duyvendak, J. W. (2011). *The politics of home: Belonging and nostalgia in Europe and the United States*. Palgrave Macmillan.

Eliassi, B. (2013). *Contesting Kurdish identities in Sweden: Quest for belonging among Middle Eastern Youth*. Palgrave Macmillan.

Eliassi, B. (2016). Statelessness in a word of nation-states: The cases of Kurdish diasporas in Sweden and the UK. *Journal of Ethnic and Migration Studies, 42*(9), 1403–1419.

George, R. M. (1996). *The politics of home: Postcolonial relocations and twentieth century fiction*. University of California Press.

Geschiere, P. (2009). *The Perils of belonging: Autochthony, citizenship, exclusion in Africa & Europe*. Chicago University Press.

Gilroy, P. (2005). *Postcolonial Melancholia*. Columbia University Press.

Guibernau, M. (2013). *Belonging: Solidarity and division in modern societies*. Polity.

Gustafson, P. (2014). Place attachment in an age of mobility. In C. M. Lynne & D.-W. Patrick (Eds.), *Place attachment: Advances in theory, methods and applications* (pp. 37–48). Routledge.

Hage, G. (1998). *White nation: Fantasies of white supremacy in multicultural society*. Routledge.

Hilal, S., & Petti, A. (2018). *Permanent temporariness*. Art and Theory Publishing.

Hochschild, A. R. (2016). *Strangers in their own land: Anger and mourning on the American Right*. The New Press.

hooks, b. (2009). *Belonging: A culture of place*. Routledge.

Karmi, G. (2015). *Return: A Palestinian Memoir*. Verso Books.

Kenny, K. (2013). *Diaspora: A very short introduction*. Oxford University Press.

Kundera, M. (2002). *Ignorance*. Faber and Faber.

Noble, G. (2005). The discomfort of strangers: Racism, incivility and ontological security in a relaxed and comfortable nation. *Journal of Intercultural Studies, 26*(1–2), 107–120.

King, R., & Christou, A. (2010). Cultural geographies of diasporic migration: Perspectives from the study of second-generation "returnees" to Greece. *Population, Space and Place, 16*(2), 103–119.

Kofman, E. (2005). Figures of Cosmopolitan: Privileged nationals and national outsiders. *Innovation, 18*(1), 83–97.

Mamdani, M. (2020). *Neither settler nor native: The making and unmaking permanent minorities*. The Belknap Press of Harvard University Press.

Matar, D. (2011). *What it means to be Palestinian: Stories of Palestinian peoplehood*. I. B. Tauris.

Maxey, R. (2006). "Life in the diaspora is often held in a strange suspension": First generation self-fashioning in Hanif Kureishi's narratives of home and return. *Journal of Commonwealth Literature, 41*(3), 5–25.

Pérez, M. V. (2014). Between religion and nationalism in the Palestinian diaspora. *Nations and Nationalism, 20*(4), 801–820.

Radhakrishnan, R. (1996). *Diasporic mediations: Between home and location*. University of Minnesota Press.

Radhakrishnan, R. (2012). *A said dictionary*. Wiley-Blackwell.

Radhakrishnan, R. (Forthcoming). Notes toward an exilic co-existence. *Synthesis: An anglophone journal of comparative literary studies*.

Rushdie, S. (2012). *Home*. Vintage Minis.

Sayigh, R. (1979). The Palestinian experience: Integration and non-integration in the Arab Ghourba. *Arab Studies Quarterly, 1*(2): 96–112.

Sayigh, R. (2015). Silenced suffering. *Borderlands, 14*(1), 1–20.

Sharma, N. (2014). Belonging. In A. Bridget & K. Michael (Eds.), *Migration: A compass anthology* (pp. 166–167). Compass.

Said, E. W. (1999). *After the last sky: Palestinian lives*. Columbia University Press.

Said, E. W. (2003/1978). *Orientalism*. Penguin Books.

Skey, M. (2011). *National belonging and everyday life: The significance of nationhood in an uncertain world*. Palgrave Macmillan.

Sökefeld, M. (2006). Mobilizing in transnational space: A social movement approach to the formation of diaspora. *Global Network, 6*(3), 265–284.

Walzer, M. (2001). History and national liberation. *Journal of Israeli History, 20*(2–3), 1–8.

Young, I. M. (2005). *On female body experience: 'Throwing like a Girl' and other essays*. Oxford University Press.

CHAPTER 5

Marked Groups and Hierarchies of Citizenship in Authoritarian and Liberal Democratic States

This chapter discusses processes of ethnic inclusion and exclusion in multi-ethnic societies in the Middle East and Western Europe. Nation-building processes often include by exclusion and states use a wide range of policies to deal with non-nationals or migrants through accommodation, assimilation and exclusion (Mylonas, 2012). The chapter seeks to analyze direct and indirect roles of the states or governments in including or excluding particular ethnic groups that are assumed to be non-nationals or 'non-core' groups within their territorial boundaries. In order to exemplify these processes, I aim to analyze the narratives of Kurdish and Palestinian migrants as belonging to two disparate stateless nations and the various citizenship regimes that they have experienced in the Middle East and Western Europe.

The chapter will illuminate how citizenship across these different nation-states is conceived, valued and experienced by Kurdish and Palestinian migrants. The Palestinians who have been interviewed in this study do not have or wish to have an Israeli citizenship. Therefore, I will focus on the Swedish context and their experiences of Swedish citizenship and how it enables their mobility in the context of immobile Palestinians under Israeli occupation and surveillance. In this respect, the question of border and mobility become central in Palestinian lives. In order to

B. Eliassi, *Narratives of Statelessness and Political Otherness*, Minorities in West Asia and North Africa,
https://doi.org/10.1007/978-3-030-76698-6_5

understand the identity formation of different migrant groups, it is important to consider the group position of migrants and national contexts in which they have been situated prior to and after immigration. Whereas the national contexts in the Middle East are by and large characterized, although in different forms and scales, by authoritarian and undemocratic political arrangements, Sweden and the UK are often hailed as world-leading liberal democracies (Eliassi, 2013, 2016). While discussing multicultural policies and redistribution in a broad Western context, Kymlicka praises Sweden for being "one of the strongest and most consistent proponents of a multicultural approach" (Kymlicka, 2010, p. 264). In a European perspective, Sweden is viewed as having the most liberal citizenship law and civic integration requirements (Goodman, 2010). Nevertheless, the exceptional image of Sweden as a tolerant and a multicultural country exempted from racial bigotry and ethnic discrimination has been contested (Pred, 2000). It is argued that ethnic discrimination prevails and affects negatively the life-chances of non-white groups in the wider Swedish society (Eliassi, 2013; Schierup & Ålund, 2011). Mulinari (2009) argues that Sweden has traditionally pursued and practiced an inclusive integration policy vis-à-vis immigrants but the principle of this inclusion has been built upon subordination of immigrants. Since 2000s, Swedish governments and political parties have gradually moved toward assimilationist rhetoric and policies, where Muslims are portrayed as a difficult group to integrate into the Swedish society. The shift toward assimilationism has been enabled by the political success of far-right parties in general elections and the wider society in portraying non-European migrants as a political threat and an economic burden. The inclusive subordination of immigrants has also led to systematic denial of racism within different societal arenas (Mulinari, 2009). Equally, Britain is generally considered as a multicultural state. Since the Second World War and as a result of migration, the United Kingdom has moved from being consisted of an overwhelmingly white and Christian constituency, to a new demographic composition pervaded by diverse ethno-religious communities. In this respect, multiculturalism has come to stand for this demographic change in Britain and how the state can or should respond to this change politically, culturally and legally. This concretely implies what the British state does in relation to the existing diversity, in relation to different modes of dress, language policy, race relations, religious freedom and immigration. In Britain, integration of different ethno-religious communities has been viewed as an important path to an inclusive society marked by diversity (Aschroft & Bevir, 2018). For a long time, Britain's race relations were mainly debated in relation to the Caribbean and South Asian communities and their descendants. This rendered invisible the experiences of migrants from the Middle East. However, this has changed and contemporary Britain's concern with integration and polarization focus predominantly on Muslim migrants. There are various studies that show that racism continues to shape the lives of minoritized groups and subordinated white migrants from Eastern Europe (see Back et al., 2012; Meer & Modood, 2009; Rattansi, 2011). Muslim migrants have come to be viewed as a suspect community that establishes ghettoized and parallel lives incompatible with the liberal values of the British society (see Hickman et al., 2012). In Britain, the critique of multiculturalism has gone so far that political debaters blame multiculturalism for endorsing domestic terrorism (Meer & Modood, 2009). The presumed nexus between Muslim migration and terrorism in Britain has led to stigmatization of multiculturalism where politicians and opinion makers endorse policies based on 'integration', 'muscular liberalism' and 'community cohesion' as a solution to the divisive effects of multiculturalism. By focusing on community cohesion and integrationist discourses, the issues of socio-economic inequalities and racism have been marginalized (Rattansi, 2011). In a comparative perspective, Britain is viewed as a country where ethnic and religious diversity is more accommodated and accepted (Heath & Demireva, 2014). While religion is deployed as a marker to create ethno-national hierarchies of belonging in both Britain and Sweden, unlike Britain, the question of whiteness is intensely under-communicated in Swedish public debates when ethnic discrimination and racism targeting non-white migrants are deliberated. It is mostly the issues of cultural differences and lack of command of the Swedish language that are viewed as justifying the political, cultural and economic exclusion of non-white migrants in Sweden (see Eliassi, 2013).

In the context of the Middle East, Butenschon (2000) points out that *singularism* underpins political communities and citizenship regimes and the ways allocation of rights and duties is legitimized. Singularism is based on the idea of political community with a single collective identity where the state is viewed as embodying that collective identity. Turkey and Israel represent such a model as a principle of political organization and can be categorized as ethnocracies that ethnicize citizenship and stipulate rights on ethnic or religious bases (see Ghanem & Khatib, 2017; Kimmerling, 2001; Shafir & Peled, 2002; Yeğen, 2009; Yiftachel, 2006). In an ethnocracy, the principle is a state *of* and *for* a particular ethnic identity that claims ownership to the state and its citizenship and power (Butenschon, 2000). Even those Palestinian Arabs who hold Israeli citizenship are treated and considered as third-class citizens, half-citizens or stateless citizens (Ghanem & Khatib, 2017; Jabareen, 2014; Molavi, 2013; Shafir & Peled, 2002). Soon after the favorable UN vote for partition of Palestine into a Jewish and Palestinian state in 1947, Ben-Gurion puts forward a vision of the Israeli statehood that inside the new Israeli state, "there will be non-Jews as well – and all of them will be equal citizens; equal in everything without any exception; that is, the state will be their states as well" (cited in Walzer, 2001, p. 6). However, this vision became far from realized. In 2018, the Israel passed a new nation-state law that underlines that it is only the Jewish people who have the right to exercise national self-determination and downgraded the status of the Arabic language (Jamal & Kensicki, 2020). The Israeli Prime Minister Benjamin Netanyahu who was behind this new nation-state law asserted that "Israel is not a state of all its citizens" despite the original claim of Israel as being the state of all peoples who live inside it as citizens, including the Palestinians:

> Today we made it law: This is our nation, language, and flag. In recent years there have been some who have attempted to put this in doubt, to undercut the core of our being. (Netanyahu cited in Vox, 2018)

This dominant Israeli position converges well with the Turkish position on how political singularism is affirmed and heterogeneity is marginalized. The current Turkish President Recep Tayyip Erdoğan captures the idea of singularism in the following way in response to Kurdish grievances to refashion and renarrativize the identity of Turkey:

> This country is ours. That's why we have, from the very beginning, said this: we said, 'one nation', we said, 'one flag', we said, 'one homeland', and we said, 'one state'. There will be no concessions given on this. Those who think differently will be excluded. (Erdoğan cited in Hürriyet Daily News, 2012)

Singularism as a model of political organization has also been applied in Iran, Syria, and until recently Iraq, where Sunni Arab primacy is gradually replaced by Shiite supremacy. Although Iraq has adopted a federal constitution in 2005 that recognizes the political and cultural rights of the Kurds, the ideas of sharing power and resources with the Kurds are resisted by dominant Arab political parties in Iraq regardless of their religious orientations. Until 2003, Sunni-Arabs were the dominant others of the Kurds but following the American occupation of Iraq, the Shia-Arabs were empowered and control main institutions and power resources in Iraq. Accordingly, Kurds in these four countries can be described as pseudo-citizens (Yeğen, 2009), which means that they cannot translate their citizenship status into full political, social, cultural and economic rights. Iraq and Syria are first and foremost imagined as Arab countries and thus silencing the diversity of people and identities that live within these states. In the Iranian context, Persian identity and 'Iranianness' are intimately conflated since the official history, language, culture, and educational system reflect the dominance and maintain the privilege of Persian-speaking people in Iran. These states in the Middle East have historically privileged the interests of a particular community (Arabs, Persians and Turks) although claiming a discourse of brotherhood (rarely sisterhood) among different people within their territorial boundaries. Relatedly, Kymlicka and Pföstl (2014) depict a gloomy prospect regarding multiculturalism and minority rights in the Arab world (this can also be applied to Iran and Turkey) and argue that minoritized groups are often stigmatized when they formulate their political demands in transformative terms. Rather than accommodating their political grievances, minoritized groups like the Kurds are portrayed as 'agents' of Israel and the United States (Kymlicka & Pföstl, 2014). Moreover, Kurds have historically been treated as "a fifth column needing to be closely supervised for recidivist separatist tendencies" (Houston, 2001, p. 99). In general, nation-building processes in the Middle East are not characterized by "inclusive and solidaristic sense of nationhood" (Kymlicka & Pföstl, 2014, p. 13) across differences but authoritarian rules and exclusivist nationalist ideology based on 'one nation', 'one state' and 'one language'. Unanimist notion of nationhood in the Middle East can illuminate why political mobilization of minoritized groups is viewed as a security threat to the state and its identity. Non-dominant ethnic or religious groups in the Middle East rare treated as 'marked citizens' (Pandey, 2006) "whose political mobilization is viewed with distrust if not outright repression" (Kymlicka and Pföstl, 2014, p. 6).

Against this background, whereas the Kurds live in their historical homeland in the Middle East and have been the dominated other of ethnic Arabs, Persians and Turks for almost a century, a large section of Palestinians have been forced or evicted from the land they consider as their homeland. This is not to say that Kurds in large numbers have not been displaced and dispossessed, as the Turkish invasions of the predominantly Kurdish regions of Syria have contributed to in 2018 and 2019. The majority of the Kurds are formal citizens of Iran, Iraq, Syria and Turkey, while there is no effective or formal Palestinian citizenship, Palestinians are often treated as refugees, migrants or pseudo-citizens in Arab countries where they live. Unlike the citizenship status of Palestinians in Jordan and Syria, where they have been treated rather fairly by the Jordanian and Syrian governments, the Palestinians in Lebanon are generally treated as a burden and a demographic threat to the sectarian balance in Lebanon. Following immigration to Sweden and the UK, both Kurdish and Palestinian migrants occupy new political positions as both citizens and racialized and inferiorized migrants, shuttled between inclusion and exclusion. It is from these different positions that the Kurdish and Palestinian migrants in this chapter frame their experiences and accounts about different citizenship or incorporation regimes. Through a comparative lens and individual narratives, we can discern those different political conditions that stipulate and determine inclusion and exclusion in multiethnic societies in the context of nation-state and how the nation-state continues to be an important locus of power in regulating the processes of political membership and belonging.

Citizenship and Its Others

The concept of citizenship has contested and multiple meanings. Citizenship has been described as the central framework for democracy and national identity and functions as the "core institution of the nation-state" (Nordberg, 2006, p. 525). What lies at the heart of citizenship is membership that provides institutional rights. Membership in a political community is often understood as necessary and unavoidable for the majority of people in a world of nation-states (Bellamy, 2008). According to Marshall and Bottomore (1992), the modern citizenship that is associated with the nation-state was achieved during three different historical periods; the civil rights in eighteenth century, the political rights in nineteenth century and the social rights during twentieth century. The civil rights provide the citizen with a legal status and protection, the political rights entail access to political institutions and the social rights involve right to welfare and entitlement to social security. These three sets of rights constitute the modern citizenship. By and large, citizenship is viewed as a desirable device of inclusion through which political membership can be established (Butenschon, 2000; Somers, 2008). Marshall did not uncritically embrace citizenship and pointed to the citizenship as "the architect of legitimate social inequality" and "as an instrument of social stratification" (cited in Chatterjee, 2020, pp. 52–53). Nevertheless, the outline of the modern citizenship developed by Marshall has been criticized for operating as a mask to endorse and consolidate the political, cultural and economic interest of a particular group and has concealed different forms of oppression based on class, gender, ethnicity, race, age and ability (Bilsky, 2008; Eliassi, 2013; Isin & Wood, 1999; Redclift, 2013). The modern citizenship despite its promises of inclusion has been subjected to criticism for concealing different forms of oppression based on class, gender, ethnicity, race, age, and ability (Isin & Wood, 1999).

The development of citizenship from the Ancient Greece via Roman Republic to the modern citizenship has been due to those struggles that different groups (e.g., women, slaves, minorities) have carried out in order to achieve equality and justice (Bellamy, 2008). These inequalities still persist in the context of hierarchical citizenship in the international nations-system. Castles (2005) provides an interesting model to understand how citizenship is configured in the world of unequal nation-states and can lead to varying power of states in political, cultural and economic terms. People from different countries are thus embedded unequally in a hierarchy of rights and freedom, where different passports and identities have varying power and values. Castles argues that nation-state and citizenship are global norms and there is a marked hierarchy among the nation-states. In this hierarchy, US is the leading state, followed by EU-member states, Japan, Canada, New Zealand and Australia, and transitional states like Russia. Below these states, we find the less 'developed' countries of the South and on the bottom of this hierarchical nation-state system, stateless people like Kurds, Tamils and Palestinians are located (Castles, 2005). In a similar vein, Mignolo (2006) has argued that as a result of a Western colonial order, non-white peoples are more often stopped at borders due to their different religion, skin, language and nationality. Racism functions often as the device to distinguish between the 'people' and the 'citizen'. Mignolo continues that "the conditions for citizenship are still tied to a racialized hierarchy of human beings that depends on universal categories of thought created and enacted from the identitarian perspectives of European Christianity and by white males" (p. 313). These structural inequalities between different groups are not only practiced between nation-states but also within the same national boundaries. In this context, Bosniak (2006) contests the universality and boundedness of citizenship and argues that nationally bounded citizenship is often assumed as being hard on the outside and soft on the inside, since citizenship is expected to be applied universally within the national boundary and to mark its exclusiveness toward those who are situated at the community's edges. For Bosniak, this understanding of citizenship is highly problematic because "citizenship's exclusionary commitments are not always confined to state's territorial perimeter but are often brought even within the nation's territory. When this happens, principles of universal citizenship and bounded citizenship occupy the same (internal) terrain" (Bosniak, 2006, p. 99). Part of the problem with this hierarchical citizenship is rooted in the ideology of birthright citizenship that contributes to unequal distribution of political voice, wealth, mobility and opportunity on a global scale. Birthright citizenship following Shachar (2009) resembles a feudal system that sanctions inherited property where allocation of birthright citizenship "regularizes, naturalizes, and legitimizes distinctions between jurisdictions, but also between vastly unequal bequests" (Shachar, 2009, p. 4). This implies that focusing solely on the formal status of an individual and a group can render invisible "the inequality of actual life chances attached to citizenship in specific political communities" (Shachar, 2009, p. 9).

Inspired by Nordberg (2006, p. 524) who has studied marginalized voices on citizenship, identity and belonging, I am interested in the ways the research participants make claims about their citizenship status and whether their legal status entails recognition, representation and rights as political members of the nation-states in which they have lived and currently live. Accordingly, national citizenship models can enable or constrain citizenship rights, agency and participation due to their historical and ideological construction of nationhood and citizenship (Nordberg, 2006). According to Isin and Wood (1999, p. 4), citizenship can neither be conceived as a purely legal concept nor as a purely sociological concept but constituted through a combination of a sociological and a politico-legal definition. A narrow understanding of citizenship as merely a right-bearing status tends to overshadow the everyday understanding of citizenship as a social practice (Fein & Straughn, 2014) and social processes that focus on "norms, practices, meanings and identities" (Isin & Turner, 2002, p. 4). As Miller-Idriss (2006) argues, we cannot study the meanings of citizenship only through examining citizenship policies and naturalization laws, but "we must also investigate how such policies are interpreted, reacted to, and acted upon by ordinary citizens in everyday life" (Miller-Idriss, 2006, p. 561). Hence, in order to gain more knowledge about how different citizenship models in Middle Eastern and Western contexts and their everyday constitution, I explore how individuals with Kurdish and Palestinian backgrounds make sense of their citizenship status on a micro-level. The individual narratives can cast light on larger political processes of political membership and belonging.

The Other Side of Citizenship: When the Particular Masks Itself as the Universal

Let us move to the interviews and examine how different citizenship is lived, experienced and valued. The majority of the research participants argued that the citizenship regimes of Iran, Iraq, Syria and Turkey included the Kurds on subordinated terms and did not represent Kurdish identities in an effective way. The Kurdish interviewees asserted that they do not identify with these states because they have been oppressed and discriminated due to their ethnic differences. Hence, Kurds cannot achieve equality if they want to live their differences publicly and make political claims to cultural, political and economic rights. Although these states have historically excluded and subordinated the Kurdish identity, their exclusionary policies have taken different forms due to different notions of nationhood in each of these states. While Syria and Turkey explicitly privilege Turkish and Arab identity, the Iranian and Iraqi states attempt to display an inclusive strategy in including the differences of non-dominant groups. Yet, these political strategies have not been successful in persuading the Kurds that these states can represent their political, cultural and economic interests. In this section, I will present the narratives of the interviewees and the different ways they relate to and interpret different citizenship regimes in the Middle East following their lived experiences. The meanings that the research participants attribute to their citizenship status often inform pattern of identification and sense of belonging. When asked about his experiences and understanding of the Turkish citizenship as a Kurd, Aram provided the following account:

> Claiming a Kurdish identity in Turkey was like putting yourself behind prison bars. If you define yourself as a Kurd, it was like resisting all resources that the Turkish state could offer its citizens. Not many people wanted to take this risk. Many Kurds wanted to have an open door and go on. Asserting yourself as a Kurd meant that you were anti Turkish citizenship and you were a traitor. And a traitor cannot expect to enjoy the societal resources in Turkey. The best thing for you to do if you were defined as a traitor was to leave Turkey (Aram, a 48 years old man, Kurdistan-Turkey, Sweden)

Aram's dilemma illustrates the ways the micro and macro levels can be bridged to emphasize the role of the Turkish state in repressing the Kurdish identity. It also shows how individual agency is constrained by state policies that punish those individuals and groups that deviate from the political order. Note, how 'Kurd' and 'traitor' are used in the account of Aram as interchangeable in the constitution of Turkish citizenship and national identity. Consequently, Kurds cannot claim their rights as rightful constituents of Turkey since the universal Turkish citizenship does not transcend or accommodate differences and particularities of different groups but embodies, defends and represents the particularity of ethnic Turkish identity (see Young, 1995, p. 175). Challenging the particularized universalism of Turkish citizenship is viewed as a treacherous act and dealt with through political exclusion, imprisonment and forced exile by the Turkish state (Butenschon, 2000, p. 20).

The history of citizenship is a history of the dominance of particular groups that "have articulated their identity as citizens and constituted strangers, outsiders, and aliens as those bête noire who lacked the properties they defined as essential for citizenship" (Isin, 2002, p. 22). In Turkey, culturalization has been an important political tool for the state to establish the parameters of Turkish citizenship. In order to achieve these 'essential properties' and qualify as a citizen, state institutions in Turkey forced Kurds to acculturate and affirm their loyalty and pride over their adopted Turkish identity. The Kurdish interviewees from Kurdistan of Turkey talked vividly and sometimes painfully about their experiences of cultural stigmatization in both everyday life and institutional contexts (e.g. educational system and military service). This is an issue that I will engage with in detail in Chapter 6.

The subordination of Kurdish identity in Syria resembles the Turkish case above. In the context of Syria, Lezgin talked about his experiences as growing up as a Kurd in the Arab-dominated Syria, where Kurdishness was a highly stigmatized identity both in everyday life and institutional settings like school, where he was bullied for having a Kurdish name. Lezgin provides a perspective that particularizes the universal Syrian identity and citizenship during his encounter with Syrian Arabs:

> I have argued with Arabs that we do not have the same position under Bashar al-Assad's regime. I tell the Arabs: In Syria you receive education in Arabic, the TV is in Arabic, the music is Arabic, the movies are Arabic, and the culture is Arabic. Whenever you travel in this country, you can use your Arabic language but we Kurds are nothing in Syria. How can we talk about equality between Arabs and Kurds in Syria? They do not understand what equality is. For them equality is about becoming like them, an Arab. Equality should mean equal rights in every aspects of the society. I had Syrian citizenship but I never felt that Syria was my homeland. I did not feel belonging to Syria because I did not have rights in that country. I know that human rights did not exist in the entire Syria and affected both Arabs and Kurds, but beside that Kurds were second-class citizens in Syria. All this makes me feel that Syria is not my state although I spent 25 years of my life there. I never felt that country was mine. (Lezgin, a 33 years old man, Kurdistan-Syria, Sweden)

Accordingly, ethnic differences and citizenship are not lived equally and non-hierarchically in Syria. Generally, Kurds have historically been deprived of cultural recognition, economic distribution and political power under the Baath regime in Syria. The Syrian *Arab* citizenship as it is called in the Syrian constitution does not transcend or accommodate differences and particularities of different groups in Syria but asserts the dominance of ethnic Arab identity. Equality is thus assumed through accepting the sameness that the Syrian Arab Republic dictates (see Phillips, 2015; Scott, 1994; Young, 1990). In other words, Arab identity is practically designed as the universal identity of all Syrians and gains primacy in everyday life and social institutions through political and ideological power. While citizenship is often assumed to be bounded and soft on inside, the experiences of the interviewees converge with those studies that dispute the universality and softness of citizenship within the framework of the nation-state and underline its discriminatory and hierarchical constitution (Bosniak, 2006; Shachar, 2009). Citizenship has historically implied the embodiment of virtues that dominant groups have inculcated and it is this particular point of view that can assume "a universal point of view" (Isin, 2002, p. 21) which allegedly serves everybody's interest. As Butenschon (2000, p. 5) underlines, the power and the value of citizenship are best recognized by those who are deprived from it, since they know how it feels to not have a passport, not having the right to abode, to own property, to enjoy political membership in a state and lacking power to influence the society. Although Lezgin rejected the Syrian Arab citizenship, he viewed it as an important asset compared to those Kurds who lack citizenship and occupy a stateless position within the Syrian society. He rhetorically asked if he who held a Syrian citizenship did not feel belonging to Syria, how would those stateless Kurds feel toward Syria in the of all those injustices and rightlessness they faced in their everyday life. In the narratives of Lezgin above, the questions of equality, representation, recognition, homeland, human rights and belonging are all present and interconnected. First, Lezgin attempts to reveal and undo the invisible, normative and naturalized political, social and cultural privileges that Syrian Arabs enjoy, to which many of them are unaware of. These privileges have been naturalized to such a degree that they are assumed to be common sense and natural(ized) order of things. Second, Lezgin attaches the issues of lack of rights to lack of belonging and emotional attachment to Syria. Homeland (in this case a nation-state) becomes a political home when it can provide its citizens with rights. The Syrian state is explicitly defined as an Arab state, since its official name is the '*Arab* Syrian Republic' and the nationality of the republic is named as 'Syrian *Arab*'. In Syria, official and everyday notions of membership converge and render the Kurds a subaltern position. For Kurds to become citizens in Syria, they have to accept the dominant Arab identity. This illustrates how the Syrian state equates sameness with equality and thus prevents different ethnic groups to live their differences relationally and non-hierarchically. In order to weaken the political position of the Kurds, the Syrian state has deprived more than three hundred thousand Kurds from Syrian Arab citizenship (see Allsopp, 2014). Hence, within Syria both stateless Kurds and Syrian Arab citizens of Kurdish background can be found. This illustrates well how the Syrian state has directly played a central role in excluding Kurds from achieving citizenship rights. Several Kurdish interviewees who had lived in Syria referred to police brutality that they had experienced as Kurds. For instance, Mustafa, a 34 years old man, argued that in Syria, "as a Kurd, you cannot expect respect but will be treated like an animal with no rights". According to Mustafa, his dog in England has more rights than the Kurds in Syria.

Unlike the states of Turkey and Syria that can easily be traced to the ethnic primacy of Turks and Arabs, the name Iran might be more elusive and appear as less ethnic and more inclusive, while in reality concealing the dominance of ethnic Persians. A widespread myth surrounds the idea of Iran as a harmonious multiethnic and multireligious society. So how does this alleged universalism work in practice in Iran? Growing up in Iran, Persian or Persian-speaking children will gradually realize that their Persian identity is represented by and shape all social institutions in Iranian society. From the day these children take their first steps into Iranian schools, they will learn that the language of instruction is Persian, history belongs to Persians, the art is Persian, literature is written and read in Persian, the songs are Persian, the anthems are Persian and geographical names are either Persian or Persianized. In other words, Persian children learn that their life-worlds at home and in public spheres are consistent and convergent. If we consider non-Persian children like Arabs, Turkmens, Baluchs and Kurds, they will on the contrary realize that their identity is not represented by these social institutions but are urged to internalize the values and language of the dominant Persian group since the very goal of social institutions such as schools in Iran has been about Persianizing the Iranian society. This is why Persian language/identity is often interpreted as the true marker of 'Iranianness' while Kurdish and Baluchi languages have been regarded as 'corrupted' dialects of the Persian language. Azeri, Turkmen and Arab languages are on the other hand, regarded as 'foreign' elements in the Iranian society. Representatives for the Iranian state has on different occasion discarded the Kurdish language as an autonomous language and belittled it to a dialect. In 2014, the Iranian Consulate based in the Kurdistan Region of Iraq released an announcement and degraded the Kurdish language. The Consulate argued that the"Kurdish dialect is not an autonomous language but belongs to the Iranian languages and is a mixture of Arabic, Turkish and Persian languages". While borrowing words and exchange are part of the historical development of languages, it is striking that the Iranian/Persian Consulate mentions the question of "mixture" when the Persian language and its vocabulary are largely dominated by Arabic words and influences. The main aim of the Iranian Consulate was to disqualify Kurdish claims to nationhood and sovereignty in a region pervaded by Arab, Persian and Turkish mastery. When it comes to Kurdish children and their lack of sufficient knowledge in Persian, Rezwan Hakimzadeh, the vice president of Iran's Department of Education argued in 2019 that this lack can be equated with a biological defect. In 2019, the Iranian authorities imprisoned the Kurdish language teacher and human rights defender Zara Mohammadi, for teaching Kurdish. Mohammadi was accused of "forming a group against national security". The minority quest for right to education in non-Persian languages is regarded as undermining national security, social cohesion and the territorial integrity of Iran, as for instance some members of the Academy of Persian Language and Literature have underlined (see Eliassi, 2014). This aversion toward Kurdish quest for ethnocultural rights illustrates that the Iranian regime and its intelligentsia both denigrate and securitize Kurdish identity and language in the name of an undemocratically imposed Perso-Iranian identity.

When it came to the experiences of Iranian citizenship, Lorin who is a 26 years old woman pointed out that although her parents were born in Iran and were formally citizens of Iran, she cannot identity with its citizenship because when she thinks of an Iranian, it is not a Kurdish person that comes to her mind, but a Persian person. In the same context, while discussing the political position of Kurds with a young Iranian woman, Evin underlines why universalism in Iran means denial of Kurdish rights:

> The other day, I had a discussion with a young Iranian woman who said that Kurds in Iran can live their lives and identities freely. I told her that is not true. And she said there are no differences between Kurds and Iranians in Iran. I told her that we Kurds want to be recognized as a people and have right to education in Kurdish language and self-rule. She could not understand that Kurds face political problems in Iran since she was saying that in Iran there are many groups but they are all Iranians. (Evin, 28 years old woman, Kurdistan-Turkey, Sweden)

It is true that Iran is indeed comprised of different ethnic and religious groups and popular nationalism is not always convergent with the official nationalism, and a state that claims unity in diversity, but the Iranian citizenship and national identity virtually privilege Persian-speaking people or ethnic Persians. In this respect, I will draw upon the work of Krishan Kumar (2000) to discuss how Iranian nationalism works at a rhetorical and practical level. The Iranian nationalism based on Persian supremacy can be labelled as an imperial or missionary nationalism, which entails that "there is the attachment of a dominant or core ethnic groups to a state entity that conceives itself as dedicated to some larger cause or purpose, religious, cultural, or political" (p. 580). Persian or Iranian politicians and leaders often avoid to talk about Persians as the ruling identity and constituency and emphasize that Iran as a country nurtures peace, brotherhood, diversity and Islam in the Muslim world. When minoritized groups politicize the ethnic and religious inequalities that they suffer in Iran, the Iranian regime and parts of its intelligentsia tend to describe these plights as Western and Zionist fabrication with the aim to divide Iran. Kumar argues that if a dominant group is in charge, they "do not need to beat the drum or blow the bugle too loudly. To do so in fact would be to threaten the very basis of that commanding position, by reminding other groups of their inferiority and perhaps provoking them to do something about it" (ibid., p. 590). Though, this dominant ethno-nationalism becomes conspicuous when its ethno-symbolic power is challenged, as in the case of the 'Persian Gulf', when Arabs want to rename it as the 'Arabian Gulf'. The drums of the agents of Persian nationalism become louder and the concealed dominance of Persian particularity becomes prominent. If we cast the net wider, Kumar posits that English nationalism is also facing similar dilemma in an era where the British Empire no longer holds a global economic and political power and is challenged by multiculturalism and Scottish secessionism. If the English have not historically needed to define themselves, they are now pressed to do so and invent an identity, which explains the rise of English nationalism (ibid., p. 593). Consider for instance, how a white English male laments the 'oppression' that the English are supposedly experiencing in a multinational state:

> I once talked with an English man and he told that "we English are also oppressed in the UK". I told him how can you be subordinated when you are ruling this country? He said: "the Scots have their own parliament but we have a British government and not an English government". I told him, my friend, that British is just a decoration of English control over this state. (Alan, a 45 years old man, Kurdistan-Syria, the UK)

One can also aptly say that the Iranian identity is a decoration of Persian political, cultural and economic control over Iran (see Soleimani & Mohammadpour, 2019). When Hassan Rouhani was elected as Iran's

President in 2013, the Kurds expected from Rouhani a new political language characterized by increasing political and cultural rights. But as soon as he was elected, he underlined that in Iran, there is only one ruling identity and that is an Iranian identity and added impassively that there are 'subcultures' in Iran below the Iranian identity. Defining non-ethnic Persians as 'subcultures' can be understood as a political strategy to deprive them from claiming nationhood and self-governance but also subsuming them under the imposed universality of Iranian identity. Kurdish claims to expand the notion of the Iranian citizenship to be more inclusive have been dealt with as a national security issue that supposedly erodes the communal bond among different groups of Iran and serve imperialistic interests. Concurrently, Kurdish political parties that are struggling against the Iranian state are often viewed as lacking political subjectivity and primarily functioning as the political 'toy' of Israel and the United States, to destabilize the allegedly harmonious Muslim world devoid of ethno-religious hierarchy. To illustrate how Kurdish identity holds an inferiorized position within the Iranian context, Birkar narrated his experiences of non-recognition in institutional contexts when Kurdish migrants are not allowed or obstructed from giving Kurdish names to their children. In Birkar's words:

> I am a Kurd from Eastern Kurdistan (Iran) and was born in a refugee camp in Iraq. I was given a Kurdish name by my parents. My family moved back to our village in Kurdistan. In Iran, me and two younger brothers had to change our Kurdish names and the authorities replaced them with Persian and Arabic names. In school, I was always called by my Persian name but at home and with friends, I was hailed with my Kurdish name. When I got married to a Kurdish woman in Sweden, one of the first things I did was to get back my Kurdish name on my Swedish identity cards. I visited the Iranian embassy to issue an Iranian passport for my newly born son. They asked me which name I had chosen for my son. I replied: Kardo. The embassy told me that they cannot accept this name and suggested a Persian name, Ardashir. I refused and one of the staffs at the embassy told me indignantly. "Today you ask for a Kurdish name, tomorrow you will be asking for a Kurdish state like those (Kurds) in Iraq". But I told them, this is the name we have chosen for our son and nothing more. They reluctantly accepted it when we had to prove that the name was not an anti-revolutionary name.

Although this is an individual experience, but it has wider and generalized value since this sense of superiority and priority of Persian identity is a central feature of the Iranian political order. This is also reflected in diasporic contexts where minorities are viewed as undermining the unity of Iran through their assumedly parochial, provincialized, divisive identities. Birkar's experience demonstrates how oppression and symbolic violence operates across national borders targeting stateless nations, where they are obstructed from naming their children. Some of the Kurdish interviewees did not want to be associated with Iran, when they had the opportunity to do so. This aversion toward the Iranian state and its dominant identity is primarily informed by their experiences and feelings that their identity and rights were safeguarded within Iran:

> I have taken away Iran from my passport as the place of birth and put the name of my town there. I do not want Iran on my passport because I am not from Iran. I am not Persian. Why Should I have Iran on my passport? I do not feel belonging to the Iranian citizenship. I had a conflict with an Iranian girl who is also my friend. We were in secondary school. The religion teacher asked the student to take stance through yes or no when she made a statement about death penalty. The teacher asked us: "Should Hitler receive death penalty?" Both of us said yes and went and stood beside each other to show our common stance. Then the teacher asked: "Should Saddam Hussein receive death penalty?" I said yes but the Persian girl said no. I told her why did you say yes to execution of Hitler but not to Saddam? It was obviously not important for her that Saddam had killed hundred thousand Kurds. (Sheno, a 26 years old woman, Kurdistan-Iran, Sweden)

> I do not want an Iranian citizenship or passport because I do not like it. I feel more Swedish than Iranian. The Iranian passport is one of the most devalued passports in the world. When you show your passport at international airports, you are treated as a terrorist or suspected. People look down at you. (Masoud, a 31 years old man, Kurdistan-Iran, Sweden)

The decision to remove the name Iran from their Swedish passport is guided by their disidentification with Iran as site of their belonging and the negative political associations (such as terrorism, autocracy and religious fundamentalism) that the name Iran triggers when they travel in different parts of the world. The very existence of the name of Iran on their highly valued 'Western' passports is also viewed as a potential risk to complicate their mobility and devalue the reach and power of their passports. There are different experiences of encounters with ethnic Persians, Arabs and Turks in diasporic contexts. For the Kurdish interviewees, it was evident that Turks tend to be more inclined toward racism and aggressive nationalism when Kurds assert their existence as an ethnopolitical reality. Lana, a 32 years old Kurdish woman from Kurdistan of Turkey argued that mentioning the name Kurdistan for the Turks "is liking dropping a bomb" and "asking for division of Turkey". State nationalism and popular nationalism go hand in hand in Turkey and at transnational levels. However, this nationalist stance was also existent among certain ethnic Persians and Arabs who could only accept the Kurds as a contained and subordinated minority but not as an equal nation with right to self-rule. The Kurdish interviewees pointed out that some Persians in Sweden expect you to speak their language and if you do not want to or cannot speak Persian, it becomes easily interpreted as 'separatism'. It is partly due to these encounters with these three dominant ethnicities that Kurds understands what hierarchy of citizenship and belonging prevails in Iran, Iraq, Syria and Turkey and how Kurds are assigned a subaltern position within these imagined communities.

Unlike Iran, Syria and Turkey, the Iraqi state has carried out paradoxical policies in relation to the political demands of the Kurds. In Iraq, Kurds have achieved cultural rights and the Kurdish language has been recognized, yet met with fierce resistance and aversion from part of the Arab constituency. Currently, the Kurdish language holds an official status in the Kurdistan Region of Iraq and it is imprinted on the Iraqi passport, but it might be a matter of time before it can be removed due to the idea that Kurdish language allegedly decreases the value of the Iraqi passport. Nevertheless, it is in Iraq that Kurds have been largely exposed to genocidal acts by the Iraqi state during Saddam Hussein's rule in 1980s. When I asked Rezgar and Aras what the Iraqi citizenship meant to them, they responded in an uncompromising way that Kurdistan is not Iraq and Iraq is not their homeland:

> I do not see myself as an Iraqi. I do not even want that citizenship or carry it. But the thing is that Kurdistan is part of Iraq today and you automatically become a citizen of Iraq. I do not feel any form of belonging to that state or feel as an Iraqi. For me Iraq means torture, killing and eradication of my people. (Rezgar, a 63 years old man, Kurdistan Region-Iraq, Sweden)

> I cannot say that I am an Iraqi. I am from Halabja and if I say that I am an Iraqi, that is the greatest denigration toward my identity as a Kurd. My city was gassed by the Iraqi army. Both me and my father were tortured in Iraqi prison. I do not consider Iraq as my homeland or state. It is a form of infidelity if I say that I am an Iraqi. If I say that I am an Iraqi, I am humiliating the blood of our martyrs. If I say that I am an Iraqi, then I accept the Iraqi identity and what has been done to me and my nation in the shadow of the Iraqi state and its flag. (Aras, a 53 years old man, Kurdistan Region-Iraq, the UK)

This view was shared among Kurds from Iraq who regarded the Iraqi state as synonymous with political oppression and genocidal acts against the Kurds. This discourse was also widely deployed to separate Kurdishness from Iraq since Iraq for the Kurds is equated with Arab identity. Another interviewee shared his non-belonging to the Iraqi state in the following way:

> Iran was a foreign country for us Kurds but when they attacked Iraq (1980-1988 war), we were applauding the Iranian aircrafts. That is a good way to express our lack of belonging to Iraq. When you read history books in Iraq, you felt that you (Kurds) were not existing as a people and of course you ask why do Arab exist everywhere while Kurds do not appear in the textbooks. We Kurds have come from somewhere so how come that we do not exist in books? The Iraqi history books talked about Somalia, Maghreb and Arab tribes but they did not talk about the Kurds although we were living within the same boundary. All this made you feel that this is not your homeland or your state. How do you want me as a Kurd to identify with a state that you define as Arabic? I cannot feel belonging to that state. I read in many places that Iraq was an indivisible part of the Arab homeland. How can I feel that Iraq is my homeland? We were living under fear all the time. So you cannot feel belonging to a state that you are afraid of. (Sherzad, 49 years old man, Kurdistan-Iraq)

The states often endorse history textbooks that reflect particular views that have gained hegemony and serve the interests of the dominant group. History textbooks are not politically innocent but often used by states and government to include and exclude different histories, identities, experiences and cultures (see Kirmanj, 2014). Sherzad's experiences show how Iraqi citizenship was shaped and constituted as representing Iraqi Arabs (mainly Sunni-Arabs) and muted other identities that did not fit within Iraqi Arab nationalism. When Iraq was founded in 1923, many Iraqi Arab nationalists imagined Iraq merely as a political home to Sunni-Arabs. In sum, lack of political recognition, power-sharing, safety and security can explain why so many Kurds from Iraq do not identify with the Iraqi state since its citizenship according to the interviewees, reflects a negation of political presence of Kurdish identity and existence within Iraq.

Citizenship, Welfare and (Im)mobility

Above, I discussed how the overarching nationalisms and national citizenships of Iran, Iraq, Syria and Turkey have not been able to accommodate Kurdish grievances in pursuit of inclusionary citizenship regimes in multi-ethnic societies. In this section, I will also include the narratives of Palestinian migrants holding a Swedish citizenship and how they understand and value this citizenship. In addition, I shall discuss how the Swedish and British citizenship is contrasted with Middle Eastern citizenship regimes and how these citizenships are experienced and inform patterns of belonging and identity formation in the context of immigration and multiculturalism. Unlike the discussed states above in the Middle East, Sweden and the UK are often hailed as international role models for their successful political arrangement of democracy and multiculturalism (see Kymlicka, 2010). An important question that needs to be considered is that the Swedish and British citizenships and passports are highly valuable compared to those of the Middle East when it comes to rights, freedom and mobility in a world of unequal nation-states. I posit that one of the reasons behind the uncompromising political stance toward the states of Iraq, Iran, Syria and Turkey is the democratic arrangement of the Swedish and British society where Kurds can relatively express their political identity without state harassment. The Swedish and British citizenship that can be acquired through 'the right of blood' (*jus sanguinis*) or 'by residence' (*jus domicile*) was discussed in relation to political and cultural rights but also in regard to security. In this regard, Kardo who has grown up in Sweden talks about the Swedish citizenship as given but explains why his parents appreciate the Swedish citizenship in a comparative sense:

> They appreciate the Swedish citizenship and its passport that you can travel with wherever you want to. They appreciate it because they compare it with what they had in Turkey. They were formally citizens of Turkey but they were not treated as citizens in Turkey. They could not exercise their

> culture, identity and freedom in Turkey. They did not have right to education in their Kurdish language. Kurds had more duties like doing military service but they did not get much back from the state. (Kardo, a 34 years old man, Kurdistan-Turkey, Sweden)

All citizenship regimes are formally built upon the philosophy of providing rights and requiring duties from their citizens. While Turkish citizenship is equated with negation of Kurdish identity and rights, the Swedish citizenship both provides mobility and limited recognition of Kurdish identity. Lezgin points out that his friends in Kurdistan of Syria cannot believe him when he tells them that in Sweden, Kurds can publish in their language and receive education in Kurdish and have right to establish Kurdish associations with funds from the municipality and the state. He explains that he experienced a 'clash' between his experiences in Syria as a formal citizen and now as a migrant in Sweden with a permanent residence permit:

> Now, I have lived in Sweden during 4 years and my sense of belonging to this country has grown a lot. I feel secure in Sweden. In this country, there is respect for humanity. From the first day I came to Sweden, when I was at the Migration Board, they gave me a form and info about my asylum application in Kurdish, but Kurdish language is forbidden in Syria. Syria is supposedly my homeland but I do not have rights there. Now I have come to Sweden which is not my homeland, but I have rights. When I said to the Swedish authorities that I am Kurdish, they said that they will bring a Kurdish interpreter. They gave me a leaflet in Kurdish about the asylum procedure. This really made me to rethink my life and my country (Syria). I was punished in Syria because I was a political activist, but in Sweden I am respected and given rights. I strongly feel attached to Sweden. I really feel that I belong to Sweden (Lezgin, a 33 years old man, Kurdistan-Syria, Sweden)

These experiences and policies to accommodate to different ethnic groups in Sweden illustrate why Sweden is so often hailed as a stronghold of diversity and equality, particularly when Sweden is contrasted to repressive and authoritarian states in the Middle East. Citizenship does not always entail belonging but it can strengthen or weaken belonging to a polity depending on its exclusiveness or inclusiveness, as Lezgin shows while comparing Syria with Sweden. Similarly, Sherzad argues that Kurds as a stateless nation should claim Sweden as their homeland:

> Although I do not speak Swedish so well, Sweden is my second homeland. I love Sweden as much as I love Kurdistan. Sweden has given me everything. I do not say that it is perfect. It gives me more than what I have got from my homeland Kurdistan. In Kurdistan, I have struggled for my rights and fought for the freedom of my people but still do not have so many rights in that country but here in Sweden without spending a cold night in the war front for defending Sweden, it has given me so many rights. Is not that a crime to not consider yourself as a Swede or as a citizen of this state? Sweden has adopted us (Kurds) because we were like orphans and treated us like its children. Therefore, we cannot be disloyal to this father. (Sherzad, a 49 years old man, Kurdistan Region-Iraq, Sweden)

This account raises many questions about how membership can be achieved in different political communities and political homes. To be accepted as a Swede requires embodying certain properties that are defined as central to constitution of Swedish identity. Immigrants in Sweden are often viewed as deficient subjects lacking properties like adherence to democratic and liberal values and lack of knowledge of Swedish language. This indicates that despite the democratic arrangement of the Swedish society, immigrants face different thresholds that prevent them from achieving equal political status. When Sherzad mentions the Swedish language, he shows awareness about discourses in the Swedish society that wants to make knowledge of Swedish language to a requirement in order to be entitled to Swedish citizenship. The state in Sherzad's narratives embodies a masculine figure that takes care of stateless Kurds and adopts them as orphans. Sherzad also asserted that since Kurds do not have a state, the Swedish citizenship and passport can compensate lack of rights in the Middle East. Swedish citizenship was generally viewed as a tool that could guarantee security "as long as racists do not control this country", which pointed to the rise of anti-immigrant political party Sweden Democrats that depicts Muslims and Islam as the greatest enemies of Sweden since Second World War.

For the majority of the Kurdish interviewees, the Swedish welfare system provides protection and safety that cannot be currently secured or achieved in the Middle Eastern states from which they have migrated. Despite romantic images of Kurdistan, the Swedish welfare system can suspend the very idea of return, even if it is possible:

> I cannot value the Swedish welfare system by words. I really appreciate it. My father has been telling us during the last 30 years that we will go back

> to Kurdistan. It is his goal but at the same time he regrets and says: "No, this social security does not exist in Kurdistan". It is enough to live in Kurdistan during a week in order to understand that you cannot buy this welfare system even if you have money in Kurdistan. I value it a lot. The health care, the insurance system, the police in Turkey are all catastrophic. (Heval, a 30 years old man, Kurdistan-Turkey, Sweden)

For the Kurdish research participants, despite their strong desire to return and settle in their countries of origin, there is a strong awareness that they might jeopardize the well-beings of their children and themselves by returning to a volatile region that lacks rule of law and an effective welfare system. Accordingly, return and the homeland can be temporarily suspended in anticipation of better times and governance in the countries of origin. A common idea that was shared by several Kurdish and Palestinian interviewees was that the British or the Swedish citizenship that they held, was "just a piece of paper". Of course, this choice of wording did not entail that possession of a Swedish or a British citizenship was useless, as we will see in relation to mobility. This critique of the formal citizenship primarily regarded its inability to be translated into equality and belonging. When asked, what the British citizenship meant, one of the interviewees described its value in the following way:

> Well, I do not feel British because I am Kurdish. A citizenship does not change my identity. But I use the British passport to travel. The British passport makes your life easier. You can work as you wish. I can travel anywhere I want to. I compare myself with the Kurds who are living here and they do not have residence permit. They cannot even rent a house. The landlords want you to prove your identity. People do not even give them a room to rent. Many of them work in places where they are really underpaid. People treat your better when you have legal documents and when you have residence permit. (Huner, a 26 years old man from Kurdistan Region-Iraq, the UK)

Citizenship does not necessarily mean belonging to an identity that it is associated with, as Huner illustrates above. Citizenship and legal statuses have multiple meanings and can either enhance or constrain one's opportunity and actual life chances in particular political communities (Shachar, 2009, p. 9). As Huner clearly indicates 'this piece of paper' called citizenship has important social, economic and legal consequences for those people who have it or lack it. Rozhgar, a 19 years old man who migrated to Britain and currently lacks residence permit, described the divergent realities of those Kurds who hold citizenship/residence permit and those who lack it:

> There are a lot of differences between me who lack residence permit and those who have it. They can travel to another country if they want to. Now summer is impending and I would love to go on a holiday and enjoy my time. I have an Albanian and a Pakistani friend who have decided to travel to the Netherlands. They asked me if I wanted to accompany them to the Netherlands and have a nice time there. I told them that this summer I am busy and I will be working and training. So, I lied to them because they do not know that I do not have residence permit and that is the main reason why I am not following them. I am ashamed if I say that I do not have residence permit. They look down at you if you say that you do not have residence permit. I am ashamed to tell them that I did not come to England in a legal way. I feel ashamed to tell them that I hid myself in a truck where I could hardly breathe. I cannot tell them that I was starving while crossing different borders until I reached England. I feel ashamed to tell that I have suffered all this just to come to this country and still do not have residence permit. I cannot travel outside of the UK and that is why I feel that I am living in a big prison in the UK. I do not feel that I am a human being now because there are many things that I do not have right to do. I cannot continue my studies if I do not have a residence permit. This obliges me to wash cars. Indeed, when you do not have a residence permit you are not counted as a member of humanity in this country.

This account indicates that there is a distinct internal hierarchy of statelessness among the Kurds who make claim to statelessness. The questions of shame, rightlessness and immobility seem to encircle the world of the undocumented people. Rozhgar uses his precarious condition as stateless and undocumented to depict a liberal democratic state like Britain as "a big prison", for the way it denies him the right to have rights in Britain. Rozghar's experiences aptly fit within an Arendtian definition of statelessness since he is contained in exile as homeless, and lacks basic rights, state protection and political rights (Blitz & Otero-Iglesias, 2011). Rozhgar's narrative testifies the global inequality of citizenship in relation to how mobility is unevenly distributed, experienced and lived. Citizenship might just be a paper but it is a paper that has the power to determine who counts as a member of humanity and treated as co-human being and who can be expelled from the domain of rights and mobility.

An important feature of citizenship is the question of mobility and the reliance on the Swedish state to help its citizens when they encounter difficulties abroad:

> I see it as freedom. I feel safer with a Swedish passport when I travel around Turkey and Kurdistan than having a Turkish citizenship or passport. /.../ The Swedish passport means a lot to me when I am abroad and when I need help from the Swedish embassies if something goes wrong. (Lara, a 24 years old woman, Kurdistan-Turkey, Sweden)

It is thus the citizenship that provides us with a political status that is often a nationality or a state identity. A (wo)man that is "nothing but a man [sic] has lost the very qualities which make it possible for other people to treat him as fellow-man" (Arendt, 1951, p. 300). However, the Palestinian interviewees were not sure that the Swedish embassies will help them if they get trapped in a war zone. Many of them referred to the Israel war on Lebanon in 2006, when many Palestinians and Lebanese migrants with Swedish citizenships wanted to leave Lebanon. For them, it took long time before they received the support they expected as citizens of Sweden. In Sweden, white popular sentiments were not supportive of the Swedish Foreign Department to support these trapped citizens and made the argument that these people should blame themselves to visit their countries of origin. The very basis of this critique was that these peoples were not true Swedish citizens but people who exploited the Swedish citizenship for their own benefits without any sense of belonging to Sweden.

Based in Britain, Lana who is a 32 years old woman from Kurdistan of Turkey pointed out that she would rather use her British passport and pay an extra fee when she enters Turkey than using her Turkish identity card that would allow her free entrance into Turkey. This has of course created problems for her with Turkish staffs at the airport who know by looking at her place of birth on the passport that she was born in the Kurdish part of Turkey but refuses to declare her devotion to the Turkish identity. It is not uncommon for Kurds to get thoroughly searched at Turkish airports. Sometimes, they have also been obliged to show their cellphones, in order to see if the person carries symbols and objects related to Kurdistan and Kurdish identity. For instance, it has also occurred that Turkey has sent back Swedish citizen with Kurdish background who has carried the name 'Kurdistan'. Mustafa offers an account why he appreciates his British citizenship and passport:

> The British citizenship means a lot. It means freedom and I have freedom of speech. I can travel wherever I want without people looking at me and be disgusted of me and my Syrian passport. People respect me whenever I go. When they look at my British passport, they have respect for me. I was in Syria in 2012. We had big problems with Turkish police because they did not want to let us in Syria from the Turkish border. The Turkish police were swearing at us all the time. So I told them to stop swearing because I am a British citizen and I have rights and you cannot treat me as a Kurd. My power came from my British citizenship. I told them if they would touch me I would contact the British embassy. They let us in. I never spoke Kurdish or Arabic with them but English. They wanted to hear that I am Kurdish so they could treat me badly. (Mustafa, a 34 years old man, Kurdistan-Syria, the UK)

This account highlights the value and the power of the British passport at different borders. Mustafa is well aware that his Kurdishness entails immobility at Turkish borders in deep contrast to the power and privilege of the British passport that can open doors and borders for him. According to Salter (2004, p.72), the passport functions as a "request by one sovereign to another sovereign to aid and protect a nationally identified bearer", even if the bearers of these passports happen to be people who challenge the sovereignty of these states by embracing Kurdish or Palestinian identities. These experiences were not absent among the Palestinians who carried the Swedish passport while visiting Lebanon. Muhammad who is a 37 years old man living in Sweden shared his experience of flagging this passport in the political context of Lebanon where Palestinians are highly stigmatized:

> The Swedish passport means a lot to me. Without that passport, I would not have been able to enter Palestine and see where I am from. I am thankful that I can be in Sweden. I have built up a life here. I have family and children. Sweden is now my homeland. I was born in Lebanon but the Lebanese tell me that I am not Lebanese but Palestinian. I have this discussion with Lebanese on daily basis at my workplace here in Sweden. There is no chance that they can accept you as a Lebanese. The Lebanese look down on us Palestinians. When I travelled to Lebanese with my family,

> my father told me to not speak Arabic because the Lebanese police want to mess with you. They stop you for hours. I spoke English and they asked me why I do not speak Arabic. I said that I live in Sweden. When I passed by the police. They swore at me in Arabic in order to provoke me but I did not care. He wanted me to give him money because it is easier for them to ask you for money if you are Palestinian. The Lebanese would love to have my passport. The Swedish passport allows you to be free and can travel wherever you like to go. The passport provides me with a belonging to Sweden. Despite the political climate now in Sweden with anti-immigrant debates, I feel belonging to Sweden, but I have to say that they make you feel like a real immigrant.

Muhammad is well aware that Palestinians are positioned between different exclusionary regimes in the Middle East and Western Europe that hierarchize belonging and claim-making to the place designated as the political home. However, like the Kurds who cherished the Swedish and the British citizenship, the Palestinians considered the Swedish citizenship as far more enabling and empowering their rights and mobility than the Lebanese citizenship that is not accessible to Palestinians who continue to live a precarious life in Lebanon. It is interesting that both Mustafa and Muhammad in the above accounts used the English language, in order to facilitate their mobility and enhance their attachment to the Western citizenships and passports that they carry and underscored their detachment from the Middle Eastern states that oppress their identities and deny them equal citizenship rights. While rights can enhance the sense of belonging to a state, its lack can activate and nurture disidentification with exclusionary state and societies. Despite his rights in Sweden, Muhammad knows that he is seen and treated as a foreigner in Sweden. For both Palestinian and Kurdish interviewees, holding a Swedish or a British passport made them into "important persons" when they travelled to their home countries. Some of the interviewees talked about the questions they received from their families and friends whether the Swedish or the British passport could take them anywhere they wanted. This curiosity and sense of inequality can explain why migration to affluent Western countries is desirable among the younger generations of Kurds and Palestinians who want to enjoy the privilege of travelling and welfare and escaping the immobility in which they are embedded within the boundaries of the existing states in the Middle East. A few Kurdish and Palestinian research participants were critical of the international order that stigmatized certain groups and complicated their mobility due to the citizenship that they held:

> Nobody asked me when they designated citizenship. For me as a human being it should not be important to be a citizen of a particular state. It does not mean anything to me, but this world has been constructed in such a way that you cannot survive without a passport. It obliges you to have a state. I am accidently born in this world where citizenship and passports are important but I have not chosen them. (Dilar, a 28 years old woman, Kurdistan-Turkey, Sweden)

> The Swedish passport means freedom. I just came home from Dubai the other day. I saw people standing in the airport and fully interrogated and looking into different cameras, but for me I got a stamp on my passport and they said hello and I just entered Dubai. Those people did not have Western or European citizenship. You feel that you flow through all controls. It feels as you come in wherever you go, thanks to this little passport. It also felt annoying because when you have Swedish passport, you become treated as a better human because nobody suspects you. I also wanted to stay in the same queue as those people and take those pictures that they took and I wanted to be interrogated as much as them. This is an annoying privilege. Of course, it is nice that you are treated so well, but it was annoying because you think why should I have this privilege but not those people. (Dalia, a 23 years old Palestinian woman, Sweden)

Both Dilar and Dalia are well aware of the uneven world order they inhabit and how different passports and citizenship can imply respect or disrespect, mobility or immobility, privilege or oppression. These individual reflections illustrate that people can oppose the political order and destabilize the assumed normalcy and basis of the unearned privileges that they enjoy. Pease (2010, p. xi) rightly argues "that unearned privilege is a source of oppression and that it entrenches social inequality and damages the lives of people who do not have access to it". One could say that having a sovereign citizenship or a passport would not be considered as a privilege unless some other is proven juridically and legally unworthy of a passport or a state citizenship. Few democratic and liberal states in the world would challenge the claim that all human beings are equal but none of them are prepared to suspend their borders to provide equal movement and access to their countries by people who seek protection (Mau, 2010). By protecting their borders from unwanted migrants, states endorse a citizenship regime that resembles a feudal system where people inherit citizenship as a birthright privilege (Carens, 1992; Shachar, 2009, 2014). Carens (1992, p. 26) has argued that to hold a Canadian citizenship is like "being born into the nobility", while being a citizen of Bangladesh is "like being born into the peasantry in the Middle ages". In this respect, Hindess has aptly described the "citizenship as a conspiracy against the rest of the world" (Hindess, 2000, p. 1489). The West continues to use its political power to maintain the inequality of mobility between the global north and the global south. Hence, the image and the talk about a 'borderless world' continue to be a fiction (Mau, 2010, p. 353), as long as the passport holders from the West can enjoy the world and foreign spaces for work or leisure, while the rest of the world remains ghettoized within their borders. For poor people from the global south, their passports lack value and meaning, when they are denied visa. People who come from countries that are viewed as poor, less democratic and engaged in armed conflicts, continue to face significant thresholds when they want to use their passports as a device of mobility and entering foreign spaces (Neumayer, 2006).

The Palestinians in the Middle East have considerable experiences of immobility due to their precarious situation as an occupied people. Hazem, who is an 18 years old Palestinian man talked about the agony of waiting and harassment that Palestinians experience when they want to cross the border between Gaza and Egypt. According to Hazem, there are two ways to get out of Gaza, either by smuggling yourself via tunnels or the Egyptian border control. Since his father already held Swedish citizenship as a Palestinian refugee, Hazem was granted residence permit and attained Swedish citizenship. When I asked him about the value of the Swedish citizenship, he chose to point to the value of the Swedish passport:

> This Swedish passport helps me to travel to Palestine and there I can show them this red passport and they respect me. When you have this red passport, they treat you like president. This applies to both Egyptian and Palestinian border officers because they cannot treat you badly as they wish to. Europeans are like king for the Egyptian border officers but we Palestinians are like shit for them. They do not care about us.

It is evident that white European figures can both enjoy foreign spaces and mobility in a respectful way, without much interruption and harassment. Consider, how Hazem uses the metaphors of 'king' and 'shit' to describe the divergent realities and hierarchical treatments that Europeans and Palestinian experience at Egyptian border. Respect was underlined as central to carrying the Swedish passport and affected the conduct of police borders. This is due to the fact that there are hegemonic cultural beliefs at a global level that affirms the status of Western citizenship regimes and confers respect to their citizens, when they move across borders and foreign spaces. Western citizens or holders of Western citizenships are well aware that they are valued higher and globally acknowledged as worthier or more competent than others. Samira described this situation in the following way:

> The first time we travelled to Jordan, we did not have Swedish passports. When we came to the passport control, they tried to pretend that they are somebody and started asking us where we were from and if we had Jordanian citizenship. They wanted to humiliate us. But last time, when we travelled to Jordan, we carried Swedish passport, my father showed his Jordanian passport and they were telling my father that it was expired, then my father asked me to give him the Swedish passports, and when the officer saw the Swedish passport, he said: "Welcome brother!", "you are very welcome to the country". My father could not understand him because the officer was very rude at the beginning and now very welcoming and kind. Just because you are from Europe, you are very welcome to the country and they greet you very well. When I was at the airport, I wanted to go to the restroom and the toilets were catastrophic and I told a police officer that there is no door to the toilet and he told: "who are you?" and later on when he saw my Swedish passport, he started calling me "the Madame". This is because I am from Europe that they treat me better and I have Swedish passport. There is no humanity in this treatment. You are simply a king. You are more valued than others who do not have that passport. And that is wrong because all human beings should have equal value. It is such a pity that a human being is more valued than another because one has a Swedish passport. It is amazing how a passport can change the way people look at you and treat you. It is sick! (18 years old Palestinian woman, Sweden)

In contrast to white citizens, racialized citizens need to prove their status as worthy of respect, by showing that they are in possession of highly valued passports when they travel across the world. For some of the Palestinians, the Swedish citizenship opens doors to Palestine and facilitates their entrance into the Palestinian Territories and Israel. However, this is not to say that they do not encounter resistance and aversion from the Israelis (Gabiam, 2015) who know very well that these persons who carry this Swedish citizenship are people who have attachments and claim to Palestine as their homeland. Muhammad narrates his experiences of carrying a Swedish passport while returning to Palestine in 1997:

> When we came to the Egyptian-Israel border, it was full of Palestinians who were not allowed to enter Israel. When we came to the border control, they look at us. My mother is veiled. You could see in their eyes telling us what are you doing here. But when we showed them our Swedish passports, then they did not know what to say. They did not have a choice and could not deny us an entrance into Israel. They were trying to find different excuses to not allow us in. There was a bag that my sister had packed in her hair dryer and hairbrush. Their borders control looks like going into an airport in the way they inspect your luggage and your body. They really scan you. They were suspecting my sister's bag and started asking: "who has packed this bag?" My father said that it was her daughter. They took my sister who was 10 years old and started to investigate her. She was scared to death when armed people were investigating her.

This account demonstrates how the Palestinian figure is securitized as a threat to Israeli security and existence. The Palestinians who hold Western citizenship might have found a temporary way out of the immobility and stoppage that Israel has created for Palestinians by erecting walls and checkpoints and suspension of their return to their homeland. Although all Palestinians face certain forms of immobility when they arrive in Israel, racialized and gendered bodies run higher risk of being interrogated and stopped. Dina, a 23 years old Palestinian woman uses the experiences of her mother as an example of how skin color matters when people are stopped at the Israeli border:

> My mother does not look like an Arab. She is blonde and has blue eyes and white skin. It is often me who are stopped by the Israeli and have to suffer humiliation and interrogation. Indeed, your skin color affects the way you are treated at the Israeli border. When they see my mother, they think that she is from a European country or they might think that she

> is originally Swedish. They do not want to get problem with the Swedish embassy.

If the British and Swedish passport primarily serve and represent the white constituencies, then they also become mainly white passports due to their association with white bodies. This is convergent with the hierarchical citizenship regimes inside Britain and Sweden where whiteness structures rights, ethno-national hierarchies and belonging. For instance, Leyla who is a 56 years old woman from Kurdistan of Turkey talked about her statelessness and the limits of the British citizenship due to the intimate bond between British identity and whiteness. Leyla argued that "If I show my British passport, people will suspect my identity because I do not look like a British person who is white". The question of being stopped at borders and airports have an important gendered dimension. Women who are veiled and adhere to Islam become more target of racist discourses and more often stopped and searched than unveiled racialized women:

> Me and my colleague passed the through security at Arlanda in Stockholm and *miraculously* it did not alarm because it does so all the time. Since I wear the veil and I have pins in my veil, it does alarm. My colleague came after me and she is Swedish. But in her case, it alarmed three times and she had to go through the control three times. When I wanted to pick up my stuff, a female security officer came and said that she wanted to touch my veil. She grabbed my head and started squeezing my head without even explaining why she was doing that. Then she just left without saying anything at all. I was so shocked. When I am at Swedish airports, people often speak to me in English and say "where are you going?" and I tell them: hello, I am still on Swedish territory and have not yet left Sweden, so we can continue speaking Swedish. I often pray to god so it does not alarm when I go through the security control. You get use to it. (Mona, a 30 years old Palestinian woman, Sweden, emphasis added)

In her theoretical deliberation about whiteness, Ahmed (2007) argues that the social effects of whiteness are lived, material and real. Whiteness is highly visible for those people who do not inhabit it but to a large extent overlooked by those who are used its inhabitance. It would be not an exaggeration to claim that the world is oriented toward whiteness as we saw clearly how white citizenship regimes and passports are privileged. When a world that is primarily inhabited by whiteness and privilege white bodies, the non-white bodies will "feel uncomfortable, exposed, visible, different" (ibid., p. 157) when they enter its domain. For racialized persons who hold Swedish and British passports, they risk being stopped and searched more often than white bodies. For Ahmed, "stopping is both a political economy, which is distributed unevenly between others, and an effective economy, which leaves its impressions, affecting those bodies that are subject to its address" (ibid., p. 161). It is not uncommon for brown bodies to feel the distress of being stopped and interrogated despite holding valid passports. When certain bodies are marked out as different, dubious and dangerous, having "the 'right' passport makes no difference if you have the wrong body or name: and indeed, the stranger with the 'right' passport might cause particular trouble, as the ones who risk passing through" (ibid., p. 162). If racialized people protest, they are often told that they have been randomly selected for screening and nothing to do with racial profiling but guided by their regular passenger profiling. In the next section, I will continue to discuss the discomfort of being a non-white citizen in white-oriented societies.

The Discomforts of Being a Non-White Citizen in White Countries

Many of the Kurdish interviewees were clear over the fact that they identified more with Sweden and Britain than the Middle Eastern states that oppress the Kurds. Despite holding a positive view of Sweden and Britain, there were a fear among the interviewees that Sweden and Britain could not be certain homelands due to exclusionary discourses, which activated a sense of estrangement and statelessness. The interviewees were aware that they were not accepted as a full-edged member of the Swedish and British society. Intersubjective experiences of ethnic discrimination complicate the sense of belonging to the Swedish society:

> Ethnic Swedes remind you in everyday life that you do not belong to this place. There is an old Swedish lady in the residence area where we are living. Since I have been 10 years old, she has commented my ethnicity. I chose to wear the veil when I was 9 years old. Because that is the first thing people think that I wear the veil and therefore I am not Swedish. She has told me: 'Go back home! You will be forced to a marriage with a cousin! You will lose hair because of the veil and you do not fit in the Swedish society.' (Rojin, a 20 years old woman, Kurdistan-Turkey, Sweden)

> Despite the fact, that I am here and have grown up in Sweden, there is always a risk that one day I might not be allowed to stay in this country. Where should I go then? That fear exists. It is starting to become scary here in Sweden when you hear political parties talking about sending home Muslims and non-Europeans. The wider society questions my presence in Sweden (Sheno, a 26 years old woman, Kurdistan-IranY, Sweden)

In dominant Western representation and imaginations, the Muslim woman is primarily conceived as an object of Muslim male tyranny, allegedly waiting for white saviors to introduce her into modernity and individual emancipation. Despite their ideological differences, liberal and right-wing political debaters and politicians in the West, often deploy racist discourses to target sexism and gender-based oppression within the Muslim communities. This is a contradictory route to feminism since the West cannot claim to endorse the well-being of Muslim women by using racism, when racist practices target both Muslim men and women in different societal arenas (see Delphy, 2015). In 2021, while discussing the question of multiculturalism and segregation in Sweden, Richard Jomshof, a leading member of the far-right political party Sweden Democrats and a member of the Swedish parliament, advertised blatantly on public Swedish TV that "Islam is a detestable ideology and religion". Racism as a divisive ideology and idea has crossed the borders between the far-right and the mainstream political parties in Western Europe and embraced by an increasing section of European societies (Kallis, 2013). This is not to say that there is no opposition to the rise of racism and anti-Muslim racism, but the problem is that mainstream political parties due to the fear of losing their votes, tend to fall into the traps of the far-right by using more and less the same interpretative framework to depict (Muslim) migration as posing a threat to the welfare state, national identity, democracy and gender equity in the West. Muslim migrants are often believed to expect rights and exploit the welfare system but not fulfil their duties as citizens or residents of European states. When Islam is portrayed as a 'detestable religion', it is an invitation to member of the dominant constituency to pit against Muslim migrants and provide the natives with the 'license to hate' (see Kallis, 2013). The ascribed and experienced immigrant status affects how people experience their political membership and citizenship (Anderson, 2013). Contemporary anti-Muslim discourses in Europe have a negative impact on Muslim immigrants and their relation to the Western societies where they are living. It is in the everyday life that people can translate their political status as citizens into rights and claim-making to places that they inhabit. It is obvious that the Swedish and the British society share a thorny way to accept to the presence of Swedish and British citizens with Muslim and immigrant backgrounds. This is a political dilemma that many European states face in regard to accepting Muslim immigrants as full-edged members of their societies. Although Swedish and British governments and mainstream political parties use rhetoric of equality at a formal and juridical level and assert commitments to fight and ban racism, they tend to reduce immigrants to social problem objects that need political solutions, often called integration policies. Moreover, essentialist notions of Swedishness and Britishness like appearance make it difficult for the Kurdish immigrants to claim a Swedish and a British identity:

> I will never be accepted as a Swede because I have an appearance that does not look Swedish. When you think about a Swede, you imagine a certain appearance; blonde and blue-eyed people. When I am abroad and I say that I am Swedish, people laugh at me and tell me that I do not look like a Swede. (Kardo, a 34 years old man, Kurdistan-Turkey, Sweden)

> The thing is that people do not know that you are British citizen or care about that. In your daily life, the whites see that you have a different appearance. You are darker and they treat you differently at the workplace in regard to the way they speak to you or behave toward you. You feel that you are not welcome in their community and there are many barriers between you and them. You are not allowed to become part of the British society, you can see it in on their body language and feel it. You can see many signals that you can see in their eyes. (Aras, a 58 years old man, Kurdistan-Region-Iraq, the UK)

Racialized people who live in societies where racism is prevalent gradually learn to detect and read the signals, language, body gestures and gazing practices of the dominant group that inform racial othering and objectification. Whiteness was raised a central marker of belonging in the Swedish and British context. This indicates that despite the idea that these societies reject racial distinction between different groups based on biology and appearance, whiteness still is the line that divides the inside from the outside. This is not to say that whiteness is a monolithic category with no internal hierarchies, but in relation to the non-white and migrants from the global south, it is the key marker of belonging in a white-centered society. Lack of command of language also matters when everyday racism is spouted in the face of non-white migrants. Bjar vividly remembers how he was bullied by white English students for not knowing English as a newly arrived refugee from Kurdistan:

> Although you have citizenship, you are not treated in the same way as those who were born here. This is why I do not feel British. You encounter racism in your life and you are not treated as good as a white person because we are not white. I was bullied by white students when I came to England because I did not speak English and I always had to fight because I could not stand people bullying me. There were also some Pakistanis and Indians who acted like whites. I have also been treated badly by white bus drivers. They can become angry when you do not have change or the way they look at you. They treat white passengers much better and politely, but when they see dark people, you can see that they do not fully respect you. (21 years old man, Kurdistan-Region-Iraq, the UK)

While language is a central key to access rights and institutions, racism will not disappear if migrants learn the language of the dominant society. Heval, a 30 years old Kurdish man who speaks with a regional Swedish dialect and currently works as a police officer in Sweden referred to his experiences of racism when he was younger. This account testifies that whiteness matters more than the question of language when rights and exclusion are determined in Sweden:

> I was looking for part-time job when I was a university student. So I called a place and told them that I would like to work part-time. They were very happy and said it is fantastic and I could come to an interview. When arrived there, the woman that I spoke to opened the door. I will never forget her gaze because it was telling me: "Have you come to the right place? You cannot be the person I talked to." Then she told me that I do not have any accent when I speak Swedish. I told her that if that is an obstacle, I can speak with an immigrant accent. I have many friends with similar experiences, veiled women who have been denied work because of their appearances.

Racism as an ideology assigns hierarchical meanings and values to differences. It is a relational practice of power abuse and domination. By gaining power in the wider society and over its institutions, racism becomes a highly relational form of justifying and normalizing privilege and exclusion. It would be naïve to assume that these experiences of racism by the interviewees are incidents of individual racism or pathologies since "racism is by definition the expression or activation of group power" (Essed, 1991, p. 37). Above, Bjar raised the position of some Pakistani and Indian youth who "acted like whites" when they targeted him as a non-white migrant while not speaking sufficient English. This is not something unique for the British context but also highly salient in Sweden when certain racialized and minoritized groups internalize the prevailing racial hierarchy that in its turn informs their negative discourses and behaviors toward newly arrived migrants and refugees (see Eliassi, 2013). While Huner was vocal about white racism, as I will return to, he was also disturbed by the fact that certain Indians and Pakistanis living in Britain viewed themselves as 'better immigrants' than those who have arrived relatively late to Britain:

> It is not only the white English who are racist but also Indians and Pakistanis who treat you in a negative way because they believe that this is their country and they have been here before people like me. The Indians and Pakistanis think that they are from here but they also came here. When I see them, I always ask to be served by a white person because you get a better service. If I have the possibility, I change to a white customer service. They are polite and treat you better. The black Caribbean are better than the Indians and Pakistanis in the way they treat you. (26 years old man, Kurdistan-Region-Iraq, the UK)

This account points to the strategies of certain racialized groups to position themselves favorably within a continuum of desirability, by becoming harsher and less welcoming toward newly arrived migrants and refugees. This harshness toward new migrants and refugees is a projection of what they themselves or their parents have experienced as subjugated migrants in a predominantly white-oriented society. Internalized racism informs the subjectivities of minoritized groups who look at themselves, identities and language through the political grammar and lens of the dominant white group (see Pyke, 2010). By embracing the racial grammar of the dominant white group, racialized groups do not challenge the hierarchical order but reproduce and reinforce the exclusiveness of whiteness. In Sweden, there are established migrants who view the arrival of newly arrived refugees from Syria and Afghanistan as the cause behind the increased level of racism and the success of the right-wing political parties with clear anti-immigrant political agendas. They are anxious that they can be mistakenly treated as a newly arrived migrant or refugee in Sweden.

Racism not only complicates the sense of belonging to the wider society but also entails and justifies material inequality for racialized groups. In effect, racism functions as a device to legitimize ethnic chauvinism of the dominant group and socially reminding the minoritized groups to accept their subordinated position in the social hierarchy. Moreover, racism does not need to be experienced directly but can inform the consciousness of racialized groups that they belong to a group that runs the risk of becoming target of racist and oppressive practices (see Young, 1990):

> I have a Swedish citizenship. A Swedish girl once asked me in the corridor where we live, whether I was Swedish. Indeed, she told me that I was Swedish but I told her that I am not Swedish and she told me that she regarded me as a Swede. I understood that she had difficulty in understanding me that I did not want to be Swedish. I told her that I am Kurdish. I explained for her that identity is not only about what I think about myself since it is a collective phenomenon. When I go out and apply for a job in the Swedish society, they will be looking at my name or my appearance. I will not be hailed, seen or treated as a Swede. (Dilar, a 28 years old woman, Kurdistan-Turkey, Sweden)

> Sometimes people show their racism the way they treat you if you are not white English. Sometimes when I finish my work, white people use slurs against me and say that immigrants have taken their jobs and tell me: "go back home to your own country!" "what are you doing here?" Sometimes, when you look for a job and you do not get the job because you do not look like white. (Huner, a 26 years old man, Kurdistan Region-Iraq, the UK)

The accounts clearly illustrate that racism targets migrants socially, economically and spatially and reinforces their sense of non-belonging to the dominant white societies in Sweden and the UK. There is a risk that by rejecting the position of 'Swedishness' and 'Britishness' that migrants can be blamed for their own ghettoization and marginalization in the wider society and neglecting the structural ethnic and religious exclusion that migrants face in the society. It is one thing to be nominally Swedish or British but a totally different things to be effectively viewed and treated as a legitimate member of the Swedish or the British society.

The principles of Swedish and British integration policy and multiculturalism are based on an inclusive subordination (Mulinari, 2009). Hassan, a 53 years old Kurdish interviewee underlined the discrepancy between having a British citizenship and the way a British identity was imagined and experienced. According to Hassan, when people imagine a British person, it is not a Kurd or Middle Eastern that come to their mind, but a person who is Scottish, English, Welsh and Northern Irish. For him, "a citizenship is a paper" and cannot be translated into being a British. He speculated if he was really British and Britain was his homeland, why was he subjected to racist slurs and imperatives like: "Paki!" "Go back home to your homeland". Hassan said that this was so recurrent since he runs a kiosk with daily encounters with people and used every effort to avoid confrontation.

This explains why reinforcing a Kurdish identity in the diasporic context can become a political strategy to escape alienation and otherness. Marivan provides a framework where he utilizes such a strategy:

> I can go to any authority in Sweden and prove that I am a Swedish citizen on paper. But the question is whether I am Swedish or not? Because when I walk on the streets in Sweden, I always feel that I am a second-class citizen. In this country, I have never been in the category of first-class citizens. I speak Swedish, have a university degree and I might have more knowledge about Sweden than certain Swedes. But that does not matter because I am a second- class citizen because this is related to the fact that I am not from this place and I receive very often the question 'where are you from?' In Sweden, there are some statistics; the second most posed question in Sweden is the question "where are you from?" All this explains why I do not want to be number two in a society. I do not think that I am a deficient person to be treated as a second-class citizen. One of my strategies to deal with this situation that I do not accept in my mind that my state [Kurdistan] is occupied. I cannot accept the current boundaries where my homeland is divided by four states. I want to be Kurdish and have a Kurdish identity but also be number ONE in my homeland (Marivan, a 28 years old man, Kurdistan Region-Iraq, Sweden)

As Bosniak (2006) puts it, the national citizenship is not only hard on the outside but it can also be hard inside against members of different groups who are not viewed as qualified to attain equal citizenship rights. It is in this context that we can distinguish between the citizenship status as 'a real Swede' and 'Swedish on paper' (Eliassi, 2013). Attainment of a Kurdish state is viewed as a political strategy to break with two forms of domination, as a Kurd in the Middle East and as an immigrant in Sweden. The example above illustrates why nationalism is perceived as an important political device to achieve statehood and political equality in a world of nation-states that subordinate stateless peoples and renders them a marginalized position both in the countries of origin but also in the context of migration. However, if the antidote to the position of being "number two in a society" is by becoming "number ONE" in the putative homeland, then the cycle of oppression and exclusion will be reproduced by targeting new groups who become ethnic strangers and denied equality in the society. After all, the very idea of being "number ONE", as Marivan desires, is about spatial management and mastery over the place called home, and creating the basis for a hierarchical citizenship that Marivan himself wants to escape. This process of othering that Kurdish and Palestinian migrants experience affect also their engagement and attachment to their ascribed identities:

> Sweden cannot accept me as a Swede. If I had been accepted as a Swede and there were no differences between me and the Swedes, I would not have the need to struggle ten times more than an ordinary Swede. Maybe my feeling about Palestine would have been different. (Mona, a 30 years old Palestinian woman, Sweden)

Both the Kurdish and Palestinian interviewees shared experiences of otherness in the context of different hierarchical citizenship regimes. Certainly, the British and the Swedish citizenship provided them with more rights and enhanced their mobility in the world than the Middle Eastern citizenships, but daily experiences of racism also reminded them about their impermanent presence in Sweden and the UK. We can make the argument that the Swedish and the British citizenship is both hard and soft on the racialized group, which create both comfort and discomfort for Kurdish and Palestinians migrants in occupying the position of the citizen in an uneven way. It is not uncommon for Arab states to refuse providing the Palestinians with citizenship rights due to the fear of depoliticizing the Palestinian cause and suspension of the politics of return for Palestinians who live in exile and refugee camps. In the wider context of stateless diasporas, the Tibetan diaspora partly opposes the act of taking up citizenship of other states since it allegedly undermines the "very foundation of legitimacy of the exile struggle" (Choedup, 2018, p. 213) and can "weaken moral and political support for the common Tibetan cause both within the Tibetan society and in international communities" (ibid. p. 211). For the Kurdish and the Palestinians research participants, attainment of Swedish or British citizenship was not considered as a negation of the Kurdish or the Palestinian cause or interruption of their experiences and positions as two stateless peoples. In contrast, attainment of Swedish and Palestinian citizenship was viewed as a political tool to enhance their rights, legal status and mobility without negating their Kurdish and Palestinian identities. The status of Britain and Sweden as uncertain homelands and daily lived experiences of discomfort, racism and non-belonging triggered and strengthened their sense of otherness, statelessness and alienation. Hence, the solution to statelessness is not merely about providing a person or a group with formal citizenship and particularly if that citizenship conceals the dominance of a particular group that has generalized and nationalized its ethnicity or racial identity within a state through political and ideological dominance (Radhakrishnan, 2003).

References

Ahmed, S. (2007). A phenomenology of whiteness. *Feminist Theory, 8*(2), 1464–7001.

Allsopp, H. (2014). *The Kurds of Syria. Political parties and identity in the Middle East*. I.B. Tauris.

Anderson, B. (2013). *US & THEM? The dangerous politics of immigration control*. Oxford University Press.

Arendt, H. (1951). *The origins of totalitarianism*. Shocken Books.

Aschroft, R. T., & Bevir, M. (2018). Multiculturalism in contemporary Britain: Policy, law and theory. *Critical Review of International Social and Political Philosophy, 21*(1), 1–21.

Back, L., Sinha, S., & Bryan, C. (2012). New hierarchies of belonging. *European Journal of Cultural Studies, 15*(2), 139–154.

Bellamy, R. (2008). *Citizenship: A very short introduction*. Oxford University Press.

Bilsky, L. (2008). Citizenship as mask: Between the imposter and the refugee. *Constellations, 15*(1), 72–97.

Blitz, B. K., & Otero-Iglesias, M. (2011). Stateless by any other name: Refused asylum-seekers in the United Kingdom. *Journal of Ethnic and Migration Studies, 37*(4), 657–573.

Bosniak, L. (2006). *The citizen and the other: Dilemmas of contemporary membership*. Princeton University Press.

Butenschon, N. (2000). State, power, and citizenship in the Middle East: A theoretical introduction. In A. B. Nils, D. Uri & H. Manuel (Eds.), *Citizenship and the state in the Middle East: Approaches and applications* (pp. 3–27). Syracuse University Press.

Carens, H. J. (1992). Migration and mobility: A liberal egalitarian perspective. In B. Brian & E. G. Robert (Eds.), *Free movement: Ethical issues in the transnational movement of people and money* (pp. 25–47). Pennsylvania State University Press.

Castles, S. (2005). Nation and empire: Hierarchies of citizenship in the new global order. *International Politics, 42*, 203–224.

Chatterjee, P. (2020). *I am the people: Reflections on popular sovereignty today*. Columbia University Press.

Choedup, N. (2018). Statelessness as a form of citizenship among Tibetan exiles. In C. M. Lyon & F. G. Allison (Eds.), *Citizenship and place: Case studies on the borders of citizenship* (pp. 187–219). Rowman & Littlefield.

Delphy, C. (2015). *Separate and dominate: Feminism and racism after the war on terror*. Verso.

Eliassi, B. (2013). *Contesting Kurdish identities in Sweden: Quest for belonging among Middle Eastern youth*. Palgrave Macmillan.

Eliassi, B. (2014). *Kurds are portrayed as linguistic bastards*. https://yourmiddleeast.com/2014/05/15/kurds-are-portrayed-as-linguistic-bastards/. Accessed 5 March 2021.

Eliassi, B. (2016). Statelessness in a word of nation-states: The cases of Kurdish diasporas in Sweden and the UK. *Journal of Ethnic and Migration Studies, 42*(9), 1403–1419.

Essed, P. (1991). *Understanding everyday racism: An interdisciplinary theory*. Sage Publications.

Fein, L. C., & Straughn, J. B. (2014). How citizenship matters: Narratives of stateless and citizenship choice in Estonia. *Citizenship Studies, 18*(6–7), 690–706.

Ghanem, A., & Khatib, I. (2017). The nationalization of the Israeli ethnocratic regime and the Palestinian minority's shrinking citizenship. *Citizenship Studies, 21*(8), 889–902.

Goodman, W. (2010). Integration requirement for integration's sake? Identifying, categorizing and comparing civic integration policies. *Journal of Ethnic and Migration Studies, 36*, 753–772.

Heath, A., & Demireva, N. (2014). Has multiculturalism failed in Britain? *Ethnic and Racial Studies, 37*(1), 161–180.

Hickman, M. J., Thomas, L., Nickels, H. C., & Silvestri, S. (2012). Social cohesion and the notion of 'suspect communities': A study of the experiences and impacts of being 'suspect' for Irish communities and Muslim communities in Britain. *Critical Studies on Terrorism, 5*(1), 89–106.

Hindess, B. (2000). Citizenship in the international management of populations. *The American Behavioral Scientist, 43*(9), 1486–1497.

Houston, C. (2001). *Islam, Kurds and the Turkish nation state*. Oxford: Berg.

Hürriyet Daily News. (2012). Erdoğan: No concession to "one nation, one flag". http://www.hurriyetdailynews.com/erdogan-no-concession-on-one-nation-one-flag-37832. Acessed 27 March 2019.

Isin, E. F., & Wood, P. K. (1999). *Citizenship & identity*. Sage Publications.

Isin, E. F. (2002). Ways of being political. *Distinktion: Scandinavian Journal of Social Theory, 3*(1), 7–28.

Isin, E. F., & Turner, B. S. (2002). Citizenship studies: An introduction. In I. E. Engin & S. T. Bryan (Eds.), *Handbooks of citizenship studies* (pp. 1–10). Sage.

Jabareen, H. (2014). Hobbesian citizenship: how the Palestinians became a minority in Israel. In K. Will & P. Eva (Eds.), *Multiculturalism and minority rights in the Arab world* (pp. 189–217). Oxford University Press.

Jamal, A. & Kensicki, A. (2020). Theorizing half-statelessness: A case study of the nation-state law in Israel. *Citizenship Studies*. https://doi.org/10.1080/13621025.2020.1745152

Kallis, A. (2013). Far-right "contagion" or a failing "mainstream"? How dangerous ideas cross borders and blur boundaries. *Democracy and Security, 9*(3), 221–246.

Kimmerling, B. (2001). *The invention and decline of Israeliness: State, society, and the military*. University of California Press.

Kirmanj, S. (2014). Kurdish history textbooks: Building a nation-state within a nation-state. *Middle East Journal, 63*(3), 367–384.

Kumar, K. (2000). Nation and empire: English and British national identity in comparative perspective. *Theory and Society, 29*(5), 575–608.

Kymlicka, W. (2010). Testing the liberal multiculturalist hypothesis: Normative theories and social sciences evidence. *Canadian Journal of Political Science, 43*(2), 257–271.

Kymlicka, W., & Pföstl, E. (2014). Introduction. In K. Will & P. Eva (Eds.), *Multiculturalism and minority rights in the Arab world* (pp. 1–24). Oxford University Press.

Marshall, T.H. & Bottomore, T. (1992). *Citizenship and social class*. Pluto Press.

Mau, S. (2010). Mobility, citizenship, inequality, and the liberal state. *International Political Sociology, 4*, 339–361.

Meer, N. Modood, T. (2009). The multicultural state we're in: Muslims, 'multiculture', and the 'civic re-balancing' of British multiculturalism. *Political Studies, 57*, 473–497.

Mignolo, W. (2006). Citizenship, knowledge, and the limits of humanity. *American Literary History, 18*(2), 312–331.

Miller-Idriss, C. (2006). Everyday understandings of citizenship in Germany, *Citizenship Studies, 10*(5): 541–570.
Molavi, S. C. (2013). *Stateless citizenship: The Palestinian-Arab citizens of Israel*. Brill.
Mulinari, D. (2009). "Den andra" familjen: Genus, nation och migration. In F. Janet & L. Åsa (Eds.), *Välfärd, genus och familj* (pp. 201–224). Liber.
Mylonas, H. (2012). *The politics of nation-building: Making co-nationals, refugees, and minorities*. Cambridge University Press.
Neumayer, E. (2006). Unequal access to foreign space: How states use visa restrictions to regulate mobility in a globalized world. *Transactions of the Institute of British Geographers, 31*(1), 72–84.
Nordberg, C. (2006). Claiming citizenship: Marginalised voices on identity and belonging. *Citizenship Studies, 10*(5), 523–539.
Pandey, G. (2006). *Routine violence: Nations, fragments, histories*. Standford University Press.
Pease, B. (2010). *Undoing privilege: Unearned advantage in a divided world*. Zed Books.
Phillips, A. (2015). *The politics of the human*. Cambridge University Press.
Pred, A. (2000). *Even in Sweden: Racisms, racialized spaces, and the popular geographical imagination*. University of California Press.
Pyke, K. (2010). What is internalized oppression and why don't we study it? Acknowledging racism's hidden injuries. *Sociological Perspective, 53*(4), 551–572.
Radhakrishnan, R. (2003). *Theory in an uneven world*. Blackwell Publishing.
Rattansi, A. (2011). *Multiculturalism: A very short introduction*. Oxford University Press.
Redclift, V. (2013). *Statelessness and citizenship: Camps and the creation of political space*. Routledge.
Salter, M. B. (2004). Passports, mobility, and security: How smart can the border be? *International Studies Perspectives, 5*, 71–91.
Shachar, A. (2009). *The birthright lottery: Citizenship and global inequality*. Harvard University Press.
Shachar, A. (2014). Introduction: Citizenshop and the 'right to have rights.' *Citizenship Studies, 18*(2), 114–124.
Schierup, C.-U., & Ålund, A. (2011). The end of Swedish exceptionalism? Citizenship, neoliberalism and politics of exclusion. *Race & Class, 53*(1), 45–64.
Scott, J. W. (1994). Deconstructing equality-versus-difference: Or, the uses of poststructuralist theory for feminism. In S. Steven (Ed.), *The postmodern turn: New perspectives on social theory* (pp. 282–298). Cambridge University Press.
Shafir, G., & Peled, Y. (2002). *Being Israeli: The dynamics of multiple citizenship*. Cambridge University Press.

Soleimani, K., & Mohammadpour, A. (2019). Can the Non-Persian speak? The sovereign narration of "Iranian identity." *Ethnicities, 9*(5), 925–947.
Somers, M. R. (2008). *Genealogies of citizenship: Markets, statelessness, and the right to have rights*. Cambridge University Press.
Vox (2018). *Israel's hugely controversial 'nation-state' law, explained.* https://www.vox.com/world/2018/7/31/17623978/israel-jewish-nation-state-law-bill-explained-apartheid-netanyahu-democracy Accessed 1 March 2021.
Walzer, M. (2001). History and national liberation. *Journal of Israeli History, 20*(2–3), 1–8.
Yeğen, M. (2009). "Prospective-Turks" or "Pseudo-Citizens": Kurds in Turkey. *The Middle East Journal, 63*(4): 597–615.
Yiftachel, O. (2006). *Ethnocracy: Land, and the politics of identity Israel/Palestine.* University of Pennsylvania Press.
Young, I. M. (1990). *Justice and the politics of difference.* Princeton University Press.
Young, I. M. (1995). Polity and group difference: A critique of the ideal of universal citizenship. In B. Ronald (Ed.). *Theorizing Citizenship* (pp. 175–207). New York: State University of New York Press.

CHAPTER 6

The Weight of Assimilation and the Confines of Resistance in Diaspora

The Turkish state was founded in 1923. Since its inception, the Turkish state has attempted to coercively assimilate the Kurds. Turkishness was cherished and proclaimed as the master identity of this new Republic through a negation of the existing non-Turkish constituencies that were historically present within this political geography. For many decades, the Turkish state and mainstream media have deliberately denied the Kurds a political voice to represent themselves as an ethnopolitical reality. Through describing political claims by the Kurds as an expression of 'feudalism', 'barbarianism' and 'backwardness', the Turkish state has attempted to prevent the Kurds from achieving recognition as an ethnopolitical identity or asserting themselves as the second territorial-linguistic community after the Turks (Yeğen, 2009). After 1980, the Turkish state and media frequently referred to political and armed Kurdish dissent led by the Kurdistan Workers' Party (PKK) as a case of 'terrorism' (Demir, 2014).

In order to craft a homogenous entity, the Turkish state initiated and implemented population policies and social engineering among non-Turks as a technique of nation formation. The predominantly Kurdish regions were imagined as the 'badlands' of the Turkish Republic that assumedly needed to be tamed and civilized through a Turkification process. Following a colonial discourse, the Kurds were imagined as the

B. Eliassi, *Narratives of Statelessness and Political Otherness*, Minorities in West Asia and North Africa,
https://doi.org/10.1007/978-3-030-76698-6_6

'Red Indians' of America who were deemed as culturally and economically unfit for the modern world and would either undergo gradual assimilation or elimination (Üngür, 2011). Accordingly, Kurdish identity was devalued as not having a place in the modern world and urged to subsume itself under the universality of Turkish identity that not only claimed to be the universal identity of Turkey but also the root of "all world civilizations and languages" (Demir, 2014, p. 388).

Although the Turkish assimilation policies have been quite successful, the Kurds remain the main force that challenge the sovereign Turkish identity and seek to reformulate the political principles of inclusion in Turkey (Ergin, 2014). In sum, coercive assimilation policies, displacement, destruction of Kurdish villages, violence and denial have thus structured Turkish politics against the Kurdish population (Eliassi, 2013). As a consequence of deprivation and military confrontation between the PKK and the Turkish state, several million Kurds have left their homes in Western cities of Turkey. Thousands of villages have been destroyed and over 2.5 billion acres of forest have been burned by the Turkish state (Houston, 2001). This forced displacement, whether economically or politically motivated, has contributed to formation of a Kurdish diaspora in Western Turkey. The Kurdish diaspora in Western Turkish cities has been viewed as a 'Kurdish invasion', where Kurds are racialized both in public and popular discourses as inferior (Ergin, 2014) and viewed as culturally incompatible with modern city life due to their supposedly backward, criminal, violent and separatist identity (Saracoglu, 2009). Many Kurds have co-opted these negative images and equate Kurdishness with ignorance, incivility and with an interest in their ostensibly parochial identity (Houston, 2001). This orientalist discourse deployed against the Kurds aims to create a hierarchical political order and buttress the idea of Turkish identity as the master identity that needs to be embraced by the Kurds in order to enter a civilized social order (Zeydanlioglu, 2008). Paradoxically, while the existence of an ethnopolitical Kurdish identity has been historically denied, muted and punished by the Turkish state, ordinary Turks both recognize the Kurds as a different ethnicity and vindicate exclusionary discourses with reference to their real or alleged differences. In popular Turkish representation, Kurds are both viewed as disrupting security and benefiting scroungers (Saracoglu, 2009, 2010). Following negative media and political representations that either define the Kurds as a problem or non-existent, the Kurdish diaspora in these Turkish cities are both de-constituting themselves as Turkish by adapting and assimilating into a Turkish identity and/or constituting themselves as Kurds as a form of resistance toward assimilation (Houston, 2001).

From the 1970s onwards, as a result of political oppression and violence and economic deprivation in Iran, Iraq, Syria and Turkey, hundreds of thousands of Kurds have migrated to Western Europe in search of political, cultural and economic rights and security. It is in the context of liberal democracies and multicultural integration policies in Western Europe, juxtaposed with processes of globalization and the proliferation of information technologies, that a highly politicized Kurdish diaspora has emerged. Migration has been a transformative experience for many Kurdish migrants who have fled Turkey and have attempted to shake off their imposed Turkish identity and/or alter their pattern of identification with the Turkish state. Against this background, this chapter will engage with the ways Kurds have experienced Turkish assimilation policies and the meanings that they assign to these experiences in diasporic contexts. Moreover, this chapter will explore the politics and limits of resistance that aim to destabilize Turkish assimilation discourses and reclaim Kurdishness in the context of political violence in Turkey.

Molding National Sameness Through Assimilation

The concept of assimilation can be best understood within the context of modernity and the nation-state. Through design, manipulation, management and engineering, modernity aimed to impose order upon the society and remove ambivalence that the differences of ethnic minorities represented (Bauman, 1991). Modernity has not only made the need for recognition central in human lives but also produced conditions in which recognition is often denied (Markell, 2003). The term assimilation, which means making alike or similar, was first applied within biology. The first usage that can be dated goes back to 1578 and referred to assimilation as "acts of *absorption* and *incorporation* performed by living organisms. Unambiguously, 'assimilation' stood for *conversion*, not a self-administered change; it was an action performed by a living organism on its environment. It meant convert into a substance of its own nature" (Bauman, 1991, p. 103, emphasis in original). It was first during 1837 that the term of assimilation was generalized and became common currency due to the escalating nationalisms. Bauman argues that what made assimilation so attractive to its advocates was the asymmetry of assimilation as a social practice and the unequivocal unidirectionality of its process. The subordinated cultural groups thus needed a radical change to transform themselves in order to become more identical with the dominant identity that functioned as a normative point of reference. The objective to achieve cultural and linguistic uniformity within the realm of the nation-state involved a far-reaching cultural crusade and intolerance to difference. The modern nation-state functions as a designing power that fosters similarity and uniformity through defining what is order and chaos, filtering the proper from the improper and legitimizing one form of life as superior to others. In order to achieve these political goals, the nation-state resorted to assimilation policies (ibid.). Assimilation as such became a declaration of war on ambiguity and those who were deemed as "*foreign* or not *sufficiently native*" (p. 105, emphasis in original). This required a nationalizing project to distinguish between the fitting and worthy national from the unfitting and unworthy non-national. It is in this context that *core* members/citizens were filtered from the culturally and linguistically *marked* and stigmatized subjects of the nation-state.

The political vision that assimilation represented lured the culturally different and victim to fall into the trap of ambivalence with the idea that the putative marked subject can gain an admission ticket "to the world free from the stigma of otherness" (p. 102). This requires inferiorized groups to obliterate the ascribed stigmatizing differences that they carry in order to meet the conditions that the gatekeepers of the dominant group had set. This situation can create distress for inferiorized groups who are objectified and meticulously examined and assessed by the dominant group that determines the meanings of their conduct. When an inferiorized group applies for an entry into the dominant group through its adaptation to the values of the dominant group, it effectively provides the dominant group with a position to act as "the *arbitrating power*, a force entitled to set the exams and mark the performance" (p. 106). The project of assimilation and its mechanism can be summarized as a nationalization project that seeks to create legal, linguistic, cultural and ideological unification within the territorial boundary of the nation-state. In order to deal with cultural heterogeneity, the nation-state often responds with cultural crusades, impatience and intolerance against differences that supposedly threaten national and political integrity of the state. Since the states were nationalized and nations were *etatized*, the state stipulates the conditions for citizenship through political loyalty, trustworthiness and devotion to cultural uniformity. This leads to a nexus between citizenship and cultural conformity (pp. 140–142).

The main Turkish strategy to assimilate the Kurds has been through language. For the founder of the Turkish republic, Mustafa Kemal Atatürk, a person who claimed to be a member of the Turkish nation, must unconditionally speak the Turkish language. Although nationalism and racism can be formulated in different ways due to specific political and historical contexts, they can easily collaborate in constructing an exclusionary political community (Gökay & Aybak, 2016). Consider how the first Prime Minister of Turkey, Ismet Inonu, expressed his idea about the Turkification process of non-Turks: "Nationalism is our only factor of cohesion…In the face of a Turkish majority other elements have no kind of influence. We must Turkify the inhabitants of our land at any price and we will annihilate those who oppose the Turks" (ibid., p. 108). According to Aslan (2015), the predominantly Kurdish region has functioned as 'an area of dissidence' that continues to challenge the Turkish state in establishing its territorial dominance over the Kurds. In order to govern the Kurds and achieve its dominance over their territories, the Turkish state has historically adopted:

> a thick definition of national belonging and aimed at an "extreme" makeover" of the society, dictating the dos and don'ts for daily behavior. The state's ambitions turned out to be the most comprehensive for the Kurdish citizens as they represented not only the largest linguistic minority within the boundary of the Turkish republic but also a society that the state's elite perceived to be in most need of modernization. (p. 15)

Turkish assimilation policy was both comprehensive and intrusive in the daily and private lives of the Kurds in Turkey. The Turkish national policy vis-à-vis the Kurds manifested itself as a colonial ideology based on a "civilizing mission that aimed at transforming Kurdish values, language, dress, tastes, and habits" (ibid., p. 16). In order to achieve this goal, the Turkish state has embraced a variety of discursive resources to disqualify the Kurds as a nation with their distinct language but speaking a spoken language corrupted by Turkish and Persian words. This shows the centrality of language as a means of erasing and oppressing Kurdish existence. Hence, being Kurdish and becoming a future Turk through violent assimilatory practices have produced wounded Kurdish subjectivities within the boundary of the Turkish state and in transnational and diasporic contexts. It is also in relation to these violent state policies that Kurdish movement and resistance have established themselves to oppose the Turkish hegemony over Kurdish lives and psyche. Diaspora is both a place and a social location from which Kurds frame their understanding of what assimilation meant to them as Kurds in Turkey and what it means to them now living in diaspora and how they respond and resist its power on their subjectivities. Unlike the state-linked Turkish diaspora that often reinforces Turkish statehood and the dominant position of the Turkish language and identity, the stateless Kurdish diaspora frequently challenges the Turkish state and attempt to subvert the Turkish mastery and refashion the hierarchical order that denies non-Turks the right to be legitimate members of the society.

Below, I will draw upon the narratives of the interviewees to show how assimilation has structured the subjectivities of the Kurds during their childhood and adulthood and how they respond to the persistent and internalized effects of Turkish assimilation policies on members of the Kurdish diaspora in Sweden and the UK.

Dehumanization and Foreignization of Kurdish Identity

The main strategy of the Turkish state has been based on a cultural war juxtaposed with military violence to erase the biographies of the Kurds in Turkey. Kurds have both consented to and violently opposed these assimilation practices, which impinge on Kurdish identity formation in its different forms. This entails that life for a Kurd in the Turkish nation-state has been and is still difficult and at times very dangerous. Kurdish assimilation into a Turkish identity has not been a simple journey since it has been based on coercive and violent practices (Houston, 2001). From the moment the state defines who is the assimilator and who is the object of assimilation, a hierarchy is constructed between different members of the nation-state (Bauman, 1991). Memo, who was a teacher in Mardin before migrating to Sweden, talked about the difficulty of being a Kurd in Turkey and recalled events and lived experiences of state and popular violence targeting Kurds. He underlined how Turkishness has entailed construction of Kurdishness as an outlawed identity:

> In my homeland in Kurdistan, I was a foreigner. In my homeland, my name was forbidden, my language was forbidden, my flag was forbidden, naming our homeland and children were forbidden. We were a forbidden people. (Memo, a 50 years old man, Kurdistan-Turkey, Sweden)

The account above converges with the formulation of Bauman that assimilation entails a form of war on identities and languages who are viewed as a threat to national community and national sameness (Bauman, 1991). It is worth noting that Kurds and other non-Turkish groups were not foreigners to these lands but *foreignized* through Turkish representations that endeavored to spatially erase non-Turkish cultures, religions and peoples. Leyla evoked her father's move to Bursa from Kurdistan and the way he was treated when declaring his Kurdishness to a Turkish family as new neighbors:

> During the 1970s when my father was living in Bursa, he told a Turk that he was Kurdish. The Turk told him: "Do Kurds eat people?" They were afraid that our family would cut their heads while they were sleeping. We lived as neighbors during 3 years and he became so sad when we moved from the neighborhood and lamented about his earlier perceptions about the Kurds to my family. He said that he has been brainwashed and taught to not see Kurds as human beings. (Leyla, a 56 years old woman, Kurdistan-Turkey, the UK)

This story indicates how negative stereotypes and stigmatization shape dominant Turkish perceptions of the Kurds not only in the past but also at present times, where Kurds are viewed as a security problem by unsettling the ontological security of the Turkish nation and its discourse of ethnic homogeneity. Moreover, this intersubjective encounter above reveals both the power of stereotypes and dehumanization of the Kurds and the productive and positive transformation in the relationship between member of the dominant Turkish group and the minoritized Kurds. In a similar context, Evin, who was born in Lebanon but grew up in Izmir, shared her experiences of otherness as a Kurd in Izmir:

> I remember it was taboo to say that I am Kurdish in school or speak Kurdish because it was Turkish that was the rule. In school everybody knew that you were Kurdish. It was during a gymnastic class that a teacher asked me the meaning of my name. She said that name cannot be Turkish and I said that it was Kurdish. She did not like the word Kurdish. Everybody

> in the class got a good grade in gymnastics except me. The funny thing is that I was the most sportive student in my class. Our Turkish neighbor told us once in Izmir: "I hope that a bee can sting your tongues so you can never be able to say the word Kurd." (Evin, a 39 years old woman, Kurdistan-Turkey, Sweden)

This entails the institutional discrimination often collaborated with popular and everyday discrimination against the Kurdish identity. Through these institutional and everyday encounters and experiences that Evin referred to above, Kurds were pushed to undervalue their Kurdishness in order to become somebody or attain some form of mainstream intelligibility in the gaze of the dominant Turkish group. In the context of postcolonial identity formation and subjugation, Radhakrishnan (2003) contends that it is important for identities to enjoy legitimacy both in the eyes of themselves and others. Otherwise "they are bound to languish within their histories of inferiority, deprived of their relational objective status *vis-à-vis* the objective conditions of other identities" (p. 19, emphasis in original). These histories of inferiority become more tangible when the interviewees discuss and remember the experiences of their denied Kurdish identity within the boundary of the Turkish jurisdiction, as the next section of this chapter will demonstrate.

Internalized Racism and Domination

Turkish supremacy has been largely constructed at the expense of non-Turkish constituencies through political violence and cultural conquest. The state power uses different social institutions to constitute a group by "imposing on it common principles of vision and division, and, thus a unique vision of its identity and an identical vision of its unity" (Bourdieu, 1992, p. 224). By creating this identical vision of unity, the Turkish state managed to displace and alienate Kurdish identity. To become a Turkish citizen, Kurds were urged to show that they had erased traces of Kurdish biographies and deculturated in institutional and everyday life. Aram provides an account of how his father invested in Turkishness and strived to attain the status of a 'civilized citizen', an experience that resembles a colonial situation:

> We had a shop where I worked as a tailor and it was close to the police station. Several of my customers were Turkish police officers. When these

> police officers came to our shop, my father urged us not to speak Kurdish but Turkish. He was ashamed of speaking Kurdish and he wanted to assert himself as Turkish and modern in front of the Turkish police officers. Speaking Turkish was considered as being a civilized person. You could see this attitude among both younger and older generations of Kurds. (Aram, a 48 years old man, Kurdistan-Turkey, Sweden)

This demonstrates that while the Kurdish identity or language was assumed to represent backwardness, Turkishness was conflated with civilization and modernity. This instilled a sense of cultural inferiority that the Turkish state has sanctioned. It is not a question of individualized experiences but has wider relevance that cut across generations. Hassan, who is an Alevi Kurd, painfully remembered his subordination due to his ethnic and religious background, given that the majority of Turkish and Kurdish population are Sunni Muslims. Hassan provides an account about the effects of Turkish assimilation on Kurdish subjectivity:

> I went to school when I was 5 years old. You do not realize this thing as a kid until you go to school where everything was in Turkish. When we Kurds spoke Kurdish with each other we were beaten up by the teachers. This was during the 1970s. I mean you go to school and the teacher asks you something in a language you do not understand and then he smacked you because you do not understand Turkish or the question. Gradually, your Turkish becomes better and you forget your own Kurdish language. It feels awful that you are Kurdish and you cannot speak your own language. Turkish language was everywhere, in the street, in the literature, radio and TV. Many people from my village say that they are Turkish because they deny their Kurdish identity. The Turkish state has really worked on making this people to lose their Kurdish identity. The Kurds start to be ashamed of their Kurdish identity and think that Turkish identity is a superior identity. I remember when we were kids and when some of us spoke better Turkish, that person was viewed as better than others. We were systematically beaten by the teacher when we did not speak good Turkish. When I was 10 years old and moved to Istanbul, I was ashamed of not speaking Turkish with a good accent because my friends were all Turkish and they could do remarks about my pronunciation. But I learnt to speak without any accent. The education system in Turkey makes you push yourself to be as Turkish as possible so you can fit in. (Hassan, a 53 years old man, Kurdistan-Turkey, the UK)

Hassan's experiences illustrate how assimilation works and how the Turkish identity due to its hegemonic state-sponsored position punishes non-Turkish identities and conquers non-Turkish bodies and minds. Hassan attempts to construct an interpretative framework to understand how Turkish identity gains hegemony in the wider society as the master identity that shapes institutions, appraises and hierarchizes differences as well as structures and conquers the subjectivity of the Kurdish subject. In the context of intensive and coercive Turkification processes of non-Turkish identities and spaces, the Kurds needed "to struggle to inhabit a world, which has been made for others" (Treacher, 2005, p. 50). This is one of the central issues that the leading postcolonial writer Franz Fanon has engaged with in the context of French colonialism and the desire of colonized black subjects to assume a white identity in order to enjoy the privileges of whiteness in some forms (Fanon, 1952, 2008). Post-colonial scholars often affirm the centrality of language for the colonial and postcolonial experience (Britton, 1999). For instance, consider the convergence between Hassan's account of the way Turkish language was assumed as the desirable symbolic object to be attained in order to gain respectability and acceptance, and the way Fanon talks about the black subject and (white) language, in this case French:

> Among a group of young Antilleans, he who can express himself, who masters the language, is the one to look out for: be worry of him; he's almost white. In France they say "to talk like a book". In Martinique, they say "to speak like a white man". (Fanon, 1952/2008, pp. 4–5)

For Fanon, language is one of central vehicles through which the colonized is radically transformed. The more the assimilated subject knows and speaks the language of power, the more he or she is assumed to have escaped the 'bush'. Mastery and knowledge of the dominant language provides the colonized subjects with credentials to different forms of privilege and recognition at the cost of those colonized subjects who have failed to alter and transform their subjectivity by learning and embodying the culture and language of the master identity (ibid.). According to Bourdieu (1992), states use education to construct, legitimize and impose a language in order to craft national sameness, common consciousness and mental structures. Aram provides a context how the symbolic power of Turkishness affected Kurds through education:

> In school, we were humiliated on a daily basis. This humiliation was normalized since we as Kurdish children had to declare that we were Turks and that we were prepared to sacrifice our lives for the Turkish nation and state. As a Kurd, you feel that *you are mentally raped by the Turkish state*. This was an extreme form of humiliation. If you could not master the Turkish language in a good way, you were also exposed to negative treatments by the teacher but also ran the risk of receiving a low grade. You could also be punished if you could not express yourself well in Turkish, which many Kurdish children could not because their parents could not speak Turkish so well. The teachers consisted of both Turks and Kurds. There were very few Kurdish teachers who were aware of their Kurdish identity. Many Kurdish teachers were stricter against the Kurdish students because they wanted to show that they were loyal to the Turkish nation and state. (Aram, a 48 years old man, Kurdistan-Turkey, Sweden, emphasis added)

The experience of Aram is clearly in line with the arguments of Aslan (2015) that the Turkish state has intruded deeply into the lives and identities of the Kurds. Aram above uses a sexualized language to depict the penetration of Turkish language and identity into the minds and bodies of the Kurdish children and the everyday humiliation they were subjected to. In her reading of the postcolonial writer Edouard Glissant, Britton (1999) argues that language can be used as a vehicle to achieve control and command. While colonized subjects might politicize language as a means of struggle and a basis for political mobilization against the colonizer, it is also true that educated elites within the colonized group due to the feeling of inferiority can use the dominant language for social promotion and mobility and to overcome the instilled colonial subjection. For the Kurdish teachers in Aram's account, one way of gaining recognition among the Kurdish teachers was expressed through asserting themselves as super-Turks by being guardians of Turkish mastery and language. It is this situation that explains how the dominant group gains the position of being the "the *arbitrating power*, a force entitled to set the exams and mark the performance" (Bauman, 1991, p. 106, emphasis in original). In a similar context of cultural and racial inferiorization, hooks (2015, p. 69) argues that racialized people might dissociate themselves from their identities, in order to undertake an attitude of superiority, and show that that the only to succeed is to assimilate into the dominant cultural values. For these racialized people who assume assimilation, it becomes urgent for them to not be seen as attached and linked to a racialized subject position. A central logic of Turkish assimilation is to eradicate the Kurdish self and embrace a Turkish self, a process that entails severe psychological distress for the Kurds (see hooks, 2015, p. 67). Assimilation as such becomes a social legitimation of Turkish supremacy. Despite the attempts of these Kurdish teachers, Aram pointed out that they could not conceal their Kurdish identity while speaking Turkish due to their distinct Kurdish accent. Ambivalence constitutes Kurdish identity formation. If they would invoke that they are Turkish as the political vision of the assimilation represented in order to be admitted a national ticket to the privileged Turkish identity, they would not be accepted as legitimate and core members of the Turkish community due to their accent and differences that revealed their Kurdishness. In addition, if they would choose to affirm their differences and demand rights, public recognition and acceptance of their Kurdish identity and language in everyday and institutional life, this could entail further exclusion and arbitrary violence and incarceration.

The interviewees above have talked about individual Kurds who have been exposed to practices of assimilation that have heavily affected the definition of self and other. To cast the net wider, the Kurdish movements that have at different times opposed the Turkish state have not been able to escape the domination of the Turkish language even when they frame a political template for political liberation of the Kurds. Aram, who was a member of the Kurdish party *Ala Rizgari* (The Liberation Flag) during the 1980s, talked about this contradiction and the penetrating depth of the Turkish assimilation:

> Even our political party that was revolutionary and wanted to create a free and an independent Kurdistan communicated its relationships and dialogue through the Turkish language. Many of our comrades could not speak Kurdish or spoke a very limited Kurdish and could not express themselves properly. We wrote, read and discussed politics in the Turkish language. We spoke Turkish as much as we could. The Turkish language was instilled into our spinal cords and we were deeply indoctrinated by the Turkish state. Sometimes within our party, somebody could suggest that we could speak Kurdish, but that person was immediately considered as a chauvinist and nationalist. It is very contradictory, because you fight for an independent Kurdistan, and you do not have the will to speak Kurdish. Why should you have an independent Kurdistan when your people speak Turkish? (Aram, a 48 years old man, Kurdistan-Turkey, Sweden)

In relations of cultural inequality, speaking an oppressed language like the Kurdish language becomes associated with a subversive identity that violates the bonds of solidarity between different constituencies that Turkish language allegedly promise to establish. Such a romantic conception of the Turkish language as a neutral and a vehicle of communication in a multilinguistic context conceals the historical and the present violence that has been constitutive to Turkish nation-building. The Kurdish resistance or aversion is not directed toward the Turkish language as such but against the way it has been appropriated by the Turkish state to stigmatize and inferiorize Kurdish language and identity. In the context of language and oppression, hooks (1994, p. 168) maintains that English language is "the language of conquest and domination" and functions as a mask to hide the history of many lost languages in the US. In this respect, hooks discusses the relation between language and oppression in the context of displacement and cultural dispossession:

> I know that it is not the English language that hurts me, but what the oppressors do with it, how they shape it to become a territory that limits and defines, how they make it a weapon that can shame, humiliate, colonize. Gloria Anzaldúa reminds us of this pain in *Borderlands/La Frontera* when she asserts, "So, if you want to really hurt me, talk badly about my language". (ibid.)

In a similar context, Havin, whose parents were born in the Turkish city of Konya, talked about Kurdish families moving there more than hundred years ago to establish disparate Kurdish communities and adopt different cultural positions vis-à-vis the state-backed Turkish identity. Havin contrasted her own village with another Kurdish village around the same city that had made efforts to assume a Turkish identity by depicting Havin's village as "uncivilized farmers". While both villages consist of relatives, their position regarding the Turkish identity is different since members of the other village speak only Turkish and try to act more sophisticated by creating a Turkish atmosphere in their homes. Havin, who has assumed a strong political position against the Turkish state, talked about her visit to the predominantly Kurdish city of Amed (Diyarbakir) and the question of language for the pro-Kurdish party The Peace and Democratic Party (BDP) that has now ceased and been replaced by The Peoples' Democratic Party (HDP):

> When I was in Amed, I was told as a form of a joke that "if you want to learn Turkish, you should go to BDP". This was a joke circulating in Amed among members of BDP. They use irony to show the power of the Turkish language even among a Kurdish party. (Havin, a 27 years old woman, Kurdistan-Turkey, Sweden)

This leads to the question of internalized racial oppression that can function as a suitable theoretical perspective to understand the psychic and material effects of internalization of Kurdish inferiority and Turkish superiority. Internalization of Turkish superiority among Kurds contributes to the material, psychic and cultural dominance and privilege of the Turkish subject (see Treacher, 2005). It should be underlined that by focusing on internalization of Turkish superiority, my intention is not to blame the Kurds, who are the primary victims of these structures of ethnic inequalities that benefit the Turkish identity. Following Gramsci's (1971/2003), Pyke (2010) argues that systems of oppression assert themselves by coercion and overt repression in tandem with winning the consent of the oppressed group. The Turkish identity has gained its current position not only by violence but also by controlling how reality is constructed and what kind of ideology and knowledge about nationhood is produced. The dominant group's knowledge and identity often circulate across the society and shape the everyday life, institutional life, the practices of organization and the bureaucratic order (ibid.). This universalization of Turkish identity assumes itself as reflecting the interests of dominated ethnic and religious groups in Turkey. From the moment the Kurds identify with the dominant group and its institutions and hegemonic national narratives, they adopt to the repressive structural arrangements that keep them down and sustain their subjugation. This leads to the question of resistance in the context of assimilation within the framework of the nation-state but also in diasporic contexts that have created new opportunities for the Kurdish diaspora to reframe and refashion its conceptions of Turkish identity as the allegedly unifying force in a diverse but divided society.

The Parameters of Diasporic Resistance

In Turkey, following the dominant political grammar of the Turkish state, Kurds are subjected to daily political violence and misrepresentation that reduce the political struggle of the Kurds to a question of 'terror'. As I have discussed above, internalized oppression among Kurds is central to how the Turkish state secures its grip on the Kurdish population as its subject and subordinate others. However, this is not to say that Kurds are submissively adopting to an oppressive social system. The empirical data show that gender, religion and education often play an important role in assuming and framing different experiences, perspectives and narratives about how Kurdishness has been constituted. Pyke (2010) underlines that there is a theoretical fixation with resistance and that it is often adopted by scholars who pursue liberation of subjugated groups. Although Pyke agrees that it is problematic to depict a group merely in terms of powerlessness and victimhood, its position cannot entail that we can detect resistance everywhere to illustrate the ineffectiveness of power and the resilience of the dominated groups. Individuals and groups often adopt a variety of strategies like complicity, accommodation and the maintenance and reproduction of power. For instance, if we exaggerate the level and the scope of Kurdish resistance to Turkish domination, there is a risk to underestimate the oppressive structure of the Turkish state that often limits the very basis of agency. This is not to say that Kurds are not able to resist or respond to the unequal power relations that they experience.

As we will see below, there is a wide range of positionalities that Kurdish individuals can adopt to deal with like complicity or resistance to Turkish assimilation. In the context of political and cultural normativity of Sunni Islam as the binding tie of the Turkish nation, Hassan narrated a story about the strategies that the Kurdish Alevis adopted in order to pass as 'good' Sunni Muslims:

> You do not need to go to mosque if you are an Alevi. When you did not go to the mosque, people suspect that you are an Alevi, so some Alevis visit the mosques just to avoid being discriminated against. During Ramadan, Alevi families tend to wake up and put the light on late just to show that they are praying and fasting. You are fooling yourself and others around you. The Turkish system never protected the Alevi's citizenship rights because they never recognized Alevi as a religious group. Many Alevis thought that the Turkish Republic will be a better place for them than the Ottoman Empire, but the Turkish Republic committed the worst massacre against the Alevis during 1930s. (Hassan, a 53 years old man, Kurdistan-Turkey, the UK)

Alevis belong to a Muslim Shi'a community and constitute the largest religious minority in Turkey. Although Alevis are denominated as Shiites, they have their unique interpretation of Shi'a Islam that is not only repudiated by Sunni Muslims but also by other Shi'a communities. The experience of Hassan above shows the intimate link between Sunni Islam and Turkishness in constructing hierarchies of religious and ethnic belonging. The experiences of otherness and discrimination that Hassan underlined above were also shared by another interviewee Lana who remembered the isolation and non-acceptance that her Kurdish Alevi family (from Malatya) experienced while living in Istanbul. Whereas Lana's family disclosed to their Turkish Muslim neighbors that they were Alevis and Kurdish, another Turkish Alevi family who lived in the same building as they did not dare to disclose their religious identity due to fear of discrimination and isolation. Lana points out that her mother was very politically aware in Turkey and did not want to accept the position of otherness that was assigned to Alevis and Kurds. This political consciousness has been transmitted to Lana who offers a critical stance toward Kurdish Alevis who endorse the Kemalist ideology that is by definition and in practice anti-Kurdish:

> I am so ashamed of some Alevi people because they still believe in Kemalist ideology and many of them vote for the CHP (Republican People's Party). Have they forgotten who committed the massacres against the Alevis? I cannot understand them and will never understand how Alevis can vote for this party. They believe in their perpetrators and they are insulting me as an Alevi. I have these arguments with my Alevi friends and distant relatives in Turkey about this issue. Some Alevis are more dangerous than the Sunni Muslims because they can be more Kemalists than anybody else. They think that voting for CHP is the way to protect them from Islamism. Why do not you vote BDP [current HDP] that is secular and very women-friendly. (Lana, a 32 years old woman, Kurdistan-Turkey, the UK)

This illustrates how differently members of the same constituency can take a stance toward the Turkish Republic despite experiencing collective sufferings due to their ethnic and religious identity. However, this also shows that while Lana views both Islamism and Turkish nationalism as a threat against Kurdish Alevis and women, many Kurdish Alevis vote for the CHP as a strategy to obstruct and resist the dominance of Islamism and downplaying if not outright rejecting their Kurdish identity. However, in both cases, they view their political positions as *resistance* toward political and religious ideologies that pose an existential threat to the Alevis and Kurds. A potential effect of these disparate ideological orientations is division and weakening of bonds of solidarity among

Kurdish Alevis. While talking to Lana, she confidently asserted that PKK has given her a home that functions as a site of resistance to think about her identity and her place in the world as a woman and as a Kurdish Alevi. Lana is very critical of Kurds who facilitate the normalization of the Turkish identity and demonization of Kurdish identity. Below, we see two examples of how she sees assimilation as a danger both in Kurdistan and in diaspora:

> I refuse to go to some restaurants in Northern London because the people are Kurdish and they call them Turkish restaurant or food. I told them to take away the Turkish and put Mediterranean food or restaurant. Because all this food cannot be Turkish. Some of them must be Kurdish or influenced by Kurdish food. I feel that I belong to Kurdistan and when I go there, I feel more as a Kurd than I ever do. I was in Diyarbakir last year with my friend. I love Diyarbakir and I feel that I belong to that city. We were going around and revisited some of the places that I have seen. We stopped at one very historical building called Hassan Pasha Hani and it is very popular now for its food and the historical building itself. When we were there, we were looking around and said that we are in Kurdistan, right? She said, yeah. But I said that people are talking Turkish. We turned around and we saw a Turkish flag. We said that this is Kurdistan only in our hearts and if we want to change this, we have to change it rapidly. Otherwise this occupation will not go away. It is not something that can change with a click of a finger. The Kurdish movement (PKK) has achieved successes. Now in Turkey, Kurds can say that they are Kurdish. People can request for the right to education in their languages. People can listen to Kurdish music. This is a reflection of the struggle of the Kurdish movement. It did not happen over one night. Lots of people have lost their lives, their homes and their children for the sake of the Kurdish struggle. (Lana, a 32 years old woman, Kurdistan-Turkey, the UK)

In the narrative accounts that Lana offered above, Turkishness intrudes into the minds of the Kurds through language, food and spaces. Lana was not the only interviewee to react negatively toward those Kurds who named their restaurants as Turkish. There were two major reasons why they chose Turkish names. The first reason is related to the success of Turkish identity to exteriorize itself and gain political legitimacy as the master identity of the nation-state, Turkey. The second reason behind this naming was the fear of the Kurdish restaurant proprietors that Turkish, Arabic and Persian customers would avoid these restaurants for having "political names". In other words, while names belonging to the dominant nations are assumed to be unifying and creating social cohesion, Kurdish names were feared to be viewed as 'divisive', 'parochial' and 'secessionist' by members of the Turkish diaspora and to a lesser extent by Iraqi and Iranian diasporas. This strategy of naming by Kurdish proprietors is also based on economic pragmatism, a stance that was harshly rejected by some interviewees as a 'bad excuse' by 'Kurds who sell their identity for Turkish money'. Naming a place or a shop is also about making public claims. Choosing Turkish names for restaurants and shops is more common among Kurds of Turkey than for instance Kurds of Iraq who enjoy a relatively autonomous Kurdish region where Kurdish identity is not penalized but publicly endorsed and lived. This is a good example of how oppression and assimilation can have transnational effects on people whose identity has been othered culturally and linguistically. For Leyla, it is not comprehensible why some Kurds continue to endorse Turkishness in England when the Turkish police is not around and telling the Kurds to not give Kurdish names to their children and restaurants:

> The Turkish police are not here in the UK to torture you if you choose Kurdish names. If Kurdish men and women have children and bring up their children with the idea that we Kurds are an ancient people in the Middle East and we have a rich food culture then you do not have people who are ashamed of their Kurdish identity like some of the people in Northern London. Kurds go to a restaurant if it is called Turkish but not the other way around. Who is the problem then? It is the Turks who cannot accept anybody else than themselves. Then why should we adopt their names when they are so racist? We should dare to name our restaurants as Kurdish because when we do that, we are asserting ourselves as Kurds and show that we exist. (56 years old woman, Kurdistan-Turkey, the UK)

Racialized groups who are objects of colonial practices can display a subjectivity characterized by "a profound and visceral schizophrenia, mingling stubborn self-pride with an imposed self-rejection, typical products of colonial ambivalence" (Shohat, 2017, p. 115). Accordingly, it would be perfidious to put Kurdish and Turkish nationalism in the same political basket, given that Kurdish nationalism is not about targeting the Turks as such but countering the Turkish state that hegemonizes Turkishness at the expense of the Kurds and non-Turkish constituencies.

For Lana, the PKK is the political movement that has created a politically conscious Kurdish subject that challenges the dominance of the Turkish identity and has constructed a resilient subjectivity among Kurds. Although Havin underlines the importance of the PKK and HDP for the Kurdish identity, she could not understand why command of Kurdish language was so poor among people who viewed themselves as Kurdish and fought for Kurdistan:

> I am not a member of the PKK or BDP (current HDP), but I am critical of their language policy. I usually meet Kurds who are supporting the PKK and BDP, but do not speak good Kurdish. I tell them even if you go up in the mountains and fight and become a martyr for the Kurdish case, I am more Kurdish than you because as long as I speak Kurdish, I am maintaining my difference and identity that Turkish has tried to destroy. I know that these are strong words and very provocative. I am not saying this because I do not have respect for martyrs. If there is something that I believe in, it is our Kurdish language. I find it funny when I see Kurdish politicians in the Turkish Parliament advocating for the Kurdish question, but barely or do not speak Kurdish. I am so ashamed of these people. They should start learning Kurdish and then their claims become more legitimate. When you do not want to learn Kurdish, you have accepted that you are a Turk, and not a Kurd although you fight for the Kurdish question. (Havin, a 27 years old woman, Kurdistan-Turkey, Sweden)

Havin discursively constructs a hierarchy among different forms of resistance that Kurds can adopt. It might not come as a surprise that Havin chooses the Kurdish language as the major site of resistance given that it has been the main target of the Turkish state. What might contradict Havin's approach is the fact that despite lack or poor command of the Kurdish language, these putative Kurds have not given up their communal belonging given that Kurdish identity is still criminalized and punished in institutional and everyday life. Moreover, while many interviewees talked about experiences of shame for not knowing the Turkish language during childhood and adulthood, Havin expresses her aversion toward Kurds who do not speak Kurdish. This is the opposite direction of how Kurdish subjectivity can be constructed that does not tolerate Turkish superiority or Kurds who speak Turkish in their everyday life. Although Havin directly blames the PKK for not endorsing the importance of the Kurdish language, it is worth mentioning that it was largely thanks to the diasporic activism and transnational practices of PKK supporters that Kurds launched their first satellite channel (Med-TV) in 1995. Med-TV came to be seen as a national television station due to its ambitions to include the diversity of Kurdishness in terms of culture, music, history, language and dialects (Hassanpour, 2003).

While diaspora is a risky place for groups who struggle for cultural rights and survival in the country of origin, there are persistent members of Kurdish diasporas who view maintenance of the Kurdish language in exile as a victory against the oppressive states in the Middle East. This idea is strongly promoted and popularized among the Kurdish diaspora in Sweden, most notably by the Swedish-Kurdish stand-up comedians Özz Nûjen who argues that Kurds did not flee Turkey and came to Sweden to become Swedish but to continue being Kurdish. This can, however, be easily interpreted by nationalist forces in Sweden as the reluctance of the Kurds to integrate or assimilate into the Swedish society and invest in cultural ghettoization. Despite the significant differences between Turkey and liberal democracies like Sweden and the UK, Kurds as a culturally endangered group face the pressure of assimilation with varying intensity in the countries of origin and in diasporic contexts. In Sweden, there are influential political parties like Christian Democrats and Sweden Democrats that view mother tongue education for children with migrant background as undermining integration and social cohesion in Sweden, an assimilationist discourse that shares the same logic as the Turkish state's policy vis-à-vis minoritized groups in Turkey. However, migration can become a transformative force in the context of liberal democracies that provide some form of space for cultural recognition of ethnic minorities. Consider how Memo frames this transformation following his migration to Sweden and the productive encounters with Kurds from other parts of Kurdistan who speak Kurdish:

> A Turkish lawyer who was working for a human right organization visited Sweden and we went there to listen to him and see what he had to say about the situation of the Kurds in Turkey during 1990s. There were many Kurds there from different parts of Kurdistan. I wrote down some questions that I wanted to pose to this Turkish lawyer. There were around 100 persons listening to his speech. He was speaking Turkish and there were Kurdish and Turkish interpreters. Kurds from Southern Kurdistan (Iraq), Western Kurdistan (Syria) and Eastern Kurdistan (Iran) were asking their questions in Kurdish and the interpreters translated their questions into Turkish. I had written my questions in Turkish and I felt what a shame that I as a Kurd have to pose my question in Turkish. I asked myself why

> cannot I pose the questions in Kurdish about Kurds? I became so angry and sad. I felt guilty as not being able to speak my Kurdish language. Why cannot I express my feelings, decisions, and words in Kurdish? I took the paper on which I had written the questions in Turkish, tore it into many parts and threw them away. I said that I will not pose any questions. Then I swore to myself: by God, by God, by God, I will start as soon as possible so I learn Kurdish and will not let an invader language take over my life and control my tongue. I wanted to become a Kurd who can express his feelings in Kurdish. I was so upset and in pain. The day after, I went to the library and during six months, I was there from 10 o'clock to 3 o'clock and studied Kurdish by my own. I read all the Kurdish books in the library. After six months, I became a new human being. I gained my language and not only that, I have even become a teacher in Kurdish language and teach Kurdish kids in Sweden. If you really want to learn Kurdish, then you will learn it but you need a strong will and a strong sense of Kurdishness.(Memo, a 50 years old man, Sweden)

Politics of emotion as a social force are central to constituting and strengthening a Kurdish identity, particularly in times of crisis and existential threat that the states pose to the Kurds in the Middle East. It becomes illustrative of how guilt, shame and pain enter the politics of Kurdish identity as transformative social forces in diasporic contexts, as Memo illustrated, from not knowing Kurdish to learning and teaching Kurdish to Kurdish children in Sweden. Memo also points out that representatives of the Gülen movement contacted him in 2012 in order to open a school and hire him as a teacher. During the meeting, Memo continues, they represented themselves as intellectuals and asserted their willingness to support Turkish students in Sweden. Memo viewed them as fostering Turkishness and asked them about their political goal. The representatives of the movement replied that they wanted to serve God and Islam. When Memo asked them about the language of instruction and what flag to use, they replied the Turkish language and the Turkish flag. But Memo said that he could not work under a Turkish flag. The representatives of the movement lamented and said "in what way will it hurt to have a Turkish flag"? Memo countered them with a question: "in what way does the Kurdish language and Kurdish flag hurt your Turkish feelings, not now but for almost a century"? According to Memo, this movement wants to synthesize Islam with Turkishness.

Kurt (2018) maintains that Islamic governmentality in the Kurdish region of Turkey and colonial rule goes hand in hand to legitimize state authority, but also to mute Kurdish claims to justice, representation and equality. Dominant Turkish representations have succeeded to produce a discourse about 'bad Kurds', who supports the PKK and HDP and 'good Kurds' who are against the PKK and support the ruling Justice and Development Party (AKP) in Turkey. In order to achieve the status of 'good Kurds' and escape the stigma of Kurdishness, many Kurdish individuals present themselves as Muslim Kurds who supports Islamic brotherhood and unity by underlining their aversion toward the PKK and the Kurdish movement. While Kurdishness is rendered absent and assigned societal stigma, the AKP has managed to produce and strengthen a division among Kurds in terms of goodness (desirable) and badness (undesirable) through an Islamic discourse that sustains and asserts the superiority of Turkishness. Kurt (2018) argues that there are two main reasons why this AKP strategy can be successful. The first reason is related to decades of discrimination and impoverishment experienced by Kurds and the survival strategies that they have adopted in order to 'pass' as 'good and loyal citizens' of the Turkish state. The second reason for this support of assimilationist discourse concealed in religious terms is linked to the strong religiosity and social conservatism that prevail in the Kurdish region. In the same vein, Gurses (2015) contends that the role of Turkish Islam as peacemaker in Turkey has been overstated given that the Islamists movements in Turkey are heavily marked by Turkish nationalism in their approaches to the rights of Kurds. Hence, Islam in Turkey not only can provide an alternative to Turkish nationalism and the Turkish nation-state as a political template, but also functions as a political tool to undermine the Kurdish opposition and rights in the name of a deceptive Islamic universalism.

It is not only Kurds from other parts of Kurdistan (Iran, Iraq and Syria) who do not consider the century long politics of assimilation and criminalization of Kurdish identity in Turkey by blaming Kurds of Turkey for not speaking Kurdish or investing time and energy in learning the Kurdish language. However, this critique came also from some Kurds of Turkey who viewed assimilation as a 'betrayal' of Kurdishness and an indication of 'mental enslavement'. Indeed, this division also creates categories like 'good Kurds' who stick to its identity and language and 'bad Kurds' who stick to the so-called enemy language or the 'invader language'. Consider how Heval frames his understanding and attitude vis-à-vis the Turkish language when spoken as the main language among Kurds in Turkey:

> When we go back to Turkey and Kurdistan, our relatives in Turkish cities speak more Turkish and I don't want my children to play with them because I get so angry at those parents who have not been able to teach their children Kurdish, but in this village in Kurdistan (Mardin) where my parents come from, they speak Kurdish. My relatives think that if they speak Kurdish, they cannot be included in the Turkish society, exactly in the same way as immigrants are having it in Sweden, where you speak Swedish so you become integrated. However, there is a major difference. Sweden allows and even gives you right to receive education, at least for now, in your mother tongue. We fled from Turkey because we could not have a Kurdish identity or speak Kurdish. I do not mind people speaking Turkish, but I do mind when Kurdish parents speak only Turkish to their children when they for instance cook. My parents have always talked to me in Kurdish. I travelled to Turkey this summer with my youngest son who is five years. My oldest cousin who is almost 40 years old started speaking Turkish with me and I told him, I feel ashamed when I see that my youngest son speaks Kurdish and you are talking to me in Turkish. He realized how wrong it was. I told him, shame on you, you are Kurdish, speak Kurdish! Language is so important for us Kurds. I told my cousin, that I would not visit him again if he spoke Turkish with me next time. He agreed to speak Kurdish. (Heval, a 30 years old man, Kurdistan-Turkey, Sweden)

While Havin earlier attacked Kurdish politicians and the Kurdish political movement for being allegedly indifferent toward the Kurdish language, Heval directs his harsh critique against those individual Kurds and parents who do not speak Kurdish and thus fail to transmit the Kurdish language to their children. Moreover, Heval provides an interesting account about how integration is framed in the context of the nation-state and majority-minority relations. Integration in both the Turkish and the Swedish context, although framed differently, does not dissolve the ethnic hierarchy that exists but constructs hierarchies of belonging by measuring how much members of minority groups adhere to the dominant cultural values (Bauman, 1991). Inclusion in the national community is stipulated by dominant culture, language and history-writing. Yet, the Swedish state has been more inclined to accommodate ethnic pluralism than the Turkish state which has viewed minorities as a threat to political and territorial integration of the Turkish nation. In Sweden, Kurdish children have the possibility to receive education in the Kurdish language one hour per week until they graduate from upper-secondary school. Heval's case shows that members of the diaspora can have leverage and affect the subject positions of Kurds living in Turkish cities and Kurdistan, by highlighting the primacy of the Kurdish language to maintain the Kurdish identity. This is an expression of identity politics, but an identity politics that occurs in the context of denial and subordination. Heval not only reinterprets history and culture in Turkey that have devalued Kurdishness, but also attempts to redefine and change the prevailing identification patterns of Kurds that have been structured by the Turkish state. While Kurds can be contained territorially by the nation-state borders of Turkey, Iran, Iraq and Syria, the diaspora provides a unique opportunity to engage in constructing boundaries that underlines the communal bonds of the Kurds as an oppressed nation. This has been further enabled and facilitated by the proliferation of Kurdish satellite channels and social media. It is in diasporic contexts that Kurds from different parts of Kurdistan can encounter and negotiate their commonalities and differences.

The Turkish state, following the footsteps of colonial states, has been aware that Kurdish children and particularly Kurdish girls and women need to be the main targets of cultural assimilation via education. This is, of course, related to the idea that women are often viewed as the biological and cultural reproducer of national boundaries and cultural symbols (Yuva-Davis, 1997). It was in the educational context that proud and loyal Turkish subjects could be crafted in the Kurdish regions of Turkey. Aram reflects on how his father's treatment of his mother in relation to her 'poor' command of the Turkish language has been transmitted to his brother in the city of Diyarbakir, which is often times viewed by the Kurds as the capital of Kurdistan of Turkey:

> The indoctrination of Kurdish men and women were different because Kurdish women were mostly at home and you speak mostly Kurdish when you are at home. The assimilation of women was not as aggressive as of the men. Kurdish men were out in the public, worked, studied, and sat in the coffee shops and adopted the Turkish language even more. But the Kurdish we spoke was also very limited because we did not have right to develop our Kurdish language in school. It was a Kurdish for daily conversations without depth. But it is thanks to the mothers that some Kurds still speak Kurdish. Some Kurdish women were also bullied by their Kurdish husband for not speaking Turkish. My father used to tell my mother: "You have lived all your life in Turkey and Diyarbakir but you still do not speak Turkish". My older brother is still like that. Last summer (2013), when I was in Kurdistan he told his wife: "why don't you speak good Turkish when you have lived in Diyarbakir for 50 years?" A person who does not

> speak Turkish is regarded as a deficient person. My brother does not question why Kurds do not speak good Kurdish but questions the Kurds who do not master the Turkish language. I told my brother that his wife was more normal than he is because she speaks Kurdish in a city inhabited mainly by the Kurds. He felt ashamed when I said that because nobody has ever told him that in that way. He is becoming more aware of this. (Aram, a 48 years old man, Sweden)

Diyarbakir holds a special place in Kurdish history in relation to the oppressive structure of the Turkish state. Kurdishness was not only banned and stigmatized in the public spaces like schools but also in Turkish prisons where speaking Kurdish was severely punished. A big sign in Diyarbakir Penitentiary hailed the imprisoned Kurds: "Speak Turkish, talk a lot" (Sungun, 2013, p. 234). Sungun points out that the Turkish state targeted Kurdish women in order to reproduce a culturally racist discourse that devalued Kurdishness and celebrated Turkishness as a superior identity. Thus, the Turkish state framed the Turkish language as a means of 'civilizing' Kurdish women in Turkey. In order to achieve this, Turkish institutions encouraged detaching Kurdish women from their allegedly 'backward' and 'primitive' Kurdish identity and language. Kurdish women were not only encouraged to transmit Turkishness to their children, but also to discourage and prevent their children from joining the PKK and picking up arms against the Turkish state. Kurdish women who joined and served Turkish institutions came to be represented as guardians of Turkish patriotism (ibid.). The Turkish fear of Kurdish women still reverberates given that the PKK has attracted thousands of young Kurdish women to its rank who fight both the patriarchal structure of the Kurdish society and the Turkish state violence against the Kurds in general.

Since Kurds do not enjoy the political freedom live and institutionally endorse their Kurdish identity and language in Turkey, Kurdish diasporas viewed Sweden and the UK as important places to formulate resistance against the Turkish state and invest in the Kurdish language. For instance, Hassan talked about himself as being active on Facebook and sharing news about the Turkish atrocities against the Kurds. When a former Turkish friend found him on Facebook and requested friendship, it did not take long before his Turkish friend sent him a message underlining the link between terror, Kurds and the PKK and unfriended him. One of the moments in which they enacted resistance toward being named as Turkish or speaking Turkish was while visiting Turkey and being stopped at Turkish airports. Several of the interviewees spoke only English, pretending not to know Turkish and refused to speak Turkish, which infuriated the Turkish staffs at the airport who in turn harassed and denigrated the Kurdish citizens of Sweden and the UK. Heval provides an illustrative account of how this encounter can take shape:

> I visited Turkey when I was 16 years old. In my Swedish passport, the place of my birth is written. They know that it is the Kurdish part of Turkey. They started speaking Turkish to me, but I spoke English with them. I told them that I am Kurdish and if you can speak Kurdish, I can speak Kurdish with you. My father got scared that I was assertive because he had experiences of being beaten up by Turkish gendarmes. The Turkish staff told me that I was a Turk and I should speak Turkish. He spat in my face and called me a traitor. What Could I do? Nothing. (Heval, a 30 years old man, Kurdistan-Turkey, Sweden)

Although Heval talks about his incapability to respond to the disdainful act and violence of the Turkish staff for spitting in his face, he has already provided a form of resistance to the Turkish state through his individual act in resisting to speak the language of power and reminding the dominant group that the subaltern Kurdish language is still alive despite decades of oppression and criminalization. While many of the encounters with Turkish immigrants were conflictual and sometimes dismissive and harsh, there were also Turkish voices who expressed fear and worry about the decline of a unifying Turkish identity for Turks and Kurds:

> In 2013, I talked with a Turk from Istanbul who I met in Stockholm. We talked about the Kurds and PKK and the conflict between the Kurds and the Turkish state. He said that when he was younger, things were so much better. His father was a general located in the Kurdish region. As a child, he had seen the Kurdish region. He said that when he was younger there were no such things as Turks and Kurds, and we could talk to each other and play with each other. I told him that it is exactly the major problem that you do not recognize anything else than Turkish and the people you were talking to were Kurdish but you could not accept their differences, so they had to be Turkish. I told him that for you in order to exist, you had to adhere to a Turkish identity. This is why there were no differences. Today you cannot continue with your denial. I told him that we can continue talking to each other, but this time I speak to you as a Kurd and not as a Turk. He could not understand why we wanted to be Kurdish and not just Turkish. (Dilar, a 28 years old woman, Kurdistan-Turkey, Sweden)

This shows how Turkish universalism is decoded as cultural and linguistic sameness where equality and difference are perceived as conflicting in constituting equal identities in a multiethnic society like Turkey. In a society structured by Turkish dominance, language, cultural values and history writing, it is not comprehensible how equality can be achieved without undoing the dominance of Turkish mastery and sense of entitlement and privilege. It is this sense of paranoia among Turkish subjects and the fear of waning ethnic privilege that have reinforced Turkish nationalism and resentment (see Ware, 2008) toward the Kurds as an 'internal enemy' that allegedly aims to harm the fragile Turkish nation. As a consequence of this discourse, the dominant Turkish constituency adopts a victim identity to endanger minority rights that Kurds are seeking to achieve. This also illuminates why the Turkish state can so easily gain popular support to wage military and cultural war against the Kurds inside and outside of the Turkish borders. The very quest of Kurds to linguistic, cultural and political rights continue to be interpreted in dominant Turkish representations as 'a question of terror' and 'plots' to undermine the existence of Turkey and the Turkish people.

The Continuation of the Cultural War Against the Kurds

Cultural assimilation, political exclusion, economic deprivation and military violence continue to shape Turkish policy vis-à-vis the Kurdish dissent. Kurdish quest for cultural equality continues to be seen as a threat against the national security of the Turkish state and its national masters. It is mainly by fearing and securitizing the Kurds that the security of the dominant Turkish nation can allegedly be secured. The Turkish state often uses a discourse of fear in order to justify political, cultural and military violence against the Kurds. As a consequence, the Turkish state creates an institutionalized and structural subordination of the Kurds and prevents them from achieving effective political, cultural and material power in the society. This is the ideal of national sameness (Nagel, 2009) that the Turkish state pursues at the expense of Kurdish language and lives. The profundity of Turkish assimilation cannot be underestimated given that it continues to target the Kurdish psyche and minds and instilling in them a sense of cultural inferiority. A large number of Kurds in Turkey and outside of Turkey continue to embrace Turkishness and the Turkish language as a way of life, since there are no states in the Middle East that endorse Kurdishness and can provide it with positive meanings and values. Education and language have been the main vehicles of the Turkish state to produce national sameness and foreignizing the Kurdish constituency as the linguistic aliens of the Turkish nation-state. Since Kurds have been subjected to several decades of assimilation, the Kurdish movements face a double challenge. First, they need to mobilize against assimilation, which paradoxically and in initial stages at least needs to use the language of the assimilators to reach the assimilated Kurds and reverse assimilation through a linguistic struggle. These two tasks need to go hand in hand in order to achieve some success in preventing the dissolution of Kurdish identity and language. By resisting the pressure to assimilate at individual and collective levels, Kurds are engaging in a struggle to alter or end Turkish supremacy (see hooks, 2015).

Kurdish demands for recognition of their identities and languages cannot be equated with simple essence-making claims. There is no way that Kurds can liberate and restore a pure essence that Kurds have supposedly lost due to political oppression of the states in the Middle East. Kurdish claim-making can also have important political effects like "self-naming and other-naming in the mapping out of antagonism. Claims to essences should always be placed in terms of their particular context of particular strategies, such as the struggles against domination, rather than be considered in abstraction" (Smith, 1994, pp. 173–174). Due to the political vulnerability of the Kurds and the continuous violence they encounter and experience in the Middle East, anti-essentialist claims to Kurdish identity are viewed as perilous by many members of Kurdish diasporas since they potentially deepen an already fragmented Kurdish identity and benefit the political agenda of the states that reject Kurdish claims to political freedom and equal standing in the society.

In order to illustrate the Turkish state's double standard regarding which group that qualify as object of assimilation and who are viewed as eligible to constitutional rights against cultural assimilation and erasure, it is apt to return to the contemporary ethnocratic and Islamist regime of Turkey led by Erdoğan. In 2008, while addressing an audience of 20,000 diasporic Turks, gathered in Cologne, Erdoğan asked his exiled countrymen to resist assimilation in Germany and added that nobody could expect them to assimilate since Turks in Europe should "be constitutional elements and not just guests" and "assimilation is a crime against humanity" (The Local, 2008). One can of course wonder if Kurds will ever be given a place within the discourse of humanity in nationalist Turkish representations and imaginations regardless of their secular or religious frameworks. Denial and erasure of Kurdish identity, language and culture continue to be the major constitutive vehicles of sustaining Turkish privileges and oppression of the Kurds across national borders. It is in such context that Kurdish demands for self-rule become intelligible. As long as Turkey use its power as a state to institutionally, emotionally and materially invests in Turkish identity at the expense of the Kurds, Kurdish resistance at individual and collective levels become critical as an antidote against the pressure of cultural and linguistic assimilation that Turkish supremacy endorses.

References

Aslan, S. (2015). *Nation-building in Turkey and Morocco: Governing Kurdish and Berber dissent*. Cambridge University Press.

Bauman, Z. (1991). *Modernity and ambivalence*. Polity Press.

Bourdieu, P. (1992). *Language & symbolic violence*. Polity Press.

Britton, C. M. (1999). *Edouard Glissant and postcolonial theory: Strategies of language and resistance*. University Press of Virginia.

Demir, I. (2014). Humbling Turkishness: Undoing the strategies of exclusion and inclusion of Turkish modernity. *Journal of Historical Sociology, 37*(2), 381–401.

Eliassi, B. (2013). *Contesting Kurdish identities in Sweden: Quest for belonging among Middle Eastern Youth*. Palgrave Macmillan.

Ergin, M. (2014). The racialization of Kurdish identity in Turkey. *Ethnic and Racial Studies, 37*(2), 322–341.

Fanon, F. (1952/2008). *Black skin, white masks*. Grove Press.

Gökay, B., & Aybak, T. (2016). Identity, race, and nationalism in Turkey—Introduction to the special issue. *Journal of Balkan and Near Eastern Studies, 18*(2), 107–110.

Gramsci, A. (1971/2003). *Selections from the prison notebooks*. London: Lawrence and Wishart.

Gurses, M. (2015). Is Islam a cure for ethnic conflict? Evidence from Turkey. *Politics and Religion, 8*(1), 135–154.

Hassanpour, A. (2003). Diaspora, homeland and communication technologies. In H. K. Karim (Ed.), *The media of diaspora* (pp. 76–88). Routledge.

hooks, b. (1994). *Teaching to transgress: Education as the practice of freedom*. Routledge.

hooks, b. (2015). *Talking back: Thinking feminist, thinking black*. Routledge.

Houston, C. (2001). Profane intuition: Kurdish diaspora in the Turkish city. *The Australian Journal of Anthropology, 12*(1), 15–31.

Kürt, M. (2018). "My Muslim Kurdish brother": Colonial rule and Islamist governmentality in the Kurdish region of Turkey. *Journal of Balkan and near Eastern Studies, 21*(3), 350–365.
Markell, P. (2003). *Bound by recognition*. Princeton University Press.
Nagel, C. R. (2009). Rethinking the geographies of Assimilation. *The Professional Geographer, 61*(3), 400–407.
Pyke, K. (2010). What is internalized oppression and why don't we study it? Acknowledging racism's hidden injuries. *Sociological Perspective, 53*(4), 551–572.
Radhakrishnan, R. (2003). *Theory in an uneven world*. Blackwell.
Saracoglu, C. (2009). "Exclusive recognition": The new dimension of the question of ethnicity and nationalism in Turkey. *Ethnic and Racial Studies, 32*(4), 640–658.
Saracoglu, C. (2010). The changing image of the Kurds in Turkish cities: Middle-class perceptions of Kurdish migrants in Izmir. *Patterns of Prejudice, 44*(3), 239–260.
Shohat, E. (2017). *On the Arab-Jew, Palestine, and other displacements*. Pluto Press.
Smith, A. M. (1994). Rastafari as resistance and the ambiguities of essentialism in the 'new social movements.' In L. Ernesto (Ed.), *The making of political identities* (pp. 171–204). Verso.
Sungun, E. (2013). Langauge as a means of "civilizing" the Kurdish Women in Turkey. In P. Celine-Marie (Ed.), *Social inequality & the politics of representation* (pp. 229–242). Sage.
The Local. (2008). *Turkish Prime Minister says: "Assimilation is a crime against humanity"*. https://www.thelocal.de/20080211/10293. Accessed 29 March 2019.
Treacher, A. (2005). On postcolonial subjectivity. *Group Analysis, 38*(1), 43–57.
Üngör, U. U. (2011). *The making of modern Turkey: Nation and state in Eastern Anatolia 1913–1950*. Oxford University Press.
Ware, V. (2008). Towards a sociology of resentment: A debate on class and whiteness. *Sociological Research Online, 13*(5): 117–126.
Yeğen, M. (2009). "Prospective-turks" or "pseudo-citizens": Kurds in Turkey. *Middle East Journal, 63*(4), 597–615.
Yuval-Davis, N. (1997). *Gender & nation*. Sage.
Zeydanlioglu, W. (2008). "The White Turkish man's burden": Orientalism, Kemalism and the Kurds in Turkey. In R. Guido & I. Anne (Eds.), *Neocolonial Mentalities in contemporary Europe? Language and discourse in the construction of identities* (pp. 155–174). Cambridge Scholars.

CHAPTER 7

Critique and Dissent as a Transnational Obligation: Diasporic Appraisals of the Kurdistan Region of Iraq

It is often argued that diasporas are important non-state actors in international relations and affect the nation- and state-building processes in their imagined or real homelands (Mügge, 2012). Diasporas have either been one-sidedly criticized for supporting an irresponsible militant long-distance nationalism (Conversi, 2012) or viewed as key actors in building peace and/or perpetuating conflicts (see Shain & Barth, 2003; Sheffer, 2003). The Kurdish diasporas in Sweden and the UK that inform the empirical context of this chapter have adopted both roles in homeland politics and resisting authoritarian nation-building states in the Middle East (Eliassi, 2013). In our globalized world, many states also engage with their diasporas in order to secure political advantages since diasporas give "an additional source of power and a sphere of influence that extends beyond the physical borders of the nation" (Adamson, 2016, p. 293). Likewise, the Kurdistan Regional Government (KRG), mainly led by the Kurdistan Democratic Party (KDP), has tried to engage with the Kurdish diasporas and organized conferences inside and outside Kurdistan on how different members of the Kurdish diaspora can contribute to the development of the region and implicitly support its current political framework and governance. However, these efforts have significantly decreased due to the economic crisis that is facing KRG. The attempt by KRG to reach out to the Kurdish diaspora is to extend its political power beyond the

B. Eliassi, *Narratives of Statelessness and Political Otherness*, Minorities in West Asia and North Africa,
https://doi.org/10.1007/978-3-030-76698-6_7

Kurdistan Region and gain the loyalty of the Kurdish diasporas as well as render them governable for different political and economic motives. In effect, states attempt to reach out to those powerful members of diaspora who can function as agents of change through their political, educational and economic resources (Turner & Kleist, 2013). States deploy different means to control and contain the transnational political ties and loyalty of the diaspora. Through establishing ties with powerful and influential members (e.g., politicians, academics, writers, artists) of the Kurdish diasporas, KRG endeavors to represent itself as the legitimate political home and mouthpiece of the Kurds and reconfigure the nation-people-state trilogy including those who are living outside of Kurdistan.

Betts and Jones (2016) maintain that diaspora is politically constructed and mobilized and view the role of animators (e.g., elites) who allocate resources as central to bringing diaspora into existence by using money, networks or ideas. Moreover, Turner and Kleist (2013) point out that diasporas remain political not in relation to the rights and recognition that they receive from the states but in regard to their capacities and desires to challenge the hegemony of the states. Regardless of their complicity with the political order or their opposition, states want their diasporas to play according to the rule of the state. This is particularly important for weak and nonsovereign political entities like KRG that needs international political, military and economic support in the volatile Middle East and aspire to avoid international attention and critique on issues related to quality of government, human rights record, gender relations, the situation of journalist and free expression. Containing the political activities of the diaspora become more urgent for authoritarian states and entities that suffer from democratic deficit. In the context of Kurdish longing for sovereignty, Klein (2014) argues that KRG has understood the political game of statehood and attempts to promote a civilized image of Kurds and Kurdistan to the Western world in order to be rewarded with a certificate of statehood, external recognition and sovereignty. As a result, KRG has invested in numerous campaigns to persuade the West that the Kurdistan Region is the 'Other Iraq' and unlike other parts of Iraq, it respects and values democracy, rule of law, women and minority rights, qualities that the Turkish, Persian and Arab neighbors assumedly lack. And it is this political image that KRG wants its diasporas to endorse and sell to the countries in which they residing.

The Kurdish diasporas are not entirely autonomous in its activities but are entwined to different political parties from different parts of

Kurdistan. However, this does not preclude these political parties to make claim in the name of a unanimous Kurdish nation while formulating and setting their political agenda. Despite its short history in Western Europe, the Kurdish diasporas have been relatively successful in its transnational political and cultural mobilization. Since 2005, the Kurdistan Region of Iraq has gained considerable political authority and autonomy within the constitutional framework of a federal Iraq where a Kurdish national identity is evolving. The Kurdistan Region has been optimistically described as a state within a state (Bengio, 2013) and skeptically defined as the Kurdish quasi-state (Natali, 2015). As an autonomous political region, it is equally assumed to be a source of inspiration for Kurds in Turkey, Iran, and Syria since it can function “as a political, territorial, and symbolic reference” (Tejel, 2009, p. 138). Members of the Kurdish diasporas do not share the same political concerns when engaging with political development in their homelands. Following the political rise of KRG, the political focus of Kurdish diasporas in Western Europe does not merely challenge the centralized Iraqi/Turkish/Iranian power but equally engages with the lack of legal governance, gender and class inequalities, corruption and undemocratic political arrangement in the Kurdistan Region. There are equally many Kurds in diaspora who see the Kurdistan Region as an economic opportunity and defend the incumbent political leaders and political parties as embodying the universal political interests of the Kurds. Thus, diasporas can be reconfigured following the political, economic and social developments in the country of origin.

In light of above discussion, this chapter engages with the ways members of the Kurdish diasporas in Sweden and the UK conceive the political rise and the symbolic importance of the Kurdistan Region and KRG in the context of Kurdish statelessness and political subjugation across the Middle East. The chapter will investigate how political divisions among Kurdish diasporans and their relationship to nationalism consistently impinge on the ways Kurdistan Region is appraised, affirmed or rejected. Through analyzing the narratives of Kurdish diasporans in Sweden and the UK, I aim to illustrate the diverse, dominating, convergent and divergent political voices that exist within the Kurdish diasporas in relation to the Kurdistan Region and KRG. Moreover, these diasporic narratives can define grievances and claims that legitimize and mobilize action against KRG and/or in support of KRG. Many postcolonial states have used the discourse of national security/cohesion/unity to quell dissent and this issue is more urgent in the Kurdish case where Kurds lack a nation-state and are operating in a vulnerable geopolitical context surrounded by four nation-states who have been inimical to Kurdish self-determination. Therefore, it is important to investigate how Kurdish diaspora juxtapose the urgent issue of democracy within Kurdistan Region with maintaining stability and unity notwithstanding external threat by the neighboring countries and constituencies. The remainder of this chapter is divided into three sections. First, I discuss how the interviewees discuss the political and symbolic value of the Kurdistan Region. Second, I examine the ways KRG becomes an object of criticism by diasporic Kurds who desire a state but not a state led by political elites who endorse corruption and do not seriously consider the questions of democracy, transparency, rule of law and feminism. Finally, I conclude with a reflection about the role of critique in diaspora in relation to KRG and obstruction of authoritarianism that often makes state institutions weak through consolidating personal or family hold on power.

Kurdistan Region as the Benchmark for Kurdish Sovereignty and Statehood

It is no overstatement to state that Kurdistan Region of Iraq is a historical conjuncture in modern Kurdish history. The decreasing power of the Iraqi state, politicization of ethno-national and religious identities, and the geographical and linguistic separation between the Kurds and the Arabs have paved the way for a distinct Kurdish identity. While discussing the importance of the Kurdistan Region, a considerable number of the interviewees in Sweden and the UK praised the materialization of Kurdish political power in the Middle East and viewed it as ground-breaking:

> Now that Kurdistan Region exists, we have our own parliament. I feel that my place exists and I do not feel so lost as I used to before Kurdistan Region came to existence. Before it was not accepted to say Kurdistan but Iraq. Now people react differently when you say Kurdistan. Even Arabs cannot deny it although they want to because Kurds control that region and our flag is flying over its territory. We own our home now. (Dimen, a 47 years old woman Kurdistan Region-Iraq, the UK)

Accordingly, Kurdistan Region represents and contributes to institutionalization of Kurdish identity, language(s) and culture. Likewise, it sanctions a place-based Kurdish identity and compete with the state identity of Iraq, that has historically been dominated by Sunni Arabs and currently by the Shia Arabs. It is noteworthy to underline that many of the interviewees referred to the Kurdistan Region as validating the existence of the Kurdish identity and rarely referred to the Kurds of Kurdistan Region as a *minority* but as the *master* identity of the region although situated within the framework of Iraqi state. This is thus a break where Kurds are no longer the tail but the head of the predominantly Kurdish region, which of course has created political frustration among historically dominant Arabs in Iraq who have viewed themselves as the owner of the state (Stansfield & Anderson, 2009). However, after the Kurdish referendum in 2017, Kurdistan Region has become highly vulnerable due to Iraqi Shia aversion and regional isolation, that aim to politically and economically marginalize and disable Kurdish autonomy. For many Kurds, the Kurdistan Region is presumed to compensate this inferiority complex since it has been successful in putting Kurds on the world map and gaining international recognition through foreign representations in the capital of the Kurdistan Region, Erbil. There are currently more than 30 international representatives in Erbil including countries like the US, the UK, Japan, France, China, Russia, Turkey and Iran. This political development was viewed as paving the ground for Kurdish independence and for some of the interviewees, the Kurdistan Region is the starter and it is from here the Kurds are assumed to see the light, progress and creation of a healthy society:

> Kurdistan Region is the beginning of something bigger and means a lot for other parts of Kurdistan in order to achieve the same thing and hopefully one day to be united. I know that it is very hard. If we are united, we have greater chance to succeed. Kurdistan Region is a proof that Kurds can become independent. (Bjar, a 21 years old man Kurdistan Region-Iraq, the UK)

This narrative above converges with the fear and anxiety of the neighboring states Iran, Turkey and Syria, that a strong autonomous Kurdish polity in Iraq can inspire and send political ideas about sovereignty and self-rule to Kurds within their respective jurisdiction. The Kurds often respond that this fear must be encountered with unity, which all Kurdish political parties adhere to rhetorically but few endorse in their realpolitik. Notwithstanding his critique against KRG for its governance quality,

Michael Rubin describes the political weight and power of KRG in the following way:

> Two decades ago, most US officials would have been hard-pressed to place Kurdistan on a map, let alone consider Kurds as allies. Today, Kurds have largely won over Washington. Kurdish politicians who would once struggle to get a meeting with a junior diplomat or congressman, now lunch with the Secretary of State and visit the Oval Office. There is a growing assumption across the political spectrum in Washington that not only will the Kurds will soon their independence, but that any resulting state will be a beacon of hope in a region where stability, democracy, and liberalism are in increasingly short supply. (Rubin, 2016, p. 1)

The political ascending of KRG cannot be underestimated despite its geopolitical vulnerability and domestic democratic deficit (Gunter, 2011). Following the Kurdish referendum for independence in 2017, the idea of an impending Kurdish independence is presently dismantled by Iran and Turkey with the active support of the US and Britain, who all agreed that Kurdish independence will imply 'instability' in the Middle East and the territorial integrity of Iraq must be retained. According to Watts (2016), Kurdish political identity has gained dominance in the Middle East and this ascendancy has led to Kurdistanization of regions predominantly inhabited by the Kurds. In this context, KRG has been a central actor in flagging the Kurdish nation and the name of Kurdistan. It was not only the Kurdish interviewees from the Kurdistan Region who praised the emergence of this Kurdish polity, but also Kurds from other parts of Kurdistan who championed the importance of this entity as a potential home for other Kurds in light of ethnic oppression in Turkey, Iran and Syria. Consider the following quote by a Kurdish woman who had struggled against the Turkish state for speaking Kurdish and spending several years in Turkish prison:

> I am proud that part of my nation is living freely in their region. I am thinking that if one day I cannot go to Kurdistan in Iran, Turkey or Syria, I can go to that part and live there. I want to be in a country where people speak Kurdish and are not ashamed of being Kurdish. Kurdistan Region is a symbol for Kurdish existence. (Leyla, a 56 years old woman, Kurdistan-Turkey, the UK)

The interviewee above vividly talked about the pain of Turkish assimilation policy and how it had instilled an inferiority complex and a cultural shame among the Kurds. Kurdistan Region becomes thus a place where Kurds can allegedly regain their confidence and assert their identity without fearing ethnic persecution. In the same vein, another interviewee underlined what this entity means for the states of Turkey, Iran, Iraq and Syria:

> Kurdistan Region is very important and sacred. Now that this place is called Kurdistan, it feels like a knife in the hearts of Turkey, Iran, Iraq, and Syria. Every time they say Kurdistan, it must be painful for these states to hear it. For many years, the Turks described Masoud Barzani and Jalal Talabani as tribal leaders. Now they are leaders of Kurdistan. (Memo, a 50 years old man, Kurdistan-Turkey, Sweden)

The politics of naming is central to Kurdish politics and resistance toward the states in which they are inhabiting and resisting. For many years, Turkey refused to refer to the Kurdistan Region in its name but used "Northern Iraq" to label this Kurdish-dominated region. After the independence referendum of 2017 and its war on Kurds of Turkey, Turkey has intensified its aggressive politics of denial against the Kurds and aiming to erase the symbolic presence of the Kurds in the region. Many of the interviewees talked about the resistance they encountered in putting the name of Kurdistan on the map when people asked them about their origin. According to the Kurdish interviewees, the name of Kurdistan was harshly contested by some Turkish, Persian and Arab and Assyrian migrants who asserted that the very name of Kurdistan was insidious, divisive and secessionist. Peteet (2005) argues that choice of words in context of territorial disputes functions as political interventions and those words that circulate most effectively are often those that belong to the dominant forces. To name a territory as Turkish or Kurdish is to make a public claim. The Kurds for instance normalize the name of Kurdistan through repeating and standardizing it and thus displacing former names that was or is imposed on the territory in question. Naming and renaming become a discursive weapon and function as a way of taking possession (Still, 2010). As Jacques Derrida has insisted, "Mastery begins, as we know, through the power of naming, of imposing and legitimating appellations" (cited in Still, 2010, p. 145). Thus, it is in the field of power that names and words circulate and different actors attempt to win the struggle in the hierarchy of credibility. Moreover, different actors involved in territorial disputes endeavor to make their narratives as the most accepted, objective and legitimate, and excluding other competing narratives through describing them as propaganda or acts of 'terror' (Peteet, 2005). While elucidating the functions of names, Bhatia shows that "the struggle over representation is directly a struggle over the legitimacy of violent acts. Indeed, a site, territory, or people are first colonised by words and names before being physically occupied by soldiers, trading companies and statesmen" (Bhatia, 2005, pp. 13–14). The name of Kurdistan is no longer as subversive as it is used to be in the Middle East and many Western leaders have embraced the name and the political attitude of the neighboring countries vis-à-vis the Kurds has gradually changed although impassively. While Turkey in 2009 embraced for a short period a political opening toward the Kurds, it did not take long time before it embraced the language of denial and exclusion vis-à-vis the Kurds across the Middle East.

According to Küçük and Özselçük (2016), the word *Kurd* no longer only invokes positions such as 'victim' and 'criminal' due to the Kurdish resistance and struggle against the chocking cruelty of the Islamic State (ISIL) in Syria and Iraq since the Kurdish movements in Iraq and Syria view themselves and are viewed by many Western states to fight in the name of humanity. However, this does not mean that the neighboring states have stopped to name the Kurdish movements as 'terrorists' (Turkey) or 'Zionist toys' (Iran) that assumedly want to serve Western and Zionist interests and split the Islamic world. The Turkish state has politically invested in erasing the signs of the Kurdish struggle against ISIS and turning them into a political force that is equivalent to ISIL. The function of naming in this context becomes a device of gathering supporters and justifying acts (Bhatia, 2005) against the Kurdish right to political authority and power sharing.

While comparing the situation of the Kurdish region in Iran with Kurdistan Region, this young interviewee underlined her impressive experience of the Kurdistan Region:

> My family urged me to visit Southern Kurdistan and they even paid my trip so I could see Kurdistan and see the feeling of living in a country where to be Kurdish is not a negative thing. When I landed in Hawler/Erbil airport, I saw the Kurdish flag everywhere. It was Kurdish police and not Iranian police as in Eastern Kurdistan. This is the first time history is on the side of the Kurds. The police officers were very polite. In Iran, a man

> must accompany me when I go into town, and the men were gazing at me all the time. They also made comment about me. Kurds are living under Islamic and Iranian laws and the Kurds have adopted the Iranian laws. But when I was in Southern Kurdistan, I did not have the same feeling and people were not acting in the same way and did not comment my body. I was with a female friend and we were in town by ourselves and nobody was telling us what we were doing there. We have to become like Southern Kurdistan. Imagine the feeling that police officers speak Kurdish to you and it is the first time in history that it is to your benefit as a Kurd. Public signs are in Kurdish and not in Persian as in Eastern Kurdistan. It makes me happy to see my identity visible everywhere. You feel at home because it feels that it is Kurdistan and not a foreign country as in Iran with a different language and TV all the time. (Sheno, a 26 years woman Kurdistan-Iran, Sweden)

The interviewee above raises important issues that have been central to the political struggle of the Kurdish movement. She refers to stigmatization of the Kurdish identity, about how police functions as a punitive institution against the Kurds in Iran and how Islamic and Iranians laws stigmatize women in Iran under the cover of protecting women from sexual harassment. The same interviewee talked about the devalued status of the Kurdish language in Iran where speaking Persian was viewed as 'classy' and much more valued than the Kurdish language. Through coercive assimilation policies, the Iranian state have managed to impose and inculcate a dominant national language and rejecting other languages as local or dialects. However, due to the proliferation of communication technologies and satellite channels, Kurds of Iran are becoming more aware of the cultural freedom that exists for the Kurds in Kurdistan Region:

> I know many Kurds from Eastern Kurdistan/Iranian Kurdistan that go to Southern Kurdistan in order to enjoy its identity and celebrate Newroz because nobody suppresses you for being Kurdish. Many of them go in different squares in Hawler/Erbil and take pictures where the Kurdish flag is flying behind them and post it on Facebook. (Masoud, a 31 years old man Kurdistan-Iran, Sweden)

An important distinction that the interviewees made regarded the ways they referred to the places they visited. While Kurds from Kurdistan Region talked about visiting or traveling to Kurdistan, Kurds from other parts did not mention Kurdistan but the names of the states of Iran, Turkey and Syria. They argued that they use different names for their places of origin due to the political status of their regions. Unlike the Kurds of Iraq who control their own regions, Kurds in Iran, Turkey and until recently Syria are subsumed under the universality of these states. Some of the interviewees talked about the magic of visiting Kurdistan Region and these experiences made them to dream intensively about political and cultural freedom in their own regions:

> My father visited our village and he usually stay there for three months. So, he visited Kurdistan Region and the first thing he did when entered the Kurdistan Region was to go and kiss the Kurdish flag on the uniform of a Kurdish border officer and kissed the ground. He told them: "I love you, arrest me, do whatever you want to do with me. I am proud of seeing you guarding the borders and the territory of Kurdistan". (Heval, a 30 years old man Kurdistan-Turkey, Sweden)

This narrative shows how the political oppression of Kurdish identity and search for sovereignty as a device of attaining freedom reinforces romantic nationalism. While the narrative above assumes that KRG welcomes all Kurds and functions as an inclusive entity, in reality Kurds from other parts of Kurdistan are still hailed as 'Turkish', 'Iranian' and 'Syrian' despite continuous Kurdish media usage of terminologies like Southern Kurdistan (Iraq), Northern Kurdistan (Turkey), Western Kurdistan (Syria) and Eastern Kurdistan (Iran). When Kurds residing in the Kurdistan Region from other parts of Kurdistan criticize the political elites of the KRG, they are often reminded that they are guests' here and should not transgress the 'red lines'. Accordingly, hospitality of KRG vis-à-vis Kurdish brethren across borders is easily transformed into hostility (see Derrida, 2000). Despite the romanticization of Kurdistan Region, Kurds in diaspora do not necessarily or uncritically embrace the idea of a Kurdish statehood when KRG cannot guarantee democracy, rule of law and effective citizenship, issues that will be addressed below.

Desiring Kurdish Rule Beyond Authoritarianism and Patrimonial Power

While the earlier section dealt mainly with the positive appraisal of the Kurdistan Region as a potential political home for the Kurds, this section focuses on the quality of governance in the Kurdistan Region. It is in this context that we will see that Kurdish nationalism is losing ground due to the prevailing political corruption and authoritarianism in Kurdistan Region. The oppositional parties within the geographical boundaries of the Kurdistan Region and the transnational political and guerrilla activities of PKK pose persistent challenge to the political order of KRG. Below, I focus on those Kurdish voices that are critical of the Kurdish authorities in the Kurdistan Region and position themselves in different ways outside of the ontological jurisdiction of Kurdistan Region constituted by the two ruling parties, KDP and PUK. Although the majority of the interviewees welcomed Kurdish statehood, they were not sure that the Kurdistan Region embraces all Kurds. A young Kurdish woman from Kurdistan of Turkey illustrates how her conception of Kurdistan Region has changed:

> At the beginning it was a very positive injection and gave hope about a better future for the Kurds. The last years, they have become more and more isolated and are just taking care of their own business. Many Kurds from other parts are disappointed and think that the Iraqi Kurds have liberated themselves and do not care about other parts of Kurdistan. I share this idea because Kurdistan Region did not open up its border for Kurds of Rojava (Syria). You expected them to be more welcoming toward the Kurds. I became very disappointed with them. (Havin, a 27 years old woman Kurdistan-Turkey, Sweden)

This young woman above endorses the official PKK rhetoric that denounces the KRG as the political home of the Kurds. PKK goes so far to accuse KDP as carrying out anti-Kurdish politics to its close political and economic ties with Turkey. Another interviewee argued that the emergence of Kurdistan Region has contained the political activities of Kurds from other parts of Kurdistan in the name of maintaining its security and existence:

> For Kurds from Eastern Kurdistan, Northern Kurdistan and Western Kurdistan, when they visit Kurdistan Region, they see Kurdish police, Kurdish flag and nobody oppresses your Kurdish identity. This become like a dream for them. It is an important experience. But the Kurdistan Region has done many mistakes because it does not support Northern Kurdistan or Western Kurdistan. It is now closing its border against Western Kurdistan in the same way as our enemy Turkey is doing. *Kurdistan Region is not only an inspiration but also a problem for other parts of Kurdistan* because it wants to silence other parts of Kurdistan for its own existence and appease

> the neighbouring states. (Sherzad, a 49 years old man, Kurdistan Region-Iraq, Sweden, emphasis added)

The interviewee above is aware of the positive aspects of Kurdistan Region for safe-guarding Kurdish identity and language; however, this does not prevent him from seeing also a peril in sanctifying the Kurdistan Region as impeccable if not complicit in containing the political struggle of other parts of Kurdistan. This is particularly true for the Kurds of Iran whose political activity has for decades been checked by Patriotic Union of Kurdistan (PUK) and even collaborated with the Iranian regime in maintaining the security of the Iranian borders. In order to appease Turkey, KDP fills the same function in regard to the political and guerrilla activities of PKK in Kurdistan Region and Rojava. Turkish governments led by Erdoğan have tried to neutralize PKK's dominance in Turkey through backing up political forces close to KDP and Masoud Barzani. In this context, a supporter of PKK expressed her aversion vis-à-vis KRG in the following way:

> KRG is no different for me than the Turkish government. When KRG was formed, they did not think about other Kurds in other parts of Kurdistan. The only differences now are that the government carries the name Kurdish and its leader is Masoud Barzani. Are women recognized in Kurdistan Region? Can you see women's movement allowed to fight for the liberation of women in Kurdistan? No, they are not. There are female Kurdish politicians in Kurdistan Region but they do not have power but function as façade. Kurdistan Region is not an inspiration for me. My movement is PKK because women representation is very important for us. (Lana, a 32 years old woman, Kurdistan-Turkey, the UK)

PKK has flagged the representation of women as central to its ideological struggle, which challenges the traditional order of the Kurdish society and politics often run by men. Women appear in Kurdish politics in Kurdistan Region but they are often used in ceremonial contexts to appease international and Western representations that KRG endorses women's rights and political representation. PKK and KDP are the two main political actors of Kurdish politics and they try to extend the political clout to all four parts of Kurdistan. Eccarius-Kelly (2011) argues that KRG poses strong challenge to PKK's dominance in Kurdish regions of Turkey by gaining credibility among the Kurdish population in Turkey through creating political and economic benefits. This empowered position has increasingly changed due to the economic crisis in the Kurdistan Region as the results of the budget cut from the central Iraqi government and the assaults of ISIL.

By monopolizing KRG, KDP has the benefits of international recognition and economic and military support. While PKK is labeled as a 'terrorist' organization by the West, KDP enjoys open diplomatic relations with influential Western leaders. Until now, PKK has succeeded in preventing the emergence of a shared political space to organize and represent differences in Northern Kurdistan/Turkey and Rojava/Syria. In contrast, KDP has not been able to do the same in the entire Kurdistan Region due to the presence of powerful adversaries like PUK, Gorran movement and Islamic parties. The question of Kurdish statehood has become KDP's central discursive strategy to quell oppositional parties and political dissent. The discourse of national unity or social cohesion in Kurdistan is strategically used by both KDP and PUK to demote the democratization process and pluralism. Unlike KDP, PKK views statehood as an inadequate solution to the political subjugation of the Kurds since statehood reproduces a new master identity that leads to oppression of 'new' minorities and creation of ethnic strangers. Accordingly, PKK views the sovereign power as inherently problematic since the nation-state constructs 'core' members through exclusion of groups that are not viewed as organic members of the nation. PKK's imprisoned leader Abdullah Öcalan has formulated a project about democratic autonomy that according to himself is anti-national. Without denying the legitimacy of the already existing states, democratic autonomy promotes the idea of a highly decentralized governance where all constituencies can partake in organizing their political, economic and social life and ruling themselves (see Matin, 2020). According to Saeed (2016), this implies that the Kurdish movement in Northern Kurdistan has moved from a one-dimensional political movement to a multidimensional social movement. Relatedly, Watts contends that democratic autonomy is not anti-national but micronational since Kurds are still defined as a nation along with other nations. However, the political nationalist struggle is situated within feminist and radical democracy movements (Watts, 2016), where the nation-state, capitalism and patriarchy are described as the three ills of our world (Üstündağ, 2016). Thus, the democratic autonomy seeks to decolonize "the hierarchically instituted social relations that lead to the constitution of oppressive and privileged communities" (Küçük

& Özselçuk, 2016, p. 187). In the same context, Jongerden (2019) contrasts the Kurdistan Region of Iraq with the Democratic Federation of Northern Syria (read Rojava) and how they use different templates to organize and govern themselves. While the Kurdistan Region is assumed to rely on the idea of the nation-state, Rojava aims to create a society based on self-organization, where the rights of minorities and women are safeguarded (see also Gunes, 2020; Matin, 2020). With respect to this Kurdish referendum for independence in 2017, Jongerden argues that the referendum was not only a failure for the idea of a federal Iraq but it also entailed a failure for the Kurdish leadership led by KDP and PUK:

> In practice, clientelistic networks around families and individuals exercise strict control, not the parliament and government, and they do so without a common political agenda and coordination. Instead of bringing the parties together in their quest for statehood, the referendum exposed the clientelistic networks that determined KRG politics long the fiefdoms associated with these networks. (p. 72)

To nuance the framing by Jongerden and the distinction that exists between KDP and PUK, Aziz (2017, p. 118) explains that KDP functions as a dynasty and aim to control the revenue in Kurdistan in order to enable its rule, while the PUK is mainly consisted of a group of corrupt officials, who use economy to preserve their power and position. What is more striking about PUK, is that it elusively acts like the center of power and opposition to the power that it has endorsed throughout the history of KRG. Soon after the Kurdish referendum, due to imposed Iraqi embargo and regional political and economic threat against KRG, the same political parties and figures of Kurdistan Region who had promised the impending Kurdish independence by declaring political divorce and adieu to Arab Iraq, went out in different Iraqi media and declared their pride of being Iraqis and promising to defend the territorial integrity of the Iraqi state. The current President of Kurdistan Region, Nechirvan Barzani, who is nephew of Masoud Barzani, one of the main architects behind the Kurdish referendum for independence, declared during a meeting with the Iraqi Prime Minister Mustafa Al-Khadimi, that "the Kurds are proud of their Iraq, and they are determined to continue work for the sake of Iraq's stability, security and sovereignty" (Shafaq News, 2020). For the Kurdish people in general, KDP and PUK do not enjoy much credibility as representing Kurdish freedom and rights but viewed primarily as oligarchs that defend their economic and patrimonial power.

Despite different approaches to the question of Kurdish statelessness, talk of democracy and uniqueness of the Kurds in the Muslim Middle East, KDP, PUK and PKK have not endorsed a reliable political order based on pluralism of ideas, shared democratic space and peaceful contestation. These three political parties explicitly use regional states to strengthen their party-interests and this implies that they choose, despite their Pan-Kurdish rhetoric to ally with regional governments over the Kurds across borders (Natali, 2015). This is not to underestimate the progress made in the Kurdish society in light of geopolitical vulnerability and the short self-rule that Kurds have been experiencing in Kurdistan Region. The geopolitical and the ideological context of the Middle East is far from favorable for non-dominant constituencies like the Kurds to pursue and implement political projects that aim to be comprehensively inclusive regardless of ethnic and religious belonging. The continuous Turkish assault on the Kurds in Rojava is a telling example that endorses militancy of ethnic divisions and identities and obstructs processes of democratization, gender equity and ethno-religious pluralism.

Whereas many interviewees passionately desired a Kurdish state as the solution to the collective oppression of the Kurds, several interviewees were not sure that the current political template of the Kurdistan Region can function as a liberating or an opportunity-enhancing vehicle for the stateless Kurds:

> A state is like a home and home is a place where you want to feel free. State means freedom. But I do not like the ruling parties in Kurdistan because if you do not join them, you will not have a place in that society. I want to have a democratic Kurdish state and not a dictatorship. What should I do with a Kurdish state if I am not free? I want a Kurdish state but democratic like the UK. I hope that the ruling parties do not lie too much but work for an equal and democratic society. (Huner, a 26 years old man Kurdistan Region-Iraq, the UK)

Although stateless nations often view statehood as a political answer to their political homelessness in a nation-state-centric world, where they can achieve their political freedom and live their differences, the interviewee above illustrates that members of stateless diasporas do not necessarily embrace a blind nationalism by endorsing statehood regardless of its mode of governance. The ruling parties in the Kurdistan Region have not been very successful in crafting a national identity through promoting bonds of solidarity between the people and the social institutions where different constituencies regardless of their political, gender ethnic and religious backgrounds can exercise equal political agency. The vast economic inequalities between different groups in the Kurdistan Region encourage and force many Kurds to migrate to Europe in search of a better life. Consider Rozhgar's account of how the power abuse of the ruling political parties in the Kurdistan Region contributed to his migration to Britain at the age of 14, where he still lives as an undocumented refugee:

> When I left Kurdistan, I was not thinking about returning to Kurdistan. When I was younger, I really hated Kurdistan. I was even telling myself if I go to Europe, I would not say that I am Kurdish. The government in Kurdistan had made me to feel like that. How can I enjoy my life in a country where the president acts like a mafia? Those who rule in Kurdistan are mafias. In Kurdistan, you do not get support from the government and they do not respect young people. (19 years old man, Kurdistan-Region-Iraq)

Rozhgar expressed his aversion toward established families within these two political parties and the way their children were elegantly dressed, drove luxurious cars and went to well respected private schools, where some of them did not even learn to speak and write in Kurdish but English or Turkish. For him, this was not comprehensible given that the ruling political parties were flagging the idea of a threatened Kurdish identity in a predominantly Arab Iraq. Many of the interviewees talked about the difficulty to institutionalize democracy in light of the two ruling parties KDP and PUK:

> Kurdistan Region has been free for more than two decades. When we were under Saddam's regime, we did not expect good things from him because he was our enemy. But when it comes to a Kurdish power and rule, you must expect the best from it. The Kurdish power instead of fostering Kurdishness, they have prioritised party politics and cemented the power of KDP and PUK. This is the greatest problem of the Kurds in Kurdistan Region. In many countries people talk about political pluralism and multiparty system but in our country, there is a multiparty system but no democracy. It is all a façade for the two ruling parties. These two parties fought each other from 1994-1998 and many people were killed

> due to their wars. When they got power, instead of undermining the power of feudalism and religion, they have reinforced them. If you criticise the ruling parties, you will be harassed and called a traitor for undermining the national unity of the Kurds. You cannot have democracy without critique. Kurdish power should remember the days of suffering and make democracy to the standard of the Kurdish society. When I visited Kurdistan, I expected something better but I saw corruption was eating up the society and it is becoming more like a culture in order to survive. The families of the leaders of these political parties are becoming like lords who are getting richer and richer and talk about national unity if they are criticised. I am suffering when I see that my country is not democratic and they want to copy the political system of the Arab states where the sons take over the power when their fathers are gone. If Kurdish soil is liberated but its people are politically oppressed, Kurdistan loses it meaning for me. I want both my soil and its people to be free. (Khalid, a 42 years old man, Kurdistan Region-Iraq, the UK)

Despite his fierce critique of these ruling political parties, his first priority is to create a Kurdish state. When the Kurdish state is achieved, Khalid expressed his desire to participate in a popular movement to remove the ruling parties. For him, the importance of having a Kurdish state will solve his identity puzzle since "every time I get the question 'where are you from?', it is like pouring salt on an injury. This wound can only be healed through a Kurdish state". This stance reflects a postponing of democratization within the Kurdish society by primarily focusing on foreign powers that subordinate the Kurds. National liberation entails often a paradoxical and ambiguous project, where the dominated group needs to liberate itself from both external oppressors and internal oppressors (Walzer, 2015).

When the Kurdistan Region experienced a short period of economic prosperity, a number of Kurdish families returned to Kurdistan to establish a life there. A recent study by Paasche (2016) illustrates that corruption obstructs reintegration of the Kurdish returnees from Europe and undermines sense of belonging to the Kurdish nation and nation-building project. Despite their appraisal of Kurdistan Region, many Kurdish migrants experienced disillusionments when they encountered the cultural norms of the Kurdish society where corruption shaped their encounters with social institutions. In order to build a democratic political culture and creating trust between the citizens and the social institutions, it is crucial that institutions endorse impartiality in the exercise of public power and counteract corruption, favoritism, clientelism, patronage and nepotism. Such just and impartial institutions need administrative efficiency and meritocratic recruitment based on competence and knowledge in running the state apparatus (Rothstein, 2014) and not grounded on what party loyalty the employees have, as it is the case in the Kurdistan Region. Whereas in most democracies, party leaders are also members of the parliament, political elites of PUK and KDP without being elected as representatives in the Kurdistan parliament continue to rule the Kurdistan Region and bypass the parliament and diminish its legitimacy. Although being politically degraded and disempowered, the Kurdistan parliament functions as a political stratagem by KDP and PUK to appease domestic and international (Western states) call for democratic rule and representation in the Kurdistan Region. The democracy that KDP and PUK rhetorically adhere is in practice based on non-democratic means such as electoral fraud and a dysfunctional parliament and political repression of dissent (see Sadiki, 2002). Rezgar, a 63 years old man from Kurdistan Region lamented that "the Kurdish parties in Kurdistan think more of filling their pockets than strengthening the Kurdish identity and language. They act more like businessmen than accountable politicians". Authoritarian regimes often exploit the economy as a means to increase support and distribute benefits to those who manifest their support and loyalty to them (Sasson, 2016), which can be applicable to the Kurdish contexts where the ruling political parties attempt to 'buy' the votes of the voters during election campaigns. The armed forces in the Kurdistan Region are politicized and used by KDP and PUK to settle political disputes and contain or co-opt political dissent and opposition. It is widely argued that the Kurdistan Region is ruled as a family enterprise by Barzani and Talabani's family. Accordingly, the democracy represented by KDP and PUK is a façade democracy since rule of law, political transparency and accountability are not the political priorities of these two ruling political parties.

Diasporic Grievances and Critique

Kurdistan Region was generally viewed by members of the Kurdish diasporas in Sweden and the UK as a potential benchmark for a Kurdish state and as a key to Kurdish sovereign freedom and power. This positive stance vis-à-vis the Kurdistan Region and its leadership has undoubtedly changed after the Kurdish referendum for independence in 2017, when it became clear that the ruling political parties KDP and PUK do everything to protect their parochial family interests than addressing the national plights and grievances of the Kurds. Despite the overwhelmingly positive conception of the Kurdistan Region, many interviewees criticized the ruling political parties in the Kurdistan Region to suppress political freedom and exploit the economic resources of the Kurdistan Region in the name of Kurdish unity and nationalism. Although KRG has lost much of its political legitimacy due to lack of legality and institutionalism that act independently without intervention from the ruling families and parties, the emergence of ISIL provided KRG with a contingent opportunity to regain legitimacy for its nationalist rhetoric both in Kurdistan and in diaspora. One can say that ISIL strengthened Kurdish nationalism within Kurdistan Region in a time of Kurdish nationalism crisis. During 2015 and 2016, Kurdish diasporas in different Western states expressed their support for the Kurdish armed struggle against ISIL and held rallies in support of the Kurdish forces and Kurdish Independence. However, time will tell how long this borrowed legitimacy can last. KRG has both contributed to strengthening nationalism by flagging a Kurdistani identity in its fight against ISIL and its political opposition vis-à-vis the central Iraqi government but it has also gradually weakened Kurdish nationalism due to its quality of government, authoritarianism, corruption and patrimonial power. Instead of Kurdish nationalism, the political party functions in practice as a surrogate for the nation and exclude those forces and voices that challenge its political power through describing them as internal enemies or Trojan horses for foreign plots against the Kurdistan Region. Consequently, members of Kurdish diasporas are divided whether Kurdish independence will bring them sovereign freedom in light of prevailing patrimonial power, succession by inheritance and lack of democratic procedures in the Kurdistan Region.

Exile is a hotbed of homesickness and nationalism but it is equally a potential site of critique of homeland politics as this chapter has shown about the Kurdish diasporas. The ruling parties often repudiate critique against the political order of the KRG under the pretext of safe-guarding the 'Kurdish experience' of ruling themselves. Hence, KDP and PUK resist, punish, mute and reject rival plans for how the political community of the Kurdistan Region can be reimagined through asserting themselves as the legitimate hegemons responsible of value allocation and assignment (Sadiki, 2002). For a democratic political order to emerge, it is important that critique has a privileged position since it provides the basis of the legitimacy of a government. In this regard, Butler (2009) argues, "the state derives its own legitimacy through granting dissent, but to the extent that it cannot control the terms of dissent, it also allows for a deterioration of its own claims, a suspension of its own mandate, and even a withdrawal or compromise of its own sovereignty" (p. 793). In other words, dissent provides a powerful means to check and undo the sovereign power. It all depends on whether the state can tolerate the terms of dissent or reject oppositional and critical voices as rogue viewpoints (ibid.). On different occasions, the Kurdish diasporas as a transnational community have demonstrated their political loyalty and emotional attachment to the Kurdistan Region and Kurdish identity. However, this transnational political obligation (Baron, 2015) is not limited to loyalty but expanded by parts of the Kurdish diasporas to include the role of critique in identifying alternative ways of ruling Kurdistan and undoing unbearable forms of political arrangement of the Kurdish society. In reality, the continuous political and economic corruption in Kurdistan has made a large part of Kurdish diaspora indifferent toward Kurdish identity and the future of Kurdistan Region. For other parts of Kurdistan, the misconducts of the ruling political parties have become a reminder that it is not enough to liberate the Kurds from colonial and oppressive foreign Arab, Persian and Turkish powers, but it is equally important to liberate themselves from oppressive and self-interested Kurdish oligarchs that use the Kurdish card to justify power abuse, suspension of democracy and distributive justice. It is worth mentioning that the road to authoritarianism is enabled by citizens who stop questioning their societies, participate in reproduction of authoritarianism through their complicity and silence (Giroux, 2011). In this regard, the Kurdish diasporas can function as critical agents and obstruct the processes of authoritarianism by holding the power and authority accountable and involve in the struggle for political justice in the Kurdistan Region that until now lacks a shared democratic space for contestation and participation.

References

Adamson, F. B. (2016). The growing importance of diaspora politics. *Current History, 115*(784), 291–297.

Aziz, S. (2017). The economic system(s) of the Kurdistan regional government, Iraq. In G. Gülistan, H. Sabine, & I. S. Ferhad (Eds.), *Between state and*

non-state: Politics and society in Kurdistan-Iraq and Palestine (pp. 103–122). Palgrave Macmillan.
Baron, I. Z. (2015). *Obligation in exile: The Jewish Diaspora, Israel and Critique.* Edinburgh University Press.
Betts, A., & Jones, W. (2016). *Mobilising the diaspora: How refugees challenge authoritarianism.* Cambridge University Press.
Bhatia, M. V. (2005). Fighting words: Naming terrorists, bandits, rebels and other violent actors. *Third World Quarterly, 26*(1), 5–22.
Butler, J. (2009). Critique, dissent, disciplinarity. *Critical Inquiry, 35*(2), 773–795.
Conversi, D. (2012). Irresponsible radicalisation: Diasporas, globalisation and long-distance nationalism in the digital age. *Journal of Ethnic and Migration Studies, 38*(9), 1357–1379.
Derrida, J. (2000). Hospitality. *Angelaki, 5*(3), 3–18.
Eccarius-Kelly, V. (2011). *The Militant Kurds: A dual strategy for freedom.* Berger.
Eliassi, B. (2013). *Contesting Kurdish identities in Sweden: Quest for belonging among Middle Eastern Youth.* Palgrave Macmillan.
Giroux, H. A. (2011). *On critical pedagogy.* New York, NY: Blomsbury.
Gunes, C. (2020). Approaches to Kurdish autonomy in the Middle East. *Nationalities Paper, 48*(2), 323–338.
Gunter, M. (2011). *The Kurds ascending: The evolving solution to the Kurdish problem in Iraq and Turkey.* Palgrave Macmillan.
Jongerden, J. (2019). Governing Kurdistan: Self-administration in the Kurdistan regional Government in Iraq and the democratic federation of Northern Syria. *Etnopolitics, 18*(1), 61–75.
Klein, J. (2014). The minority question: A view from history and the Kurdish history. In K. Will & P. Eva (Eds.), *Multiculturalism and minority rights in the Arab World* (pp. 27–52). Oxford University Press.
Küçük, B., & Özselçuk, C. (2016). The Rojava experience: Possibilities and challenges of building a democratic life. *South Atlantic Quarterly, 115*(1), 184–196.
Matin, K. (2020). Liminal lineages of the "Kurdish Question". *Middle East Report* 295. https://merip.org/2020/08/liminal-lineages-of-the-kurdish-question/ Accessed 7 April, 2021.
Mügge, L. (2012). Ideologies of nationhood in sending-state transnationalism: Comparing Surinam and Turkey. *Ethnicities, 13*(3), 338–358.
Natali, D. (2015). The Kurdish quasi-state: Leveraging political limbo. *The Washington Quarterly, 38*(2), 145–164.
Paasche, E. (2016). The role of corruption in reintegration: Experiences of Iraqi Kurds upon return from Europe. *Journal of Ethnic and Migration Studies, 42*(1), 1078–1093.

Peteet, J. (2005). Words as interventions: Naming in the Palestine-Israeli conflict. *Third World Quarterly, 26*(1), 153–172.

Rothstein, B. (2014). What is the opposite of corruption. *Third World Quarterly, 35*(5), 737–752.

Rubin, M. (2016). *Kurdistan Rising? Consideration for Kurds, their neighbors, and the region*. American Enterprise Institute.

Saeed, S. (2016). *Kurdish politics in Turkey: From the PKK to the KCK*. Routledge.

Sadiki, L. (2002). The search for citizenship in Bin Ali's Tunisia: Democracy versus unity. *Political Studies, 50*(3), 497–513.

Sasson, J. (2016). *Anatomy of authoritarianism in the Arab Republics*. Cambridge University Press.

Shafaq News. (2020). *Barzani: Kurds are proud of their Iraq*. https://shafaq.com/en/Iraq-News/Barzani-Kurds-are-proud-of-their-Iraq. Accessed 17 March 2021.

Shain, Y., & Barth, A. (2003). Diaspora and international relations theory. *International Organization, 57*(3), 449–479.

Sheffer, G. (2003). *Diaspora politics: A home abroad*. Cambridge University Press.

Stansfield, G., & Anderson, L. (2009). Kurds in Iraq: The struggle between Baghdad and Erbil. *Middle East Policy, 16*(1), 134–145.

Still, J. (2010). *Derrida and hospitality: Theory and practice*. Edinburg University Press.

Tejel, J. (2009). *Syria's Kurds: History, politics and society*. Routledge.

Turner, S., & Kleist, N. (2013). Introduction: Agents of change? Staging and governing diasporas and the African State. *African Studies, 72*(2), 192–206.

Üstündağ, N. (2016). Self-defense as a revolutionary practice in Rojava, or how to unmake the state. *South Atlantic Quarterly, 115*(1), 197–210.

Walzer, M. (2015). *The paradoxes of liberation: Secular revolutions and religious counterrevolutions*. Yale University Press.

Watts, N. F. (2016). The spring in Sulaimani: Kurdish protest and political identities. In J. H. Shabnam & L. Philip (Eds.), *Political identities and popular uprisings in the Middle East* (pp. 37–57). Rowman & Littlefield.

CHAPTER 8

Seeing as the Stateless in a World of Nation-States

It is argued that social sciences have not seriously accorded attention to statelessness despite intensive and passionate engagement with issues of right, justice and human rights (Bloom et al., 2017). Relatedly, Butler (2010) asserts that statelessness is too important to be sidelined since it often arises in the context of wars, inequality and conflicts (cited in Butler & Spivak, 2010, pp. 13–14). Despite statelessness's continuous prevalence in our world, statelessness is rarely viewed as an academic topic to be studied with in the social sciences. As Butler wonders:

> If one asks: who writes on 'statelessness' these days? – the question is hardly understood. In fact, it is generally dismissed as a trend of the 1980s. It is not that statelessness disappeared but only that we apparently have nothing interesting to say about it any more. One has to wonder about what 'interesting' means in such a context. (Butler & Spivak, 2010, pp. 13–14)

Similar argument is made by Belton (2011) who maintains that "among the ranks of the non-citizen, one finds a lesser-known category of people which has yet to be considered seriously by political theory – the stateless" (Belton 2011, p. 59). Moreover, Belton asks for a new approach to understanding statelessness as a distinct experience of non-membership by not only "looking at who is let in and what naturalization procedure should be

B. Eliassi, *Narratives of Statelessness and Political Otherness*, Minorities in West Asia and North Africa, https://doi.org/10.1007/978-3-030-76698-6_8

expanded to them, but also entails examining who has always been on the inside and to whom we need to justify their continued exclusion" (ibid.). In his essay on Kurdish identity and statelessness, Vali (1998) underlines that while the nation-state as an institution is viewed as a major achievement of modernity, statelessness and its consequences do not occupy the same privileged position within modern philosophical and political theory. As such, the stateless cannot be represented as political or as politics by the discourse of modernity and the nation-state but as a humanitarian issue. In effect, this widespread notion of statelessness neglects the fact that statelessness is a direct effect of modernity and exclusive nation-building systems (Vali 1998, p. 85). Consequently, the stateless is turned into political invisibility not only in politics but also in political theory that covers issues of membership and inclusion. In his deliberation about the radical role of theory, Cole (2017) argues that theory can help us to evaluate and critique existing political order and envision a new alternative and superior order. Cole points out that statelessness needs to be understood in relation to the global political order and be grasped:

> as a leftover residue lying outside of the international system of sovereign states, either nothing to do with that system or because of some minor inefficiency of that system that can be tweaked. Or we see them as a structural failure, a product of that order, such that finding a solution to statelessness means asking radical questions about the international political order. (Cole 2017, p. 258)

Cole charges liberal political theory as exclusionary, since liberal political theory has generally adopted an insider perspective that has privileged the voices and experiences of those who are members of a nation-state and possess statehood, namely the citizen. This has entailed the exclusion of the stateless as voiceless and the voice of the citizen as the legitimate voice to be acknowledged and heard. This is not to say that the question of statelessness has not been a problem for political theory. When the stateless has been included in the theory, it has been framed as problem for the citizen, a problem that needs a solution in order to preserve the interest of the citizen. In other words, the interest of the citizen has functioned as a gravitation center when solutions are proposed to deal with the stateless. It is not only the solution to statelessness that has privileged the position of the citizen but also theory that has been structured in relation to the perspectives, voices and experiences of the citizen. Such approaches construct the citizen as the core and the stateless as the periphery of theory (p. 261). Cole suggests that in order to construct a true inclusive theoretical framework where there are no fixed points and everything as negotiable. For this to be achieved, there is a need where "all have equal voices in reaching an egalitarian settlement based on universal principles of justice" (p. 263). This entails that membership should not be taken as a point of departure but what kind of meanings are assigned to membership. For Cole, at the level of theory, it is not the idea of statelessness that constitutes the problem, but the way membership of the dominant group is constructed. Practically, this means that it is those subjects who possess membership that constitute the problem by monopolizing their positions, interests and power and not the stateless who are deprived from rights and resources (ibid.). In sum, theory can either exclude certain categories of people by disqualifying their voices, experiences and perspectives as peripheral to the existing political order or challenge the existing order by considering and highlighting the experiences, collective sufferings and voices of disenfranchised groups that might engender new inclusionary political visions about the world. It is important for a radical theory to not fall into the trap of state rhetoric by using exclusionary appellations like 'terrorist' or 'separatist' when the claims of the stateless for equality, recognition, representation and justice are evaluated as destabilizing political 'noises'. In reality, such direct or indirect complicity with the state discourse and rhetoric about the ethnocultural, other as endangering the national security of the nation and its imagined territorial boundary, can further reinforce the emergence of what Appadurai (2006) labels as a predatory majority that seeks the exclusion and erasure of minorities as a prerequisite for its dominance and privilege.

Migration studies is of particular interest for statelessness studies since scholarship on migration engages heavily with analysis of how membership, citizenship, identity and belonging are constituted within the framework of the nation-state and in transnational contexts. Although stateless people and individuals might migrate/flee from a state to another or stay within the boundary of the state in question, it is important to not uncritically equate statelessness with immigration and refugeehood that disciplines like political theory, sociology, anthropology engage with. In this regard, Arendt (1951, p. 279) reflected on the usage of different terminologies regarding the stateless and argued that by using the term 'stateless', stateless people require some form of governmental and international agreement to address their vulnerabilities and provide them with a legal status that safeguards them. The term 'stateless' was replaced by the postwar term 'displaced persons', a discursive strategy that aimed to ignore or end the talk about statelessness (Arendt 1951). Although the term stateless has not fully disappeared, it is less used than categories like refugee, immigrant or displaced people. By ignoring the self-definition of stateless people as stateless, the states reinforce each other's sovereignty and provide little space for political refuge and resistance against the state that represses and wants them back for punishment (see Arendt 1951).

As the empirical data of this study has clearly shown, statelessness is not only theoretically situated within a negative discursive field but also as a lived experience. Lack of a national identity is often equated with absence of a legitimate political home, which is symbolized by the nation-state. As Radhakrishnan (2012) argues, a people and a person without a national belonging cannot become a people and a person in a world of nation-states since "the very idea of home and being at home in the world without the armature of the nation-state has been rendered utterly insubstantial" (p. 66). It is in the same context that Gyanendra Pandey maintains that it is by having a nation, that people are considered and treated as civilized (cited in Geschiere, 2009). When different empires declined around the world, nationalism emerged as the dominant ideological force, where "every nation began to feel the need to define itself as an *ethnie*, as a self-sufficient, organic entity with its own principles of development, its own 'soul'" (Kumar 2000, p. 591, emphasis in original). According to the logic of nationalism, those who lack a collective memory and do not have a national language and national literature capturing and conveying the experiences and values of the group, cannot expect to be treated and recognized as a people (pp. 591–592). This hegemonic position of nationalism underpins Gellner's (1983/2006, p. 6) poignant arguments that lacking a nationality is a form of deficiency and a disaster for the people involved, since a man without a nation is equal to a man without a shadow that" defies the recognized categories and provokes revulsion". Mamdani (2020) laments that political modernity has created a situation in which many people are taught to believe that they cannot live without the nation-state and the nation. Those peoples who do not adhere to this political imperative and fail in achieving statehood will be denied the privileges of the nation-state and will soon find themselves as a subjugated and permanent minority. This political order creates a huge distress for stateless peoples whose national identity and lives are excluded and denied recognition and representation in a world of nation-states.

The agents of the dominant nationalisms in the Middle East are well aware that disqualification of the Kurds as a legitimate nation must start with denying their separate language, culture and history and exiling them from representation, in order to turn them into a non-people, with no significant contribution to human development (Houston, 2009). Consequently, the stateless figure is captive of a nationalist world order that he or she cannot simply opt out of. This suggests that a theory which intends to grasp the reality of stateless people needs to shoulder two important tasks through opening up "a space that is neither captive to the 'world as it is,' nor naively credulous of visions of 'the world as it should be'" (Radhakrishnan 2003, p. vi).

Since the world is normatively reduced to nation-states due to the political and ideological dominance of the nation-state model (Radhakrishnan 2003), it is 'nearly impossible to conduct successful large-scale political action outside of this mighty social organization' (Malešević, 2013, 193). Moreover, citizenship despite its valuable acquisition cannot fully accommodate the political grievances of stateless people like the Kurds and Palestinians. Although Palestinians who have been forced to flee and leave their homeland can attain citizenship in the West, the right of belonging to Palestine cannot be suspended by attaining citizenship elsewhere, since Palestinian dispossession continues to be unaddressed as a global injustice in light of Israeli minoritization, occupation and expulsion of Palestinians (Butler 2012, p. 213). However, it is not comprehensible why certain Arab countries like Lebanon continues to deny the Palestinians citizenship rights and making precarity as a feature of Palestinian life condition in refugee camps.

Despite holding formal citizenship, the Kurds have not been viewed and treated as legitimate constituents in Iran, Iraq, Syria and Turkey. Rights in these states are often viewed as political charity and deployed strategically to quell and appease Kurdish political dissent and contestation (see Matin 2020). Historically, Kurds have generally not only being exposed to structural discrimination but also lacked 'the intersubjective experiences that engender the confidence and self-assuredness required to *feel* that one has the authority to speak as full member of a political community' (Balaton-Chrimes, 2014, p. 25 emphasis in original). The reluctance of the Kurds to accept a subjugated position within these states has created a sense of ontological insecurity among these states where Kurds continue to be represented and treated as disloyal and marked citizens (see Pandey, 2006). While the Palestinian and the Kurdish suffering might not resemble each other in several respects and enjoy different levels of legitimacy in the international community, it is important to note that "any and all suffering by virtue of forcible displacement and statelessness is equally unacceptable" (Butler 2012, p. 129). It is apparent that the political sufferings of the Kurds and Palestinians in the Middle East continue to guide "the imaginative resources" (Askland, 2014, p. 324) of the Kurdish and Palestinian diasporas, in the way they organize their cultural and political activism to alter the political conditions of Kurds and Palestinians in their homelands. A result of their continuous political activism and campaigning against the state violence that targets Kurdish and Palestinians lives and homes, Kurdish and Palestinian diasporas continue to see the suffering of their peoples in the Middle East as their own sufferings. Ending occupation of their homelands and achieving political freedom underpins the continuous politicization of Kurdish and Palestinian diasporas. However, this is not to say that members of Kurdish and Palestinian diasporas will permanently return to their homelands or will automatically feel strong attachments to the people in Kurdistan or Palestine if they achieve some form of independence or self-rule, since their place-based identities and belonging are hybrid, fluid and ambivalent (see Askland, 2014, p. 330; Hammer, 2005). These are the destabilizing effects of migration, mobility and life in exile, that identity cannot be fixed spatially and temporally.

The findings of this study have clarified the role of the state in enabling and delimiting access to citizenship rights. States and government policies still matter in forging political membership and regulating the political boundaries between nationals and non-nationals. A common feature that emerges among many citizenship regimes is the idea that subordinated groups lack properties that the 'core' group often embodies as organic members of the state. It can be about lacking the 'right' language, culture, appearance, religion, history, etc. (Isin, 2002). It is in a similar context that Anderson (2013, pp. 2–3) maintains that the nation-state is conceived as a community of value, whose citizens supposedly share common ideals and behaviors, from which ascribed non-citizens are excluded. Whereas the Kurds are forcefully subsumed under the universality of Turkish, Iraqi, Iranian and Syrian citizenship, Kurdish migrants in Sweden and the UK have made a commitment and a choice when they have applied for Swedish and British citizenship. Despite their positive appraisal of the Swedish and the British citizenship regimes, Kurdish and Palestinian migrants were highly aware of the various thresholds that the society has set up to exclude non-white and Muslim immigrants from achieving equality. It is in this context that Fry and Tlostanova (2021) maintain that ethnic exclusion continues to be a major problem not only for authoritarian regimes but also for the most egalitarian and apparently democratic societies, to which countries like Sweden and the UK belong. Exclusionary citizenship regimes not only target those outside of its national borders, but also marked citizens within the same entity. Nativity according to Fry and Tlostanova "remains the main principle of citizenship and, by association, of belonging to humankind, thus creating potential internal enemies and disposable lives" (p. 45). As Anderson (2013) eloquently argues, citizenship is constitutive to the global system of inclusion and exclusion, where states adopt both a discourse of universalism and inclusion and at the same time implementing practices of closure and exclusion against national outsiders. As we have seen in this study, exclusion and closure do not only target racialized migrants who lack British or Swedish citizenship, but also those peoples who are formally citizens but reminded on daily basis that they do not belong here neither culturally nor spatially.

Given that the Swedish and the British passports occupy a highly privileged position in a world of nation-states and allow their nationals to visit more than 170 states without visa restrictions, it appears as a convenient choice for Kurdish and Palestinian migrants to attain these citizenships. For Kurds and Palestinians as members of two stateless nation, attainment of Swedish or British citizenship functions as a pragmatic citizenship that allows them to enjoy freedom, mobility and security (see Mavroudi, 2007). Least to be misunderstood, pragmatic citizenship should not be equated with 'exploiting' these citizenships, since both the Kurdish and Palestinians research participants lamented the fact that they were denied the right to be legitimate members of Swedish and British societies and participate equally in shaping the meanings of these citizenships. Moreover, a pragmatic citizenship does not imply a negation of Kurdish and Palestinian identities. On the contrary, the Kurdish and Palestinian migrants belong to highly politicized diasporas and persistently challenge the official state narratives and ideologies of nationhood in the Middle East (Eliassi, 2013). Since the Palestinians fiercely challenge the idea of being stateless or landless, the idea of Palestine is intensely embraced and repeated across generations despite their knowledge that their adversary, Israel, is investing immense energy and resources in erasing the Palestinians or containing them within a ghettoized part of Palestine in the

West Bank and Gaza. In response to Israeli denial of Palestinian property, lands, and national-political rights, "the Palestinians have fostered the collective militancy of nostalgia in exile" (Shohat, 2017, p. 105).

Let us return to the central question of this book. What is statelessness if it is not merely a negation of citizenship? Statelessness implies a definitional problem in a world of the nation-state; where the stateless person needs to explain himself/herself more than members of sovereign peoples whose identity, language, history and culture are championed by states. Statelessness is not only a structural status injury but it also haunts the stateless in their everyday life, even when the stateless people do not identify with the sovereign identity within which they are forcefully subsumed. While established nations provide their members with confidence to define and imagine themselves as a continuous people (see Billig, 1995, p. 8), stateless people both lack that confidence and are reminded of their political otherness as an ill fit in the international political order permeated by statehood and sovereignty. Although established nations can often live their nationhood without defining themselves or being defined as nationalists, nationalism as a divisive ideology is assumed to be a property of stateless peoples that claim nationhood and statehood that established nations have ironically monopolized. In contrast to the supposedly parochial nationalism of the dominated ethnic groups, the nationalism of dominating groups is often championed for creating social cohesion, political stability, 'brotherhood' and unity across differences.

It is often argued that history belongs to the victors and this also becomes evident in the case of stateless people where they do not exist as a 'proper' people in history books. When the stateless person faces the question 'where are you from?' in everyday life, he or she cannot prove his/her existence through maps that are often viewed as an objective portrayal of placed-based identities. If many non-white immigrants experience difficulty in giving a straightforward answer to the question 'where are you from?', Kurdish and Palestinians migrant find further difficulty in answering this question since their identities are significantly contested, ambiguous, denied and devalued both in the Middle-East and in Sweden. Inferiorized and marked groups often interpret the recurrence of the question 'where are you from' as a device of othering and a reminder of their non-belonging. Furthermore, the stateless person needs to act as a teacher or as a historian in order to trace the history of his/her people and how they have arrived at this point. Since the stateless person lacks a given or a secure political home, the stateless person is often deprived of having the right to define himself/herself. The stateless people are not only reduced to superfluous characters but their identity, culture, food, history and existence are dispossessed, suppressed and muted by the sovereign power that denies the stateless people the right to full public visibility, recognition and representation. It is in this context we can understand why dispossessed, threatened and endangered nations like the Kurds and Palestinians perceive statehood as an important vehicle to realize, protect and exteriorize their existence. Hence, the lives of the Kurds and Palestinians are bound by statelessness and political otherness in an uneven world. Certainly, having a formal citizenship within the current Middle Eastern states is better than not having any at all, yet there is a need to expand the notion of citizenship to include decentering the dominant ethnic identity through redefining the sovereign identity to be inclusive of all differences in a non-hierarchical way.

The problem of the stateless figure cannot be reduced to a humanitarian issue as it is often done in relation to refugees, since it is a product of political exclusion that the nation-state contributes to (Vali 1998). Politics of naming becomes thus important in the context of claim-making to statehood and sovereignty. The sovereign powers in Iran, Iraq, Syria and Turkey for instance do not allow the Kurds to claim a position of statelessness because from the moment the Kurds makes a claim to statelessness, they are asserting themselves as political and a challenge to the sovereign state identities in a refusal to be subsumed under their exclusionary universality. This is not to say that resistance does not have a limit both discursively, militarily and politically since the sovereign power can often repudiate the political claims or voices of the stateless people as 'noises', 'terrorism' and 'separatism' that allegedly disturb the political stability of national and regional/international orders. In the context of authoritarian states of Iran, Iraq, Syria and Turkey, stability has meant quelling the dissent of the minoritized groups and discarding it as foreign plots that allegedly undermine national security, territorial integrity, 'brotherhood' and national cohesion. For Palestinians, Israel emerged as a colonial settler state that imported Jewish migrants across the globe that were not historically present in Palestine in order to designate an Israeli nation based on a Jewish majority. This political project made the Palestinians into a demographic and political minority in their own homeland. While the Israelis celebrate the foundation of Israel as a victorious day for the Jewish people as finally finding a political home in which they can be its masters and avoid the risk of being collectively harassed and slaughtered, the Palestinians lament that foundation as the basis of their homelessness, dispossession and erasure. The foundation of Israel continues to torment the political subjectivity of the Palestinians and their political future and well-being as a nation inside and outside Palestine.

What is conceived as Palestine or Israel is in reality home to Muslims, Jews, Arabs, Christians, Druzes and Bedouins, so the very idea of exclusive claim to this land as just belonging to one people is highly problematic. The solution is neither to endorse a settler identity nor a nativist monopolization of this land (see Mamdani 2020), but to democratize and pluralize claim-making to this land as a non-hierarchical multi-homeland polity. Before achieving this, there is an urgent need to initiate a process of decolonization of Palestine that can compensate Palestinian losses and spatially re-structuring Palestine to represent its diverse constituencies. Although the names Palestine and Israel trigger different emotions and associations for different peoples, it is important to resist the process of ethno-religious hierarchy and mastery that have gained upper hand in the Middle East. De-ethnicization should not be equated with denying particularities and differences, but preventing political power to uniquely serve the interest of an ethnic group that promotes itself to the status of universal and obscures its hegemonic power (cf., Butler 2012, p. 23). The answer to Jewish mastery in Israel is not placing the Palestinian Arabs at the top of the political hierarchy and exiling the Jews from political power and rendering them an inferiorized position as a marked group. As Mamdani (2020) argues, it is important to privilege the future over the past so "blood enemies can become political adversaries, adjudicating their differences through a political process rather than on battlefields or in courtrooms" (p. 36). This is not to say that Mamdani neglects the past as lacking relevance to understand our contemporary world. On the contrary, Mamdani urges us to reflect on history and learn from the monstrosity of political modernity and the nation-state as well as the violence that has been committed in the name of nation (ibid.).

Nations without states that fight for their independence and self-determination are daily reminders to the states that their nationalist project is not complete but contingent and does not enjoy universal legitimacy within its borders (Guibernau; Matin, 2020). By using violence, the nation-state wants to send political message to the dominant ethno-national constituency that it is the very presence of the minoritized groups and their peaceful or violent claims and actions that justify use of violence to secure the continuous mastery of the titular nation over the territory in question. For instance, in Turkey, one of the most unifying discourses across Islamist, secular and nationalist political parties is invocation of Kurdish 'terror' and 'separatism' to mobilize the titular nation against Kurdish demands for cultural, economic and political rights. The Kurds have tasted the bitterness of the political formulae that nationalist, semi-secularist, racist and Islamist regimes have offered the Kurds in the Middle East. The discursive weapon that the states of Iran, Iraq, Syria and Turkey use against the Kurdish demands for full citizenship as a Kurdish nation is that Kurdish claims are not viewed as serving the general interests of the region or the universal national identity that is largely monopolized by a particular ethno-national constituency. The idea that Kurds can find a safe home in the context of existing system and ethno-national hierarchies is a utopian vision. A possible way to accommodate the cultural, political and economic rights of minoritized group is to reject the very idea of minority position since this tends to provide the titular nation with the power (numerical superiority) to dictate the rule of how the political order should be forged and used against those who do not play according to its rule. This is only possible when the nation-state is not the only political template for organizing political life since it has proved itself as a failure in regard to ethnic and religious pluralism. For Kurds, it is equally important to learn from history that a polity that bases its existence solely on nationalism or a reactionary religious ideology potently reproduces the predatory nationalist identity that the Kurds have historically fought and aimed to undo. And there are no political guarantees that the victims cannot become oppressors and killers if the nation-state and nationalism are embraced as the dominant guidelines of political life since the nation-state has a strong tendency to create permanent majorities and minorities (Appadurai 2006; Mamdani 2001, 2020; Pandey, 2006). Although Zionism has been crucial in constructing Palestinian nationalism, it is important to remember, as Shohat (2017) shows in her work, that Arab nationalism alienated many Arab Jews from the Muslim world who did not hold so much in common with the Zionists, mainly represented by the Ashkenazi Jews. Arab nationalism excluded Arab Jews from its sphere of belonging by not making a distinction between Arab Jews and Zionists. This alienation pushed the Arab Jews toward Israel as allegedly representing all Jews, where they ironically experience racism due to their Arabness or Oriental identity. Shohat goes so far as to argue that had Arab nationalism made a distinction between Jews and Zionists, they might have won the support of Arab Jews against Zionism (p. 112).

Although nationalism has been one of the most divisive ideologies in the world, there are certain academic attempts to attach a positive meaning to nationalism as creating bonds and love between the compatriots. It is suggested that we need to strike a balance between the civic and the ethnic basis of nationalism in order to make it more inclusive. "Why nationalism? Because nothing else works" (Tamir, 2020, p. 538). According to Cocks (2002), there is no easy and single recipe that can be offered in order to contain nationalism but it would be a failure to not envision a new political community "in which the tensions between particular and universal, majority and minority, citizen and exile, home and the world, might play themselves out less cruelly than they have done in the nation-state and less oppressively than they have done under imperial rule" (p. 158). Kumar (2017, p. 475) who has studied the emergence and the visions of the Roman, Ottoman, Habsburg, Russian, British and French empires and how they have shaped the world, maintains that today's nation-state system with its claim to sovereignty and strong tendency toward ethnic homogeneity is not a desirable recipe for managing diversity and differences in multiethnic societies.

Without negating the asymmetrical power between dominant and dominated nationalisms in the Middle East, most of these nationalisms, if not all, have emerged in a context of nationalist humiliation and resentment as well as domination by Western empires. Due to experiences of humiliation, Jewish nationalism (Holocaust) and Turkish nationalism (loss of the Ottoman Empire) adopted a dangerous path toward ethnic cleansing of weaker groups that were conceived as a danger against their territorial power. Unlike Tamir's (2020) positive embracement of nationalism, Mamdani (2020) depicts a gloomy picture of nationalism and the nation-state as sites of violence and genocide. Since nation-building often leads to making of majorities and minorities, dominance and subordination, nationalist violence becomes a vehicle through which the oppression can be maintained by dominant national groups or countered by oppressed nations. One of the main reasons, that have obstructed the process of decolonization of political modernity and nationalism as its privileged child, is related to the epistemic conception of freedom. In anticolonial discourses, independence from foreign powers was viewed as the immediate and sufficient way to bring colonization to a political end (Mamdani 2020). As I illustrated in Chapter 7 with regard to the Kurdistan Region of Iraq, there are many Kurds who view liberation from political corruption as important as emancipating the Kurds from Turkish,

Arab and Persian mastery. When Kurds of Iraq achieved a considerable autonomy within the federal framework of Iraq, the priority of its leadership was not to rally the society toward social equality despite its loud rhetoric about bringing light, freedom and prosperity to the lives of the Kurds (see Aziz, 2017). This is not to say that post-Saddam Iraq is a paradise for ethnic equality. Conversely, violence is central to the constitution of Iraqi Arab identity. After 2003, the Shiite Arab constituency asserted themselves as the masters of Iraq and are economically and militarily involved in othering practices and discourses against the Kurds as a people who jeopardize Iraq's territorial integrity and exploit the Iraqi state for its economic benefit. Mamdani (2020) maintains that decolonization should be understood "as a two-sided process: externally, the assertion of political independence from the colonial power and a claim to membership in the community of states in the world at large; internally, the reimagination and redefinition of the political community" (p. 34). For the Kurds, despite the colonial division of Kurdistan, it might not be directly the colonial power that Kurds want to liberate themselves from but it is principally the states of Iran, Iraq, Syria and Turkey, that "are centres of power primarily responsible for violent mastery, both ideological and political, over the Kurdish region" (Houston, 2009, p. 20; see Matin 2020). If there is a political will beyond economic self-interest, the West can play an important role in endorsing a just solution to the Kurdish and Palestinian question given that the US and Europe still play an important political, economic and military role in the region. This proposal might go against the very idea of Mamdani (2020) who views political modernity, national sameness and colonialism as Western fabrications, spread and embraced zealously by the rest of the world.

In a world that is pervaded by a multiplicity of differences, national sameness functions as a threat against those who are not viewed as belonging. Although belonging is important for human well-being, it is equally imperative to create a polity based on equality (Butler 2012). Since many Middle Eastern states suffer from intractable ethno-religious conflicts, they can choose another political formula than the exclusionary nation-state to settle these conflicts. For instance, they can adopt a federation based on multiple nationalities so "it becomes quite literally impossible to conceive of a nation or its actions outside the context of a plural and concerted action" (ibid., p. 146). Within the framework of this federation, sovereignty cannot be based on the will of a single nation since this polity can commit itself "to a form of political life that would demand power sharing, concerted action, the dissolution of sovereignty into plural power, and a commitment to equality across national ties" (ibid.). Hence, such a federation can become important in order to realize a difference-friendly Middle East, where cultural, gender and religious differences are not stigmatized and the expectation of assimilation to dominant norms is not the price for gaining equality and respect (Fraser, 2006, p. 7). Recognition of differences should not exclusively be dictated by the polity, whether it is a state or a federation, but the people themselves who are not reduced to passive recipients of recognition but also highly active in debating the terms of recognition (cf., Modood, 2008, p. 49). This political formula might create constructive communal bonds between different constituencies without the need to resort to arms and violence to assert their public presence and demand their rights. In order to achieve this, laws, values and institutions need to work together so the very idea of ethno-national mastery can be delegitimized and the notions of reciprocity, acceptance and respect to be embraced across differences. Yet, it remains to be seen if conviviality between different constituencies in the Middle East and the wider world can gain a chance to become a "condition of our political life" (Butler 2012, p. 23).

There is a strong need to expand the notion of statelessness from a mere acquisition of a nationality/citizenship to include other rights and issues is to enable non-sovereign identities to flourish and avoid becoming objects of structural and everyday inferiorization (Radhakrishnan 2003). In her seminal work, Arendt (1951) equated statelessness with the loss of a political home, government protection and political rights. Somers (2008) has further expanded Arendt's definition through referring to citizenship to include not only civil, juridical and social rights but also "the primary right of recognition, inclusion, and membership in both political and civil society" (Somers, 2008, p. 25). While Somers (2008) provides an important framework to create a more inclusionary membership, her approach to citizenship and statelessness does not preoccupy itself with decentering and de-ethnicizing the sovereign identity in multinational and multicultural societies, but expanding its framework to be more inclusive. In contrast to Somers, Vali (1998), takes the issue of statelessness to another theoretical level in order to explore the political situation and exclusion of the Kurds in the Middle East. According to Vali, sovereignty is often assumed to define the identity and the legitimacy of the political power while also being outside of the state's conduct.

Moreover, the sovereign citizenship often bears the identity of the dominant ethnic group and it becomes the "primary locus of unifying functions of the state within the juridical framework of sovereignty, and hence the primary means of exclusion of non-sovereign political and cultural identities from the political process" (Vali 1998, p. 86). In other words, as long as the dominant ethno-national constituency is assumed as the actualized master identity within multinational countries, which sets the rule of the game in an uneven playing field that permeates this unequal relationship, non-sovereign identities cannot expect equality, even if they pursue their rights peacefully within constitutional framework of the state. If non-sovereign identities enter the coercive national equation in light of lack of popular-democratic legitimacy or popular sovereignty, political, cultural and economic inequalities will persist since they will not be able to alter the normativity of the sovereign political identity that dominate all societal structures that privilege a particular identity but claim universality (Eliassi; Matin 2020; Radhakrishnan 2003). The universality, that for instance Persian, Turkish or Arab political identities claim in each of the states where Kurds live, "obtains only a borrowed presence through the distorted means of its investment in a certain particularity" (Laclau, 2006, p. 648). Certainly, 'a borrowed presence' would be a euphemism to use in the context of highly authoritarian states like Iran, Iraq, Syria and Turkey where state violence is an immediate tool to assert the hegemony of the dominant ethno-national constituency. These states tend to urge the Kurds to adhere themselves to the universal or the overarching identity of the states as Iraqis, Iranians, Turkish and Syrian Arabs. Despite claims to universalism, none of these three constituencies have eliminated their particularities and transformed themselves into an inclusive universality (see Laclau, 1992). The states in the Middle East have made strong efforts to render the Kurds the position of a non-people and preventing them from being equal partner in the constitution of the universal by muting and punishing their differences. The cultural and linguistic norms of the dominant constituencies continue to shape the states and present themselves as functioning in everybody's interest. However, this is not a generous invitation to the Kurds to be included but a requirement by the states that Kurds need to assimilate to the norms of the dominant constituency and the state that it has realized in its own cultural image. As a reaction to this exclusion from an alleged universalism, a politicized Kurdish identity has emerged as a major challenge to the sovereignty and the territorial power of these states. For the Kurds, it is only by breaking those dominant ethnocultural norms apart that universalization does "have a chance to renew itself within a radically democratic project" (Butler 2012, p. 23). A multilateral universality according to Butler (1994) needs to be internally diverse and inclusive and a "site of permanent political contest" (p. 159). In order to evade new and future exclusions, universality "would have to be left permanently open, permanently contested, permanently contingent, in order not to foreclose in advance future claims for inclusion" (ibid). It is often said that if just the Kurds left aside their parochial particularity and ethnic demands, their lives and region would experience more prosperity and stability. This is what Saddam Hussein tended to tell the Kurds of Iraq, while destructing their homes and gassing them to annihilation (see Kirmanj, 2013).

This leads us to the question of equality and difference and the idea of who can qualify as a human being and embraced by rights, recognition and respect. Historically, many peoples have been sidelined by different ideals of universality and denied the status of a human being. When minoritized groups like Kurds and Palestinians declare that they are also human and worth recognition as nations among other established nations, they are asserting themselves as claimants to equality and justice and challenging those divisions and hierarchies that sustain their subordination, an issue that Phillips (2015) meticulously engages with in her book *The Politics of the Human*. Phillips maintains that there is a strong ethical ideal by denying the importance of contingent differences like culture, skin color and sexual orientation and asserting our common bonds as human beings, since this can function as a discursive weapon against the divisive ideologies of racism and sexism. Nevertheless, for Phillips (2015), the conception of a common human identity constitutes a danger to the idea and realities of being different. For instance, if minoritized and racialized groups are called upon to sideline or see beyond their particular grievances in the context of persisting ethno-national hierarchies, there is a danger that we privilege the already privileged and dominant group (see Young, 1990). It is not a coincidence that is, but not only, marginalized groups who are predominantly concerned with their stigmatized and unrecognized differences. Telling excluded groups that they are also human without altering and democratizing power relations, "is at best an empty sentimentality, and at worst Sartre's 'ideology of lies'" (Phillips 2015, p. 38). As Phillips eloquently puts it with respect to why minoritized groups insist on their differences:

> If you are already more securely established in the hierarchies of power, it is much easier to set your particularities aside. They do not thereby vanish, but they require no special attention because they are already more incorporated into what is understood as the human norm. (Phillips 2015, p. 13)

This illustrates how a false universalism works that reproduces itself by asserting its hostility to marked groups who want their differences to gain institutional and public recognition, respect and representation. What the dominant ideology requires from excluded group is undoing their particularities, in order to achieve the status of the human or the universal that the nation-state supposedly bestows. Predictably, marked groups often press the powerful and the states to extend the scope of equality to embrace their perspectives and experiences. When stateless peoples challenge the states to reverse, transvalue and redefine their ethnonational hierarchies, they assert themselves as political by making judgment between justice and injustice (Isin, 2002) and interrupt naturalized forms of domination (Rancière 1999). Certainly, statelessness as a political injury is not an accident in the lives of the Kurdish and Palestinian peoples but direct effects of colonial nationalism and exclusive nation-states (Matin 2020). Equality beyond national sameness can be achieved if we politically and legally alter those institutions and discourses that deny, inferiorize or exclude the differences of subjugated groups who strive to gain equal public recognition and respect. It is in such a political context, that to be a human being, equal and different do not need to be seen as incompatible and opposing (Scott, 1994). As long as the inequality and denial continue within the realms of the nation-states, few societies can achieve lasting peace, conviviality and stability, since inequality and denial are fertile ground for cultivating polarized identities in a world where certain groups establish themselves as subjects of rights and privilege at the expense of racialized and stateless groups. At the end, it is mainly by altering the political normativity of the nation-states and hierarchical citizenship regimes, that a new inclusionary political future can be envisioned and enacted beyond political mastery and subordination.

References

Anderson, B. (2013). *US & THEM? The dangerous politics of immigration control*. Oxford University Press.
Appadurai, A. (2006). *Fear of small numbers: An essay on the geography of anger*. Duke University Press.
Arendt, H. (1951). *The origins of totalitarianism*. Shocken Books.
Askland, H. H. (2014). 'It was all about independence': Loss, division and rejuvenation among the East Timorese in Melbourne. *The Australian Journal of Anthropology, 25*, 321–336.
Aziz, S. (2017). The eeconmic system(s) of the Kurdistan regional government, Iraq. In G. Gülistan, H. Sabine & I. S. Ferhad (Eds.), *Between sstate and non-state: Politics and society in Kurdistan-Iraq and Palestine* (pp. 103–122). Palgrave Macmillan.
Balaton-Chrimes, S. (2014). Statelessness, identity cards and citizenship as status in the case of the Nubians of Kenya. *Citizenship Studies, 18*(1), 15–28.
Belton, K. A. (2011). The neglected non-citizen: Statelessness and liberal political theory. *Journal of Global Ethics, 7*(1), 59–71.
Billig, M. (1995). *Banal nationalism*. Sage.
Bloom, T., Tonkiss, K., & Cole, P. (Eds.). (2017). *Understanding statelessness*. Routledge.
Butler, J. (1994). Contingent foundations: Feminism and the question of 'postmodernism.' In S. Steven (Ed.), *The postmodern turn: New perspectives on social theory* (pp. 153–170). Cambridge University Press.
Butler, J., & Spivak, G. C. (2010). *Who sings the nation-state?* Seagull Books.
Butler, J. (2012). *Parting ways: Jewishness and the critique of Zionism*. Columbia University Press.
Cocks, J. (2002). *Passion and paradox: Intellectuals confront the national question*. Princeton University Press.
Cole, P. (2017). Insider theory and the construction of theory. In B. Tendayi, T. Katherine, & C. Phillip (Eds.), *Understanding statelessness* (pp. 255–266). Routledge.
Eliassi, B. (2013). *Contesting Kurdish identities in Sweden: Quest for belonging among Middle Eastern youth*. Palgrave Macmillan.
Fraser, N. (2006). Social justice in the age of identity politics: Redistribution, recognition, and participation. In F. Nancy & H. Axel (Eds.), *Redistribution or recognition? A political-philosophical exchange* (pp. 8–109). Verso.
Fry, T., & Tlostanova, M. (2021). *A new political imagination: Making the case*. Routledge.
Gellner, E. (1983). *Nations and nationalism*. Cornell University Press.
Geschiere, P. (2009). *The perils of belonging: Autochthony, citizenship, exclusion in Africa & Europe*. Chicago University Press.

Guibernau, M. (1999). *Nations without states: Political communities in a global age*. Polity Press.
Hammer, J. (2005). *Palestinians born in exile: diaspora and the search for a homeland* . University of Texas Press.
Houston, C. (2009). An anti-history of a non-people: Kurds, colonialism, and nationalism in the history of anthropology. *The Journal of the Royal Anthropological Institute, 15*(1), 19–35.
Isin, E. F. (2002). Ways of being political. *Distinktion: Scandinavian Journal of Social Theory*, 3(1): 7–28.
Kirmanj, S. (2013). *Identity and nation in Iraq*. Lynne Rienner Publishers.
Kumar, K. (2000). Nation and empire: English and British national identity in comparative perspective. *Theory and Society, 29*(5), 575–608.
Kumar, K. (2017). *Visions of empire: How five imperial regimes shaped the world*. Princeton University Press.
Laclau, E. (1992). Universalism, particularism, and the question of identity. *October, 16*, 83–90.
Laclau, E. (2006). Why constructing a people is the main task of radical politics. *Critical Inquiry, 32*, 646–680.
Mamdani, M. (2001). *When victims become killers: Colonialism, nativism, and the genocide in Rwanda*. Princeton University Press.
Mamdani, M. (2020). *Neither settler nor native: The making and unmaking permanent minorities*. The Belknap Press of Harvard University Press.
Malešević, S. (2013). *Nation-state and nationalisms*. Polity.
Matin, K. (2020). Liminal lineages of the "Kurdish Question". *Middle East Report* 295. https://merip.org/2020/08/liminal-lineages-of-the-kurdish-question/ Accessed 7 April 2021.
Mavroudi, E. (2007). Palestinians and pragmatic citizenship: Negotiating relationships between citizenship and national identity in diaspora. *Geoforum, 39*, 307–318.
Modood, T. (2008). A basis for and two obstacles in the way of a multiculturalist coalition. *British Journal of Sociology, 59*(1): 47–52.
Pandey, G. (2006). *Routine violence: Nations, fragments, histories*. Standford University Press.
Phillips, A. (2015). *The politics of the human*. Cambridge University Press.
Radhakrishnan, R. (2003). *Theory in an uneven world*. Blackwell Publishing.
Radhakrishnan, R. (2012). *A said dictionary*. Wiley-Blackwell.
Rancière, J. (1999). *Disagreement: Politics and philosophy*. University of Minnesota Press.
Scott, J. W. (1994). Deconstructing equality-versus-difference: Or, the uses of poststructuralist theory for feminism. In S. Steven (Ed.), *The postmodern turn: New perspectives on social theory* (pp. 282–298). Cambridge University Press.

Shohat, E. (2017). *On the Arab-Jew, Palestine, and other displacements*. Pluto Press.

Somers, M. R. (2008). *Genealogies of citizenship: Markets, statelessness, and the right to have rights*. Cambridge University Press.

Tamir, Y. (2020). Why nationalism? Because nothing else works. *Nations and Nationalism, 26*, 538–543.

Vali, A. (1998). The Kurds and their "others": fragmented identity and fragmented politics. *Comparative Studies of South Asia, Africa and the Middle East, 18*(2), 82–95.

Young, I. M. (1990). *Justice and the politics of difference*. Princeton University Press.

Index

B. Eliassi, *Narratives of Statelessness and Political Otherness*, Minorities in West Asia and North Africa,
https://doi.org/10.1007/978-3-030-76698-6

The manufacturer's authorised representative in the EU is Springer Nature Customer Service Centre GmbH, Europaplatz 3, 69115 Heidelberg, Germany. If you have any concerns regarding our products, please contact ProductSafety@springernature.com

Printed and bound by CPI Group (UK) Ltd, Croydon, CR0 4YY
30/09/2026
02225457-0015